Engaging Reason

On the Theory of Value and Action

JOSEPH RAZ

OXFORD
UNIVERSITY PRESS

This book has been printed digitally and produced in a standard specification in order to ensure its continuing availability

OXFORD
UNIVERSITY PRESS

Great Clarendon Street, Oxford OX2 6DP
Oxford University Press is a department of the University of Oxford.
It furthers the University's objective of excellence in research, scholarship,
and education by publishing worldwide in
Oxford New York
Auckland   Cape Town   Dar es Salaam   Hong Kong   Karachi
Kuala Lumpur   Madrid   Melbourne   Mexico City   Nairobi
New Delhi   Shanghai   Taipei   Toronto
With offices in
Argentina Austria Brazil Chile Czech Republic France Greece
Guatemala Hungary Italy Japan South Korea Poland Portugal
Singapore Switzerland Thailand Turkey Ukraine Vietnam

Oxford is a registered trade mark of Oxford University Press
in the UK and in certain other countries

Published in the United States
by Oxford University Press Inc., New York

© in this volume Joseph Raz 1999

The moral rights of the author have been asserted

Database right Oxford University Press (maker)

Reprinted 2010

All rights reserved. No part of this publication may be reproduced,
stored in a retrieval system, or transmitted, in any form or by any means,
without the prior permission in writing of Oxford University Press,
or as expressly permitted by law, or under terms agreed with the appropriate
reprographics rights organization. Enquiries concerning reproduction
outside the scope of the above should be sent to the Rights Department,
Oxford University Press, at the address above

You must not circulate this book in any other binding or cover
And you must impose this same condition on any acquirer

ISBN 978-0-19-924800-1

ACKNOWLEDGEMENTS

The following chapters are published separately as indicated:

'When We are Ourselves: The Active and the Passive', *Proceedings of the Aristotelian Society*, suppl. 91 (1997).
'Incommensurability and Agency', in Ruth Chang (ed.) *Incommensurability, Incomparability, and Practical Reason* (Harvard University Press, 1998).
'Explaining Normativity: On Rationality and the Justification of Reason', in *Ratio*, 12(1999).
'Notes on Value and Objectivity', in Brian Leiter (ed.) *Objectivity in Morality and the Law* (Cambridge University Press, 1999).
'Moral Change and Social Relativism', *Social Philosophy and Policy*, Cambridge University Press, 1994.
'Mixing Values', *Proceedings of the Aristotelian Society*, suppl. 85 (1991).
'The Truth in Particularism', in Brad Hooker and Margaret Little (eds.), *Moral Particularism* (Oxford University Press, 1999).
'On the Moral Point of View', in Jerome B. Schneewind (ed.), *Reason, Ethics and Society* (Open Court, 1996).
'The Amoralist', in Garrett Cullity and Berys Gaut (eds.), *Ethics and Practical Reasoning* (Oxford University Press, 1997).
'The Central Conflict: Morality and Self-Interest', in Roger Crisp and Brad Hooker (eds.), *Well Being and Morality: Essays in honour of James Griffin* (Oxford University Press, 1999).

CONTENTS

Introduction	1
1. When We are Ourselves	5
2. Agency, Reason, and the Good	22
3. Incommensurability and Agency	46
4. Explaining Normativity: On Rationality and the Justification of Reason	67
5. Explaining Normativity: Reason and the Will	90
6. Notes on Value and Objectivity	118
7. Moral Change and Social Relativism	161
8. Mixing Values	182
9. The Value of Practice	202
10. The Truth in Particularism	218
11. On the Moral Point of View	247
12. The Amoralist	273
13. The Central Conflict: Morality and Self-Interest	303
Index	333

Introduction

Aspects of the world are valuable. That constitutes reasons for action. Because we are rational animals, ones with the power of reason, we are able to conduct ourselves in the light of those reasons. Being rational is being capable of acting intentionally, that is, for reasons, as one takes them to be, and that means in light of one's appreciation of one's situation in the world.

This book, collecting essays written over the last eight years, explores some aspects of the complex interdependence of value, reason, and the will. The first essay, 'When We are Ourselves' paints with broad brush a simple, and simplified, picture of a person relying on the thought that our life is our own when it is under our control and that means when our various emotions, hopes, desires, intentions, and action are guided by reason. Intentional action is action for reasons. Possession of features which show actions to be good in some respect constitutes reasons. 'Agency, Reason, and the Good' defends the connection between intention and reason on the one hand, and between reason and the good on the other, from objections based on people's ability to choose the bad, and to act intentionally in an expressive but unreasoned way. 'Incommensurability and Agency' adds some details to the picture by laying the foundation for an understanding of the relations between reason and the will. The theses of these essays keep cropping up, explicitly or implicitly, in all the others.

It was rather presumptuous of me to call the following two essays 'Explaining Normativity'. I plead in my defence that explanation is always relative to a puzzle, and these essays seek to explain some of the puzzles which preoccupied me, explaining them in ways which, however incomplete, satisfy me. As their titles suggest, the first deals with two topics. First, the relations between rationality and reasons. Clearly there is a connection, but what is it? Does rationality convey success in action for right reasons, or success in acting according to reasons as one sees them, or an attempt to follow reason, or success in the use of rules or reasoning? There are other possibilities. The essay does not offer a complete account of rationality. Its aim is to delineate some elements in such an account in order to help make sense of the views expressed in this book. These reflections led to a consideration of the connection between reasons and principles of reasoning, and to the second part of the essay, concerning the possibility of justifying these principles. The second of the two essays rounds up the discussion of the relations between reason and the will started in the first couple of essays.

The essay on objectivity generally, and on the objectivity of value in particular, marks a transition from the subjective to the objective end of the complex phenomena explored here, from examination of people's ability to be guided by the valuable aspects of the world[1] to an examination of the possibility of there being value in the world. I say advisedly 'the possibility' of the existence of value, for it is not part of the brief of this book to argue for the existence of any particular value, nor to show which aspects of the world as it exists are of value. Throughout I use examples, sometimes not stopping to warn that those who disagree with the suggestion that what is claimed to be of value is of value should choose alternative examples. But at no point does my argument depend on the choice of example. Naturally, sometimes it does depend on the existence of cases of the type instanced. While the arguments do not extend to vindicate any value claims, they indirectly contribute to the vindication of claims about the existence of types of valuable objects and options, particularly those whose existence depends on shared social practices with shared meanings. This theme is first touched upon in the essay on the objectivity of values. Having explored the nature of objectivity, and dismissed various spurious reasons for doubting the objectivity of value, it sketches four ways in which values may depend on social practices.

The fact that some values depend on social practices for their existence raises many difficulties. 'Moral Change and Social Relativism' adds to the discussion of two of these, which is begun in the objectivity essay. It considers the degree to which the fact that the existence of some values depends on sustaining practices means that these practices feature in the explanation of the value of the values concerned. It also considers whether the dependence of value on practice, such as it is, is consistent with the universality of values.

The relations of some values and social practices are further explored in the essays on 'Mixing Values', and 'The Value of Practice'. They deal with the same problems, and with others. In part my aim is to establish the social dependence of some values, which I call mixed value goods, that is goods whose excellence consists in instancing several other good qualities, the way the goodness of a novel may consist in the excellence of its language, plot, characterization, humour, and more. I try to show how our evaluation of

---

[1] And to avoid the bad and valueless aspects of it. Like many writers I accentuate the positive, and often assume without words that with appropriate modifications what is said of the good will be read to apply to the bad as well.

mixed value goods is genre-dependent, and why it is that genres are historical creatures. These are key facts in the understanding of the practice-dependence of some values.

The question of the universality of values is central to much of the argument in Chapters 6 to 9. It is posed centre stage in 'The Truth in Particularism'. In some ways this essay belongs with the first four in the book, being concerned primarily with what it is to be guided by a reason, as well as with the results of the fact that reason often underdetermines outcome. I placed it here, however, to mark the movement beyond the social dependence of value to the ways in which individual agents make a difference to the reasons they have. There is much more to be said on this topic. Here I merely take the theme explored by Winch in his 'Universalisability', and transform and adapt it to my use. The way in which people's character affects the reasons they have, without being itself a reason, is analogous to the way social practices affect agents' reasons without being themselves reasons.

Throughout the book no distinction is drawn between moral and other values. I do not believe that there is a context-free theoretically interesting difference between moral values and others. The vindication of this view is the subject of the last three essays. Their aim is to emphasize the unity of reason by arguing against two common distinctions. 'On the Moral Point of View' and 'The Amoralist' argue that the distinction between morality and other practical domains lacks theoretical significance. In particular I claim that there is no valid conception of morality according to which morality, or some master moral perspective or argument, is a source of values, or of principles of action. My arguments are directed against some conceptions of morality, and do not touch others. In this regard the essay on 'The Central Conflict: Morality and Self-Interest' is more radical. It aims to establish the complementary thesis that there is no viable conception of self-interest or prudence according to which it is a source of value or reasons. If successful these three essays illuminate the reach of the conclusions of the rest of the book. They apply to moral and to non-moral reasons and values.

All but three of the essays collected here have been published separately,[2] though several have been revised for republication. The revisions are very minor in all but one case: the first essay has been somewhat expanded to strengthen its argument. Chapter 8 'Mixing Values', is followed by an appendix, written in 1991, highlighting the central contentions of the essay, and replying to a criticism of it by James Griffin. All the essays have been

---

[2] The exceptions being Chapters 2, 'Agency, Reason, and the Good', 5, 'Explaining Normativity: Reason and the Will', and 9, 'The Value of Practice'.

written over the last eight years. My first attempt to develop and put together a body of thoughts relating to the matters here discussed was in 1992, in lectures at Oxford, and, in the following year, while giving the four lectures expected of the short-term visiting Mellon fellow at Princeton. These early lectures provided the foundation for many of the essays in this book. The fourth lecture, however, was never published. It provides the basis of the essay on 'The Value of Practice'. Rereading this essay today makes me realize how much more I hoped to accomplish when I first prepared those essays, how many of the problems I was troubled by then I am still troubled by today. For me this book is a progress report, reminding me as much of what remains to be done, of tensions in the views here set out and of problems they raise, or problems solutions to which they presuppose, as of what they accomplish.

I have acknowledged my debt to many friends and colleagues who helped me with these essays in the notes to the various essays where their help was particularly important. I would like to thank here the students who attended my seminars on these topics at Oxford and at Princeton for their interest and trenchant questioning. I am grateful to Stephen Everson for many discussions during his time at Balliol, and some later, and to Don Regan, for discussions during my visit to Ann Arbor in 1994, and on one or two other occasions. Their insightful comments were a source of stimulation and encouragement. I am afraid that the book does not live up to their demanding standards, but I hope that they will find enough of value in it to be pleased to have helped with its conception.

I

When We are Ourselves: The Active and the Passive

Is it an accident, or a matter of mere linguistic interest, that life is associated with activity, and death with its absence? Accounts of the nature of persons have to explain two inter-related boundaries: the boundary between what is me and what is outside me, part of the environment within which I live, but not part of me; and the boundary between my life as I lead it, and what happens to me in my life. They go a long way towards explaining what we may call the sense of self, the sense a person has of who he or she is, as well as other aspects of our notion of a person. In this chapter I will comment on some aspects of the second distinction. I will use the contrast between active and passive as a help in characterizing that distinction. The active/passive distinction is associated with a variety of ideas and metaphors. There is no need to think that they all come to one basic distinction. There may be several boundaries we rely on for different purposes. In this chapter I will proceed on the assumption that we need only one distinction to mark the boundary between what is and what is not part of my life as I lead it, although this is likely to be a distinction admitting of degrees. I will return to this question in concluding.

Three qualifications to begin with: First, it is not to be assumed that necessarily the distinction applies to all episodes in our lives. There may be some episodes, events, or aspects of our lives regarding which we are neither active nor passive for the distinction does not apply to them at all.

Second, many of those who have addressed these issues recently, including Harry Frankfurt, who did more than anyone to draw attention to the issue and to contribute to its understanding,[1] connect the active/passive

---

This is a revised version of a paper presented to the Joint Session of the Aristotelian Society and the Mind Association, July 1997, and printed in the supplementary volume to the *Proceedings of the Aristotelian Society* (1997). I am grateful to Penelope Bulloch, Thomas Baldwin, John Campbell, Peter Hacker, John Hyman, and Sophia Reibetanz, for helpful comments on an earlier draft.

[1] See in particular his 'Freedom of the Will and the Concept of a Person', 'Identification and Externality', and 'Identification and Wholeheartedness', all included in his *The Importance of What We Care About* (Cambridge: CUP, 1988). All page numbers in the text are to this book.

distinction with questions of moral responsibility. The thought is that we are responsible for the life we lead, but not for desires or actions which force themselves on us in spite of ourselves. This I think is a mistake. No doubt the boundary between the active and the passive is relevant to questions of responsibility. But it does not settle them. Our responsibility extends beyond responsibility for actions, or thoughts, etc. which are our own, or regarding which we are active. We are sometimes responsible for actions which we rightly disavow as not being 'us'. When such actions are wrong, responsibility for them may be attenuated and may not amount to guilt. But it may well give rise to duties to make amends, the sort of duties which only those responsible for an action or for a failure to act have.

Third, like many contrasts (real/unreal; objective/subjective, etc.) the contrasting words 'active' and 'passive' are used to draw several different contrasts. Clarifying the sense used here is among the purposes of the chapter. In testing its suggestions one should be aware, however, that not every case which does not fit them is a counter example. It may belong to a different use made of the terms. For example, in terms of the distinction I have in mind, a bird-watcher keeping still in his observation hide-out is active. In a familiar sense he is of course passive. Similarly a person taking criticism without responding is thereby being passive in a sense different from the one I am interested in, and is active in the sense explored here. On the other hand, when shoplifting a kleptomaniac is active in one sense, but passive in another. There is something in him which makes him act in spite of himself. What he does is in some sense not part of his life as he leads it. It is an episode which disrupts his life in spite of himself. Finally, are we active when breathing? Yes, and yet no: *qua* living organisms we are active, but *qua* persons we are not. Our breathing, like our digesting, is not part of our life as we lead it.

Frankfurt offers the following instance as illustration of the phenomenon we are concerned with:

In the course of an animated but amiable enough conversation, a man's temper suddenly rushes up in him out of control. Although nothing has happened that makes his behaviour readily intelligible, he begins to fling dishes, books, and crudely abusive language at his companion. Then his tantrum subsides, and he says: 'I have no idea what triggered that bizarre spasm of emotion. The feelings just came over me from out of nowhere, and I couldn't help it. I wasn't myself. Please don't hold it against me.' (p. 63)

Frankfurt's example helps in fixing the intuitive distinction we are trying to elucidate. He remarks on the fact that he believes that even though the passions are thought of as in one sense passive, the distinction he is after cuts across them and divides our emotional experiences into active and passive. Frankfurt uses the internal/external distinction interchangeably with the active/passive one. This is another sign that the distinction he is seeking to explain should not be too rigidly aligned with all the associations of the active/passive distinction. I will follow his example, though, of course, this does not mean that the choice of the terminology of activity and passivity is arbitrary.

I

I will travel towards my destination along a somewhat circuitous route. I will start with an old chestnut: can we choose to believe? Can we decide what to believe and what not? Are our beliefs voluntary? There is reason to think that the answer to all these questions is affirmative. People can sometimes truly say 'I will not believe that', 'I will go on believing this in spite of everything', 'It is difficult (or easy) for me to believe that'.[2] The explanation of these statements may seem to bear directly on the question of whether one can choose to believe. In particular it may seem that if one can refuse to believe something then one can also agree to believe it, and that sounds very much like saying that one can decide what to believe.

Nevertheless the dominant consensus, to which I subscribe, is that we cannot. This question is often discussed in the context of an examination of Hume's view that belief is involuntary. For Hume, and for some of those who followed him, the assertion that belief is not voluntary was an expression of the empiricist view that belief is passive, that it is an impression. Hume's empiricist account of belief and belief formation has long been discarded. Are there other reasons for denying that we can decide what to believe? An influential argument was offered by Williams. He thinks that the responsiveness of belief to truth and to evidence is inconsistent with people being able to decide what to believe:

If I could acquire a belief at will I could acquire it whether it was true or not; moreover I would know that I could acquire it whether it was true or not. If in full consciousness I could will to acquire a 'belief' irrespective of its truth, it is unclear that before the event I could seriously think of it as a belief, i.e. as something purporting to represent reality.[3]

---

[2] These examples are taken from H. H. Price, 'Belief and Will', *Proceedings of the Aristotelian Society*, suppl. (1954). See also Jonathan Bennett's discussion in 'Why Belief is Involuntary' *Analysis* (1990), 87. My own views set out below diverge from those of both of them.

[3] 'Deciding to Believe', *Problems of the Self* (Cambridge: CUP, 1973), 148. For the purposes of this discussion I will use 'choose to believe' and 'decide to believe' as interchangeable. The two main differences between choosing and deciding are: (1) we can choose

This is not the end of his argument, but as it already includes one dubious juxtaposition and a non-sequitur we may stop here. It may be true that if we could acquire a belief at will, we could acquire it whether or not it is true, and we would know that. But even now (and remember that we cannot acquire beliefs at will) we can acquire false beliefs, and we know that. Williams believes that 'If it were possible to acquire a belief regardless of its truth, and if we knew this to be possible, it would follow that we could decide to believe a proposition regardless of whether we thought that it is true.' This is a non-sequitur. To render his argument valid one has to accept an additional premise, namely that: 'The power to decide what to believe includes the power to decide what to believe while being indifferent to the truth of such beliefs.' Given this premise Williams would be right in concluding that we do not have such a power for, as he has pointed out earlier in his article, for advanced language users, to believe a proposition is to believe it to be true.[4]

Williams's argument seems to presuppose that the notion of decision or of choice implies unrestricted freedom to opt for any option which in principle is a possible object of choice or decision. That is not so. Both choice and decision are subject to rules of rational constraint, the most important of which is that one can only choose or decide for a reason, i.e. for what one takes to be a good reason for the option chosen.[5] Even irrational choice is choice for a reason (which the chooser believes to be at least a good prima-facie reason).[6] This places a limit on what one can choose in any given situation. I cannot choose to have coffee because I love Sophocles. I must believe something which intelligibly can be taken to be a reason for that choice. If one were able to choose to believe it may be that only evidence bearing on the likelihood that the proposition in question is true can intelli-

---

only when we have acceptable alternatives, but we can decide even when we have no acceptable alternative; (2) we can choose an action by performing it. The choice can consist in its performance. Deciding to perform an action is separate from the act one decides to perform, and must happen, if at all, before it is performed. For our purposes the differences can be taken as read, and need not be dwelt upon.

[4] 'Believe that p' and 'believe that p is true' are not the same proposition for one can have beliefs, but not beliefs that something is true, without possessing the concept of truth. But for those creatures whose conceptual ability includes possession of the concept of truth, the conditions under which we can ascribe to them belief in either proposition are the same.

[5] One's reason, if valid, establishes the good in choosing the option one does, though it may not be sufficient to show that the chosen option is superior to all its alternatives. Sometimes the reason for the option is merely the good of choosing the option, or of choosing in a certain manner. These exception cases do not affect my argument.

[6] This proposition has often been defended. For my own attempt to argue that one cannot want anything except for a reason see 'Incommensurability and Agency' (ch. 3).

gibly be taken to be such a reason.[7] If so then one would be able to choose to believe only for such reasons or for what can be interpreted as such reasons. It follows that Williams's argument fails for it rests on a false premise.

I do not endorse the suggestion that belief is forced on us by what we take to be decisive rational reasons. There is a latitude in the space of reasons, both for action and for belief. There are many cases in which there are reasons to believe a proposition which are not decisive, meaning that while they make it rational to believe it, they do not make it irrational to withhold belief. In such cases just as our choices (when underdetermined by reason) reveal our character and tastes so do our beliefs.[8] When we believe a proposition or withhold belief because not to believe, or not to withhold belief, would be irrational, all that is shown of our character (barring special circumstances) is that we are normal rational persons. But whether or not we believe something when neither belief nor withholding it would be irrational can show us to be suspicious, indecisive, envious, trusting, naive, and so on. In this, coming to believe is analogous to choosing. It is also like choosing in that the character traits are in part formed by the fact that we tend one way or another when reason is indecisive.

Moreover, the character traits which affect beliefs or choices cannot be cited by the agents as reasons for them. I may know that I believe a certain proposition whereas you do not because I am more trusting of people than you are. But I cannot give my trusting nature as a reason for believing that proposition. It is not a possible reason for belief.

One may think that the character traits that I mentioned as explaining why we believe a proposition even when it is not irrational to withhold belief are all defects of character, and that is why they cannot be reasons for belief. Possibly virtuous character traits, which explain when we do and when we do not come to believe this or that when reason requires that we do so, will be citable as reasons for these beliefs. But that is a mistake. The alleged 'virtuous' character traits are simply those which show that we follow reason (trust people just to the right degree, suspect them just when one ought to do so, etc.). When we follow reason our reasons, rather than the character traits which enable us to discern them, are our justification. And by the nature of the case such virtues cannot explain when we do or do not believe

---

[7] For an argument that other reasons may be relevant see Jack Meiland, 'What Ought We to Believe? or The Ethics of Belief Revisited', *American Philosophical Quarterly*, 17 (1980), 15.

[8] Naturally, irrationally induced beliefs are also liable to reveal one's character and dispositions. Such beliefs may be induced by fear, or self-deception, or wishful thinking, and other motivated irrationalities. My point is that the same is true of our rationally held beliefs.

where the latitude of reason means that either would be rational. Besides, character traits which explain what we believe only when reason does not compel belief are not necessarily defects of character, as they would have been had they led us to believe against reason.

II

Having rejected Williams's argument, do we have to conclude that our beliefs are voluntarily chosen or decided upon? Not necessarily. The evidence for this proposition mentioned so far was that we can, on appropriate occasions, make true statements such as 'I will go on believing this in spite of everything', 'It is difficult (or easy) for me to believe that'. These statements, however, do not imply that it is up to us to choose or decide what to believe, even though other similarly constructed utterances (e.g. 'I will not Φ', 'I will go on Φ-ing in spite of everything') do have such implications. These examples, and others like them, show that belief has many conceptual connections with the active. They show that normally beliefs belong to the active rather than to the passive side of our life. For the most part beliefs are not dispositions with which we are landed or afflicted. We form beliefs, we come to believe. We are not overcome by them, as we may be by a sudden flash of anger, or a mood of despair. They do not just happen to us, we are active in reaching them.

The thought that our beliefs are up to our will, that we choose them or decide which ones to have, is due to the thought that the active is to be explained by reference to the will. That grew out of the very mistake a variant of which, I claimed, led Williams astray, the mistake of taking our will to be free of all *rational* constraint, of thinking that it is the genuine expression of ourselves, because, it is sometimes thought, it is the manifestation of our spontaneity. 'Choice is', in Aristotle's words, 'either desiderative reason or ratiocinative desire' (*NE* 1139^{b}4). Or, as Aquinas puts it: 'Reason comes before the will and directs its activity' (*ST* II-I Q.13a.1). But if so, then freedom from rational constraint does not explain the active character of the will, and we have no reason to think it the only paradigm of the active. Indeed it makes sense to suppose that it is active only when it responds to reasons as we see them, that is, to an active belief.

A spurious reason for denying that beliefs can be active arises out of the view that actions are the paradigm of the active. As beliefs are neither actions nor, since they are not adopted by decision, are they adopted by actions, then they cannot be active. The category of the active is, however, both wider and narrower than that of actions, as the examples I gave in my introductory remarks show. Or rather, they show that there is a notion of the active which does not depend on action.

The distinction between the active and the passive, in the sense in which we are interested, depends, at least in part, on our responsiveness to reason (which is, like the notion of the active itself, a matter of degree). In other words, the distinction depends on the appropriateness to our circumstances of the mental states, events, or processes concerned. We should believe only when reason warrants, be afraid only when in serious danger, feel pride only when we have something to feel proud about, etc. We are active when our mental life displays sensitivity to reasons, and we are passive when such mental events occur in a way which is not sensitive to reasons; or at least this is part of what accounts for the distinction. In these terms beliefs are—pathological cases excepted—on the active side of our mental life.

This does not mean that we form beliefs only as a result of deliberation. We may form them because—with our senses—we perceive how things are, or because through subconscious processes we come to have or to form them. All of this is consistent with the active character of believing, or having beliefs. What does that active character consist in? As indicated, it consists largely in the fact that our beliefs are responsive to reasons. To believe a proposition is to have a view as to how things are, and coming to believe that the evidence shows that things are not so *is* ceasing to have that belief. Even when we form perceptual beliefs, or when we come to have certain beliefs without being aware of the fact, the beliefs are responsive to reason. This responsiveness is manifested in two ways. First, in that unconscious processes of belief formation, just like explicit deliberation, depend on absence of awareness of sufficient reasons against the belief, and—normally—on awareness of adequate reasons for it. When it seems to me that I see a cat I—without deliberation—believe that there is a cat there. But if I believe that I am in a magic show, then I do not form that belief. Second, when I deliberate and come to the view that the evidence is that a proposition I believe is false, the very process of coming to that conclusion is also a process of ceasing to believe it. By their responsiveness to reasons believing and beliefs belong to the active side of the active/passive divide.

Does it follow that belief is voluntary? The voluntary/not voluntary distinction or more precisely the distinction between the non-voluntary and that which is not non-voluntary, is related to the active/passive distinction. But to illustrate this we have to tread carefully as it has complicated contours. Irrelevant to our purpose is the use of 'voluntary' in which it contrasts with unwillingly, under pressure, reluctantly, etc. Furthermore, there are contexts in which we cannot use 'voluntary', but can use 'non-voluntary', that is cases in which 'non-voluntary plays the role of an affirmative term, and its negation is 'not non-voluntary'. Finally, not only actions can be non-voluntary. While it would be wrong or misleading to say that any emotions are voluntary, and most emotions are neither voluntary nor non-voluntary, some of them are non-voluntary. I may feel irritated with, or jealous of, my friend when the irritation or jealousy is unjustified. I may excuse myself by the fact that these feelings are non-voluntary. Here non-voluntary tracks the passive: the emotion seized me in spite of myself. I was passive in the matter.

In spite of these considerations, the distinction applies to beliefs only when stretched. It is as odd to say of a belief that it is non-voluntary as to say that it is voluntary. Though it is possible to call a pathological belief, a belief which persists in spite of the fact that the agent knows it to be false, a non-voluntary belief, it is equally or more natural to deny that it is a belief at all. 'I cannot help thinking that the house will fall down although I do not believe that it will' is a more natural way of expressing such dissociation. It seems that there is less room for people to dissociate from their beliefs than from their emotions, desires, and actions. One reason for this will emerge below. But the full explanation cannot be explored here.

Whatever the verdict regarding the voluntary character of belief, the considerations adumbrated above show that, even if beliefs are not non-voluntary, it does not follow that they can be chosen. Emotions are not a possible object for choice, not even emotions which are not non-voluntary.

III

If, however, beliefs belong to the active side of our mental life why can they not be chosen? One explanation, pertaining to an important subclass of beliefs, relates to the nature of perception.[9] Paradigmatic perceptual beliefs are not acquired on the basis of the examination of evidence for them (though they are subject to review in the light of evidence of perceptual mistakes, etc.). While we have them, and continue to be aware of their perceptual origin, we cannot choose to abandon them. All this follows from the nature of perception, and need not detain us here. None of this shows, however, that we can never choose or decide to believe.

As choice and belief are analogous in being both, at least sometimes, underdetermined by reason, and since where this is so what one chooses or comes to believe may reveal some traits of character, what explains the fact that we cannot choose to believe? As I argued, the explanation does not lie in the responsiveness of belief to reasons. The significance of the distinc-

---

[9] The point I am pursuing here is roughly B. Williams's second reason for why we cannot decide to believe. See *Problems of the Self*, 149.

tion lies elsewhere. It lies not in the distinction between the active and the passive (where normally choice, decision, and belief are all, in different ways, on the active side) but in the fact that choice applies primarily to actions, and to what can be accomplished through them.

Choice is exercised by acts which constitute choosing: in taking one course of action rather than its alternative we choose it, or we may have chosen it earlier by deciding to take that action. Beliefs we do not acquire by performing actions. Though there may be actions preceding their acquisition (investigating the evidence, etc.) the beliefs themselves we form (or 'we come to believe'), rather than adopt, decide upon, or choose.[10] We decide and choose what to do in the world: to build or to travel, to wage wars or to make friends, to eat or to give up overeating. We do not decide nor choose how to feel, what emotions, attitudes, and beliefs to have.

We can choose to perform or not to perform mental acts, in which action has to do with thinking, and with what we do by thinking. Perhaps the thought that we can choose to believe was made plausible to those who thought that we can acquire beliefs only by thinking, and that therefore, since we can often choose when to think, we can choose what to believe. This argument is guilty of two mistakes. First, we acquire many of our beliefs—probably the vast majority—not through thinking and deliberation. Perceptual beliefs—special cases excluded—are but one prominent example. Second, while we can choose when to think and of what, it does not follow that we can choose the results of our thinking. Having thought of an incident I can become angry with John, or frightened of him, or I can come to believe that it was his fault and not mine—all these may be rational conclusions of my thinking, yet none of them is chosen by me, nor can they be.[11]

Things are not altogether straightforward. There are the instances of people deciding not to be angry any more, or not to be irritable, etc. To unpack the meaning of such decisions requires some sensitive delineation of complex arrays of features. Crudely, we cannot stop feeling angry by deciding not to feel angry. But we can decide to take action to abate our anger, for example by not dwelling on it, and we can take action to avoid the circumstances in which we become angry. And we can decide to try to improve our character, to be less prone to certain feelings, or at least to

---

[10] ' "Belief" may . . . refer to a psychological act—to the fact that a man *accepts* a proposition, or *takes* it to be true.' Chisholm, 'Lewis's Ethics of Belief', in *The Philosophy of C. I. Lewis*, ed. P. A. Schlipp (La Salle, Ill.: Open Court, 1968), 223, cited by Bennett, 'Why Belief is Involuntary'). But to the extent that this is so it refers not to an act of believing but to an act of accepting a proposition, which is discussed separately below.

[11] 'Concluding', when referring to the coming to believe in a conclusion as a result of deliberation, is not an action.

suppress various expressions of our emotions and feelings in action.[12] Sometimes the very decision to take action not to feel angry causes my anger to abate.

For our purposes more important are apparent exceptions of a different kind. In certain contexts it is certainly possible to talk of choosing what to believe. We can choose to believe one witness or one report or piece of evidence rather than another. Therefore, in contexts of examining evidence we can choose what to believe on the basis of the evidence. The *Oxford English Dictionary* offers the following example: '1713 Guard. No. 39, I shall not retract any advertisement till I see those verses, and I'll choose what to believe then . . .'. But such uses are special to certain contexts. They bear implications which do not contradict the general conclusion. We can mention two contexts of this use. First, the assertive or defiant use: 'You are not to tell me what to believe. If I choose not to believe in science that is my business.' Second, we accept (for reasons) propositions to serve us as premises in deciding what to do or what to believe when doing so answers a need but we neither believe nor disbelieve these propositions nor do we think we have sufficient reason requiring us to do either. Familiar cases in which such a need arises are when a judge has to decide who bears responsibility for an event, or an employer which candidate to employ. Their decisions are sometimes based on evidence which, though relevant, is less than conclusive. They may then be forced to choose which evidence, and thereby which conclusions, to accept.

In neither context does one choose to believe a proposition. In the first type of context one is not choosing anything. Instead, one asserts one's right to come to one's conclusions by oneself, rather than follow someone's opinion, pressure, or diktat. One would then form one's beliefs in the usual way, that is, in response to reasons as one sees them. In the second type of context one is choosing, but not choosing to believe. One is choosing to accept a proposition without necessarily believing it.

IV

The upshot of the argument so far is to divide the laurels between those who thought that we can and those who thought we cannot decide what to believe. The verdict supports the latter view: we cannot choose or decide what to believe. But regarding the deeper underlying issue the former view

---

[12] An additional complication is that while we cannot literally decide not to feel angry, we can resolve not to feel angry. Here, as on many other occasions, 'resolving' differs from 'deciding'.

prevails: belief belongs to the active part of our nature and our life. The perception of this fact is at least part of what led to the 'voluntaristic' view of belief. The false view of the will as (relatively) free of subjection to reason misled both camps to adopt or reject the view that belief can be chosen, depending on whether they emphasized that belief is active or that it is governed by reason. In fact it is both and no dilemma is involved once one realizes both that the will itself is subject to reason and that choosing and deciding are not the only manifestations of the active.

The initial account of activity I have presented so far is simplified. According to it for the most part our beliefs are a product and an aspect of our active nature because they are responsive to reasons, the exception being those pathological 'beliefs' which we persist in even though we know that they are unfounded. In such cases it is somewhat inaccurate to refer to us as entertaining beliefs at all. Rather it is a case of being haunted by thoughts, being unable to shake off certain propositions, being afflicted by feelings (fears, etc.) the cognitive component of which one knows to be unwarranted, and so on. In this picture, in other words, beliefs which are not sensitive to reasons are hardly beliefs at all. (Typically, people would deny, when aware of the fact, that pathological beliefs are beliefs of theirs, but the circumstances may warrant others to hold that they are). But the shape of our beliefs is more complicated than that. It includes many degrees and kinds of dissociation, which we cannot explore here.

Beliefs are not events in our life, but they are on the active side of the divide because, and to the extent that, in our life we respond properly to reasons as we understand them. Our beliefs are an important element in the formation of our feelings, emotions, attitudes, and desires, and a major determinant of our hopes, aspirations, goals, and actions. It is, therefore, reasonable to expect that whether or not our emotions, moods, thoughts, desires, and actions are active or passive, whether or not they are part of our lives as we lead them, will depend at least in part on whether the beliefs which inform them are active or not. At least it seems reasonable to assume that

(1) if the beliefs are ones which intrude on us rather than being wholly ours then so are the thoughts, desires, emotions, or actions which presuppose them.

Similarly it is reasonable to assume that to be active those states of mind must meet a second condition, namely,

(2) we must judge them proportionate to the reasons we think we have for them.

If these points provide the core of an account of the active it would appear that we are active when we are responsive to reason. Is the active/passive distinction the same as the rational/irrational? This view has a distinguished philosophical history, though it has to be reinterpreted as our understanding of rationality changes. It has much to commend it. It plays down the significance of the fact that the triggering event comes from inside us (e.g. being thirsty versus being confronted with a sudden danger). It relies instead on the appropriateness of our response to the triggering circumstance. It is not a rationalistic view for it does not assume that reason alone determines our responses. What emotion we feel when in danger depends in part on the accident of the case and in part on our emotional constitution, both as members of the human species and as individuals with our own temperaments. Reason merely sets the limits of the rational, limits which are themselves sensitive to our biological and social nature, and thus determines when we are active.

Yet though the two contrasts (rational/irrational and active/passive) are related, they are not identical. I will consider only one important difference between them, which will help to disambiguate some of the earlier formulations: we are irrational but often active when we act against our better judgement, through weakness or impetuosity. Similarly self-deception and wishful thinking can lead us irrationally to have certain beliefs, without consigning them to the fringe of pathological beliefs which are not really our own.[13] We are active not when we are *properly* responsive to reason but when *we think* that we are. We are active so long as we appear to ourselves to be conducting our life rationally, or as I shall say so long as we live under semblance of rationality. When our beliefs are induced by self-deception, wishful thinking, or other forms of irrationality which we do not recognize as such, we are active even though we are irrational. We are responsive to reasons as we see them, or as we see it we are responsive to reason. That is the core account.

The statement of the core account is liable to mislead. It does not mean to suggest that we are active only when we are self-reflective and explicitly hold views about our rationality, let alone that we are active only when we have views about the nature of rationality. We believe that we are properly responsive to reason whenever we would, if challenged, resist, at least

---

[13] I have in mind occasional irrational conduct, emotions, intentions, etc. A person who is generally irrational is not leading his own life even while he may think that he does. This is the case e.g. of a severely paranoid person who suffers hallucinations, and who persistently believes that terrorists, let us say, are hunting him and he is hiding from them. He appears to himself to be leading his own life in a rational way. But he is not. Nor is a demented person whose memory is confined to a few minutes, and who, being unaware of his dementia, thinks that he is generally reacting reasonably to situations he is in. Having a unified personality and being in general rational are presuppositions of being oneself, and being able to lead one's own life.

initially, claims that our conduct, intentions, emotions, etc., are irrational or unreasonable.

Self-deception and wishful thinking are typical causes of irrational beliefs which remain active because they appear to us rational. Their very ability to deceive us depends on that. Only while our beliefs maintain the semblance of rationality can they deceive us. Weakness of the will, and impetuosity too, often remain within the active. This is so, for example, when our weakness manifests itself by making rationalizing excuses (there is no harm in having one cigarette from time to time; this one will be my rare cigarette). There are accounts of akrasia (e.g. Davidson's) by which an akratic will is always active. If so, then giving in to an addiction-related desire is not a case of akrasia. The addict who tries and fails to shake off his addiction is not in charge of his life. He does not control it. He is passive for, while his desire for, say, heroin is backed by reason (as are all akratic desires and actions), nevertheless it is not, in his own eyes, proportionate to reason.[14]

V

My account of the notion of the active, it may be objected, is too objective. However, if the remarks above are correct then to want to be rational is to want to be a person. It is a desire that almost all people have; even those who want to die want to remain persons until they die. Note that the desire to be rational is consistent with wanting to be irrational on this or that occasion. As we just saw, there is another way in which the charge is not accurate: we are active to the extent that *we believe* that we are properly responsive to reason. Yet the account is objective in not depending on

[14] One possible objection to the core account concerns the case of the happily irrational person. Imagine someone who says (to himself or to others): 'I know that it is irrational to smoke, but, Ho Ho, let's do it and have fun.' Is there any reason to think that such a person is not being active in leading his own life according to his own lights? I agree. I feel that in all such cases we would find that the agent is mistaken about his own irrationality. In the example I gave I suspect that the person is not irrational at all. He simply values his health (or his longevity) less than many others, and is willing to risk them for the pleasure of smoking. This is not irrational, though he thinks that it is and therefore feels guilty about his conduct. This is expressed in the defiant bravura of his thought. Other examples will reveal different mistakes. Perhaps the most interesting is the case of a happy immoral action. Imagine a person who happily beats up an old lady believing this to be immoral and therefore irrational conduct. I suspect that he does not really believe it to be irrational. He may believe it to be immoral, but also believe that he is entitled to express his anger even in an immoral way. The motivation for interpreting all such cases as involving mistakes will become clear in the concluding pages of this chapter.

people's desires or feelings about how they are, or how they want to be. The reasons emerge when we recall the reasons which made Frankfurt admit that his very subjective account is incomplete.[15]

Frankfurt's central idea is that desires and emotions are internal to a person if and only if he identifies with them. This determines the subjective character of his account. Externality is determined by one's own attitude to one's desires and emotions. The problem as he sees it is how to understand identification. His first suggestion was that we identify with a desire if and only if we decisively want it to move us to action (pp. 15, 18). There is a sense in which every desire contains or implies a desire that (other things being equal) it move one to action. The presence of this desire marks 'desires', when the term is used narrowly to exclude hopes, or wishes. Frankfurt's suggestion must be taken to mean that a person identifies with a desire if and only if he desires it, rather than any of the competing desires he has, to move him to action. Before long, however, Frankfurt realized that this characterization would not do. When I want a refrigerator and also want a dishwasher, but, not able to afford both, I form the desire—using Frankfurt's formulations—to be moved to action by, let us say, the desire for a refrigerator, and not by the desire for a dishwasher, it does not follow that the desire for the dishwasher is not really my own, that I relate to it in the way an addict relates to the craving to satisfy his addiction which he resents and tries to shake off without success.

This problem may incline one to characterize identification as a desire to have a desire or an emotion (rather than the desire that it move one). But Frankfurt was always careful not to confuse, as this suggestion does, one's wishes to have or not to have certain characteristics, emotions, or desires with the phenomenon of identification that he was after (pp. 15, 63–5). A person who regrets that he is envious, and who wishes not to be, may be anguished precisely because he knows that he really is an envious person, that he cannot claim that envy is an external force which possesses him. So later on Frankfurt drew attention to the need to characterize the elusive notion of non-identification neither by reference to a desire not to have a desire or an emotion, nor by a desire not to be moved to action by them, but by their outright rejection (p. 67), a notion which he felt unable to analyse.

The reason Frankfurt found no way to solve the problem is that, once

---

[15] In doing so we should bear in mind that Frankfurt has a number of different goals in his sights: he is trying to explain the notion of a person, to explain the nature of freedom of the will, as well as to explain when our will and passions are truly our own, employing for this last purpose the distinctions between the active and the passive, the internal and external. My concern is only with the last of these. His success in achieving his other goals is immaterial here.

he identified externality with absence of identification, he made it dependent on people's own attitude to themselves, and made it impossible to distinguish externality from people's disapproval of the way they are. Nor does his approach allow for a solution to a second problem he alerts us to: if a desire's being really mine depends on another desire of mine, can the second desire determine the fate of the first even if it is itself not really mine? This is implausible, as is the supposition that these second-order desires cannot be external. But then what authenticates the authenticators? What determines whether second-order desires are really internal? We can agree with Frankfurt (pp. 167–9) that an agent who stops at a second-order desire, and does not form higher order desires about it, need not be doing so arbitrarily. But that does not solve our difficulty.

Here we can see the advantage of the approach I have been recommending. Its central notion is that activity is related to the proper functioning of the processes which govern our mental lives, our beliefs, moods, emotions, desires. That proper functioning consists in proper responsiveness to reason. That provides the key to the account of what it is for people to live their lives as they lead them. We do so to the extent that we believe that our thoughts, beliefs, emotions, and desires are properly responsive to reason. This account avoids the pitfalls of Frankfurt's approach. Nothing here is up to us. Conflict is not part of the account, which, since it does not rely on making mental states our own by adopting them, does not encounter the difficulty of establishing that the adopting state is ours.

Cannot Frankfurt's problem be replicated within the framework of the core account? If we are active while we are, as we see it, responsive to reason, does it not follow that our view that we are responsive to reason need itself be, as we see it, responsive to reason? If so, we are back in an infinite regress with no obvious reason to stop at any particular stage.

One response views a person as leading his own life so long as he rationally, even if mistakenly, sees his beliefs, conduct, emotions, etc. as responsive to reason. There is no regress of any kind here, though a justification which would motivate this response is required. I tend, however, to favour the simpler position which I presented as the core position: we are ourselves so long as, as we see it, we are responsive to reason. We may be irrational in thinking that we are responsive to reason. What counts, however, is not the justification or rationality of our view, but the view itself: We are ourselves and we lead our own life so long as we see ourselves as rational agents, so long as we conduct our life under the semblance of rationality.[16] This is not an altogether subjective condition. To believe that we are

---

[16] Remember though the earlier caveat, namely that this is so only so long as we are in general truly rational.

responsive to reason requires understanding of what counts as relevant evidence, what are relevant reasons and what not, and an at least rough competence in evaluating their bearing. Those who do not possess that competence and that understanding cannot be said to see themselves as responsive to reason. If they claim that they are, this is merely because they do not understand what they claim. So, to see oneself as subject to reason is to be responsive to reason to a minimal degree. That still allows room for one to believe, mistakenly, and even irrationally, that one is responsive to reason. And this would be enough to satisfy the condition of my core account.

The problem with Frankfurt's account is not that it is subjective, but that it is subjective in the wrong way. The key to my account is the objective notion of proper functioning, explained in terms of responsiveness to reason. The relatively subjective element is that the active depends not on proper responsiveness, but on what a person takes to be proper responsiveness. The psychological phenomena explained are of agents who are landed with mental states which are not their own, which they have in spite of themselves. The explanation lies in witnessing a breakdown of the proper functioning of our faculties, and that consists in thinking that we are not properly responsive to reason.

It may help bring out the rationale of the account if we consider the relations of self-control and self-understanding. Both, when properly understood, are central to the notion of the active, of one's life as one leads it. My life is mine to the extent that I am in charge of it. It is not mine if I lose control, if urges and emotions invade me which are out of my control. When they are under my control they are intelligible to me. I understand them, and why I have them. That understanding is not the one gained from science. It is not the understanding a kleptomaniac may have that some enzyme deficiency makes him a kleptomaniac. Rather it is the understanding a smoker has of what attracts him to cigarettes. It is belief in the presence of what we take to be the good in an action, or desire, of the rationale of a belief or an emotion, that is, belief in reasons for our wants, beliefs, emotions, etc. Reason makes us intelligible to ourselves. Through it we direct our lives, we are in control. Sometimes this means acting, or choosing, etc., in light of reason, sometimes it means no more than forming beliefs or emotions where they are reasonable, where their formation and persistence is under the control of our rationality, even though there is no self-awareness or decision.

In cases of motivated irrationality, we abuse reason, we are motivated to believe flattery, presenting it to ourselves as reasonable appreciation, we are motivated to smoke against our better judgement, inventing spurious exceptions or excuses. In such cases we are motivated to make ourselves appear to ourselves, however momentarily, as functioning reasonably. We are then still active, living our lives as we lead them. When the emotion, or desire, etc., is incomprehensible because of its incomprehensible object (an urge to lick the wall) or strength (why can I not resist the desire for heroin as I can the desire for chocolate, simply by resolving not to do what I know is bad for me?), we lose the ability to understand ourselves and to control our life.

The phenomenology of the passive aspects of our life is complex and the cases are diverse. Occasions of finding ourselves with moods, emotions, or intentions, or finding ourselves acting in ways which are unintelligible to us, are many. They differ from severe cases of schizophrenia (where people may behave in ways which they have no phenomenal account of, no sense of what it feels like) to common phobias, and to many moods where the way it feels is clear, but one is at a loss as to why one should feel like that. We are alarmed by the extreme and unusual manifestations of such cases, and take in our stride the more common ones. Not all of them are abnormal or undesirable. While they differ in many ways they are united in their opaqueness to ourselves, in the fact that they are unintelligible to us for they are not based on reasons, and therefore while they may be subject to self-manipulation they are not subject to our direct control. Regarding them we are passive.

Our life as we lead it is just our life, except that some elements in it seem like intruders, interpolators. Some thoughts we have, emotions we feel, some of our beliefs, desires, and actions are experienced as not really ours. It is as if we lost control, as if we were taken over, possessed, by a force which is not us. Such cases are the exception, but they are real enough. The difficulty in explaining their nature is not in explaining the exception, but in explaining the normal case: in what sense are our normal feelings and emotions, desires and beliefs, etc., 'ours' or 'under our control'? My suggestion was that life is activity and we are active in so far as, as it seems to us, we function well, that is in so far as, as it seems to us, our moods, emotions, beliefs, desires, etc., are properly responsive to reason.

Does the notion of the active outlined here account for all cases of psychological dissociation? I doubt it, but I feel unable to form a clear view. To do so we need more details of the notion I sketched and, of course, a thorough phenomenology of the psychology of dissociation. We also need a better account of rationality and of irrationality than is currently available. Meanwhile my suggestions can only be tentative.

2

Agency, Reason, and the Good

One approach to the explanation of agency, with origins in the writings of Plato and Aristotle,[1] takes acting for a reason[2] to be the distinctive and central case of human[3] agency. Other forms of action are either irrelevant (e.g. 'as I fell I hit the vase and shattered it', 'my breathing got heavier') or to be explained by reference to the central case (e.g. 'I opened the door by mistake', 'I hurt him inadvertently'). Reason is then explained in part by invoking value: valuable aspects of the world constitute reasons.[4] This

---

[1] So far as I know much of the interest in it in recent philosophical writings is due to Anscombe's *Intention* (Oxford: Blackwell, 1957).

[2] Whenever I refer to reasons I will have reasons for action in mind. In fact the conclusions here advanced apply equally to all practical reasons (reasons for attitudes, emotions, etc.), that is to all reasons other than reasons for belief.

[3] Where this way of identifying the kind of agency involved is not meant to imply that only human beings are capable of such actions (nor that all human beings are), but only to pick out the class of action as one which is typical of humans.

[4] 'Reason', like 'father', is both a one-place and a two-place predicate: 'People's vulnerability', one may say, 'is a basic moral reason.' But if that is so it is because some relational application of the predicate is true (e.g. 'that people are vulnerable is a reason for us all to protect them from harm'). This example presents reasons as a relation between two facts: the fact that people are vulnerable is a reason for (the fact of) people protecting others from harm (to obtain). Alternatively, and more naturally in many contexts, we conceive of reasons as a relation between a fact which is the reason (when used as a one-place predicate), a (class of) person(s), and an action(-type). It is also possible to claim that all reasons are properties of the action for which they are reasons, i.e. properties which make it *pro tanto* good. Here 'reasons' is given a slightly different, though closely connected, sense. I doubt that much illumination can be derived from a careful study of the grammatical or logical form of reason-sentences.

Note that in regarding facts as reasons (as explained here) one indicates that reasons are aspects of the world only in the sense that it is not a fact that so and so unless the world is such and such (e.g. unless a certain action was performed, or an event occurred, or unless some object has some property, etc.). In this way identifying reasons as facts is neutral regarding the ultimate 'ontological' character of reasons. I believe that events, acts, states, and more can be reasons, and that nothing much turns on that. Some may object to this way of conceiving of reasons on the ground that while identity of reference establishes identity of acts, it does not establish identity of reasons. Anselm Müller argued to that effect (in lectures in Oxford during 1999). For example, Abe may say: 'I will help Bertie because he is my partner.' Eve may say: 'I will help Bertie because he is Abe's partner.' They have different reasons. Abe's is that *Bertie is my partner*. Eve's reason is that *Bertie is Abe's partner*. The propositions expressing the reasons are different, but they refer to the same fact. Hence reasons are identified by the same criteria as are propositions rather than as facts.

approach, the classical approach, it may be called, can be characterized as holding that the central type of human action is intentional action; that intentional action is action for a reason; and that reasons are facts in virtue of which those actions are good in some respect and to some degree.[5]

This way of understanding the connection between action, reason, and value has been challenged by various writers.[6] Suppose for example that in a fit of rage at my unfaithful husband I gouge out his eyes in his photograph (which I find while going through his wallet) and then tear it up. I did that because I was mad at him, but I do not claim that the action was good or wise, or even permissible. I agree that I should never have touched his property, and that the whole thing was foolish if not worse. Nor do I claim that I had a reason for doing what I did. I did it because I was mad at him, but not in order to accomplish anything (not even to hurt him—I did not for a moment believe that it would), nor in the belief that the action was a worthwhile or good action. Actions like this are not particularly rare and, it is claimed, they show the inadequacy of the classical approach. They are intentional, but neither done for a reason, nor seen by the agent as good.

I will examine this challenge in two stages. First, I will consider the possibility that reasons need not be connected to value in the way the classical approach alleges.[7] Then I will consider the case for denying the identification of intentional action with action for a reason.

I believe that this argument is mistaken. The difference between Abe's and Eve's reasons is real enough but left unstated in their statements so far. It is made explicit when Eve amplifies the statement of her reason: *Bertie is Abe's partner, and Abe is a dear friend*. Nor is it the case that Abe's reason is made clear only when using a reflexive demonstrative. I can know what his reason is and explain it to you by stating: *Bertie is Abe's partner*. But, you may object, is it not the case that Abe may know that (i.e. may know that *Bertie is Abe's partner*) and yet not know that he (Abe) has any reason? And would that not show that the reason is not correctly or not fully stated that way? Yes, and no. Abe may know that Bertie is Abe's partner and not realize that he, Abe, has a reason, for he may not have the knowledge which he would express by saying *I am Abe* (and which no one else can have). But that shows only that he will not realize that he has a reason when the reason is pointed out, for to understand that the fact pointed out is a reason he must know something which he does not. It does not show that that fact is not the reason. If *I am Abe* is part of the reason then only he can know that he has that reason, which is patently false.

[5] The agents' belief that there is a reason for their action, or a specific belief of theirs in something which they take to be a reason can also be said to be a reason, in a slightly different sense which I will call an 'explanatory reason'. An explanatory reason may exist even when there is no reason for the agents to do what they did (i.e. when they mistakenly believe that there is a reason for their action). Nor can a reason explain agents' behaviour unless they were aware of it (though not necessarily of the fact that it is a reason).

[6] e.g. Rosalind Hursthouse, 'Arational Actions', *Journal of Philosophy*, 57 (1991).

[7] The challenge to be examined relates to the type of examples mentioned. I will not consider objections arising out of belief in the conceptual or other independence of deontic considerations, which can constitute reasons while not being related to the good, etc.

1. REASON AND THE GOOD

(a) The Objection

Let me start with what I will take to be a common assumption. Generally speaking, humans have the capacity to act in light of an appreciation of their situation in the world. That capacity is primarily manifested in intentional actions: they are actions under the control of the agents who take them. They are undertaken because of what the agents believe about themselves, and the world around them, and that means that they are intelligible to their agents. So, typical intentional actions are actions about which their agents have a story to tell[8] (i.e. actions manifesting an internal viewpoint about what one is doing, or is about to do), a story which explains why one acted as one did. Moreover, and this point is crucial, the explanation makes intelligible not only why the action happened; it makes it intelligible as an action chosen, or otherwise undertaken, by the agent. It is a story which shows what about the situation or the action made it, the action, an intelligible object of choice for the agent, given who he is and how he saw things at the time.

I have put the point in as vague a way as I can for the task of explaining human agency is precisely the task of making sense of this common assumption. The classical approach is one route one can follow in attempting such an explanation. According to it the 'story' is of what the agents took to be facts which show the act to be good, and which therefore constitute a reason for its performance, making it eligible.

At this point the objector comes in. The classical approach, he contends, confuses the features which make an action an intelligible object of choice with what might make it a good action. True, what makes it good also makes its choice intelligible. But good-making features are just one kind of feature capable of explaining the eligibility of actions, that is their possible attraction for an agent. That an action will cure someone's illness makes it eligible because it makes it good. But that an action hurts another makes it an intelligible object of choice too, says the objector. Those who understand people understand that a desire to hurt, and to watch the other being hurt, exercises great appeal for many people. That an action is hurtful does not make it good, but it makes it intelligible by making its appeal to some agents intelligible. Another example: that one has a duty to perform an action is a reason to perform it, which also shows it to be good, at least in some respect. But that an action will violate one's duty, or that it will break all the norms, also makes it an intelligible object of choice. Again, we know that often

---

[8] Or they are parts of sequences of action—getting up, walking to the left, stopping at the door, turning the handle, etc.—about which one has a story to tell.

people do what they do precisely because it is the wrong thing to do, because it is the anomic choice.

Once we draw a clear distinction between features which show an act to be an intelligible object of choice and ones which show it to be good or of value we will see, the objection continues, that reasons belong with the first, and not with the second. People will acknowledge, or brag, that they did something because it would hurt X, or because it was against all the rules. These are often their openly avowed reasons. And that is how it should be, for reasons are those considerations which make the act eligible from the point of view of the agent, and not necessarily those which make it good.

(b) Some Background

To deal with the objection, using the examples I have given, we need some initial simplifications and clarifications. First, the kind of case we are dealing with is often complicated by the presence of multiple reasons and motives, ambiguities in their interpretations, and by occurrences of self-deception and rationalization. We will just assume that our examples are not infected by any of these.

Second, sometimes people act to hurt others, etc. because they mistakenly believe in what they take to be values, for example, they may believe that women whose husbands betrayed them should kill their children and commit suicide. Such women are acting for what they regard as good reasons, reasons, that is, which make their actions the best or the right actions in the circumstances.[9] While many such actions are bad and wrong, and some even monstrously bad, they are not counter-examples to the classical approach, for in the eyes of their agents they are good. The objection relies on cases where agents intentionally do what they take to be bad because, as they see it, it is bad.

Third, reference to mistaken beliefs in reasons serves to remind us that while, according to the classical approach, reasons are facts which endow an action with some good-making properties, when we explain actions by the reasons for which they were undertaken the focus is on the agents' beliefs that they had such and such reasons, beliefs which may be false. In explanatory contexts we sometimes refer to such beliefs themselves as reasons, and we always do so when we take those beliefs to be false, that is, when we think that (in the primary sense of the term) the agents had no

---

[9] In this chapter I do not deal with another objection to the classical approach, namely that right action (or that some categories of right action) has to be understood independently of the good, that deontic considerations are independent of considerations of value. I assume that whatever one must (or must not) do for deontic reasons is at least also good (or bad).

reason for their actions. Even then their actions are susceptible of explanation by reasons, which here means by their beliefs in reasons. I will leave it to the context to clarify whether reference to reasons is really to reasons or to belief in them.

Finally, it may be objected that the alleged counter-examples above fail because they are incomplete. That an action will hurt another is no reason for performing it for if it were then everyone would have such a reason, and those who did not act for them would be irrational. That is absurd, and therefore the examples fail to embarrass the classical approach. How is this response to be squared with the fact that some people will openly admit that they did what they did solely because they knew that it would hurt someone? The argument is that this states only part of their reason. They also believed that their victims deserved to be hurt, or that they had a duty to hurt them. Once the missing component of their reason is added the case is seen to be clearly consistent with the classical approach.

There is no doubt that this analysis is true of some cases, but it need not be true of all. The objection to the classical approach is based on the possibility of cases in which agents would deny any thought that what they did was right. They acted to hurt others and never thought that what they were doing was other than bad or wrong. This, one may reply, still leaves their reasons incomplete and therefore incomprehensible. Surely, if asked 'Why did you do what you did?' they will say 'Because we wanted to hurt'. Their desires are their reasons, and that an act will satisfy one's desire makes it *pro tanto* good. This reply is, however, not available for defenders of the classical approach, for they deny that agents' desires are (some special cases apart) reasons for their actions at all, let alone that they are good-making reasons.[10] Moreover, the classical approach allows that in any given situation people may well be confronted with quite a number of incommensurate options, so that there is no reason to expect every rational agent in a similar situation to choose the same. This is as true when the options are entirely benevolent (going to the theatre, collecting for a charity, working out, etc.) as when they are hurting others, acting immorally, etc.

(c) Refuting the Objection

With these clarifications let us turn to an examination of the objection. It is aimed at the classical approach, while accepting the common assumption, that is, the assumption that reasons make actions eligible by making

---

[10] For my arguments to that effect see Ch. 3. See also W. Quinn, 'Putting Rationality in its Place', in his *Morality and Action* (Cambridge: Cambridge University Press, 1993).

their choice intelligible from the point of view of their agents. The objection is, therefore, committed to the availability of an explanation of how it is that non-good-making qualities make an action eligible. I find it difficult to imagine such an explanation. For example, suppose one were to say that the intelligibility of certain reasons lies simply in the fact that we know (or believe) that human beings are often motivated by them. We know that people are often motivated to hurt, whereas they are not commonly motivated to swallow pieces of paper. Therefore, we find it intelligible that people act to hurt, and strange if they swallow pieces of paper (for no further reason).

But this explanation misses the point of the common assumption. Naturally, when we know that a certain pattern of conduct is common we are not surprised when it happens. That does not make it intelligible, except in that we assume that, if it is intentional, then it is intelligible to the agents. They have reasons, we assume, even though we do not know what they are, nor are we interested in finding out. Contrariwise, if the conduct is rare it may be more difficult for us to imagine what reasons the agents had for their conduct, but the rarity of the conduct is no proof that it is unintelligible, irrational—not even proof that the agents' action is based on false beliefs in reasons.

It is not surprising that applying the distinction between different kinds of explanations, those giving the agents' reasons and those which are from 'outside', from an 'external point of view', is not always easy in practice. Our interest in explanations is of many kinds, and when we provide an explanation we often try to cater for a demand whose nature is not always perspicuous, or one which may be ambiguous in nature. This is true even when it is our own interest or curiosity that the explanation is meant to satisfy. Consequently explanations themselves are often ambiguous, and multipurpose. Besides, sometimes the very divide between reason-based and other explanations is rather thin. Pleasure provides the clearest example. We know that many people prefer sweet food, and if we plan marketing, investing, etc. that is all we need to know. But we understand why a person prefers sweet food from that person's point of view only if we discover, for example, that sweet food gives them pleasure, that they enjoy such food. That taste is, as I said, common. Suppose however that someone claims to have pleasure in chewing paper. We will be surprised, but once we are convinced that the claim is truthful we will accept it. There is no accounting for taste, we will say.[11] Here, as with pure pleasures of the senses generally, there is not much rational depth to the reason. We cannot ask for

---

[11] I am not suggesting that such claims cannot be empirically tested, nor that people cannot be wrong about what gives them pleasure. But that is another story.

further and further rational explanations (as we can when someone does something because it is only just to do so, for example). It is merely a matter of one's physical constitution. But that should not disguise the difference between 'many people prefer sweet food' and 'many people enjoy eating sweet food'.

The difficulty in explaining the eligibility of actions in ways other than by reference to good-making qualities may make one doubt the objection. But is it just failure of imagination which makes the classical approach seem the only coherent account to have? I do not think so. The problem is of finding conceptual room for an alternative. Suppose we concede the objection and allow that one has reason to hurt others. It would seem to follow that those who do not hurt others, or who deny that the fact that an action would hurt others is in and of itself a reason to perform it, are irrational, or at least imperfectly rational, for they fail to acknowledge such reasons. If cogent this argument constitutes a refutation of the objection, its *reductio ad absurdum*. The refutation cannot be avoided by claiming that bad-making properties are permissive reasons. They are not, and it is wrong to follow them. The objector may try to avoid the *reductio* by pointing out that it presupposes what he denies, that is it presupposes that reasons not only render actions eligible for choice by the agent, but that they also *pro tanto* justify them. According to the objector everyone may find hurting people attractive just as everyone may find bananas tasty. It does not follow that doing what is attractive is justified.

But does this way of explaining reasons independently of value preserve the normativity of reasons? Does it account for the fact that defying reasons is irrational, that one may disregard a reason only to follow a more stringent one? The problem is not in the reality of the example the objector produces in support. The problem is in providing a coherent account of reasons, which allows for agents (*a*) believing that possession of properties other than good-making properties can provide reasons for actions, and (*b*) allows for the normative force of reasons, i.e. for the fact that failure to conform to them is a fault.

The classical approach allows that a gap may open between what is good and what attracts agents. But it accounts for the gap by the fact that agents can make mistakes. Certain actions appear to them attractive because they appear to them to possess good-making properties, but in fact they do not possess them. The gap acquires a stronger, more troubling profile when the mistake is due to motivated irrationality, such as self-deception, or wishful thinking. The objection, on the other hand, fails to provide an account of the attractiveness of the reason-constituting properties which preserves their normativity.

(d) Are There Reasons which are Neutral in Value?

Yet the force of the counter-examples is still troubling, though they may well be suspected of overkill. Why, we may wonder, need one go for reasons which involve badness? If the argument is that reasons need not be related to the good the natural counter-examples would be cases where reasons are simply neutral regarding the good, cases where reasons are neither good nor bad. Yet such examples are much harder to come by. What could be such an example? That a person when at home closes the door to the room he is in because he feels queasy and uncomfortable being in an open rather than a closed room, or the other way round, that one opens the door because . . . Or suppose that, walking in the street, I hear people singing round the corner, and curiosity makes me deviate from my route to see what is going on. Entirely intelligible, but does it show that the action is good in any respect?

It seems fairly clear that such reasons do not make the action morally good, nor do they manifest any moral virtue in their agents. Nor do they realize any other important impersonal value (beauty?), nor manifest any non-moral virtue or skills of their agents. Does it mean that these reasons are not constituted by good-making properties? Some may say that there is just one other way in which they can be good: they can be good because they contribute to the well-being of their agents, that is to the overall success (or quality, or what not) of their lives. But then, conformity with the reasons in my examples does not contribute to the agents' well-being either.

I do not want to get hung up on the examples I used. If you disagree choose your own. Imagine, however, that the person who, when at home, closes the doors to the rooms he is in, would, were he not to do so, soon become absorbed in whatever he is doing and forget that the door remained open. His closing the door does not affect his well-being for it does not affect his life. Or think again of the person who makes a momentary detour to see who is singing round the corner. His life is not affected one way or another by his action, which he will completely forget a few minutes later, and which has no other consequences. Some people would insist that such actions do favourably affect the person's well-being. They merely do so to a minuscule degree, so that the difference they make escapes our notice. Well-being, however, is in part about how people feel about their life, and in part about the values of their actions. Factors which make no difference to either do not affect their well-being. I will accept therefore that there are cases of people acting for reasons which are morally neutral, contribute to no Value, not even to the well-being of their agents, manifest no virtue, moral or other, and display no skill or accomplishment of any note.

Does not that disprove the classical approach? I do not think so. I do not believe that for an action to be of value, or to be good, it must possess a good-making property connecting it to big Values, like justice or beauty, or well-being or any other value for which we have an abstract name. Small goods are small but good none the less, nor need they be trivial instances of big values. This is a conceptual point, about the nature of concepts of value, and of what is valuable. It is not, of course, to be tested entirely by its conformity to the meaning of the words 'value' or 'good', though they are relevant to the issue. The notion of value used here, and in many philosophical discussions of axiological issues, does duty for a whole range of English words and expressions: 'value', 'good', 'best', etc., are just some of them. Others include many (but not all) uses of 'important', 'worthy', 'significant', 'meaningful', 'useful', 'meritorious', 'attractive', 'estimable', 'a good thing to do', and others. The notion is meant to generalize over the concepts of the pleasurable, enjoyable, of beauty, etc. We learn its scope by example, and we fix its contours by understanding its function within an explanatory account.[12] Theories falling within the classical approach do so, and they are not to be faulted by the counter-examples, for those presuppose that small values must be instances of big values, a supposition the classical approach is of course committed to denying. It should be admitted that talk of value in the context of what I call 'small values' is an extension of the normal use of the term, and may mislead. But the cases involved are cases where we may well say that the person's action was a good one, or use some other related expression.

(e) The Objection to 'Small' Values

A possible objection to this 'small values' view runs as follows. The small values view loses the concept of value altogether. It collapses into the concept of a reason, and is no longer an independent concept which provides part of the explanation of the concept of a reason for action. So long as the notion of value is tied to what I loosely call big values we have a grasp of its meaning which is partly independent of the role of value in providing reasons for action. We know roughly how to argue about beauty, justice, freedom, well-being, and other values. The moment the essential link to big values is severed—the objection proceeds—we no longer have any way of understanding value except through the maxim that whatever constitutes

---

[12] In other words, the concept is not hostage to the linguistic accident of the existence or absence of an abstract noun naming one value or another.

a reason is of value. Value now is entirely dependent on reason and plays no independent explanatory role.

The objection is, however, unjustified. As it recognizes, all the concepts involved—intention, reason, rationality, intelligibility, and value—are interdependent. We cannot but explain one in terms of the others. This interdependence, far from being vicious, is the reason for our ability to explain each of them by means of the others. This ability is lost if one concept entirely depends on just one other. This is, according to the objection, what happens to the notion of 'being of value', if it is not to be understood as tied to what I called big values as well as to reasons. But the objection overlooks other contexts to which value is central, such as the contexts of justification and of evaluation, and thus it also overlooks the connection between value and rationality. To put the point briefly: values not only show how certain actions are intelligible but also how they are justified. It is central to the classical approach that the same concept is crucial both for intelligibility and to justification (and therefore also to evaluation). Of course, intelligibility and justification can come apart. Intelligibility depends, according to the common assumption, on how things looked to the agents at the time. Justification and evaluation depend on how things really were at the time, though they allow for different types or dimensions of evaluation which take greater or lesser account of the agents' subjective perspective.

According to the classical approach, the role of values in justification and evaluation allows us to check on any claim that some consideration is a reason because it makes an act an intelligible object of choice: if this is so then the same consideration must also show that the act is justified or at least that there is something to be said in its justification, something that in the absence of contrary considerations makes it justified. Justifications (at least some kinds of justifications) do not depend on the agents' perspective, and do not depend on the reasons for which agents actually acted. We have a (relatively) independent grasp of the notions of evaluation and justification, and therefore the objection fails.

(f) Anomic Tendencies

The argument so far has disposed of the objection to the classical approach in so far as it relies on the claim that features which make an action an intelligible object of choice need be neither good nor bad. This may seem to offer little comfort to the supporters of the classical approach for it fails to dispose of cases relying on the intelligibility of actions for reasons which the agents acknowledge not to justify the actions (special circumstances always excluded). Hence, the challenge to the classical approach is not yet answered. When people take what they believe to be bad-making features to be their reasons I will say that they act for anomic reasons.

Some may be tempted to deny the possibility and intelligibility of action for anomic reasons. We can understand people saying 'I am doing this because it is bad', if what they mean is 'because it is conventionally taken to be bad', or if another reinterpretation is available. Otherwise we must judge them to be conceptually confused. Literally speaking, they say nothing in uttering the sentence 'I am doing this because it is bad', that is, they are totally incoherent. I do not, however, believe that such reinterpretations are always adequate to the phenomena. That is, I think that there are cases of action for a reason where the best description or explanation of what the agents did is that they took those actions because they believed them to be wrong or evil. True, the classical approach judges these ways of describing or explaining the agents' action to involve a degree of conceptual confusion and incoherence. But not all confusions render the thought totally empty, nor beyond all comprehension. Many people's beliefs include contradictions, and while the notion of believing in a contradiction is to a degree incoherent, it is nevertheless not devoid of all content. It provides the best description of many people's state of belief.

The objector to the classical approach does not, of course, regard anomic reasons as incoherent. Rather, he regards them as disproving the classical approach. But there is no reason to agree with him. The objector faces two difficulties. First, he has to explain why, if the classical approach is mistaken, if the possession of good-making characteristics is not the only thing which can constitute reasons, we do not have reasons which are neither good nor bad. It seems to follow that only what has value or disvalue can constitute a reason. Secondly, he has to provide an alternative explanation of what makes an action an intelligible object of choice. I am facing the proverbial saucer of mud, and proceed to eat it, moving my hands and mouth as I would normally do when eating. Something has gone wrong with me. In the absence of any good-making characteristic which I believe eating the mud possesses I will not be able to understand what I am doing. I will be more horrified at myself behaving in this way than other people will be. For to me this will signify that I have lost control over myself, that I am possessed by something which makes me act in ways I do not understand, ways which I disavow, protesting that it is not really me. The objector agrees with this description of the saucer-of-mud case. His task is to explain how it differs from cases in which agents have reasons which make their actions intelligible to themselves, but which are not conceived by them as good-making. This is where he fails. He has no explanation as to how reasons not conceived as good-making differ from the mud-eating example. He can neither identify what would count as such reasons (why not the fact that what is in the saucer is mud?), nor explain how they function as reasons, as factors rendering actions intelligible objects of choice.

These two difficulties are inter-related. Had the objector been able to answer the question about the intelligibility of actions he would have been able to produce examples of reasons where the factors which render actions intelligible are neither good nor bad. His failure to do so makes it possible to deal with anomic reasons as an anomalous, degenerate case.

What the objector promises, or at any rate what he must deliver to succeed, is a new account of normativity of reasons, independent of their relations to value. The objector should be able to specify what we have a non-value-dependent reason to do in a way which is free from any reference to values. All he delivers are anomic reasons, which are clearly not independent. They are generated from real reasons by inversion. There is no way of understanding them except as an inversion of values. That establishes that they are a degenerate case, an exception which proves the rule, rather than an objection to it. They are non-reasons (that is, facts which are of the wrong kind to be reasons) which through some corruption of a psychological process are taken for reasons. As an anomaly we can understand anomic reasons and their allure, to the extent that any incoherent thought can be understood. We know what they are, how to identify them: by inversion of true reasons. And we know how to explain their allure, by the appeal of contrariness.

The appeal of contrariness is an established psychological phenomenon.[13] Not being psychologists it does not fall to us to explain it. Its existence is well attested in a wide range of otherwise very different types of cases. Nor is it either good or bad in itself. Much creativity arises out of contrariness. Knowing of its existence we should have predicted the existence of anomic reasons even before we came across them. The only doubt might have been whether conceptual constraint set a limit to the possibility of contrariness. But we know from other cases that it does not. Contrariness quite often leads to nonsense. Had nonsense been totally beyond comprehension, anomic reasons would have been impossible, there would have been no content to them; but it is not. As I have just remarked, sometimes the best description and explanation of people's beliefs and actions involve conceptual confusions. That is what makes anomic reasons

---

[13] Notice that I am not claiming that people who act for anomic reasons act in order to be contrary, if that means that the contrariness of their action is their reason for it. This too may sometimes happen, but it misses the point of actions for anomic reasons. It represents them as undertaken for what are perceived to be good-making features (even though the perception is mistaken). Anomic agents perceive themselves as acting in pursuit of the bad, not the good. I invoke contrariness not as a reason, but as a psychological explanation of their action.

possible, and what enables us to understand them up to a point. Anomic reasons are possible, and we can understand them, only because they are a degenerate case of the normal. They vindicate rather than challenge the classical approach.

But does contrariness explain in the right way how the bad can be appealing, that is, how it renders actions an intelligible object of choice for certain agents? If it does not, if it merely provides an explanation from 'outside', it fails to explain anomic reasons. The answer is yes and no. The classical approach denies that anomic reasons are really reasons. They are a perversion of reasons. They are non-reasons masquerading as reasons. Therefore, there is no call to extend the notion of the normative, and explain how possession of non-good-making characteristics can be a reason. What is needed is an explanation of how they can masquerade as reasons, that is, an explanation of what attraction they can hold for agents who take them to be bad. Contrariness delivers that explanation, or rather a full phenomenological description of it would. It can do that because it works by inversion. It takes some elements of the norm and ascribes them to the opposite of the norm. Of course, when it transgresses conceptual constraints our ability to understand the process is limited. In those cases it descends into incoherence. What we expect is that the phenomena will reveal the same impenetrability, the same resistance to complete understanding. Anomic reasons, the claim is, do just that. We can understand them only so far, but not completely.

The fact that contrariness is a general and structural psychological tendency, working by inversion, means that it is capable of generating forms of behaviour providing apparent counter-examples to any norm. Had the classical approach been misguided, had the true explanation been different, contrariness would have generated not anomic reasons, but some other reasons being apparent counter-examples to the true approach. In other words, whatever the nature of reasons, we would expect contrariness to produce degenerate cases of non-reasons masquerading as reasons. Reasons generated by contrariness are not counter-examples for accounts which are psychologically acute and sensitive. These accounts allow that, given that human beings are capable of self-understanding, their conduct can be influenced by knowledge of explanations of human conduct, influences leading to a whole range of deviations, of which action for anomic reasons is just an example. This means that explanations consist of explaining the standard case and some of the possible ways in which deviations can be generated.

(g) *A Moderate Objection: On Degrees of Intelligibility*

At this point a moderate objector may break rank with the others to deny that my argument against the objection affects him. He does not wish to extend the normative beyond its dependence on good-making qualities. He agrees that actions for anomic reasons are irrational. But they are actions for real reasons. My suggestion that these are non-reasons masquerading as reasons is not credible. Nor are actions for anomic reasons that exceptional. They are just one type of irrational action, similar in many respects to akratic actions. That is why I am wrong in thinking that the classical approach can absorb their existence unmodified, taking them to be a degenerate case of the norm.

On one point the moderate objector and I agree, namely that actions for anomic reasons are irrational, and therefore exceptional. They are, however, a good deal more exceptional than typical akratic actions. I say, 'typical akratic actions' for what kinds of psychologically deviant actions should count as akratic, or as displaying weakness of the will, is of course a controversial matter. Typical akratic actions are actions for ordinary reasons: smoking because one enjoys it or to avoid the unpleasant sensations and feelings induced by nicotine deprivation, being disloyal to a friend because doing so advances one's career or job prospects, etc. What makes them akratic is that the agents judge them to be wrong or unwise. They act against their better judgement. Moreover, given that they are irrational they are not entirely open to explanation by reason. We can understand why the action was done for it was done for a reason which we can understand. But we also cannot understand why it was done, cannot understand it from the inside. For the agents themselves say that they knew they should not have done it, and there was nothing to prevent them from following their judgement. So why did they do it after all? Akratic agents are themselves in the same situation. They understand their akratic actions in the sense that they know what attracted them, and they felt the force of the attraction. But on the other hand, they do not understand why they acted as they did, in spite of the fact that they thought that they should not. They do not understand why it is so difficult for them to resist the temptations, or the fears, or whatever it is that makes them act against their better judgement.[14]

Akratic actions fit the classical approach. The reasons for them are ordinary reasons, and their irrationality, being an irrationality, should not be eliminated by an alternative account which makes it more intelligible and rational than it is. Action for anomic reasons is not akratic, for the agents may not display the internal conflict typical of akrasia. They may be

[14] Complications and qualifications abound. Here are two. (1) Both the akratic agents, and others observing them, may have a different kind of understanding of the situation, an understanding consisting of familiarity: they may know what it feels like. They may even predict how they or others will react to the temptation. (2) Sometimes the irrationality of weak-willed actions is hidden from their agents by self-deception, or faulty reasoning. For example, people may say: 'Overall we should not have this cigarette, but it would be so good to have it, and there is nothing wrong in not doing what one should do overall once in a while.'

entirely happy acting as they do. It is also more anomalous than akrasia for it is intentional action for a pseudo reason, rather than for a real reason (that is, for a fact which renders the action, in the eye of the agent, bad—at least to a degree—rather than good). But, given that both akratic actions and actions for anomic reasons can be accommodated by the classical approach, the moderate objector's claim that they require a modification to it remains unproven.

2. EXPRESSIVE ACTION

(a) Reason and Expression in Action

Was the example with which I introduced this chapter, in which I find a photograph of my husband and in a rage gouge out his eyes, a case of action for anomic reasons? It is not detailed enough to tell. It might have been, or it may be a case of akratic action. It is clear, however, that not all its features which seem at odds with the classical approach have yet been explained. It requires an examination of the second challenge to the classical approach: allowing that reasons are facts which show the act to be good in some respect and to some degree, that is allowing that reasons are essentially related to the good in this way, the second challenge denies that all intentional actions are actions for reasons.

Various reasons prompt people to doubt the thesis that to act intentionally is to act for a reason. Some actions are too spontaneous or their effects too negligible to count as actions for a reason. For example, what is my reason when I instinctively move my arm across my face when becoming aware of a fly hovering above my nose, or turn my head to the left when becoming aware of something moving on my left? Some actions are part of a whole sequence of actions where there may be a reason for undertaking the sequence but not for a particular step in it. What is my reason when I put one foot in front of the other in the course of getting out of the room?

I will not discuss these objections here.[15] They seem to be based on a misguided notion of what it is to act for a reason (parallel to the denial of small values we discussed above), leading to the conclusion that one acts for a reason only when one's action is preceded by deliberation about what to do. They also misunderstand the role of routines (such as moving one's leg to walk, or following a familiar route across town when returning home from work). While routines require the finessing of reason-based explana-

---

[15] They are partially discussed in Ch. 10.

tions, they also require, for the same reasons, finessing our understanding of intentional action. The case I wish to examine is of expressive action, that is action which is intentional at least in part because—it would seem—it is expressive, not because it is undertaken for a reason. The most persuasive example of this kind of action may well be the simplest: in the course of a conversation I suddenly get annoyed by something said, or by a recollection, and I bang the table in exasperation, for example. But before I examine such cases a few general observations about reason and expression in action.

We can start by picking up where the previous section left off, for a word of explanation arising out of that discussion may connect the two parts of my argument. I emphasized that in as much as intentional actions are actions for reasons they are intelligible, that is, they can be understood from within, their agents and others can understand what, in the eyes of the agents, made the actions eligible. Naturally not all aspects of people's actions are intelligible in that way. When I drive a car I do not have a reason to corrode its tyres, nor do I have a reason for the precise posture in which I sit in the car. The wearing out of my tyres and my body posture are both side-effects of my driving. Why does the fact that many aspects of our actions are not susceptible to reason-based explanations, that they are not intelligible in the way aspects of actions which are reason-based are, why does that not undermine the relevance and importance of reasons for the understanding of agency? Furthermore, many actions are not intentional, and thus they too cannot be explained by reasons (at least not by reasons alone). I do things by mistake, or accidentally, or inadvertently, and so on. Does that not show that the emphasis on the internal perspective, on the intelligibility of the action as an object of choice, is misguided? And if reasons are as central as the classical approach suggests, why do we not consider these actions as irrational as we do akratic actions, actions for anomic reasons, and others?

These matters require much more detailed analysis than they can receive here. In principle, however, the answers are not far to seek. In many of these cases we do not mean to control certain aspects of our actions, we just let the body, or the environment, take care of itself. This 'not meaning' may be reasoned ('I cannot significantly affect the rate of erosion of my tyres', 'I will be even less comfortable if I try to sit in a posture of my choice, than if I let my body determine my posture') or not. Cases of action other than intentional ones are mostly either the bringing about of further consequences by intentional actions (in which case they are further aspects of the intentional action we did not mean to control) or they are cases of failure in an intentional action (or both). But these failures (as in action by mistake, inadvertent action, etc.) are not failures of rationality, but of execution.

Being unintended failures[16] they cannot be explained from the inside, even though an external explanation is often easy to find.

These observations leave one important class of case: intentional action undertaken in the belief that the reasons against the action (or for some incompatible alternative to it) are not worse than the reasons for it.[17] In these cases one understands (or thinks one does) what renders the action eligible. But one also understands (or believes one understands) that incompatible alternatives are also eligible, and not inferior to this action. It follows that one cannot understand from the inside one's preference for this particular action. So far as reasons can enlighten one, one might just as well have chosen one of the other options. These cases, however, are not irrational for one is not defying reason. Reason, so to speak, has exhausted itself. One cannot explain one's choice from the inside for there is no inside story to tell on that point. (I can explain why I chose to drink spirits rather than wine, but not why the Macallan rather than the Balvenie—though sometimes I can do that too. Sometimes I may well have reason to choose one rather than the other.) Some people find this puzzling and in need of explanation. But it is just a fact of life. We can explain how it is possible that reason will not determine all aspects of one's choices (it would have been very surprising if it could), and explain which aspects it fails to determine in a particular situation and why. Beyond that it is just a fact that when there is no internal story to have we have none.

The fact that so many aspects of actions are not explained by the agents' reasons makes it possible for them to express people's character, their personality traits, and tastes.[18] This statement suggests a greater bifurcation between reason and expression than is the case. In acting rationally we express our rational nature. Much more, however, is expressed by the manner of our actions (willing or grudging, eager or hesitant), by involuntary aspects of conduct (posture expressing confidence, for example), or by choices among options where reason does not indicate that any of them is better than all the others (which may show taste for adventure, sense of fun, physical exuberance, and much more).

(b) Purely Expressive Intentional Actions: The Relevance of Control

When we have an interest in our own actions or those of others, it may be both in the reasons for which the actions were done, and in the way they express the agents' personality. In many cases one or the other interest

---

[16] Cases of unconscious intentions excluded.

[17] Though not better either. Where they are believed to be better the action is akratic.

[18] Needless to say, not all aspects of our actions which are not controlled by reason do that. Normally I express nothing when, in driving my car, I wear out its tyres.

dominates. But in all cases, according to the classical approach, it is people's responsiveness to reason which accounts for their ability to act intentionally. Moreover, to identify people's intentions one needs to identify their reasons. They fix the intentions. What the action expresses may dominate our interest in it, but it does not determine the intention with which it is done.

This is doubted by the second objection to the classical approach. According to it actions can be intentional in virtue (in part at least) of being expressive, and not merely because they are undertaken for reasons. The clearest evidence to start the argument will be cases of actions which are intentional even though they are not undertaken for reasons, cases of purely expressive intentional actions. My kicking or banging the table in frustration is an example of such cases. The actions in question typically express emotions, feelings, and moods. If they express character or personality they do so through expressing emotions, etc.

I call such actions purely expressive to distinguish them from actions undertaken in order to express something. Some expressive actions are communicative actions: since it is the anniversary of the revolution I fly a flag on top of my house. Or, I turn my back on a person, to express my disapproval of his conduct. I fly the flag, and turn my back, to communicate to others that I mean to express whatever it is I mean to express. But expressive action may be undertaken for reasons not involving a communicative intention. Seeing me teeming with anger you may say to me (they do so in films) 'Why do you not smash some crockery?' and in order to relieve my tension I do just that. My examples are different. They are cases in which people just act, or if you like, they just act out their frustration, or anger, or joy, and so on. They do not do what they do in order to express their emotions. They just act and their actions express their emotions.

This distinction is real enough, and it is the basis of the claim that purely expressive actions are not done for reasons. Yet they are intentional actions. Their intentionality can be established by the fact that they are under the control of their agents, control that is manifested in two crucial respects. First, the initiation of the action is up to the agent, and second, the execution of the action is also under the agent's control. Let me take the second point first. A mother hits her child in exasperated rage. Her arms hit the child: their movements could be as well directed and controlled in strength as they would be were she acting for an ordinary reason, for example, giving a demonstration. Expressive actions need not be marked by any lessening in control over the manner of their execution. They can display as much skill and dexterity as any action.

Similarly, turning to the first point, their initiation and continuation is under the agents' control. People who smash an object in anger usually choose one which is not very expensive. If they choose one which is very expensive this is deliberate, it is understood to show the strength of their feeling. Strong reasons to desist coming to mind at the last minute will typically cause one to desist, and so on. I describe control over the initiation partly as ability to stop it or to avoid it. But that does not equate such acts with semi-voluntary acts like breathing, which count as our acts at all only in a marginal sense, and only because of a limited ability to suppress them, or control their manner (fast breathing, etc.). The body's autonomous system initiates breathing. All we can do is exercise a limited degree of control. There is nothing comparable with purely expressive acts. If they happen they do because we choose them. But we are reluctant to describe it like that because that makes them more like actions for reasons than they are. They are more spontaneous. They explode within us, we feel. That is why it is easier to concede that we can suppress them than that we initiated them, chose them. But we did, or else they would not be intentional.

But while control is necessary to intentional action it is not sufficient. To show that an act is intentional it is not enough to show that its initiation and conduct are under the agents' control. They also must have a story to tell about it, a story which makes its performance intelligible. It explains why they exercised their control to perform it, rather than to avoid it. That is where the expressive aspect of the action comes in and provides the missing element which in other actions is filled by the reason for which the action was performed.

This, then, is the challenge to the classical approach's claim that intentional actions are actions for reasons. Pure expressive actions express emotions, feelings, or moods but are not done in order to express them, nor for any other reason. In spite of this they are intentional for they are under the control of their agents. This challenge is stronger than the challenge based on anomic reasons, for it contains the germ of an alternative account of intentionality based on control and expressiveness. Still, even this challenge is not without weaknesses. We expose them when examining the connection between control and reason. To be convinced of the strength of the challenge we need to be convinced that acting for a reason and being in control of the action, while clearly different concepts, are not inter-related in application. The reason why this is a potential weak point is that while we feel that there is some awkwardness in describing purely expressive actions as actions for reasons, we also suspect that they involve some loss of control.

I conceded that there is no respect with regard to which purely expressive actions necessarily involve loss of control. Yet they typically involve some loss of control. We expect people expressing emotions by throwing the crockery at the door or at a person, or a picture, to be less successful in finding their target than the same people would normally be. We expect people kicking the table to miss the table's leg more often than they normally would. We also expect such people to be less good in judging the prudent degree of force to apply, and are not surprised when often they hurt themselves (physically) more than they expected the action to hurt them, or cause more damage than they expected to cause. Could it be that while there is no necessary loss of control in any specific respect, a purely expressive action must involve some loss of control somewhere?

First, note that many aspects of purely expressive actions are not merely subject to their agents' control, but are also governed by reason. Even if the mother hitting the child does not do so for a reason, the action merely giving vent to her frustration, and even if people throwing crockery at others with whom they quarrel do so just in anger, and not for any reason, they aim at the child or at the people with whom they quarrel *because* they are the appropriate target for their expressive action. What counts as expressive action is in part a matter of cultural convention. In some cultures you can express contempt for a person by spitting in their direction. In other cultures this would not express anything. Is it surprising that only where it is recognized culturally as expressive do people express themselves through such actions? Purely expressive actions are not merely under our control, they are also under our guidance and we guide them to be what they are, that is, to be purely expressive, and to do no more, not to cause too much hurt to ourselves or to others, not to make us look ridiculous, etc. Even if we do not undertake them for a reason, we are guided by reasons when we engage in them. Given that in so many respects purely expressive actions are guided by reasons, why do we feel that there is something odd in taking them to be actions for a reason?

Possibly the answer, and with it the key to the explanation of purely expressive actions, is that they involve a small loss of control, and that is why they are not typical examples of actions for a reason. This brings me back to the question left hanging in the paragraph before last: do purely expressive actions necessarily involve loss of control? The answer, I am afraid, is yet again both yes and no. First the yes: I think that it is not just that some diminished control over the execution of purely expressive action is typical. I suspect that it is necessary. Purely expressive actions are nonidentical twins of actions for a purely expressive reason, that is actions one undertakes when the emotion swells within, and one says to oneself, 'Why should I not let rip? It will do me good', or 'I am entitled to', or something like that. That is, when the action is just a tiny bit more calculated it is an ordinary action for a reason, albeit a purely expressive one. The hesitation in saying that purely expressive actions are identical with their twins is that they explode from within without this element of calculation. But that explosion is a matter of diminished control over the initiation of the action.

The diminished control I identified is not located where I looked for it above. There the question was whether there is some diminution in agents' control over the manner and skill involved in purely expressive acts. My tentative answer is that in principle no such diminution is required, but that in practice it will be difficult to convince anyone, including the agents themselves, that an action which is perfectly controlled in manner and execution is not under perfect control at the point of initiation, and is therefore purely expressive. Since conceptual boundaries in such matters cannot be sharp, it may be too sharp, too definitive, to say that purely expressive actions need involve diminished control only over their initiation, but not over their manner and skill in execution. But they certainly involve the first kind of diminished control.

(c) Do Purely Intentional Actions Refute the Classical Approach?

Why then did I answer no as well as yes? For one thing, I had to. If purely expressive actions are actions over the initiation of which we have no control they are not intentional actions.[19] They will be more like breathing, that is, semi-voluntary actions, in virtue of our limited control over their execution. I need not deny that there are expressive actions which fit the bill. There are times when we lose control over ourselves altogether. We are subject to irresistible impulses which we cannot control, or something like that. There is no need to consider such cases here. They are the sort of exceptional cases which do not require a revision in the classical approach, nor in any other approach, but exist as (one hopes) exceptional breakdowns of human agency, rather than as examples of it. The challenge that purely expressive actions pose to the classical approach is that they are supposed to be ordinary intentional actions, and yet not actions for reasons. If they are ordinary intentional actions they are actions the initiation of which is controlled by their agents. The examples of purely expressive actions used throughout this chapter are not cases of total loss of control over the initiation of the action (I will not throw the vase in rage if I realize at the last minute that it is a very expensive one, etc.), and are meant to be ordinary intentional actions.

There is another way of seeing why the thought that agents do not

---

[19] Admittedly they can be borderline cases: even if their agents cannot control their initiation, to the extent that they control and guide their manner and execution, and especially if they can and do not terminate them, they possess characteristics of intentional actions and can be said to be more or less intentional.

control the initiation of purely expressive actions of the kind our examples illustrate is incorrect. In all these examples the agents do not disapprove of their actions. Of course, one can regret having kicked the table, as one can regret any other action one may have performed. But at the time of action the agents are not conflicted. Their actions are not akratic for they do not believe that they should not perform them. No doubt there can be purely expressive actions which are akratic as well, but that is not part of their nature. So let us confine our attention to those which are not akratic, to normal purely expressive actions. People who perform them are as happy with the fact that they performed them as with any other normal intentional actions.[20]

This last point seems to me to provide a clue to an explanation of purely expressive actions. It suggests that people who perform normal, purely expressive actions have, in the terms of the common assumption with which we started, a story to tell about their performance. They know why they did what they did. They are, at the time of action, content to have done as they did. Moreover, their explanations as to why they acted as they did are based on the same direct, non-evidential knowledge as we have of our reasons, intentions, decisions, and their like. Finally, their explanations invoke considerations which are in fact reasons for actions, and which could have been their reasons. For example, they may say that they acted out of rage, adding, or more commonly implying, that the action was an appropriate expression of rage. Typically such explanations invoke motives rather than reasons, but they state facts (that I was enraged and the action was an appropriate expression of my rage) which are also reasons for the actions thus explained.

In all, purely expressive actions are almost like actions for reasons. They differ in that while they do not involve loss of control over their initiation they involve diminution of that control (that is the Yes side of the answer, which was explained above). This makes it somewhat awkward to say that they are actions for reasons. It makes them differ slightly from their non-identical twins, in which the factors invoked by agents to explain their actions actually serve as reasons for those actions. The difference between the twins is in a slight loss of control in the purely expressive twin. But their similarity is so great that in spite of the difference the purely expressive actions are actions with a story from the point of view of the agent, a story which can serve as a reason—it merely did not function as a reason. Can we describe how it did function in a way which will bring out both the similarity and the difference between the twins? My suggestion is that we

---

[20] Nor are they in fact irrational, at least not necessarily so, for there may be good reasons for the agents to act expressively, even if they did not act for these reasons.

can think of people who perform normal purely expressive actions as people who let themselves express their emotions, feelings, or moods in action. They permit themselves to do so. They allow their emotions, feelings, or moods to express themselves in action, rather than taking an action in order to express their emotions. It is as if their will is less active (less in control) than in ordinary actions for reasons. Normally, we will the actions because of, what we take to be, the reasons for them. When we act for an expressive reason we take the fact of our emotion to be (part of) a reason for an action appropriate for its expression in the circumstances. In the case of purely expressive actions we merely allow the emotion to express itself, the will acting as a non-interfering gate-keeper.

These metaphors show, I hope, how subtle and thin is the difference between the twins. Does it justify regarding purely expressive action as an objection to the classical approach? I do not think so. In part the difference between such actions and normal actions for reasons is just too slight to make this case any more than a small modulation of the classical approach. But even this is to allow purely expressive actions the wrong role in the argument. The crucial point is that the very loss of control which makes them cases of letting oneself act for a reason rather than cases of acting for a reason also makes them somewhat less than typically intentional. This is where their use as an objection to the classical approach goes wrong. Control over the initiation of the action is an element in intentional action. When this control is absent the action is not intentional. When it is slightly impaired, and it is no more than that in our case, it is no longer a paradigmatic intentional action. Hence, the intentionality of actions and their character as actions for reasons go hand in hand, even if their alignment is not entirely tight.[21] This is what the classical approach maintains.

3. HOW STRONG ARE THESE ARGUMENTS?

The argument of this chapter, and much of the argument of the book, aims at establishing essential features of some of the concepts which play a key role in our thought. If successful they achieve a dual goal: in as much as they provide an account of these concepts they contribute to an explanation of some central features of people's lives as rational agents. In as much as the concepts they explain are those we commonly use when thinking about ourselves and others as rational agents, they explain some central features of our self-understanding. They can succeed in one goal only if they

---

[21] This remark is meant to acknowledge that we feel more clearly that they are not typical actions for reasons than that they are not typical intentional actions.

succeed in both. Given that the understanding of people as rational agents which we seek is an understanding gained through the use of concepts which are pivotal to our thinking about ourselves, their analysis cannot contribute to the explanation of human beings as rational agents unless it contributes to the explanation of our self-understanding, and vice versa.

No claim is made here, however, that it is impossible to understand humans in any other way, through the use of other sets of interlocking concepts. Arguably a complete understanding of rational agents requires success in the dual task. That is, no explanation which is alien to people's self-understanding can adequately account for their character as rational agents. But it is also possible that in some cultures past or future, or in the past or future of our own culture, people's self-understanding may depend on the use of different sets of concepts. If so then the conclusions expounded here are not undermined. The truths which different set of concepts enable us to grasp are consistent, or they would not be truths. But the explanations they provide are, on that assumption, incomplete. They have to be complemented by an account of those alternative ways of understanding people's rational nature. Cultural histories serve to remind us of this need. But so long as new ways of conceptualising ourselves may emerge in the future the task of explanation is inherently incomplete, incomplete not in having left undone something which can and needs to be done, but because changes in the ways persons conceive of themselves will require new explanations to enable us to understand them. Even if we succeed in stating the preconditions of any way of conceptualizing rational thought these preconditions will not be sufficient in themselves to explain all the puzzles to which their specific instantiations give rise. Claims of philosophical success are not to be seen as claims of philosophical finality. The ever open possibility of conceptual change is but one reason for the conclusion that the thought that the task of philosophical explanation can be discharged once and for all is illusory.

3

Incommensurability and Agency

Incommensurability is the absence of a common measure. It has acquired currency as something of a philosophical term of art used in relation to a variety of topics and problems, depending on what is the measure whose alleged absence is of significance. The incommensurability that I will be concerned with is the incommensurability of value: the possibility that the value of two items, or that the goodness of two options, is incommensurate, in that neither of them is better than the other nor are they of equal value.[1]

When speaking of both items and options whose value is incommensurate. I will be referring to specific options or specific objects.[2] Occasionally I will refer to the value that possession of a certain property lends to an object or an option (e.g. that being sweet endows an apple with additional value). I will not be concerned, however, with the comparative goodness of abstract values, such as freedom, justice, beauty, fairness, and the like.

This chapter will suggest that a proper understanding of human agency, and in particular of the relations between the role of cognition and volition in human agency, presupposes that there are widespread incommensurabilities of options.

I am grateful to Jonathan Dancy for very helpful comments on an early draft.

[1] I will use 'incommensurable' and 'incommensurate' as stylistic variants, and if needed to alleviate monotony I will also use 'incomparable' as meaning incommensurable. Strictly speaking, of course, incommensurability does not imply incomparability. Items whose values have no common measure may be comparable in a variety of ways: of two paintings whose value is incommensurate, one may be more colourful than the other, or older, etc. Besides, the most common use of 'incomparable' is to indicate great superiority of one of the items, i.e. it entails their commensurability. 'How can you compare', one may say, 'Mozart and Salieri? Clearly Mozart is incomparably the better composer.' Which he is. Hence, incommensurability is not to be confused with incomparability.

[2] I use 'option' to refer to an action that an agent is both able to perform and has an opportunity to perform. For example, going to Lincoln Plaza cinema for the late show next Sunday is an option for me today. The specificity of options does not entail that all their aspects are specified or decided upon. How to get there may be left undecided. Nor need a specific option be for a simple action like opening a window. It could be a complex course of action such as going on a skiing holiday next January.

1. PROBLEMS AND DIRECTION

An understanding of values is central to both our understanding of the world and our understanding of human action. This dual aspect of our interest in values and valuables is, of course, not accidental. Paradigmatically human actions aim at achieving some good or averting some bad. The capacity for human action is—I join many in believing—the capacity to act knowing what one is doing and doing so because something in one's situation makes this action a reasonable, or a good, or the right thing to do.[3] In other words, it is the capacity for intentional action, the capacity to act for reasons. Values 'control' reasons in that one can have reasons for an action only if its performance is, or is likely to produce, or contribute to producing, good or if it is likely to contribute towards averting something bad.[4] Thus the concept of reason for action connects those of value and agency. I will approach the issue of the incommensurability of values from the perspective of the explanation of action. From this vantage point, the incommensurability of values is seen as leading to the incommensurability of reasons for actions.[5]

I will contrast two conceptions of human agency, which I will call the *rationalist* and the *classical*. In broad outline, the rationalist holds that paradigmatic human action is action taken because, of all the options open to the agent, it was, in the agent's view, supported by the strongest reason. The classical conception holds that the paradigmatic human action is one taken because, of all the options the agent considers rationally eligible, he chooses to perform it. There are, I shall argue, three crucial differences between the two conceptions. First, the rationalist conception regards reasons as requiring action, whereas the classical conception regards reasons as rendering options eligible. Second, the rationalist conception regards the agent's own desire as a reason, whereas the classical conception regards the will as an independent factor. Third, the classical conception presupposes the existence of widespread incommen-

---

[3] This essentially Aristotelian conception has been powerfully revived in recent times by G. E. M. Anscombe, *Intention* (Oxford: Blackwell, 1957), a book that influenced many further constructive writings on the subject.

[4] This is true of deontic reasons as well, for while what is deontically required may not be one's best option, it is invariably an action that is good in some way or avoids some bad consequences.

[5] The primary context in which we refer to reasons is when debating what to do. Secondarily we refer to them to explain what we or others think or thought they have reason to do. Reasons, in short, are considerations that bear on the desirability or otherwise concerning the case for or against options. Or, in the secondary usage, they are considerations believed by the people under discussion to bear on the case for or against options.

surabilities of reasons for action, whereas the rationalist conception, if not committed to complete commensurability, is committed to the view that incommensurabilities are relatively rare anomalies. The three differences come down to a contrast between the rationalist view that generally rational choices and rational actions are determined by one's reasons or one's belief in reasons and are explained by them, as against the classical conception that regards typical choices and actions as determined by a will that is informed and constrained by reason but plays an autonomous role in action.

The will is the ability to choose and perform intentional actions. We exercise our will when we endorse the verdict of reason that we must perform an action, and we do so, whether willingly, reluctantly, or regretting the need, etc. According to the classical conception, however, the most typical exercise or manifestation of the will is in choosing among options that reason merely renders eligible. Commonly when we so choose, we do what we want, and we choose what we want, from among the eligible options. Sometimes speaking of wanting one option (or its consequences) in preference to the other eligible ones is out of place. When I choose one tin of soup from a row of identical tins in the shop, it would be wrong and misleading to say that I wanted that tin rather than, or in preference to, the others. Similarly, when faced with unpalatable but unavoidable and incommensurate options (as when financial need forces me to give up one or another of incommensurate goods), it would be incorrect to say that I want to give up the one I choose to give up. I do not want to do so. I have to, and I would have equally regretted the loss of either good. I simply choose to give up one of them.[6] In what follows I may on occasion refer to people deciding to do what they want from among eligible options. Such references should be qualified as meaning 'what they want or what they choose without wanting'.

My case for the existence of widespread, significant value incommensurabilities is connected to a way of understanding the role of the will in intentional action. This should not be surprising. If of the options available to agents in typical situations of choice and decision, several are incommensurate, then reason can neither determine nor completely explain their choices or actions. Nor can the action be predicted on the assumption that, since the agents are well informed and rational, they would do what they have most reason to do. The bar to such predictions is not that people are not rational or well informed. Even if they are, this method of explaining

---

[6] Choices made by institutions form a special case. It is hardly ever appropriate to refer to the institution choosing to do what it wants. See 'On the Autonomy of Legal Reasoning' in my *Ethics in the Public Domain* (Oxford: OUP, 1994).

and predicting action, which underlies so much work in the development and application of decision theory, is unavailable when the options that agents face, or some of them, are incommensurate. The will comes into play at this stage (though, as has already been noted, that is not the only role it can play in action), and typically agents choose from incommensurate options one that they want to perform. In any case, whatever they do, they do because they choose to, not because they ought to perform that action on the balance of reasons.

Rationalists would find this understanding of the relations between reason and the will distorted. They would gladly agree that the reasons for or against various options, the agents' own desires excluded, will often be incommensurate. But the agents' own desires are among their reasons for action. Some people think that ultimately the agents' desires are the only reasons there can be. Others may not go so far but will insist that the agents' desires are among the reasons that should and do guide their actions. Once we see that, we readily see that there is no room for incommensurabilities among the options open to agents, for when push comes to shove, the need to choose will concentrate the minds of the choosers, who will realize (or will think that they do) that they want one of the options more than the others.

Rationalists have powerful arguments to support that view of desires. The most compelling is that if they are not reasons, then the classical conception of action is right and there are widespread incommensurabilities. It is their abhorrence of incommensurabilities that makes rationalists what they are. They do not suffer this vacuum in the space of reason, and they have powerful arguments to deny its possibility. To rationalists, the fact that intentional action is undertaken in the light of the agent's understanding of his situation suggests that the agent must always be capable of finding an answer to the question, 'What am I to do?' There are always factors—we call them reasons—that guide the agent's choices and decisions. If there were incommensurabilities, then actions would be unintelligible to the agents who perform them. They would not be able to explain why they performed the action they did rather than one of the other options open to them. All they would be able to say is: 'We saw that there is no reason to prefer A to B, or the other way around, and we did A.' The obvious gap in this explanation will baffle not only the observer who is trying to explain or predict people's behaviour. It will defeat the agents themselves, who would regard their choices as a mystery, as something that happens to them rather than something they do. According to the rationalist, incommensurability is inconsistent with the fact that intentional actions are under the control of the agents, that they are determined by their choices.

2. BRUTE WANTS

Practical reasoning, reasoning about what is to be done, has two aspects.[7] It is concerned to establish how things are and how—given that that is how they are—one is to act. I will be concerned with its second aspect only.[8] According to the belief/desire account of reasons for action, that aspect of practical reasoning has to do with determining what, in the instant situation, one desires most, or what is, or is to be, one's all-things-considered desire, given all one's desires and beliefs about how things are. As this account gives desires the most extensive role in practical reasoning, I will take a simple version of it as the target for my argument.[9] The simple version regards brute desires—desires that we have not because we see reason to have them—as the only kind of reason to perform an action, other than for instrumental reasons. In other words, according to the simple version of the belief/desire account, the only reason an agent has is to do what will satisfy his brute desires. I will rely on two arguments against it.[10]

The first argument concludes that the simple version assumes that people reason about what they should do, given that they have conflicting desires—desires that, the world being as it is, cannot all be completely satisfied—but that it is incapable of making sense of such reasoning. The simple version has to maintain that when facing conflicting desires, people should do what they most want to do. There is, according to that account, nothing other than desires that can be a reason for action, let alone a reason capable of adjudicating between conflicting desires. So the question of what

---

[7] What is to be done, either by the person deliberating or by someone else, and either now or at a later time, or if the opportunity arises—and one need not expect that it will, nor that it may arise—or at a time past, as when one examines one's youth, or someone else's past action.

[8] Without thereby implying that they can be neatly divided. The distinction is meant as a rough-and-ready working distinction, not one capable of bearing much theoretical weight.

[9] Note, however, that the discussion will concern only the belief/desire account of *reasons for action*, and not belief/desire accounts of intention or of the explanation of action.

[10] I will not discuss the most common charge against the belief/desire account: that it cannot explain the fact that we can reason about what goals we should have in a way that is not entirely dependent on the goals we already have. That is, people ask themselves what they should do and what they should desire in an unconditional way. They ask not, what should I desire to do now given that I already have the following desires? but, what should I desire now, *tout court*? Possibly they ask what I should and what I should not desire in a way that is in principle open to the possibility that all my current desires are misguided or even morally wrong. But whether or not this last question is possible for anyone to entertain seriously, the unconditional question I mentioned is one that we do deliberate about, and its consideration does not presuppose the feasibility of a complete overhaul of all our beliefs and desires. I believe that this charge is justified. But its consideration cannot be undertaken here.

to do in the face of conflicting desires must be settled by reference to those desires themselves, and as there is nothing in their content that could be a reason to prefer one of them to the others, it must be their strength to which agents must appeal when reasoning about what to do in the face of their conflicting desires. Their reasoning is, in effect, an attempt to establish what they want most.

The very thought of people deliberating about what they want most (unless it means—as I will later claim that it does—deliberating about what they should want most) is peculiar. It suggests a picture of people's wants being out of their control. They are givens that people are landed with, as they might be with tiredness or a passing depression. Given that people have the desires they have, the simple version assumes, they are concerned to satisfy them, and if it is impossible to satisfy them all, at least let the most powerful desires be satisfied. Were this a sensible view of people's wants, there would be no room for reasoning about what one should most want to do. Whatever one ends by doing, one wants most to do. In this picture of wants as powers somehow implanted in us, the winner is the want with the greatest motivational power. What else can 'wanting most'— meaning the want with the greatest motivational power—mean other than the want that we end up acting on, at least if the action is not a mishap, not an accidental slip, but the action we intended to take? Admittedly there can be a question as to whether the action one took is the one conducive to achieving what one wants most to have or to be, but that is because of the possibility of cognitive failure in identifying the action most conducive to those further goals. When we ask what of the different things we want to have we want most to have then, barring cognitive failure, bad luck, or misfired action, it is just what we would have if the action we take bears its hoped-for fruit. Therefore, we can conclude that if the purpose of the part of practical reasoning we are discussing is to establish what we want most, the simple version of the belief/desire account would lead to the conclusion that we should not reason but act. In our actions, our strongest motivating desires reveal themselves.

This is, of course, no more than a caricature of the belief/desire account of practical reason. Its proponents do not think that the aspect of practical reasoning concerned with deciding what is to be done, given that the agent has conflicting desires, is an attempt to establish which desire is motivationally strongest. What we want most means to them something like: the satisfaction of which desire will give most pleasure, or avoid more frustration, or maximize our happiness, or contentment; or satisfaction of which of our desires will lead to those of our desires that cohere best being satisfied; or they may have a different interpretation of what the phrase 'what we want most' means, and they may not even use this phrase but some other to hold this pivotal position in their account of practical reasoning. All these suggestions, I readily admit, are much superior to the caricature I criticized above. The point is that all of them suggest reasons for satisfying desires. None of them takes desires as inherently worthy of satisfaction. They are worthy of satisfaction to the extent that their satisfaction gives pleasure, or prevents frustration, or to the extent that it contributes to happiness, or to making a coherent whole of one's life. I do not wish to endorse the soundness of all these reasons, or of the others relied on in various versions of belief/desire accounts. (Why should people have a coherent life? In order to be all good, decent, middle-class folk?) Their soundness does not matter for the purpose of the argument at hand. What matters is that all of them transcend the self-imposed boundaries of the approach. All of them presuppose values whose normative force does not derive from the fact that people desire to pursue them. Were it to amount to no more than that, we would be back at the strength-of-motivation style of reasoning at one remove, with the added disadvantage that we will have acquired an additional false premise: that in the relevant sense, people desire pleasure, or the avoidance of frustration, or the coherence of their lives, or whatnot, more than they desire anything else. But if these values do not rest on desire alone, then there are values whose normative force is independent of being desired, and without them the belief/desire approach does not make sense, whereas with them it is no longer the belief/desire approach.

Notice that one cannot object that, since such values are implicitly relied on in some belief/desire accounts, then their invocation must be understood as compatible with the approach once it is purged of incautious descriptions of its nature. For the moment we admit some desire-independent values, we open the floodgates to others. Why should practical reasoning give the sole role to the values of pleasure, avoidance of frustration, or the maximization of coherence in one's life? Why should it not give equal weight to friendship, loyalty, magnanimity, justice, and so on? And above all, why should it be dominated by one value, and deny the independent force of all others?

So much for the first argument. The second argument helps explain why the simple version of the belief/desire approach fails to account for deliberation in the face of conflicting wants. It does so because it mistakes the nature of the will.[11] What we want to do, be, or have, we want for reasons. The questions 'What should we want most?' and 'What do we want most?'

---

[11] I am here repeating and elaborating arguments I have put forward in *The Morality of Freedom* (Oxford: Clarendon Press, 1986), and more specifically in 'On the Moral Point of View', in J. B. Schneewind (ed.), *Reason, Ethics, and Society: Themes from Kurt Baier, with his Responses* (Chicago: Open Court, 1996), 58–83, which is Ch. 11 below.

are normally one and the same question. When we reason about what we want most, we reason about what we have most reason to want. Since the value or the goodness of things and options constitutes the reason for having them or for doing them, their value or goodness is also the reason for wanting to have them or to do them. Normally when we deliberate about what we want most, we deliberate about what it would be best for us to want because it would be best for us to have or to do.[12]

I will return to the qualification 'normally' in the next paragraph but one. First, let it be noted that these remarks become compelling once we see that our wants are ours not merely because they are inflicted on us but because we conceived them and, as it were, endorsed them. For the most part, they are under our control, and that means that we have them only if we hold their objects to be worthwhile and that the wants disappear once that belief disappears. This feature of wants is central to them. It explains the sense in which they are under our control, rather than being states of mind visited upon us, like being overwhelmed by a sense of loss when hearing of the death of a friend. It also explains the sense in which we endorse or fail to endorse our wants. A want is ours so long as we have it because of a belief in the value of its object, and it would disappear were we to abandon that belief. Wants are not 'ours'; they are compulsions, or addictions we suffer from, when we have them, even though we do not believe in the value of their objects or the desirability of satisfying them.[13]

Our wants are, in this regard, like beliefs. Beliefs too are under our control in this way; that is, we have them when we feel justified in holding them, and once that conviction evaporates (e.g. in the face of contrary evidence), we lose the belief. We cannot want what we see no reason to want any more than we can believe what we think is untrue or contrary to the evidence. Moreover, beliefs like wants can become irrational obsessions—thoughts that inflict themselves on us in spite of ourselves when they persist independent of the evidence.

Those remarks bring out the difference between belief and desire, as well

---

[12] Exceptional cases need not be denied. One may want to want something to prove to oneself that one can want it or to win a bet, etc.

[13] It is a mistake to think, as was first suggested by Frankfurt, that endorsement by second-order desires is part of the explanation of the sense in which some desires are ours and some are forces that seize us. Second-order desires may be ours, or be inflicted on us, just like first-order desires. We can have a second-order desire, which is not 'ours' in the relevant sense, not to have a first-order desire that is authentically ours. More to the point, we need not have a second-order desire endorsing each of our first-order desires for them to be ours. Since writing this essay, I have explored these matters in 'When We are Ourselves: The Active and the Passive', *Proceedings of the Aristotelian Society*, suppl. 71 (1997), 211–29: Ch. 1 above.

as their similarities. We want to do or to have something only if we believe that it has some aspect that makes it worthwhile, makes it good or valuable. We want what we want inasmuch as it has that good aspect. We may at the same time want not to do the action or not to have the object inasmuch as they have other properties that make them worthless, or bad. In this respect, beliefs differ from wants. We cannot literally believe that p and that not-p. But there is no contradiction in both wanting to perform an action or to have an object, and wanting not to do the action or not to have the object. This asymmetry, resulting from the aspect-dependent character of wants, should not blind us to the basic similarity between beliefs and wants, which results from the way both depend on judgement—about justification of the belief and about the worthwhile character of the object of the want. As was noted, in both cases we are familiar with pathological abnormalities. Sometimes people cannot help believing what they know to be false. Sometimes people cannot help wanting what they know to be worthless and entirely without merit. In those cases, deliberation about what we want most diverges from deliberation about what we have most reason to want. But while the pathology of the will, like the pathology of belief, is important and revealing, the first and most important fact about it is that it involves pathological cases, whose understanding depends on understanding the factors that caused the deviation from normality. The pathological character of these cases accounts for the fact—to be commented on below—that in such cases, the agent concerned may well deny that he wants to perform the worthless or pointless action. Rather, he will say, he is driven towards it by a force that grips him and that he cannot control. And this too has its parallel in the cognitive case.

Some people reject the whole line of reasoning I have been pursuing. They believe that one can want anything, and not only what appears to one to be good or of value. This equates wanting something with an urge for it that attacks one. Urges, impulses, cravings, and their like are real enough, but it is wrong to take them as the basis for an analysis of wants and desires. (I am using 'desires' in the way customary in philosophical writings. Its common use makes it far closer to urges and passions. But when so understood, its proper use is far too restricted for it to do its philosophical duty; that is, in its common use, it is false that whenever one acts intentionally, one acts because of a desire to do what one does.) Unlike urges, most ('philosophical') desires do not have a felt quality. My desire to get in time to a meeting on European democracy starting in an hour's time is typical of instrumental desires, and my desire to read Ivan Klima's new novel is typical of non-instrumental ones. Neither is a felt desire; they arose because of my belief that I have good reasons for both actions, and because something in me responded to these reasons and made me want to act on them.¹⁴ If I do not get to act on them, that is most likely to be either because the opportunity did not arise or because when it arose I preferred to act for another reason. Either way, I am unlikely to feel frustration or any sense of loss. Naturally if I tried to satisfy my desires and failed, I might well feel frustrated. But that feeling of frustration is not a result of an unfulfilled desire but of a failed action, and is likely to be acute only if it is due to my clumsiness, thoughtlessness, incompetence, or the like.

Not all urges are pathological. Many of our desires are, if you like, endorsed urges. But normally we do not endorse them; they do not become our desires, unless we find them (and it may be no more than a rationalization) to be backed by reasons. If a force beyond my control propels me to take an action that I see no reason to take, then, regardless of whether I actually take the action or not, it would be misleading to say that I want to take that action. Not infrequently we prefer to satisfy an urge or a craving as a way of ridding ourselves of it. In those cases, our reason is that the craving is troublesome and the action that satisfies it will rid us of it. Acting for such reasons is sometimes akratic, but it need not be. Either way it is action for a (good, albeit not necessarily sufficient) reason.¹⁵

So if I want to count the blades of grass in my garden, I do so because I think that this will take my mind off some upsetting event, or because the action has some other good-making property. If I find myself drawn to count blades of grass but cannot think of any reason for doing so, I would certainly deny that this is a desire of mine. It is a force that seizes me in spite of myself. If I am overcome by it and perform the action, I would be right to say that I could not help it, though in a way it would be an intentional action. All I say, to repeat the point made above, is that anyone will recognize this as a pathological case.¹⁶ In the normal case, if I want to have a drink because I think that it tastes good, and am then convinced

---

[14] It could have been that I realized, or believed, that the reasons for the action are such that even when the reasons against performing it are taken into account, it would be irrational not to perform it. At the other extreme, I may conceive the desire to perform it because of its good points, even if, given the reasons against it, performing it would be irrational. But most commonly it is neither of these. The reasons that make me desire to perform an action are simply those reasons for it that I respond to, whereas others leave me relatively cold.

[15] Some expressive actions are an interesting borderline case. I kick the table in frustration, or walk up and down. Do I do so to relieve tension (conforming to the pattern I described or satisfying an urge to get rid of it)? Perhaps, but I am also expressing my exasperation, anger, or whatnot, and the fact that an action has expressive meaning is a reason to perform it when such expression is appropriate.

[16] The best analysis of such cases is provided by Harry Frankfurt, *The Importance of What We Care About* (Cambridge: CUP, 1988).

that it does not, then I no longer want to have the drink. No loss or regret is involved. The desire disappears with the loss of belief in the reason.

There is always a reason for any desire. The statement that one wants to paint potatoes green is incomprehensible, not least to the agent himself, unless there is something in the way he sees the action—in his beliefs about it, its circumstances, and consequences—that makes it appear a sensible action to him. Not everything can be desired. Only what is seen under some aspect of the good can be.

3. WANTS AND REASONS

Still, the question remains: given that there are things one has reason to do and does not particularly want to do, or feel like doing, is it not the case that if there are other things that one has reason to do and wants to do, one has greater reason to do them, other things being equal? If so, would it not show that wanting to do something is in and of itself a reason to do it, additional to the reason for doing it, which is one's reason for wanting to do it?

When put in this way, the answer seems to be yes both times, and yet the case is not so clear. First let us note that only desires that they currently have can be thought of as reasons for the people who have them. Consider the following case: I want to take up playing the piano after I retire. I want to do that because it would help pass the time in an enjoyable and rewarding way. I will enjoy facing new challenges, encountering music not merely as a listener, and so forth. All these are reasons for taking up the piano, and they are also reasons for wanting to do so. I am aware of them, and they are my reasons for wanting to do so after I retire. (I wish I could do so right away. It would be good to do it right away, but I cannot afford the time, and therefore do not want to do it now.) Is the fact that I now want to take up the piano in thirteen years time an additional reason for doing so? Suppose that in the intervening years, I lose that desire and forget about it. At the time of my retirement, a friend advises me to take up the piano. Would he be missing one reason for doing so if he does not mention among others the fact that thirteen years earlier I wanted to do so? This example tilts the other way. My friend might mention my long-forgotten desire—not as a reason for taking up the piano or as a consideration that shows the good in doing so but as proof that once upon a time I agreed with him that there are good reasons for doing so, and also to show that the thought is not alien to me, that I can—or could—see myself doing it.

Incommensurability and Agency

To suggest that an abandoned want is a reason is to put irrational obstacles to agents' changing their minds. As we know, our past conduct may bind us in the future. We may have entered into commitments from which we cannot now escape, except, perhaps, for good reasons. Or we may have built our life around certain goals and ambitions that it is silly to abandon, or worse, it may be a betrayal of all we ever cared about, of what our life was about. But these are special cases. They are not mere desires that we conceive for a while and then abandon. If a desire is abandoned because we no longer believe that the reasons we saw for having it are good ones, it would be irrational to hold that even though we are right to abandon it, we cannot do so altogether, that it leaves a shadow, in the form of a reason to perform any action that will fulfil any of our now-defunct desires. But even if we did not change our mind about the reasons for the action, and even if the reasons themselves did not change, even if all that happens is that we no longer want to do what we felt like doing before, we are—as it were—within our rights to change our mind or our will like that. There can be no rationale for holding us bound to pursue dead desires, not even when this is subject to the 'other things being equal' proviso.

But if dead desires are not reasons, nor are future desires. That is, the fact that I now want to take up the piano when I retire is no reason for me to take up the piano when I retire, or to prepare for taking it up at that time. As we saw, if when I retire I no longer desire to take up the piano, the fact that once I had such a desire will be no reason to do so. Therefore the belief that the fact that I now have the desire to take up the piano in the future is a reason for doing so (in the future) and therefore for preparing for doing so (now) can be sustained only if we have reason against changing our desires. To hold that there is such a reason is to put arbitrary obstacles to possible changes of mind. Why should my current desire commit me to its perpetuation unless I have a good reason for a change of mind? What is wrong with losing a desire to do something just because one no longer feels like doing it, even though one's judgement of the merit of the action has not changed? Of course, if my desire results from a belief that it is supported by reasons that defeat any alternative, I should not abandon the desire unless I come to believe that it is no longer supported by such reasons or that it never was so supported. But when it is merely a desire to do one of many things one could rationally do, there is no reason why I should not change my mind or inclination. The presumption in favour of continuing with one's existing desire cannot be more plausible than its opposite: the presumption in favour of periodically changing all one's (nonrationally compelled) desires. Each of these presumptions will appeal to people of a certain temperament, but neither of them is sanctioned by general principles of rationality.

It is still possible that while I have a desire, it is a reason for the action that will satisfy it.[17] One way in which this, if true, may be thought to be significant is in clarifying the way we think of resolving conflicts between our various desires. Wants and desires are to be distinguished from wishes. They indicate a disposition to perform the action, given appropriate circumstances. At the same time, one may have conflicting desires. If desires are reasons, a rational agent should, other things being equal, follow the desire (or combination of desires) that is the most stringent reason. But in what sense can one desire be more stringent than another? Presumably the desire that is backed by the weightier reasons (those whose satisfaction would be best), or whose satisfaction will give most pleasure, or whose non-satisfaction would be felt most acutely, or the desire supported by some combination of these factors, is the most stringent one. But if that is the measure of the stringency of a desire, then its stringency is determined by reasons other than itself. This is obvious in the case of the reasons that back it and the same is true for securing pleasure and avoiding frustration. Pleasure is not a general concomitant of satisfaction nor is frustration a general concomitant of non-satisfaction of desires. We may be unaware that something we strove to achieve was realized. But that does not mean that our desire was not satisfied, nor does it generally diminish the good done by its satisfaction. We campaigned for a cause and—unbeknown to us—as a direct result of our campaign, our cause has won. The good thus done is unaffected by our ignorance of it.[18]

The case of frustration is even clearer. For the most part, frustration is the result of failure in an attempt to satisfy the desire, but many desires remain unsatisfied because the opportunity for their satisfaction does not arise, or because when it does, one has better reasons, or one just chooses to do something else instead. One can feel frustrated in such circumstances, but this is not an inevitable concomitant of the desire, and I believe that it is in fact not at all common. For example, I want to spend a summer in Chamonix. This may be quite a strong desire if by that one means a desire I would not let pass unsatisfied given a decent opportunity to satisfy it. But if I never have the opportunity, I will not feel frustrated. I am aware that I have many desires of this kind; there are many things I want to do or to experience and I am aware that many, indeed most of them, will remain unfulfilled (even too many places where I want to spend a summer). It

---

[17] Therefore if I believe that I will have a desire to take up the piano when I retire, I now have reason to prepare for that event.

[18] We should, of course, distinguish the anodyne sense in which 'I am pleased to meet you'—said as part of a formal introduction to a stranger—indicates pleasure, and pleasure in the sense in which one can take pleasure in wine, dancing, or a good book. Pleasure in the non-anodyne sense is the subject of my remarks.

would be silly of me to feel frustrated every time I realize that all hope of satisfying one of them has passed forever.

If the stringency of the reasons that desires (allegedly) constitute is determined by other considerations that are reasons in their own right, and would count anyway—that is, would count even if we deny that the desire itself is a reason—what sorts of reasons are desires? Perhaps the answer is that prima facie desires are not reasons, but that one's all-out desire is a reason. That would seem to fit with the only reason we have seen so far to think that desires are reasons: that if, of a range of acceptable options, one wants—and this must refer to one's overall want—to pursue one, it would be irrational to choose one of the others. But the thought that, while prima facie desires are not reasons for action, overall desires are is riddled with difficulties. First, an overall desire is just a prima facie desire that encounters no opposition from conflicting desires or that defeats the opposition. How can its being a reason depend on whether it is opposed by other desires? I am offered a pear and a banana. I want to eat, but I cannot have both. I want to eat a pear. That fact is a reason for eating a pear if I do not want to eat a banana more than a pear. But if while wanting a pear I want a banana more, then wanting the pear is not a reason. Not merely is it a weaker reason than my desire for the banana. It is no reason at all.

Second, what I want most to do may conflict with what I know that, but for the fact that I have a conflicting desire, I ought to do. The situation of a person who wants to do something that he ought not to do, all things considered, is familiar and unproblematic. In that case one will, on pain of irrationality, do what one has a conclusive reason to do, perhaps reluctantly or with regret that one's want remains unfulfilled. The question is: is it possible that an action that, barring one's desire to perform it, one ought not to perform (one has a conclusive reason to avoid) is a permissible action just because one wants to perform it? Can one's desire for an action, or for the consequences of an action, change the balance of reasons from conclusively against to that action being as well supported by reason as any alternative?

A variety of will-related factors may indeed have that effect. That one does not want to do what one otherwise has to do may mean that one will not do it well, and therefore it may be better not to do it at all. One's disappointment and frustration at having one's desire remain unsatisfied may tip the balance the other way.[19] Naturally, the fact that doing what one wants to do will be enjoyable or pleasurable is a reason for doing it, which may

---

[19] Especially with children. We expect grown-ups to be in control of their will and emotions, and not to pander to them. But on rare occasions, the disappointment will be so great that it is right to avoid it.

tip the balance. We are familiar with these and with other ways in which factors sometimes connected with the agent's desire may affect the balance of reasons. But none of them can be equated with the fact of his having a certain desire, nor is any of them a necessary concomitant of having an overall desire.

I suspect that desire in itself cannot tip the balance of reasons and that to the extent that we are inclined to think otherwise, this is because we think of other factors that are (contingently) related to desires. 'Proving' this point is, however, difficult. All one can do is analyse examples and rely on a shared understanding. Consider the following case. I want to do something. I know that unless my desire tips the balance, I should not engage in the action, for it will hurt the feelings of someone, call him George, whose feelings I should not hurt. That factor is no more than a prima facie consideration against the action. It can be overridden or defeated by other considerations. The action may be necessary for my health, or for my prospects of promotion, or something else. In all such cases I am called on to compare the stringency of the reason I have not to hurt George's feelings (how much he will be hurt, the nature of my relations with him, etc.) as against the stringency of the conflicting reason (what damage to my health will ensue, how certain it is, etc.). We often call such comparisons 'weighing the reasons against each other'. But if the only 'reason' I have for doing the hurtful act is that I want to do it, is such 'weighing' appropriate, or even possible? It is not just that wanting it seems an inappropriate consideration even to mention as weighing against the hurt it will cause George.[20] The problem is that it is not clear what, in the circumstances, could count as weighing my desire against the reason I have not to hurt him. I can, of course, take account of the strength of my desire. But that merely sends me back to how much frustration or inner disruption its non-satisfaction will cause, how much effort (and what will be the costs of the effort) overcoming the desire will require, and so forth. These—I have allowed earlier—are reasons for action, but they are not to be identified with the desire itself, and they do not accompany all desires.

I have argued above that, in the normal case, a desire disappears[21] when the reason for it seems insufficient. Formally I cannot rely on that conclusion at the present juncture. It begs the question we are considering: whether the desire can tip the balance and thus not be insufficiently

---

[20] I do not mean that it is inappropriate to want to hurt him. I mean that it is inappropriate to consider my wanting to perform an action (when the want is based on an unobjectionable reason) as a consideration for performing it when I know that it will hurt him.

[21] Or recedes to become a desire to do the relevant act if an appropriate opportunity arose.

supported by reason. But the point is nevertheless relevant. The thought that my overall want can both be a reason in its own right as well as dependent for its continued existence on the balance of reasons is paradoxical. It requires too much by way of mental gymnastics.

The following objection may be raised: The way to assess the weight that having a certain desire has is simple. As I rightly argued earlier—the objector would say—it is determined neither by the strength of the felt force propelling one to satisfy the desire, not by the frustration caused by its non-satisfaction, nor by the pleasure its satisfaction gives. It is determined by how much one is willing to forgo in order to have it satisfied. A desire one would give up one's career for is greater than a desire one would only give up a week's holiday for, and so on.

This objection may have occurred to the reader in connection with my dismissal of the simple version of the belief/desire account. There I took motivational strength to be the only meaning a supporter of that account can assign to the notion of a strong desire. The reason that was so, the reason that the simple version cannot avail itself of the 'option value' of a desire as a measure of its strength (as I will call the objector's suggestion that the strength is determined by how much the agent is willing to forgo for the satisfaction of the desire), was that according to the simple version, options have no value except inasmuch as being desired endows them with value. The person who would not sacrifice a chance for promotion at work to save the life of his child is simply a person for whom the value of his child is less than the value of his career. It does not show that he is giving up more when he sacrifices his child, for his child has little value for him. Therefore, that he sacrifices his child to earn an extra $1,000 a year does not show that he wants money very much, for he is giving up something very valuable to get it. So long as we regard wants as the only determinant of value, we cannot resort to some independent source of value by which to measure how much one wants one thing or another.

At the present stage of the argument, however, we have left the simple version behind. We allow that value and reasons do not derive entirely from desires. Does not the objection succeed at this stage in the argument? One's first response is that the same problem is still with us. In the preceding paragraph, I assumed that if desires determine the value of options, they determine not their value *tout court*, but their value to those who have the desires. This assumption is necessary to avoid contradiction, since the same option can be open to various agents, of whom some want it and some want to avoid it. Some may say that, even though we are admitting that value is not determined by desires, value for an agent is. That is, if a person would rather give up his child than forgo an extra $1,000 a year earnings, then the child has less value for his life than the money. If this is so, it is still impossible to use value to determine strength of desire. But if this is so, nor is it ever possible to criticize a person for wanting something that is bad for him. In the next section I will suggest that what is good for someone is not determined by that person's desires. This allows for the objection to stand. It allows for a desire-independent value of what is good for an agent, which enables us to measure the strength of the agent's desire by its option value to him.

So far we can go along with the objection. We can agree that the strength of a desire can be measured in this way. This is not to accept this as the sole measure of its strength. We do assess the strength of desires in a variety of ways, and we have already encountered several of them. Their motivational force and the frustration that their non-satisfaction will cause are both among the determinants of the strength of desires. The problem we encounter in taking desires as reasons is not that we cannot make sense of the notion that desires have strength but that we have no reason to take their strength as desires as indicating their weight as reasons. This remains the case with the 'option value' measure of desires. It leaves untouched the basic point that, since desires are reason-dependent, their persistence depends on persistence of belief in the reason and that necessarily those who have them want the strength of their desires to reflect the weight of the reasons for them, and accept criticism if it does not. This implies that they do not want desires to be counted independent of the reasons that they see as backing them, and they do not want them to count at all if those reasons do not exist. You may question why I suddenly attribute importance to what people want, when my aim is to discount the importance of wants. I rely not on what people contingently want, but on what is necessarily implied by whatever they want since it is an implication of the very notion of a desire, an implication of the way it is based on belief in reasons. There is, therefore, nothing to the objection.

All the considerations canvassed over the last few pages suggest that a bare desire is not a reason for the action that will satisfy it. But they do not altogether dispose of the argument. There remains the simple point that if of two acceptable options one wants one thing and does the other, one is acting irrationally. If when offered a pear or a banana, I have reason to take one and it does not matter which one, then if I want the banana but take the pear, I have acted irrationally. Moreover, in situations of the kind just described, one can explain and justify taking the banana by pointing out that one wanted the banana, and not the pear. In such contexts we refer to what we want as we do to reasons. Here they function as reasons. In these circumstances, wants are reasons, though in being limited to this case they are very peculiar reasons.

4. VALUES AND REASONS

Wants, I have argued, are not reasons for action—not in the normal sense of the word. They are neither independent reasons in the sense of being by themselves a consideration in favour of the action that satisfies them, for we cannot have wants except where we believe there is a reason for it, nor do they carry any weight in themselves, independent of the reasons that support them. A want can never tip the balance of reasons in and of itself. Rather, our wants become relevant when reasons have run their course. Once the verdict of reason is that one option should be pursued, we can do so willingly or unwillingly, and of course we can defy reason and follow a different option through either the impetuosity or the weakness of our will. Likewise, once reason has failed to adjudicate between a range of options, we normally choose one for no further reason, simply because we want to. Sometimes, however, we choose what we do not want. This usually manifests an unconscious desire for punishment, self-hate, self-contempt, pathological self-doubt, or something else. And such manifestations are irrational. In that sense, and in those circumstances, doing what one wants is the rational thing to do. Of course, in such cases the question 'What should I do?' does not normally arise for an agent aware of the nature of his situation. Yet it makes sense for an agent in that situation to ask: given that that is how things are, would it be all right for me to do what I want? And the affirmative answer suggests that wants are here reasons. But given the concerns of this essay we can put such cases aside and accept the conclusion that wanting something is not reason for the action that satisfies it.

The fact that options have a certain value—that performing them is a good thing to do because of the intrinsic merit of the action or of its consequences—is the paradigmatic reason for actions. My wanting something does not make it good or valuable and is therefore not a reason for action. But does not the fact that I want something make it good for me?

As before, we have to avoid confusing wanting something with other features, sometimes associated with some desires. We have to distinguish what I will call 'goals' from desires. Typical examples of goals are success in one's career, success in one's relationships, possessing the entire set of nineteenth-century French stamps, or qualifying as an International Master in chess. For those who have these goals, they are, of course, things they want to do or to accomplish. But they are not mere desires. Goals are our goals because in our actions we have set on pursuing them, because they play an important role in our emotional and imaginative life, because our success or failure in pursuing them is going to affect the quality of our life.[22] The fact that goals are integrated with central aspects of our lives, that they represent what matters to us in life, makes them constitutive of our well-being. We have reason to do whatever will facilitate the pursuit of our worthwhile goals, and often we would also want to perform actions that we believe facilitate pursuit of our goals. But not everything we want does contribute to the pursuit of our goals; sometimes what we want will retard and hinder their pursuit, and not always do we want to do what would in fact facilitate pursuit of our goals, even when we know that it would. While we adopt goals through our actions, and mostly through our willing actions, we do not always feel like doing what would serve our goals any more than we always feel like doing our duty, even when we know that it is our duty.

Some goals are reasons, but the fact that achieving a high level of competence on the piano is John's goal does not make it a more valuable achievement or accomplishment than it would have been had it not been John's goal. Does not that show that the value or goodness of options is not the only fact that can be a reason for action, that goals—some goals— are reasons as well? While the fact that competence on the piano is John's goal does not affect the value of such competence, it does affect its value to John. It makes that competence something the achievement of which is good for him. In general the achievement of a goal is good for the person whose goal it is only if the goal is worthwhile.[23] In this respect, goals are like desires; having them implies belief that there is value in them, that there is a reason to pursue them independent of the fact that one does or wants to pursue them. To take up stamp collecting, or playing the piano, or being a lawyer implies believing that these are worthwhile activities or pursuits. Yet once a person has made something his goal, it acquires special importance for him. He has a reason to pursue it that he did not have before. I believe that writing poetry and teaching are both valuable activities. But as a teacher who has never taken up poetry, I have reasons for teaching that arise out of my commitment to teaching, and I do not have similar reasons for writing poetry.

This suggests a certain complexity in the relations between value and reason that cannot be explored here. For present purposes, I have to confine myself to the suggestion that the difference between the value of an option and its value to the agent covers the point we are concerned with, and lends further support to the supposition that the value of options (in general or to the agent) is a reason for performing them, whereas desires are not reasons for the actions that satisfy them.

[22] See also the discussion of goals and well-being in my *The Morality of Freedom*.

[23] See ibid., ch. 12, on the relation between goals and well-being; see also my *Ethics in the Public Domain*, ch. 1.

5. REASON AND THE WILL

Most of the argument of this chapter was designed to show that the fact that a person wants something is no reason for that person to perform the action that is most likely to facilitate the satisfaction of the want. My suggestion was that the fact that wants are not reasons for action makes it most plausible that typical reasons are facts about the value or good of options.

Given that the fact that an action satisfies the agent's desires does not endow it with value, it seems inevitable that in typical situations in which an agent faces various options, the value of some of them will be incommensurable. This is certainly not always the case. Even in typical cases, there will be options that are inferior to others. But typically once they are eliminated, agents are still left with a number of options that are incommensurate in value. If this is so, then reasons for actions are better characterized as making actions eligible rather than requiring their performance on pain of irrationality. In typical situations, reason does not determine what is to be done. Rather it sets a range of eligible options before agents, who choose among them as they feel inclined, who do what they want to do or what they feel like doing. Much work needs to be done to analyse the different ways in which our will leads us to do one thing rather than another. My only concern was to suggest that, in all of them, the will plays a role in human agency separate from that of reason, a role that neither kowtows to reason by endorsing its conclusions nor irrationally rebels against it by refusing to endorse them.

This leads to a vindication of the classical conception of human action. If reason leaves room for an independent role of the will, this is because reasons merely render actions intelligible. And that is so only if normally choice situations include a number of undefeated incommensurate options. If desires are not reasons, it is much more likely that that is indeed so. There are few credible sources of commensurating value left.[24] To be sure, much further argument is needed to make this conclusion secure. But we should by now be immune to the fear of vacuum in the space of reason that, I have suggested at the outset, is the strongest argument for rejecting the possibility of widespread incommensurabilities of options, and the classical conception of reason of which it is a part. That phobia was fuelled by the

---

[24] Two popular ideas are: (1) because what we do affects our well-being, the contribution of various options to our well-being provides a basis for commensurating them, and (2) a rational constraint of coherence provides such a basis. I attempted to refute the first in 'Facing Up: A Reply,' *Southern California Law Review*, 62 (1989), and in *Ethics in the Public Domain*, and to refute the second at least partly in 'The Relevance of Coherence', *Boston University Law Review*, 72/2 (1991), 273–321.

thought that wants are intelligible to those who have them. The argument of the chapter embraced this point and showed that the intelligibility of our wants is secured by the fact that they are based on reasons. That does not fully explain why we want one thing rather than another. Explanations by reference to reasons do not explain everything. Our chemistry rather than our rationality explains why some like it hot. That variability between people, like variations between what people want at different times, is not fully accounted for by reason. The intelligibility of our desires does not require that. It does, however, require that we have reasons for our desires and that is inconsistent with the rationalist account of the will, which is itself prey to the objection it raised against the classical conception.

The argument of this chapter for the classical conception of human agency with its reliance on widespread incommensurabilities gains support from ordinary human experience, which teaches us that quite commonly people do not survey all the options open to them before choosing what to do. Rather, they find an option that they believe not to be excluded by reason and that appeals to them and pursue it. At the very least, the case for this conception of practical rationality is to be taken seriously. That suggests that incommensurability of the value of options is a pervasive feature with far-reaching theoretical consequences.

4

Explaining Normativity: On Rationality and the Justification of Reason

Aspects of the world are normative in as much as they or their existence constitute reasons for persons, that is, grounds which make certain beliefs, moods, emotions, intentions, or actions appropriate or inappropriate. Our capacities to perceive and understand how things are, and what response is appropriate to them, and our ability to respond appropriately, make us into persons—creatures with the ability to direct their own life in accordance with their appreciation of themselves and their environment, and of the reasons with which, given how they are, the world presents them.

An explanation of normativity would explain the various puzzling aspects of this complex phenomenon. In particular it would explain how it is that aspects of the world can constitute reasons for cognitive, emotive, and volitional responses; how it is that we can come to realize that certain cognitive, emotional, or volitional responses are appropriate in various circumstances, and inappropriate in others; and how it is that we can respond appropriately. This chapter explores an aspect of the last of these questions.

1. NORMATIVITY AND RATIONALITY

The normativity of all that is normative consists in the way it is, or provides, or is otherwise related to reasons. The normativity of rules, or of authority, or of morality, for example, consists in the fact that rules are reasons of a special kind, the fact that directives issued by legitimate authorities are reasons, and in the fact that moral considerations are valid reasons. So ultimately the explanation of normativity is the explanation of what it is to be a reason, and of related puzzles about reasons.

The first version of section 1 was included in papers presented at the Philosophy Colloquium at Berkeley, at the conference in memory of Jean Hampton at Tucson, and at a conference on practical reason in the Humbolt University, Berlin. I learnt from questions and comments of many who participated in those occasions. I owe a special debt to David Silver, who was the commentator on my paper at Tucson, and to Jonathan Dancy for most helpful comments on a later version of the paper.

Reason[1] is inherently normative. That is its central characteristic. Therefore, the accounts of normativity and of reason and rationality, though not identical, are inter-related. An account of rationality is an account of the capacity to perceive reasons and to conform to them, and of different forms of conforming to reasons, and their appropriateness in different contexts. To explain the capacity to conform to reason the account must explain the possibility of error, failure to perceive reasons correctly, and of failure to respond to them once perceived. An account of irrationality is an account of some of the ways of failing to conform to reason, those which render one, or one's behaviour, or emotions, etc., irrational. The core idea is that rationality is the ability to realize the normative significance of the normative features of the world, and the ability to respond accordingly.

In one sense of 'rational', we, or anything else, are rational beings to the extent that we possess that ability, which I will call 'capacity-rationality'. The absence of capacity-rationality does not mean that a creature is irrational. It means that no judgements of rationality apply to that creature. In another sense, we, or anything else, are rational to the extent that in general we use that ability well. There is a further use of 'rationality' in which it applies to specific human responses, or their absence. Our actions, intentions, beliefs, emotions, etc., can be severally rational, non-rational, or irrational.

Rationality makes us into persons. To yield an explanation of rationality the core idea has, of course, to be hedged and refined. I will confine myself to four observations which help locate the relations between capacity-rationality and normativity.

First, to be people who are rational in the first sense, that is, to be people with the ability to perceive reasons and respond to them, we need a range of capacities which do not directly contribute to our rationality. They include some perceptual ability, and the capacity to control our movements at will. An impairment of our perceptual ability does not diminish our rationality. Nor does lack of muscular control, or other neurological or physical impairments of our ability to move at will. Possession of at least some perceptual ability, and of some ability to control one's movements at will, are presupposed by capacity-rationality.[2] But they are not themselves constituents of rationality.

---

[1] I will be using 'reason' when it sounds natural to use it. The expression refers variously to all or some of the following: people's reasoning capacity, people's use of that capacity when referred to in a general way, the reasons which apply to people on the occasion(s) discussed. I will sometimes leave it to context to identify the meaning.

[2] My claim is that their possession to some degree, during some part of the creature's life, is necessary for that creature to have capacity-rationality at all, not merely for his ability to display that capacity or exercise it. It is true, though, that beyond that minimum lacking the ancillary capacities may impede the exercise of rationality, or make it temporarily impossible.

There are other preconditions of capacity-rationality. Among them are psychological capacities, such as the possession of memory, the capacity for conceptual thought, and the capacities to form beliefs and to reach decisions. Some of the preconditions relate to capacities possession of which is a precondition of being either rational or irrational, but where their successful exercise does not render one (or one's judgement, action, etc.) rational, nor does their failure render one irrational. Perceptual failures, muscular failures, failures of memory are examples of preconditions of this kind. The abilities to form beliefs and to reach decisions belong to the other kind. Success and failure in their exercise contribute to the evaluation of the rationality of one's beliefs, actions, etc., as well as to the evaluation of the rationality (in the second sense) of the person concerned.

Not surprisingly the boundary between those who do not meet the preconditions of capacity-rationality, and are neither rational nor irrational, and those who meet the preconditions, and are irrational, is not a sharp one. Someone who lacks a minimal capacity to make up his mind about anything fails the preconditions and is neither rational nor irrational. He lacks capacity-rationality. But those who have a minimal ability to make up their minds, and constantly vacillate, finding it always difficult to make up their minds, and almost impossible not to change almost every decision they take soon after taking it, are irrational.

What is capacity-rationality in itself? It is a capacity to see the normative significance of the way things are, to comprehend what reasons they constitute, and the significance of that fact for oneself.[3] As indicated at the outset, part of the explanation of normativity consists in the explanation of this capacity. Here again we encounter the overlap between the explanations of normativity and of rationality.

These remarks lead to my second point. Some accounts of rationality identify it with a reasoning ability. That ability consists, at least in part, in the ability to recognize inferential relations. That is it consists of, or includes, an ability to figure out what conclusions follow from given premises (the active side of the capacity), and an ability to recognize that inferences are valid or invalid[4] when this is pointed out to one (the passive side of the capacity). While at least a minimal reasoning ability is among the constituents of capacity-rationality, it does not exhaust it, at least

---

[3] Needless to say, possession of this capacity itself is a matter of degree. Some humans and other creatures can recognize (the normative aspect of) some types of reasons but not of others. Some humans and other creatures can reflect about the fact that the existence of certain facts constitutes reasons, and form general views about the nature of reasons and rationality. Others can do so to a limited degree, or cannot do so at all. There is little point in trying to fix a test of personhood which will endow the concept with relatively sharp boundaries, which it does not possess.

[4] I am using these terms to designate the success and failure of any inference, not merely of deductive ones.

not if the capacity to reason is the ability to construct and understand inferences.

That a certain proposition follows from certain premises is, other things being equal,[5] a reason for not believing the premises without believing the conclusion.[6] Given that rationality is the capacity to realize the normative significance of facts, that is, to realize whether they constitute reasons, and which reasons they constitute, and to respond appropriately, the capacity to see the normative significance of inferences is high among the constituents of capacity-rationality. But what of reasoning power in general? One possibility is that the capacity to realize that C follows from P is like the capacity to see that the house is on fire. They are ways of realizing the existence of facts which constitute reasons, and their possession is a precondition of being able to become aware of the normative significance of those facts, and to respond appropriately. On this account neither perceptual capacity nor reasoning ability are themselves constituents of rationality. They are merely preconditions of its exercise. Alternatively, it is arguable that reasoning is unlike perception in that it is involved in almost any recognition of the normative significance of anything. Even recognizing that, since C follows from P one has, other things being equal, reason not to believe P and reject C, involves reasoning. The close involvement of reasoning in capacity-rationality would justify, on this view, regarding the ability to reason as a constituent of rationality.

There is no doubt that reasoning ability is closely involved with rationality, even though the pervasiveness of its involvement may be debated. Yet it is doubtful that this involvement would in itself justify the identification of reasoning ability with capacity-rationality. There is, however, a better argument for that conclusion: realizing that C follows from P is not merely realizing the existence of a fact which is a reason (as in seeing that the house is on fire). It is realizing that there is a reason.

---

[5] The existence of defeasible valid inferences requires the qualification 'other things being equal'. Typically when the inference is defeated it yields no reason at all.

[6] It is not, however, not even when the inference is a deductive one, a conclusive reason. Mere knowledge that a set of propositions is self-contradictory is a reason, if one does believe in at least some of them, to refrain from believing in one or more of them so that one's beliefs will not be self-contradictory. When one has no further information about the location of the contradiction, and the reasons for it, the only way to know that one has conformed with this reason is to refrain from believing any of the propositions in the set. When the contradictory set is large the price of doing so can be very great. Sometimes, it may be impossible to conform with this reason (e.g. if the set includes all one's beliefs). But even when it is possible it may be unjustified, given the price. After all, knowledge that the set is contradictory is no more than knowledge that one of its propositions is false. We know on inductive grounds that even if our beliefs are consistent at least one of them is false. That is no (adequate) reason to suspend all our beliefs. Why should the fact that our beliefs are contradictory be such a reason?

Understanding that C follows from P is the same, or at least involves understanding that, other things being equal, one has reason not to believe P and reject C. That is part of what it means that the one follows from the other.

This argument notwithstanding, this seems to be a case where our concepts are not as neat and tidy as philosophers may wish them to be. While possession of a minimal reasoning capacity is a constituent of capacity-rationality, that ability may be modest. In general, failures of our reasoning powers do not warrant a judgement of irrationality. Failure to see that a conclusion follows from certain premises most commonly merely shows that one is not very bright, or just not very good at reasoning. In most cases it does not show that one is irrational, as failure to realize that if a conclusion follows from premises then one has reason not to believe the premises while rejecting the conclusion does. On the other hand, failure of *elementary* reasoning does establish irrationality: failure to realize, in normal circumstances, that it follows from the fact that one's destination is not far away that it will not take long to get there, is a failure of rationality.

It follows that there is a certain distance between capacity-rationality and reasoning ability. Good reasoners can be habitually irrational, and, more commonly, perfectly rational people can be bad reasoners. They often make mistakes, but that does not impugn their rationality.[7]

The third point was anticipated in the previous remarks, and helps illustrate them. Our rationality, I claimed, consists in the ability to recognize the normativity of features of the world. That ability expresses itself in the proper functioning, in relevant respects, of our faculties. The point I am striving to make is that our rationality expresses itself not only in our deliberation and reasoning, nor in any other specific act or activity, but more widely in the way we function, in so far as that functioning is, or should be, responsive to reasons. Take a simple example. I mentioned above that habitual failure to take decisions, or to form judgements where they are called for, is a form of irrationality. Imagine that whenever Sylvia leaves her home she locks her front door behind her, walks to the gate, turns back, goes to the door and, to check that it is really locked, unlocks and relocks it, goes out of the gate and immediately turns back, goes back to the door and repeats the action, and so on several times. This form of indecisiveness amounts to

---

[7] The point discussed in the text helps in dissolving an apparent asymmetry between theoretical and practical reasons. How is it, one may ask, that practical (and aesthetic) reasons are normative on their face, being facts like: 'Doing A will give you pleasure', or 'you promised to do A', whereas anything can be a reason for belief? That there are clouds and high winds is a reason to believe that it will rain. But there is nothing inherently normative in the fact that there are clouds and high winds. The explanation is that the fact that there are clouds is no reason to believe anything, though that it follows from the fact that there are clouds, that rain is likely, is a reason, and is normative on its face.

irrationality. At some level Sylvia probably recognizes that her actions are irrational. But at the same time she is seized by anxiety and doubt. Maybe the key did not turn full circle and did not lock the door, maybe she imagined feeling the bolt move, and in fact it did not, maybe when she unlocked the door to test what she did before she forgot to relock it.

We are all familiar with the mild forms of such anxiety. Barristers are supposed to capitalize on it by undermining witnesses' confidence that they really saw what they saw, that they really remember what they remember. At the same time we recognize that the capacity for such self-doubt is itself an aspect of our rationality. It manifests our ability to monitor (mostly below the level of awareness) our reactions and their appropriateness to the circumstances, that is to monitor our responsiveness to reason. But to act rationally we need to preserve a proper balance between resoluteness and openness to doubt. It is not a balance we can decide upon. While Sylvia can grit her teeth and decide not to turn back again for the fifth time, such conscious decisions only minimize her irrationality. To be rational she must act 'automatically' in a way which allows for a proper openness to doubt without relapsing into indecisiveness and anxiety. To be rational she, and we, must function properly, and that functioning must be automatic, rather than a product of deliberation and decision.

The fourth and last point to be made here about rationality is by now obvious. I am treating rationality as a unified concept, designating a unified capacity, which straddles the divides between practical and theoretical rationality, as well as between procedural and substantive rationality, and others. Some writers believe that there are two concepts of rationality in use, and presumably they designate two different abilities. Parfit sets the distinction thus: 'To be substantively rational, we must care about certain things, such as our own well-being.' 'To be procedurally rational, we must deliberate in certain ways, but we are not required to have any particular desires or aims, such as concern for our own well-being.'[8] He does not elaborate. What could he mean? It is possible for a person[9] irrationally to fail to have desires or intentions or goals which he has adequate reason to have. It is also possible for someone who generally has the goals which rationally he should have to display irrationality often when deliberating. There is no reason to think that failures of rationality are randomly distributed among the different occasions on which rationality is called for. For example, motivated irrationality, such as self-deception, would manifest itself selectively on occasions where its existence would serve its underlying motive. Parfit's distinction may, therefore, be understood as a distinction between success in being rational in different aspects of one's life. But the context makes clear

---

[8] D. Parfit, 'Reason and Motivation', *Aristotelian Society*, suppl. 71 (1997), 99, at 101.
[9] By their nature persons are rational in the sense of having capacity-rationality.

that he does not mean it in this way. He seems to think that there are two different notions of rationality, each designating a different capacity. His discussion raises the possibility that possession of the rationality identified by one of these notions is independent of possession of the rationality marked by the other. Whether or not this is Parfit's meaning, it is a common view, and a mistaken one.

The division between substantive and procedural rationality (and between substantive and instrumental rationality) took hold among philosophers who doubted that reason is directly involved in the choice of ends, but believed that reason has a role to play in practical thought, which the notion of procedural rationality captures. Some allowed that we talk of rationality in a more extensive sense, and claimed that that is merely an ambiguity in the meaning of 'reason' and 'rationality', perhaps resulting from those primitive times when people believed that rationality affected the choice of ends as well. In fact reason affects our choice of ends and the desires we have just as much as it affects our deliberations and our beliefs. We cannot have a desire except for a reason.[10] Once that is allowed, the motivation for the division of rationality into two distinct capacities disappears. There is no reason for thinking that the capacities which enable us to discern and respond to reasons for desires are different from those which enable us to discern and respond to reasons for belief. One may well need some special abilities (discriminating eyesight, or palate, a good ear, or a capacity for empathy, etc.) to be able to discern various non-instrumental reasons. But these, while presupposed by capacity-rationality, or by the ability to use it, are not identical with it, nor are they constituent elements of it. They do not show that there is more than one concept of rationality.

It is not clear what Parfit means to include in 'to deliberate in a certain way'. The power of reasoning in and of itself does not establish any degree of rationality. Imagine a person who as a hobby picks an arbitrary collection of propositions, perhaps chosen randomly from newspapers and magazines, and works out various other propositions which follow from them. Putting on one side the suspicion that the very activity displays irrationality, does he show himself to be good at procedural rationality? I do not think so. Our person is good at recognizing the existence of inferential relations. He is not changing his beliefs in any way, not even conditionally (i.e. the story does not assume that he acquires beliefs of the sort: given the inferential relations I have reason not to believe the premises and disbelieve the conclusions). For all we know he does not understand the normative

---

[10] Though occasionally people have urges which are unreasoned. I have argued to this conclusion in 'Incommensurability and Agency': Ch. 3 above.

significance of inferences. Perhaps procedural rationality is meant to include more than such reasoning. There may be no obstacle to enriching the notion to include steadfastness of resolution and other aspects of proper functioning of the kind alluded to above. The question is whether, once enriched, the capacities included under the heading of 'procedural rationality' will be different from the capacities which make one so-called substantively rational.

To repeat: to those who believe that no rational capacities are involved in persons having goals the answer is obvious. But since we desire only what we think of as worth desiring, our desires are among our responses to perceived reasons. This is true of a desire to drink when thirsty as much as of the desire to become a good teacher. In conceiving desires and in adopting and maintaining goals we deploy all the capacities which are involved in so-called procedural rationality, and there seems to be no other capacity involved, at least none which can relate to rationality. The reasoning ability and other capacities which make people rational in forming beliefs about scientific matters, or about the weather, or anything else which can be said not to be in itself normative, are the same abilities which make people rational in the way they adopt and maintain goals. Therefore, there is only one kind of rationality.

As was allowed above, there may be factors which may interfere with the display of rationality in one area but not in another. But these will not be enough to establish complete independence of one's success in being rational in the different domains, and they will not track the supposed distinction between procedural and substantive rationality. Typical examples of such selective failures of rationality are those occasioned by motivated irrationality. They affect one's thoughts, feelings, and goals only when the motive leading to the irrationality comes into play. But they can affect one's choice of goals as well as one's 'theoretical' beliefs.

These remarks on the nature of rationality and its relation to normativity form the backdrop to the discussion that follows. They concern capacity-rationality, and though they inevitably have implications regarding the meaning of judgements that this or that action, desire, emotion, attitude, belief, etc., is rational or irrational, these implications are not straightforward. As they do not affect the rest of the argument they need not be explored here, beyond one point. Obviously to judge a belief, desire, emotion, etc., as rational is to note that having them is at the very least consistent with a successful deployment of our capacity for rationality.[11] The

---

[11] 'This was a rational belief for X to have' may mean no more than that. 'He rationally came to the belief that . . .' indicates much more. It presupposes actual use of one's rational capacity, and asserts that that has been successful. There are many variations and nuances in attributions of rationality and irrationality to beliefs, etc.

standard by which success is to be measured is far from clear. It is doubtful that there is only one standard employed on all occasions. It seems likely that we recognize a range of standards, and on each occasion we implicitly employ the one we find fitting in the circumstances. The most demanding standard regards as rational only those beliefs, etc., which are consistent with complete identification of all the reasons which apply to the situation[12] and a perfectly appropriate response to them. Everything else is judged irrational.[13] This standard seems to be used only rarely. A very lenient standard regards any belief to be rational unless holding it results from a failure (successfully) to employ one's rational capacity which involves gross mistakes, etc. Some standards relativize to one's age (what would be rational for a child to believe may be irrational for an adult), educational background (given that you have a degree in physics it is irrational for you to believe that), position in life, or to some other social variable. Common are standards which tie irrationality to blame. One's beliefs are irrational when one is blameworthy for having them. The best of those employ something like the legal test of negligence: a belief is irrational if and only if holding it displays lack of care and diligence in one's epistemic conduct.

2. THE CENTRALITY OF THE ABILITY TO REASON

When studying reasons we study normative aspects of the world. When discussing rationality we discuss our perceptions of, and responses to, reasons. Our ability to reason is central to our rationality in all its manifestations, that is regarding reasons for belief, action, emotion, or anything else.

One way to bring out the point is by reminding ourselves that emotions, attitudes, desires, and intentions have a cognitive content and cognitive presuppositions. Their rationality depends, in part, on the rationality of the beliefs which contribute to them, and which are presupposed by them. This dependence is asymmetric. Beliefs do not depend on feelings, desires, or intentions in the same manner. The rationality of beliefs enjoys a certain primacy for being involved with other forms of rationality, which it does not presuppose.

---

[12] Even this demanding standard allows that epistemic reasons vary with context. Therefore, even according to it, one's beliefs may be rational and false.

[13] There is no reason for the standard for irrationality to be the contradictory of the standard for being rational. The two can be logically independent, allowing for beliefs which are neither rational nor irrational.

More specifically, at least a rudimentary reasoning ability is involved in all rational responses to reason, simply because they are responses under the control of the agent, though admittedly I am using 'responses' loosely here, to indicate that rationality depends on appropriateness or intelligibility in the circumstances. Emotions, desires, intentions, or beliefs are rational depending on (a) whether they belong to a rational agent; (b) whether their occurrence is under the control of the agent; and (c) whether they are appropriate or intelligible given the reasons for and against them, as these reasons are, or as they are reasonably perceived by the agent.[14]

It is worth stopping to comment on the second of these conditions. It embodies several of the points belaboured in the previous section. I will address my remarks to the case of rationality in the endorsement of beliefs, but they apply with minor modifications to rationality in one's intentions, emotions, decisions, actions, etc. Control consists in the proper functioning of a person's rational faculty, the proper functioning of the person's ability to recognize and respond to reasons, rather than in any particular performance, such as an action, or a deliberate decision. Control is manifested when a belief is adopted, or endorsed in a process in which the ability to recognize reasons and respond to them (proper appreciation of and response to perception, or to testimony, for example) is active. It can be active even when beliefs are formed without deliberation or awareness, but when the agents' critical faculties would have stopped their formation had they been rationally suspect.

Is it not a distortion to claim, as I just did, that the proper functioning of a faculty, even of rationality, depends on being in control of our emotions, actions, beliefs, and the will? After all, the central use of 'control' relates to exercise of the agent's will: we control what we do, and how we do it, and we control our emotions, to the extent that we intentionally hold our emotions in check by an effort of will, etc. But there is a wider, more basic, use of control. People being out of control means that their will itself is not under their control, and our will and beliefs are out of control when they are systematically irrational.

Capacity-rationality is a more fundamental capacity than the will, which is the capacity for intentional action, for forming intentions and taking decisions. Rationality is like dispositional abilities, that is abilities which are manifested when the circumstances are right (e.g. a rope which can take a 100 kg. weight is a rope which will take weights up to 100 kg. without snapping, unless . . .). Our fundamental psychological abilities are of this kind, except that they are subject to complex possible interferences, many of them due to psychological factors: memory can fail when people are

---

[14] This point is subject to the baseline question discussed above.

depressed, etc. Rationality is like that: it is the ability to respond appropriately to (perceived) normative aspects of the world, and this means that rational beings respond appropriately to perceived normative aspects of the world, when no failure of attention, emotional upset, mood, memory, will, etc., interferes.

Like other dispositional capacities, rationality is a capacity which displays itself when the occasion presents itself, so long as no distorting factors interfere. That is what the second condition for the rationality of beliefs, actions, etc., signifies. People's beliefs (and again these remarks apply with some changes to other objects of our rationality) are rational only if they are formed and maintained while the people involved are in control of their formation, and continued endorsement—that is, while their reason controls how they come to adopt or endorse their beliefs. Reason controls the formation and endorsement of beliefs when, whether or not their formation or endorsement involves deliberations, beliefs are formed in processes which stop people from having them when their formation or endorsement is not warranted by reasons, as the agents see them, given their understanding of the situation they are in. A different aspect of control (and all these are matters of degree) is exercised when reason makes people endorse propositions which they are aware of compelling or at least adequate reasons to endorse.

Some people will say that when reason is in control we engage in subconscious reasoning. Whether or not such claims can be vindicated, the exercise of our rationality must be represented in the same way that reasoning is represented. The exercise of reason which manifests its control over our beliefs, emotions, intentions, desires, etc., is subject to the same rules that govern explicit reasoning. To that extent, capacity for reasoning is central to rationality and is involved in all its manifestations. This raises the question of the standing of principles of reasoning.

3. CAN REASON BE JUSTIFIED?

In setting out (at the beginning of this chapter) the contours of the problems of explaining the nature of normativity I did not once refer to the justification of normativity. Is not that the primary task of a theory of normativity or of reason?

It is not easy to make sense of the very request for the justification of normativity. We can ask whether this fact or that is a cogent reason for action or belief, etc. We can raise more general questions about types of facts. For example: does the law (i.e. the fact that one is legally required to perform an action) constitute a binding reason for action? Do people have good reason to conform to the practices of their country? But what is it to justify reason as such? Presumably the question is whether we are ever justified in holding anything as constituting an 'objective' reason? Or, whether it is possible for anything to be a reason? Or, whether there are any facts which are reasons?[15]

Some answers to these questions are discussed in later chapters in this volume. These explanations of the quest for the justification of normativity do not, however, dispose altogether of the difficulty in understanding it. Even once anxieties about the objectivity of reasons are put on one side questions remain. They are not dissipated by looking for the justification of statements that this or that is a reason for action or belief. Such justifications take many shapes and forms: burning the cat would be cruel (and that is a reason not to burn it) because it would inflict gratuitous suffering, and so on. These are the mundane arguments for this reason or that we are all familiar with. The quest for the justification of normativity cannot be whittled down to the normal arguments for the truth of a statement about this reason or that. It is a search for the vindication of the methods of reasoning employed in such mundane arguments, or for the discovery of a super principle which justifies confidence in the whole enterprise of reason, the whole enterprise of discerning reasons and responding to them. Is that a meaningful and a sensible request?

One common reply is that every argument to debunk reason would be self-defeating, for it would have to use reason, and thus its own validity depends on the assumption that it seeks to challenge, i.e. that reason is justified. Recently Tom Nagel has advanced a whole array of arguments in support of the objectivity, universality, and reality of reason (these are his terms) including a version of the argument that challenges to reason are self-defeating.[16] Nagel's argument rests on two pillars. First, that 'one cannot criticise something with nothing'.[17] The second is the fact that we cannot escape relying on reason.[18] Both pillars are suspect.

---

[15] Alternatively, perhaps the question meant is whether it makes sense to talk of anything being a reason? But this question comes very close to the explanatory questions I mentioned in the previous section. They explore what is the sense of normative discourse. I for one find little reason to doubt that normative discourse is meaningful.

[16] In chs. 2 and 4 of *The Last Word* (New York: OUP, 1996).   [17] Ibid. 20.

[18] Nagel is, of course, aware of the fact that the inescapability of a belief in the objectivity of reason is no proof of its correctness: see ibid. 33. He rests his case on the claim that no sceptical conclusion follows from the fact that explanation must come to an end, and that 'the language, and the truth of some other form of subjectivism is not shown by the fact that justification comes to an end at certain points at which there is natural agreement in judgements. Nothing about the framework of thought is shown by these facts' (34). I agree with these propositions. They are consistent with the less sanguine view expressed in the main text.

Reductio ad absurdum is a familiar form of argument which, at least prima facie, need not presuppose anything. It refutes a supposition by deriving a contradiction from it. As presented, *reductio* arguments quite commonly presuppose premises and rules or methods of argumentation which are accepted as uncontroversial. But need this be the case? Is there some reason why one must rely on some premises, rules, or methods of argument other than those which are refuted by the *reductio*? I do not think so. In a way no *reductio* argument does. They all take the following form: using rules (or methods) of argument R_1 to R_n a contradiction can be derived from premises P_1 to P_m. Therefore, at least one of the premises or at least one of the rules of inference is false or invalid. As I said, commonly in such arguments all but one or a few premises are accepted as being true, hence the conclusion is that at least one of the remaining ones is false. But strictly speaking such arguments do no more than impugn one of the premises and rules of inference. Of course, *reductio* arguments use rules of inference, not least in their final step: all these premises and rules yield a contradiction so at least one of the premises is false or at least one of the rules invalid. That does not matter to my point, since the rules of inference relied upon are themselves put in doubt by the argument. Nothing is relied upon without being cast into doubt at the end.

To use *reductio* to challenge the validity of reason one would reduce the number of premises to the minimum, including only logical truths or indubitable other truths, and use only the most basic rules of inference. If *they* give rise to a contradiction then it follows that at least one of them is false or invalid. Would not such a conclusion be tantamount to a sceptical argument against reason itself? For example, suppose that using substitution and modus ponens only, one derives a contradiction from (x) x = x. Could not such a proof lay claim to being a refutation of the cogency of reason?

Moreover, if we reject Nagel's claim that 'one cannot criticise something with nothing', then the fact that we cannot escape relying on reason may not be a very powerful point in its defence. It may turn out to be the case that, while we cannot avoid relying on reason, we know that we are doomed to rely on an incoherent system of thought.

From the fact that, if there is such a radical *reductio* argument, it will refute the validity of reason and the value of rationality, it does not follow that they stand refuted. One can perhaps conclude (*a*) that Nagel and others have failed to produce general reasons for the impossibility of a successful sceptical argument against reason, and yet hold (*b*) that no such argument exists, and therefore that we have no reason to doubt the cogency of reason. But that view does not seem to be quite adequate to the situation.

First, it is not entirely true to say that no challenges of the kind described exist. Paradoxes, some old, some new, such as the liar paradox, or Zeno's paradoxes, or the sorites paradox, have been known for a long time. Such paradoxes seem to be of the required kind. If not singly then cumulatively they challenge the coherence of reason. They take assumptions that lie at the very foundation of our conceptual thought and reduce them to a contradiction. They challenge the coherence of the concept of truth, the concepts of change and of time, and of the concepts of identity, of objects, and of possessing properties. It would take a brave man to say that they were all solved successfully. But we need not argue about that. What is of interest is that for long stretches of time people did not know how to solve them, and knew that they did not know how to solve them. Yet they carried on regardless. Rational thought did not stop, was not abandoned, in spite of awareness that, for all one knew, there were contradictions at its foundations. I do not know of any serious, let alone successful, argument that that was irrational, that it was irrational of people to carry on using reason, although they were aware of unresolved paradoxes concerning its basic features.

How are we to understand this reaction? I am less interested in its historical explanation than in the question whether it is a rational reaction on general grounds, independent of the specific historical context. One possible explanation is that, even if the use of reason is incoherent and self-contradictory, we are condemned to carry on using it. To be sure we can abandon reason, but we cannot reason our way into doing so. We abandon reason, or it abandons us, when we suffer brain damage, stupefy ourselves with hallucinatory and other drugs, etc. People can take action deliberately in order to be rational no more, but they cannot get there simply by reasoning their way into scepticism about reason. But that answer is unsatisfactory. If we can abandon reason, or cause it to abandon us, why is it not the case that exposing the contradictions at its foundations constitutes an argument for doing so? One cannot answer that such an argument relies on reason. It relies only on the fact that reason is self-defeating and self-contradictory.

One may point out that the step from the proposition that reason is self-defeating, and self-contradictory, or simply that it is unjustified, to 'let's blow our brains out' relies on the rationality that has just been defeated. Perhaps the bankruptcy of reason cannot be a reason for abandoning reason. But at least it means that there is no reason not to do so. We cannot conclude that we may do this if we want to, if that means that we have reason to believe that abandoning reason is permissible. But we can hold that we may do so, meaning simply that there is nothing against doing so—no reason against doing so, since there are no reasons for anything. That conclusion is devastating enough. It does not leave things in equilibrium.

It is not neutral as between abandoning reason and not doing so. For, if the debunking arguments are successful then to choose to continue to rely on reason is either to choose to be self-deluding, or to choose arbitrarily with open eyes to follow a debunked mode of life. It is to act against the spirit of the action. It is to rely on a method when by the light of that method itself it should not be relied upon. That does not establish a reason for not relying on it, but it places reliance psychologically at a disadvantage.

4. ARGUING AGAINST SUBSTANTIVE PRINCIPLES OF REASON[19]

We cannot reason ourselves into abandoning faith in reason, not because it is impossible for us to abandon faith in reason as a result of a successful argument that we should do so, but because no such argument can be sound. *Reductio* arguments of the kind I mentioned do not constitute a *reductio* of rationality. It is useful here to distinguish between the formal notion of reason, and substantive doctrines about the nature of reason. The formal notion of reason is fixed by the very abstract and essential characteristics that mark the kind of thinking which is governed by reason. We have no word for it other than 'thinking'. It is, however, thinking in a narrow sense, the sort of thinking that we refer to when saying: 'Wait a minute. I am trying to think,' and not the sort of thinking that daydreaming, free association, fantasizing are.[20] The formal notion of reason singles out a type of thinking which is marked by the discipline it is subjected to, a discipline which enables one to distinguish instances of successful thinking from flawed thinking. Possibly thinking in the narrow sense can be adequately characterized by two central essential properties:

(i) It is thinking which is subject to evaluation as correct or incorrect.
(ii) The standards by which success of episodes of thinking is judged depend on the reliability of the process of thinking which meets them in yielding justified intentions, decisions, and beliefs,

---

[19] The considerations advanced below are presented informally. I assume an interdependence of words, meanings, and concepts, but do not clarify it. Nor do I try to make more precise the notion of a principle of reasoning. Given a generous understanding of the notion, not all principles of reasoning are constitutive of meanings or concepts. That does not affect the case put here which is sound as applied to those principles of reasoning which are constitutive of meanings and concepts. If anything, the contingency of other principles of reasoning is even easier to establish, but I will not consider them here.

[20] Though other forms of thinking may borrow parts of the discipline of reason which marks the narrow notion of thinking.

that is, ones which are adequate, given the normative aspects of the world.[21]

In short, reason is a discipline which governs thinking, or a type of thinking. Thinking in conformity with reason is successful thinking, and thinking which does not conform to reason is unsuccessful as an instance of thinking of that kind. The substantive doctrine of reason spells out the content of that discipline. Rules of inference (deductive and non-deductive alike) and the central concepts they depend on are a central part of the substantive doctrine of reason.

I will argue that the paradoxes of reason cast doubt on the substantive doctrine of reason, on the cogency of the concepts and rules of inference it employs, not on the possibility of reason in itself. That is, they do not impugn formal reason. Do they cast doubt on the way we reason? Or on our understanding of the way we reason, on our theory of reason? Does the substantive doctrine of reason I referred to consist of the principles which govern our reason or our attempts at an explicit articulation of those principles?

They may do either. In any case the two are not entirely separate. Once we develop explicit accounts of the nature of reason, of its substantive doctrines, those accounts, while they never exhaust the forms of reasoning we engage in, do affect how those who are more or less aware of them and accept them reason. Solutions of the liar paradox cannot be said simply to improve our understanding of how we reason all along. They change our reasoning practices, modify the rules used in them, or restrict their application. And the same goes for solutions to most other logical paradoxes. This is particularly likely to be true of the ancient paradoxes. Regarding them, it is unlikely that the persistent failure of attempts to solve them is due merely to misunderstanding of how we actually reason, and therefore unlikely that solutions point merely to misunderstandings rather than to the need for a change in the concepts which generate the paradoxes.

If I am right then reason, i.e. the doctrines of reason, can be successfully challenged, and we respond to such challenges by modifying it, modifying reasoning practices and the principles which govern them. I am not suggesting that they are modified only in response to paradoxes and sceptical challenges. However, so long as they do not bring new paradoxes in their wake, modifications which free our practices from paradoxes constitute advances or improvement in our reasoning practices, and in the principles of reason we use.

---

[21] Notice that not all thinking aims at justifying beliefs or intentions. It can be part of the telling of invented stories, fanciful imagining, etc. It is, however, thinking of the relevant kind if it is governed by standards the use of which can justify intentions and beliefs.

On this view, reasoning principles are social principles, evolving roughly in the ways in which social practices generally evolve. But they can also be challenged on grounds of incoherence, or unreliability. They can be improved in response to such challenges. In this picture, changes in logical and conceptual principles of reasoning parallel changes in inductive clues and scientific methods of experimentation. Even though changes in principles of reasoning involving conceptual shifts occur mostly in informal ways and are harder to document, they respond to pressures similar to, though more diffuse than, those affecting scientific methods.

One reason for viewing with suspicion the claim that reasoning principles are based on practices which evolve in ways similar to that of other practices which govern our life is the familiar philosophical doctrine that regards changes in reasoning practices as nothing but corrections of mistakes. Such corrections occur when the changed practices comply more closely with the universal principles of reason. This objection admits that not only the explicit articulations of principles of reasoning can be faulted and can change, but that actual reasoning practices can be affected by contradictions and paradoxes, and can change to avoid them. But the objection denies that that process should be regarded as a process of change in *the substantive principles of reason*. They are universal and timeless. The changes we observe are in our imperfect attempts to conform to them.

The objection presupposes, however, that there is one and only one set of correct or valid principles of reason. This seems to me implausible, or at least in need of qualification, given the intimate relation between principles of reasoning and meaning and reference (i.e. given that if we abandon a principle of reason—e.g. the excluded middle—we change the meaning or content of the propositions which are governed by these principles of reasoning). If there can be systems of concepts such that (*a*) none of them is better than any of the others, and (*b*) there is no possible system of concepts and reasoning which is better than they are, then there is more than one ideal or correct system of concepts and reasoning, ideal in that they cannot be improved upon. Systems meeting these conditions also meet a further condition: namely, that each includes concepts which are not part of the others. Therefore, such systems are incommensurate.[22]

---

[22] My invocation of meaning incommensurability carries no sceptical implications. I do not claim that those who understand a system of concepts and reasoning (or, for that matter, a theory) cannot understand others which are incommensurate with it. Nor do I believe that incommensurability implies the possibility of incompatible truths, each vindicated within its own system or language, and each refuting the other. The possibility of incommensurate systems of concepts presupposes that truths that can be stated in one are compatible with truths which can only be stated in the other, though the tests of compatibility may involve extending the range of concepts in one or both to make sense of the very notion of compatibility and incompatibility between incommensurate propositions.

The mere possibility of incommensurability among systems of reasoning (expressed in different languages or segments of languages) does not cast doubt on the universality and timelessness of the principles of reasoning. However, once that possibility is admitted it becomes difficult to resist the thought that there are indeed an indefinite number of incommensurate systems of reasoning, and incommensurate languages or segments of languages expressing them. The number and identity of the historically instantiated systems of concepts, and of the rules of inference and reasoning associated with them, are matters of historical contingency. Moreover, it is possible for more than one correct system to be instantiated. That makes it hard to deny not only that the historical instantiation of principles of reasoning is a matter of contingent fact, but that the principles themselves are historical products emerging at particular points in time. The alternative is to assume the existence of an infinite number of sets of principles of reason, most of which it is impossible for us to find out about until such time, if ever, when the related new language evolves.

Let it be granted that ideal or correct principles of reason are historical products, that is, practices which arise in time, must we also concede that practices riddled with paradoxes embody principles of reason, rather than that they embody mistaken principles which are accepted as if they were principles of reason, but which are not? Admittedly it is puzzling to think that there can be paradox-ridden principles of reason. Adding that they are imperfect or defective principles of reason, rather than removing the oddity of this view, adds to it. Is it not a contradiction in terms to think of imperfect or defective principles of reason?

Nevertheless, we must accept that this is so, for the alternative is unacceptable. The first and most radical way of understanding the situation of people whose practices of reasoning are infected by paradoxes has to be rejected. It would be wrong to say that the people whose practices of reasoning were riddled with paradoxes did not have any principles of reasoning enabling them to distinguish cogent from erroneous arguments, and rightly guiding their thinking. It is evident that they engaged in thinking guided by reason just as much as anyone else does.

A more moderate understanding of their situation will have it that their practices of reasoning were mistaken, but had limited validity in being imperfect approximations of the sound principles of reason. On this view we can say that they were, by and large, guided by the sound principles of reason, except that their practices failed to incorporate and follow them adequately, thus leading them on occasion to incorrect applications of the right principles. Apart from other weaknesses, this way of understanding their situation presupposes that there is a unique set of sound principles of reason, whereas—as was suggested above—there seem to be indefinitely many incommensurate sound sets of principles of reason.

The most promising suggestion is a modification of the second proposal, to allow for a plurality of incommensurate sets of principles of reason. It says that practices of reasoning infected by paradox can rightly be regarded as mistaken approximations of some sound principle of reason or other. Being such approximations we can say, as in the second proposal, that the people who followed them could be in part vindicated. They can be said to have been imperfectly guided by the sound principles of reason which their practices approximate. This suggestion purchases the advantage of not allowing that principles of reason can themselves be imperfect at too easy a price. In the absence of further criteria, and it is not clear what they might be, any practice of thinking approximates some set of principles of reason or other. This may not be an objection to the suggestion we are examining. Possibly no practices which allow one to distinguish correct from mistaken thoughts, episodes of thinking, or transitions of thought, can be discounted. All of them are practices of reasoning in the minimal sense we are exploring, that is, they approximate some sound principles of reason, and their practitioners can be said to be guided by the sound principles these practices approximate.

Nevertheless, I find this suggestion unacceptable for it seems that any imperfect (i.e. paradox-infected) practices of reasoning approximate not one but many sound principles of reason, many of which are unknown to us or to the practitioners, and, given our time and place, many are unknowable by us or by them. In these circumstances, denying that people are governed and guided by the principles they have, and insisting that they are really guided by principles beyond these, principles which they do not know, and perhaps cannot know, is an unhelpful verbal trick to avoid saying that principles of reason can be imperfect. The suggestion serves no other purpose. The 'more honest' course is to keep the connection between principles people follow and the practices they engage in. This connection allows us to explain how people can be guided by principles which in some sense they do not know, that is, of which they are not (fully) aware, and the content of which they cannot articulate. The price of allowing that principles of reason can be imperfect seems no price at all.

The preceding argument for the historical character of principles of reason presupposes meaning incommensurability. Is the presupposition justified? The issue is complex and it is easy to argue on the one hand for and on the other hand against meaning incommensurability. Not everything which can be expressed in one language can be expressed in all others without extending their resources, either by adding new words, or phrases, or enriching their grammar. Once, however, enrichment is allowed, what is there to stop a language from being enriched to whatever degree may be necessary to enable it to express whatever the other does, and to include all the concepts of the other? Can it be enriched by simply absorbing the other language as a part? Is not that the way the 'languages of science' came to enrich the standard natural languages which, because of the existence of such specialized segments, can express what they could not express without them?

If this is where the argument resides then I suspect that there is no 'principled' solution to this problem. That is, it cannot be solved by arguments which disregard the contingent and historical nature of languages (both natural languages, and specialized segments of them like the languages of science or of law). The issue of incommensurability of meaning turns out to be the problem of the identity of languages, and that is a historical matter. Whether something is a segment of another language or a separate language can depend not on relations of meanings and of rules of grammar, but on how the two developed and who uses them and when. But if the issue of meaning incommensurability is one of historical development then meaning incommensurability is possible and therefore principles of reasoning are themselves historical products.

I will, therefore, proceed on the assumption that the substantive principles of reason are historical products which can be challenged on grounds of self-contradiction, incoherence, and unreliability, and which can change to avoid such challenges. This allows scepticism more scope than Nagel allows it. It does not, however, allow for an attack on reason or rationality itself. Such an attack would have to be addressed to the formal concept of reason, and show that it is incoherent.

Before we consider this problem here is one last word regarding critiques of substantive doctrines of reason. The preceding discussion aimed to show that such doctrines are capable of being criticized. When paradoxes are discovered principles are revised to avoid them. This in itself does not constitute a justification of those principles which are not infected by paradox. Does one not need to provide them with some justification other than the timid response 'so far no paradoxes affecting them have come to light'? Yes, and no. It is certainly possible to explain why such principles are valid. But the explanation is not of a kind normally thought of as justification. Rather the explanation will relate to the constitutive role of such principles, reconciling the fact that they are constitutive of a mode of thinking with the possibility of alternative, incommensurate, sets of principles, and noting that the validity of the principles does not guarantee that whatever thoughts they are manifested in are about 'an independent, objective reality'.[23]

---

[23] See my 'Notes on Value and Objectivity' (Ch. 6).

5. THE STANDING OF FORMAL REASON

Is it possible for a sceptical argument challenging the coherence of the formal notion of reason, or the case for its use, to be successful? Many of the attacks on reason and rationality witnessed in the course of history are meaningful and arguably justified. Such, for example, are attacks on rationalism claiming either that people have come to exaggerate what can be achieved simply by conformity with principles of reason, or that the imagination and fantasy, or feelings and emotions, are of value, as well as thought in the narrow sense. None of these nor other similar claims need be disputed. Nor need we engage in an argument about the instrumental importance of rational thought, for example, whether people or the human race generally can survive for long without it. The question is whether it is possible to prove that rational thought is inherently bankrupt. If it has instrumental value, the debunking argument goes, it has it in spite of its failure to live up to its aspiration to be a reliable guide to truth. Can one show that rational thought as such, not merely this or that substantive doctrine of rational thought, is incoherent?

Two possible routes towards this conclusion suggest themselves. Sceptical argument following the first route would prove that no account of the content of reason can escape a *reductio* argument showing it to be incoherent. While the refutation of any specific account of reason has to proceed via a *reductio* argument, an argument that any account of reason is subject to a successful refutation need not itself employ a *reductio* method of argumentation. Any form of proof would do.[24] The second line of attack would consist of arguments showing that the very formal notion of reason is incoherent. I do not believe that we have been confronted by any such arguments. But it may be useful to speculate on the effect they may, if successful, have.

Think first of the impact of the paradoxes affecting the substantive doctrines of reasoning. Their solutions did not lead to wholesale abandonment of rational concepts or principles of reasoning. Rather, they led to modifications of existing principles and practices of reasoning. This is what one would expect if one believes that all adjustments forced by arguments would tend to be the minimal necessary to satisfy the reasons forcing them. In terms of familiar metaphors: we start where we are and we proceed to adjust our position from there. We move not towards some unique ideal but towards a system of concepts and of reasoning which is readily reachable from our starting-points and which seems to avoid the difficulties which force us to move from our initial position. It seems reasonable to

---

[24] Pyrrhonist sceptical arguments are of this kind, as they aim to show that if a proposition is supported by reason so is its negation.

assume that more radical paradoxes affecting the cogency of the formal concept of reason will, if they ever materialize, lead to similar partial adjustments.

It is true that the strategies of challenging formal reason seem to allow a more far-reaching conclusion. They seem to allow the conclusion that no principles of reason whatsoever can be valid. But appearances are misleading. To entertain that thought is to entertain the thought that propositions and concepts are discrete with no logical or conceptual relations between them. That would make mastering any of them impossible. Hence the most that a challenge to formal reason can succeed in doing is forcing adjustments to the concept of formal reason.

There is, however, a difficulty in conceiving of such an adjustment as anything other than a correction of a mistake regarding the one and only notion of reason. When considering the principles of reason my suggestion was that the pressure of paradoxes leads one to move from one's initial system of concepts and of principles of reasoning, through the smallest adjustment which happens to suggest itself, to what is strictly speaking an incommensurable alternative system. Both systems are instantiations of the formal notion of reason, though the second is (so far as we know) superior to the first in not being infected by paradoxes. When we abandon, through some adjustment, our formal notion of reason such a picture is impossible to sustain, for there is no genus which covers both the earlier and the later formal notions of reason. It seems as if, strictly speaking, we must regard the previous notion as a mistaken (because affected by paradoxes) version of the second. That is, we must assume that there is but one, though possibly not yet correctly understood, notion of reason.

The imagined radical paradoxes do not lead to a change in the concept of reason, but to the correction of mistaken beliefs about its nature. We cannot distance ourselves from the formal concept of reason, and adopt another in its stead. This enterprise does not make sense. This conclusion should not be misinterpreted. It is not that we are captives of 'our' concept of reason and cannot abandon it even if it is mistaken. We can so to speak 'abandon it', though what we abandon is not the concept of reason but the views we happen to hold about its nature.[25] These views are what sceptical arguments can hope to refute. The very possibility of formal reason cannot be refuted for the notion of such a refutation does not make sense. It assumes either that concepts are discrete with no conceptual relations between them, or that there can be an alternative to formal reason, and that is nonsense.[26]

---

[25] We can of course 'abandon' it in the trivial sense of ceasing to reflect about it.

[26] Of course we can become creatures which cannot think (in the narrow sense of that word). That, however, is a fact about us, not about the concept of reason.

6. CONCLUSION

Let me take stock. We saw (in section 3) that the thought that normativity as such should be defended and justified often amounts to a demand for the justification of reason. It encompasses questions I did not touch on, primarily doubts about the objectivity of reason, and about the possibility that people may be motivated by reason.[27] Putting such doubts to one side we saw that it was possible to advance sceptical arguments against any of the principles of reason. Such principles are historical products in the same way that languages and other systems of concepts are. They can be replaced by others which are, hopefully, free of paradox. Such changes are normally achieved not through wholesale rejection of principles of reasoning and of the systems of concepts which gave rise to them, but through their adjustment and modification. There cannot, however, be sceptical arguments against reason itself. For while it is possible for human beings to stop engaging in thinking, in the narrow sense of the word, and even to lose the ability to do so,[28] it makes no sense to think that the concept of thought or of reason can be rejected or be found defective. Our understanding of it can be found wanting. It can change, but what can change is the understanding of a concept which remains the same.[29] It follows that the validity of specific normative principles can be called into question. And that we—human beings—can become creatures incapable of being guided by normative considerations. But so long as we are capable of rational thought we are capable of being normatively guided, and, while we can explain the nature of reason and normativity, there is no such enterprise as justifying normativity.

---

[27] See Ch. 6.

[28] It is plausible to suppose that we can stop thinking altogether only if we lose the ability to think.

[29] To avoid doubt let me add that throughout history the methods of reasoning employed by people have changed, hopefully improved, in many ways which have nothing to do with paradoxes, and sceptical arguments of any kind. Such improvements can happen as people's knowledge and understanding of the world they live in increase. The discussion above does not bear on such developments.

5

Explaining Normativity: Reason and the Will

The relation between reason and the will has been central to many discussions of the nature of reasons and of normativity. Can reason motivate? If so how so? If not, what is the relation between realizing that a reason applies and conforming to it? These questions are the focus of this chapter.

1. CONFORMITY WITH A REASON DOES NOT ALWAYS REQUIRE ACTING FOR THAT REASON

Aspects of the world are normative, that is, they constitute reasons for action. What does that entail for those for whom these are reasons? What must they do, how must they be to be perfect conformers with reasons?

One conforms with reason if one behaves as reason requires one to behave. Suppose that Mary never fails to conform to reason. Her emotions, beliefs, desires, and actions never flout reason. The supposition is very strong, and is not meant to be realistic. It means that Mary is not merely never guilty of having irrational beliefs, intentions, etc. The supposition means that her emotions, beliefs, desires, and actions always actually conform to reason, not only to reasons as she non-culpably, but perhaps mistakenly, supposes them to be. To avoid any complication or misunderstanding on that score let us suppose further that Mary can without too much difficulty establish what are all the reasons which apply to her. Assume further that she never suffers accidental mishaps of the sort that cause us to fail to perform actions we intended to perform. This means that the excuse of ignorance would not be available to her. If she is never at fault this is because she always conforms, with no mistakes or failures, to the

---

Earlier versions were presented at the Philosophy Colloquium at Berkeley, at a conference on practical reason in Berlin, and at the conference in memory of Jean Hampton at Tucson. I learnt from questions and comments of many who participated in those occasions. I do not remember all those from whose questions and comments I benefited. I would like however to acknowledge my debt to Erich Ammereller, Michael Bratman, Alvin Goldman, Ulrike Heuer, Barry Stroud, and most especially to David Silver, who was the commentator on my paper at Tucson.

reasons that apply to her. What can we learn from this fact about her actions, beliefs, or desires? Much less than some writers assume. In particular we cannot learn from this that:

(1) She knows all the reasons which apply to her.
(2) Her conduct, desires, intentions, decisions are motivated by all the reasons which show them to be right or justified.[1]
(3) Whenever there is an adequate reason for her to believe some proposition to be true she does so.
(4) Whenever there is an adequate reason for her to perform a certain action she does so.
(5) Whenever there is an adequate reason for her to want something (or to intend to do something) she wants it (or intends to perform that action).

I will return to theses (3) to (5) in the next section. First, I will examine the second thesis. I am assuming that if it is false so is the first. If to conform to reason Mary need not be motivated by all the (undefeated) reasons which apply to her, there is no reason to think that just because she perfectly conforms to reason she knows all the reasons which apply to her.

(a) Nonfeasance

Since Mary perfectly conforms with reason it goes without saying that she has never murdered any innocent person, never kidnapped an innocent person. It does not follow that she did not commit such crimes because she was aware of overwhelming reasons against them. It may never have occurred to her to kill or abduct anyone, and she is none the worse for it. Arguably, Mary is a better person that way than had she considered murdering someone, and desisted because after deliberation she realized that it would be wrong to do so.

If these moral examples seem contentious think of non-moral cases. Mary has reason not to eat any of the broken bricks in her garden, nor to crawl under the bed every morning, nor to throw some books out of the window every night, and so on and so forth. She does not eat broken bricks, does not crawl under the bed in the mornings, nor throw books out of the window in the evenings. The thought of doing any of these things has never

---

[1] The reasons bearing on the justification of an action are reasons either for or against it. If the action is justified the reasons for it are not defeated by those against it (not even in combination with those which are partially against it, i.e. against performing it in some circumstances, or in some manner). The undefeated reasons for a justified action are those which justify it. There may be other factors involved in the justification of some actions, factors which are not reasons for the agent, and therefore irrelevant here.

occurred to her. Her nonfeasance is simply a result of this fact. It is not motivated by awareness of reasons. She would not be more rational had she reflected on all the things she has conclusive reason not to do. Which is just as well, as it would have been impossible for her to do so. True, we can be unreflectively motivated by reasons, but not when we do not know them, and Mary may well not know many reasons for such nonfeasance. Her conformity to them need not be secured by being motivated by them.

Two general points are illustrated by this example. First, there are reasons against performing actions, or having emotions, or beliefs, etc., as well as reasons for them. To conform with a reason against some action one need not do anything. So long as one does not perform that action one conforms with the reason. Similarly, a reason against a certain emotion (e.g. against being angry with one's children when they are naughty) is conformed to so long as one does not have the offending emotion. No alternative emotion is required. The same is true of belief. A reason against believing that such and such is not necessarily a reason for believing that not such and such. One conforms with it so long as one does not have the offending belief. One need not have any other belief.

Second, in general, at least so far as reasons against actions, beliefs, or emotions are concerned, conforming with them does not require being motivated to avoid the actions, beliefs, or emotions for those reasons. We can go further: conforming with them does not require either intention or knowledge. To conform with the reason(s) against murder it has to be the case that one does not murder. One need not even know that murder is possible, nor have the notion of killing or of causing death.

(b) Overdetermination

Is the same true of reasons for performing actions, and for having beliefs or emotions? First, consider beliefs. By hypothesis, in having the beliefs she has Mary does not rely on any bad reasons. Similarly by hypothesis she has all the beliefs that she has decisive reasons to have (or all the beliefs that there are decisive reasons for her to have). But does she hold those beliefs for those reasons? Must she be aware of those reasons? Must she be aware that they are reasons, and for which beliefs they are reasons? The answer to all these questions is: not necessarily. Reasons for believing a proposition are often numerous and overdetermined, and there is nothing amiss in not taking note of all of them. For example, it is enough if one relies on reports of others, even when direct evidence for the proposition is within one's reach.

Similar considerations, and some more, apply to actions. The reasons for many actions are overdetermined and one need not know all of them to conform with all of them. One may conform with reasons when acting on advice, without knowing the reasons, even though they are reasons one could find out about with ease. Many actions are habitual or semi-automatic, and one may never have considered the reasons for them. Similar considerations apply to other reason-guided responses to the world.

(c) Unintended Action

A further consideration applies specially to actions. Not infrequently people do what there are compelling reasons for them to do without even realizing what they are doing. Their doing what they had reason to do may be a consequence or a by-product of some other action that they performed intentionally. They may intend to perform an action (for a good or a bad reason) whose performance constitutes the performance of another action that they are not aware they are performing, but which, unbeknown to them, they have ample reasons to perform. They may be lucky, but in general their actions cannot be faulted when this is the case. They conform to reasons.

Cases of nonfeasance, of overdetermination, and of unintended action establish that conformity with reason does not always require having some specific motive, in particular it does not require being aware of the reasons which apply to one and reacting directly to them. Naturally, some actions, or emotions, have to be for the right kind of reason. Some reasons are not merely reasons for action. They are reasons for acting for a particular reason. Friendship cannot survive long unless the friends act for the sake of their friends at least some of the time. Anger can be unjustified if motivated by hurt pride, and justified if motivated by injustice. But these are special cases. Less often noticed are the special cases in which we have reason not to act for a (good) reason. I have argued that the actions of officials within institutions, where there is a division of authority between different officials, are an example. Officeholders should not act for reasons reliance on which falls outside their jurisdiction. More generally I claimed that directives from authorities create for their subjects reasons not to act for certain reasons. I call such reasons exclusionary reasons.[2] But both reasons to act for a reason and reasons not to act for a reason are special cases. In general, conformity with reason requires doing the action, or having the belief, intention, emotion, or desire that the reason is a reason for, and that is all. Later we will come across additional reasons for the same conclusion.

---

[2] See J. Raz, *Practical Reason and Norms*, 2nd edn. (Oxford: Oxford University Press, 1999), especially the appendix.

It is a separate question whether people's conformity with reason can be reliable unless by and large they are motivated by the right reasons. Naturally it is highly unlikely that one could conform with reason by chance. But nor can we take for granted that the more we rely on our knowledge the more successful we will be in conforming to reason. There is good reason to think that we cannot reliably conform to reason unless much of the time we do so automatically and unthinkingly. It is an empirical question where and when that requires actual knowledge, however implicit, and to what extent the most reliable guide to conformity with reason is that the possibility to be avoided is not one which ever presents itself in fact (i.e. we have no opportunity to perform the actions), or in our thought (i.e. the thought of taking offending actions does not occur). To the extent that knowledge is not required for reliable conformity then not only is there no fault in our actions and beliefs, etc., when they conform with reason, even though they are not undertaken for the reasons they conform to, there is no fault in us either. We cannot say that while our actions and beliefs are as they should be, we are at fault for not having been guided by all the reasons which apply to us (and which were within our reach). These questions, as well as the question of when we are motivated by reason when we act without deliberation,[3] need not detain us here as they do not affect the conclusion argued for above.

2. ARE REASONS OPTIONAL?

To continue with the question of how it is that we can respond appropriately to reasons let us now turn to the remaining theses which we must reject regarding Mary, even though she conforms to reason perfectly. They were:

(3) Whenever there is an adequate reason for her to believe some proposition to be true she does so.
(4) Whenever there is an adequate reason for her to perform a certain action she does so.
(5) Whenever there is an adequate reason for her to want something (or to intend to do something) she wants it (or intends to perform that action).

I will not consider the last thesis at any length. Its rejection follows directly from the previous conclusions. In general, though not without exception, the reasons to want to do something are the reasons for that action (or doing), and once the reason to perform it lapses (because one has performed

---

[3] I discuss this in 'The Truth in Particularism' (Ch. 10).

the act, or for some other reason) there is no more reason to want to perform it. As it is possible perfectly to conform with reason without always acting for the reasons one conforms with, it follows that it is possible to conform with reasons to do what one has reason to do without wanting to do that act for that reason. It follows that it is possible to conform with reason without always wanting what one has reason to want.[4]

The brief and somewhat simplified explanation of the failure of theses (3) and (4) must be either (*a*) that in some circumstances reasons are optional or (*b*) that some reasons are of a special optional type. Reasons are optional to the extent that the fact that there are reasons for a certain response make it an eligible, attractive response, but not one which it is wrong not to adopt.

Thesis (3) and the Latitude in Epistemic Reasons

I will offer only a brief explanation of the rejection of thesis (3).[5] People can have different epistemic profiles. Think of degrees of trustfulness and suspiciousness.[6] Some people will form a belief on the basis of testimony which will leave others still doubtful. Sometimes it would be irrational either to form or not to form the relevant belief, given the testimony. But at other times it may be rational both to come to that belief, and to withhold belief in the circumstances. While being credulous or excessively suspicious are characteristics identified by their tendency to lead their possessors into irrational beliefs, or doubts, many people possess differing degrees of trustfulness, none of which tends to lead them to form or withhold beliefs irrationally. A more trusting person may come to believe a proposition in circumstances where had he been less trusting he would have suspended belief. And yet he is not irrational to come to that belief, nor would he have been irrational to withhold belief in the circumstances. These are observations of familiar features of our epistemic judgements. They show that people may find themselves in circumstances where neither believing a proposition nor withholding belief will be irrational. In such circumstances the reasons for that belief are 'optional'[7] only. They make believing (and withholding belief) intelligible, but they do not amount

---

[4] This point will be further clarified below. It will be seen that the normal reason to want something is conditional on a reason to achieve it, and it lapses once the reason it is conditional on is satisfied.

[5] I am mainly repeating my observations in 'When We are Ourselves: The Active and the Passive': see Ch. 1, above.

[6] Much of what I will say of them applies also to many other epistemic characteristics: e.g. the fact that some tend to give greater weight to statistical evidence than others.

[7] The term is not entirely happy here. In particular it does not mean that we can choose what to believe. See 'When We are Ourselves' (Ch. 1).

to a rational requirement to believe (or to withhold belief), on pain of irrationality.[8]

A possible objection to this conclusion claims that it leads to a contradiction. To describe the range of situations in which reasons for belief require neither believing nor withholding belief I said that in those situations one is justified in saying that the evidence warrants belief, and also justified in saying that it warrants withholding belief. But one cannot both believe and withhold belief. Therefore, if reason warrants belief it cannot also warrant withholding it, and vice versa.

As it stands this is no objection. It is merely a denial of the possibility I have been arguing for. The objection rejects without argument the possibility that epistemic warrant can be permissive (depending on circumstances). The objector may, however, modify his claim. He may claim that one can only see oneself as justified in forming a belief if one denies that in the situation it would be justified to withhold belief, and that one can only see oneself justified in withholding belief on the ground that in the situation it would be unjustified to form[9] that belief. But why should we accept this claim? Common experience has made familiar situations in which we recognize that reasonable people may differ in their judgements, even though they are facing the same evidence. To think this to be the case in any particular situation does not presuppose that differences in background beliefs account for the reasonableness of the difference in judgements. Therefore, we are not surprised to find ourselves in such situations. We ourselves can be one of the differing sides, both of whose positions are reasonable.

Thesis (4) and the Optional Element in Practical Reasons

The rejection of (4) follows directly from its meaning. The fact that certain actions, states, etc., are good or valuable in various ways constitutes reasons for action. The reason(s) for an action is (are) adequate if, given how things are, it is intelligible and not wrong, irrational, or unreasonable that one performs the action for that (those) reason(s). For example, other things being equal, that Julie has promised John to help him when he moves house is an adequate reason for her to do so. Other things being equal, if she helps him

---

[8] Another consequence of these remarks is that it is a mistake to claim that as between a proposition and its negation one is rationally required to believe that which is supported by the better evidence. In certain circumstances it is not irrational for a person to admit that p is better supported than not-p, and yet to withhold belief on the ground that the evidence for p leaves him in doubt.

[9] Or, to hold. It takes less to justify holding to a belief one already has than to justify forming a new one.

because she promised her action will be intelligible and not wrong.[10] We could distinguish two elements in a claim that something (Julie's promise) is an adequate reason for an action (the promised action). First the reason (the promise) is a sufficient reason in that it makes the action it is a reason for intelligible. Second, given that it is not defeated by (wholly or partly) conflicting reasons, it is an adequate reason for the action, for conforming to it is not wrong or unreasonable or irrational.

The fact that this or that (action or other thing) has properties which make it good or bad in some respect is a reason (for the people appropriately related to it) for action (as well as for desires, intentions, and emotions). Such reasons can be either conditional or unconditional. Unconditional reasons are sufficient, independently of what other reasons one has. That is, if that P is an unconditional reason to do V then it is intelligible that one does V because P, and that does not depend on the fact that one has another reason which doing V will serve, nor on the absence of reasons against doing V.

A reason for A to do V_m is conditional on another reason R to V_n if and only if it is a sufficient reason for A to V_m only if R is a sufficient reason for A to do V_n, and that explains (at least in part) why A has a reason to do V_m. The goodness of many things (or the existence of many goods) constitutes conditional reasons only. That the chair is comfortable is something good about the chair, and we can say that is a reason to sit on it, but such a reason is not a sufficient reason. If one has reason to rest one's legs then one has a sufficient reason to sit on this chair because it is comfortable. Reasons are sufficient if they are unconditional, or if they are conditional reasons whose condition is met.[11]

All instrumental reasons are conditional reasons, but they do not exhaust the category. Reasons we have to do something because doing it constitutes something else we have reason to do are also conditional reasons. If I have a reason to give you a good recent recording of Beethoven's quartets then the fact that the Emerson Quartet recording is outstanding is a reason to give it to you. Doing so constitutes (and is a way of) giving you a good recent recording of the quartets. The example illustrates the additional point: that the existence of intrinsic goods as well as of instrumental goods (i.e. those whose goodness resides in their ability to produce good consequences) can constitute conditional reasons. Our discussion concerns sufficient reasons only. For simplicity's sake I will concentrate on

---

[10] You may well feel that her reason is much more than that. Her promise means that she is required to help him, or something like that. This may be so. But it is also an adequate reason.

[11] All these terms can be relativized to a person or a class of persons.

unconditional reasons, hoping that that will not obscure the fact that they are not the only sufficient reasons.

When do we have unconditional reasons? To the extent that the question raises substantive evaluative issues we cannot go into them here. The following observations illustrate the kind of issues involved. Do I have a conditional or an unconditional reason to read *A la recherche du temps perdu*? One may say that the reason is conditional on a reason to read Proust, or to be familiar with French literature, and the like. Indeed so. But the question is: do I also have an unconditional reason to read the novel simply because it is outstandingly good? Here opinions may differ. Some would deny that I have such a reason. I have a reason to read it only if I have a reason to be a cultivated person, or some such reason.[12] Others may differ. They will say that I have (unconditional) reason to read the novel. To read it in order to become a cultivated person is to read it for the wrong reason. It may even be a self-defeating reason, as being a cultivated person entails cherishing excellence in culture for its own sake, rather than as a way of becoming a person of a certain kind. They can agree that we have a reason to be cultivated, but claim that we have (an exclusionary) reason not to act for it. They will add that, irrespective of that, we have an unconditional reason to read *A la recherche* just because of its excellence.

With these distinctions in hand let us return to the question whether a perfect conformer with reason, like Mary, would perform every action she has adequate reason to perform? What makes a reason adequate? It must be a sufficient reason, and it must not be defeated by other competing reasons, that is by reasons which cannot all be completely conformed with. It follows that Mary will not be taking all the actions she has adequate reasons to take. Whenever two competing reasons fail to defeat each other Mary will be able to conform with only one of them. Two reasons fail to defeat each other either if they are equal in strength or stringency, or if they have incommensurate strength or degrees of stringency.[13]

The discussion of the five rejected theses yields one important additional conclusion.[14] When I set out my position at the outset I said that a perfect

---

[12] Some philosophers seem committed to the view that all our reasons are conditional on having a reason to have a good life, i.e. that the only unconditional reason people have is to promote their well-being. Some support the same view with the qualification that we are also subject to unconditional moral reasons. In Ch. 13, also published as 'The Central Conflict: Morality and Self-Interest', in R. Crisp and B. Hooker (eds.), *Well-Being and Morality: Essays in Honour of James Griffin* (Oxford: OUP, 1999), among other places, I try to explain why well-being cannot play that role in our life.

[13] These definitions have to be modified to allow for the special (and partial) conflicts between reasons for action and exclusionary reasons excluding reliance on them. For the sake of brevity I omit these complications. Cf. the postscript to *Practical Reason and Norms*.

[14] This was pointed out to me by Barry Stroud.

conformer to reason would not have to live up to the ideals stated in the five theses. This, one may have thought, is a result of my weak notion of a perfect conformer as a person who never offends against reason. Granted that I am right regarding a conformer understood as a non-violator, are there not higher standards of conformity to reason which consist precisely in meeting the conditions of the five theses, and is it not better, is one not a more rational person, if one conforms to those higher standards? Several of the arguments I relied upon show that this higher standard is illusory, and impossible. The arguments against the second proposition show that there is nothing particularly desirable in attending to all the reasons which apply to one. Both those and the arguments against propositions (3) and (4) show that often the alleged ideal is logically impossible. This is consistent with holding that some goods can only be obtained if pursued for the right reasons. It is also consistent with a different ideal: of being a person who is good at discerning reasons and responding to them, when the need arises.

3. DOES INCOMMENSURABILITY RENDER REASONS OPTIONAL?

Back to our discussion. The rejection of the fourth thesis raises two questions. How important in practice are occurrences of undefeated and competing adequate reasons? And, are reasons ever optional for different reasons? Not all good- or bad-making properties are alike, and therefore, not all reasons are alike. In considering in what sense and to what degree reasons can be said to be optional I will concentrate on a certain range of examples, like the value of *A la recherche* or of a good film, or a good holiday, or the value of having (another) child, or of moving house, or changing job, and the reasons which the value of these options constitutes. Reasons of these kinds are central to people's conduct of their lives. But it may be that some classes of cases, for example, reasons of justice, do not conform to the pattern which applies to them.

A familiar belief will serve as our starting-point. Suppose that a good play is receiving a powerful performance in the local theatre tonight. For that reason Mary may well go to see it. If she does her action will be intelligible and in her circumstances, I will assume, not only be not wrong or unreasonable, but very sensible. Yet, Mary decides not to see the play. She may not feel like doing so, and, perhaps with some regret, she decides to stay at home. If she does, her action will again be intelligible and neither wrong nor unreasonable. The fact that the play is good and that it is well performed is a reason to see it. It makes going to see it an intelligible option, and if one goes for that reason the action would be explicable by reference to this fact. But that fact does not mean that one has to go. It merely makes going to see the play an acceptable option.

What I will call *the basic belief* is that this structure of reasons is most common: that most of the time people have a variety of options such that it would accord with reason for them to choose any one of them and it would not be against reason to avoid any of them. In many cases the reasons for doing one thing or another are not time-specific: the same reasons and the same opportunity to conform to them will apply on a number, sometimes an indefinite number, of occasions. This does not, however, explain the basic belief. Quite apart from the fact that delay is not costless, the basic belief applies to time-specific reasons as well. Mary, in our example, does not have to go to the play even on the last evening of its run. She may still just not feel like it and do something else instead.[15]

The basic belief applies to large as well as to small decisions. Mary may consider whether to have a(nother) child. While in some situations she may have decisive reasons against or for having a child, so that it will be wrong for her not to follow them, in many situations the decision is, as it were, up to her. There may be—let us say—reasons for having a child, and very little against doing so. Yet while if she decides for those reasons to have the child her decision will be intelligible and reasonable, if she decides against it she will not be acting unreasonably, nor doing anything wrong. She does not have to have a child just because there are reasons for having it and little against.

Common views, like the basic belief these examples illustrate, do not speak for themselves. It is difficult to ascertain what background assumptions are being taken for granted by those who hold them. This is why it is difficult to see clearly the theoretical position which they express or presuppose. Yet, the basic belief should be given credence unless it can be shown to be incoherent or inconsistent with some of our rightly entrenched views. While it affects the way many people view many concrete cases, it is not itself a belief about any particular case. It is about the structure of the practical considerations facing people on many, probably the vast majority, of occasions for action in which deliberation is possible. Moreover, it reflects the way people actually behave in most situations. They sometimes act on the understanding that in the situation in which they find themselves one of the options open to them is supported by reasons which defeat all competing options, and they have no choice but to take that option. But on

---

[15] I am not, of course, claiming that the fact that this is the last opportunity never matters. Only that sometimes it does not. The ensuing discussion will show why it will not do, in Mary's case, to say that the last night of the run was not really the last opportunity, as there will be other comparable plays in good productions for her to see.

most occasions they believe that there are many options which they can follow, and while some of them are ruled out by competing reasons which defeat whatever reasons support them, other options remain open, remain eligible. On most occasions, in other words, people conduct themselves on the assumption that they face a number of options which are all supported by reasons, without any reason which would make one of them the one which the agent must choose. The choice between them is not dictated by reason.

I take the basic belief to be true. Part of the task of explaining normativity is explaining the structure of normative thinking. Therefore, unless they are incoherent or inconsistent with each other we take structural aspects of our normative thought as given. They may require correction in details, but unless incoherent or inconsistent they cannot be otherwise flawed. The task is to explain them.

One suggestion divides reasons into two types: enticing reasons and requiring reasons. Enticing reasons make an option attractive, and render following them intelligible. But they do not bear at all on the reasonableness of not conforming with them. Failure to conform with enticing reasons is never wrong, unreasonable, or irrational. One difficulty with this position is that the very same considerations which in some circumstances seem to be enticing reasons are under other conditions requiring reasons. Mary would have to go to the play and to have a child if her situation changed and additional reasons for these courses of action presented themselves. It is possible to imagine situations in which the additional reasons alone do not dictate an outcome, but they do so when added to the reasons for the play or the child which Mary already has. In such cases Mary has a conclusive reason to go to the play or to have a child, a reason which consists of a number of reasons, none of which (nor any subclass of them) is conclusive on its own. In conjunction, however, they constitute a conclusive reason which it would be wrong of Mary to violate. The allegedly enticing reason is part of that conclusive reason. Should we say that enticing reasons are enticing one by one, but not in combination? That would abandon the objective of relying on enticing reasons to explain the basic belief. Some combinations of enticing reasons are optional in the sense explained. In the example there were several reasons for Mary to see the play. The reason to see it that night was a conjunction of all of them. Declaring that reasons are enticing only one by one, but not when combined, leaves the example unexplained.

There is a second problem with the 'enticing reason' suggestion. Mary, having decided not to go to the play, would—there and then, or later—decide what to do instead. She would be doing something intentionally, that is for a reason, instead of going to the play. Mary being a perfect conformer with reason, it follows that her reason for whatever she does instead of going to the play is not defeated by the reasons for going to the play. This would be the case if both reasons are enticing reasons. We can assume that enticing reasons are not capable of defeating any other reasons. But what if the reason for her action is a requiring reason? It need not be a very weighty reason. Suppose that she will be going to visit her mother. It would be wrong of her not to visit her mother, who is very old, from time to time. She does not have to do it that day. She has plenty of time on her hands having just retired from her job. The reason for going to visit her mother that night is, therefore, not a very strong one. But it is not merely an enticing reason. It is one capable of rendering Mary's action wrong,[16] if she fails to conform to it without good enough reason. How are we to understand her situation? If the enticing reason to go to the play could have justified her deferring the visit to the next day does it not show that enticing reasons can defeat requiring reasons? If so, would it not follow that whenever one enticing reason competes with another reason (enticing or requiring),[17] one would have to follow the stronger reason? This would make the division of reasons into enticing and requiring meaningless. And it would make it unreasonable of Mary to go to visit her mother, rather than go to the play. If the enticing reason for going to the play could not defeat the requiring reason for going to her mother how could it have been reasonable for her to go to the play rather than to her mother? I do not know how to answer these questions.

An alternative understanding of the theoretical position which makes the basic belief plausible in many situations is available. Reasons which are incommensurate do not defeat each other. That would make it both reasonable for Mary to go to visit her mother, and reasonable for her to go to the play. She has reason to do either, but she has no decisive reason either way, for the reasons are incommensurate.[18] Two competing reasons (for

---

[16] If you disagree with this choose another example. Many will do.

[17] Can one escape this difficulty by characterizing enticing reasons as those which do not defeat other enticing reasons, but which behave like requiring reasons when conflicting with other requiring reasons? That would not get us out of our difficulty either. For this to be a viable suggestion one would need independent ways of assigning reasons to one or the other of the categories. It seems, however, that there is no satisfactory way of classifying one's reason for visiting one's mother. It is natural to classify the reasons for going to the play as enticing and the reason to visit one's mother as requiring. If so then the suggestion fails for it conflicts with the basic belief which holds that the reason for visiting one's mother is 'optional' in the context imagined, i.e. that one does no wrong in preferring to go to the play. If we take our cue from this fact, and classify the reason to visit one's mother as enticing, we fail to explain how in some contexts it can trump all other reasons, and be conclusive.

[18] The same is true if the competing reasons match each other in strength. But it is relatively rare for two independent reasons to be equal in strength. See the discussion of the topic in ch. 13 of my *The Morality of Freedom* (Oxford: OUP, 1986).

specific actions on specific occasions) are incommensurate if and only if it is not true that one defeats the other, nor that they are of equal strength or stringency. They are incommensurate in strength, that is, reason does not determine which of them should be followed, not even that there is equal reason to follow either. When reasons are incommensurate, they are rendered optional, not because it is equally good (or right or reasonable) to choose the option supported by either reason, but because it is reasonable to choose either option (for both are supported by an undefeated reason) and it is not unreasonable or wrong to refrain from pursuing either option (for both are opposed by an undefeated reason). Incommensurability does not, however, render reasons absolutely optional. They are not divided into two types of reasons. Whether a reason is or is not optional is judged relative to other competing reasons. It is not optional relative to competing reasons which it either defeats or by which it is defeated. It can be said to be optional relative to competing reasons which are incommensurate with it. To that extent it can be said that (many) reasons are optional. They are not optional in themselves, but they are optional in the circumstances. They render options attractive, make their choice intelligible, but they do not make it unreasonable, let alone wrong, not to choose them.

Can we use incommensurability to explain the basic belief? In my presentation of the example I said that Mary has good reasons for going to the play and only few against. This indicated that the reasons for one option clearly defeat the reasons against it. Is this consistent with incommensurability? It all depends on whether the mentioned reasons against include the option costs of going to the play. If they do then this is not a case of incommensurability. But often they do not. The reasons against the play include the bad aspects of going to that play (the need to travel to the theatre, unpleasant people one may meet there, etc.). Typically, they will include opportunity costs when there is some specific reason to engage in some alternative activity: some office work which has to be completed by the following day, etc. But, typically, they do not include all option costs.

When we judge Mary not to be wrong in passing up the opportunity to go to the play we do so because we assume that she will have other reasonable ways of passing her time: read the newspapers, have a useful long night's rest, plan her summer holidays, or whatever—we assume that she has incommensurate options which she will later decide between. If it turns out that she spends the evening, and always intended to spend the evening, in some worthless pursuit we will revise our judgement that it was reasonable for her not to go to the theatre. So the incommensurability suggestion explains the basic belief by making certain assumptions about normal expectations people have when they rely on the basic belief in concrete situations. It does not vindicate all cases which people regard as manifestations of the basic belief. They are justified only when these expectations exist, and the conditions they set are met.

The incommensurability of reasons, in the sense I am using the term, is often misunderstood. It is compatible with extensive ranking both of values, or goods, and of the reasons they constitute. A film may be relaxing, amusing, beautifully photographed, ingeniously directed, well-acted, psychologically insightful. Its plot may be gripping and make one forget one's worries. It may have something deep to say about society. Each one of these would make the film good in one respect or another. We could also judge how good the film is overall, and as a member of some class of films (action films). Such judgements will depend on the individual good features of the film, and on how they are realized together to give it the appropriate balance and integration required of a film which is good overall, or good of a kind.

Each of the good features of the film that I mentioned, and many others, are reasons to see it. Whereas were it to be bad in any of these respects that would be a reason not to see it. But the weight of the reason that the presence of a good feature constitutes is not the same as the contribution of that feature to the overall excellence of the film. I may have more reason to see a mediocre, but highly amusing film tonight than to see a much better film which is rather heavy and lacking in humour, because after a day fraught with difficulties at work the amusing film is just what I need. In this example the reason which wins the day is a conditioned reason: I have a reason to relax and therefore I have a reason to see an amusing film. But the point holds good of unconditional reasons as well. I may have a better reason to go today to see film A for its excellent photography, than to see film B which is better overall. Film B even though better may have nothing remarkable about it. The reason to see it is not very strong. A, while a rather poor film, has extraordinary photography which is a much stronger reason for seeing it, in spite of its poor overall quality.

This point can be generalized. Whenever the presence of a property P makes its possessor T good (or bad) to a degree, or in some respect, and where the good-making aspect of P is a result of the combination or interaction of several properties $Q_1 \ldots Q_n$, which are themselves good-making properties, the reason a person has for having T because it is Q_m may be more stringent than the reason to have it because it is P.

Now let us return to the incommensurability of options and of the reasons for them. Claiming such incommensurability is consistent with believing that the goodness of films and of other things is commensurable, and that of any two films, or whatever, they are either of equal value or one is better than the other. I do not believe this to be the case. But that is beside the point. Only the commensurability of reasons is relevant to the explanation of the apparently optional character of reasons. The preceding paragraphs establish that the ranking of concrete or particular reasons does not follow the ranking of the good-making characteristics whose presence constitutes reasons. It may depend on additional features, special to the situation, or to the agent involved.[19]

4. THE WILL AND NORMATIVE BELIEFS

Many philosophers assign the will a special role in the explanation of practical thought.[20] The conclusions of the discussion thus far, which establish a certain normative latitude, help with establishing what truth there is in such views. The normative latitude established above consists of the fact that even perfect conformers with reason will not need to know all the reasons which apply to them, will not have to be motivated by all the reasons which apply to them, will not have to believe all that they have adequate reason to believe, nor do or desire all that they have adequate reason to do or desire. That latitude does not depend on the fact that reason tolerates or excuses a certain amount of ignorance and mistakes. It applies even to perfect conformers like Mary, who can readily find out all the reasons which apply to them.

The latitude of reasons points towards three conclusions regarding the relations of reason and will. To introduce them let us distinguish four groups of normative/evaluative propositions:

---

[19] It is tempting to think that, other things being equal, the ranking of a good at a more comprehensive level determines the more important reason. That means that, other things being equal, one has more reason to see the better film than the film with the better photography. But that seems not to be the case. I may go to see a film because of its photography, rather than a film which is better overall, for no special reason—just because I feel like it. Such cases seem to me to fall within the range of the optional character of reasons. If so then the two reasons that it has the better photography and that it is a better film overall are, other things being equal, incommensurate.

[20] See D. Parfit, 'Reasons and Motivation', *Aristotelian Society*, suppl. 71 (1997), 99, and R. Audi, 'Moral Judgements and Reasons for Action', in G. Cullity and B. Gaut (eds.), *Ethics and Practical Reason* (Oxford: OUP, 1997) for recent attempts to classify the different views on this issue. Among the most influential writings on the subject see R. M. Hare, *Freedom and Reason* (Oxford: OUP, 1960), Davidson, 'Intention', in his *Essays on Actions and Events* (Oxford: OUP, 1980), and B. Williams, 'Internal and External Reasons', *Moral Luck* (Cambridge: CUP, 1982). Important counter arguments were advanced by D. Brink, *Moral Realism and the Foundations of Ethics* (Cambridge: CUP, 1989) and J. Hampton, *The Authority of Reason* (Cambridge: CUP, 1998). See also A. Mele, 'Internalist Moral Cognitivism and Listlessness', *Ethics*, 106 (1995), 727. Most writers confine themselves to consideration of moral reasons; not knowing of any relevant way in which they differ from others I will disregard this distinction.

(1) That something or some act is good *simpliciter*.[21]
(2) That something or some act is good for someone. Such statements establish that someone has a (sufficient) reason for doing or not doing something.
(3) That someone has an adequate reason to act in a certain way.
(4) That someone must conduct himself in a certain manner, that he would be acting wrongly (or unreasonably or irrationally) unless he did so, that he has a conclusive reason to take one course of action in preference to all others.

The three conclusions are first, it is not the case that, necessarily, wanting A or wanting to do V is a condition of either believing that A is of value, or that it is of value to the agent, or of believing that one has an adequate reason to do V, or believing that one has conclusive reason to do V, or that it would be wrong not to do it. More generally, belief in propositions of any of the four types does not involve wanting anything. Second, it is not the case that, necessarily, a *rational* agent who believes a proposition of any of the four kinds regarding the value of an action, or the existence of a reason or a conclusive reason for it, will want to perform it. Third, belief can explain action independently of any desires.

I will not consider the first conclusion separately. If the second conclusion is true so is the first, since it is entailed by it. The truth of the second conclusion can be established by the following chain of considerations. Belief in propositions of the first type, for example that *Don Giovanni* is a great opera, that hill walking can be invigorating, healthy, and refreshing, is not in itself a belief that one has any reason to do anything. It does commit those who have those beliefs to certain further evaluative beliefs and attitudes: thinking well of people who engage with the good in the right way, etc. But it commits them to no contingent desires of any kind. The condition of wanting everything which one believes to be (unconditionally) good is not only not a necessary concomitant of rationality in belief, it is a highly undesirable condition of extreme avarice. Hence belief in propositions of type (1) does not involve any desire as a concomitant, or precondition, let alone as a constituent.

If something is an unconditional[22] good *simpliciter* then it is good for any person who has the opportunity and ability to engage in it in the right way. In general one has a sufficient reason to do whatever is good for one. In addition to believing that an option is good, belief that it is good for one

---

[21] Such statements often establish the existence of a conditional reason for action. As will be seen below, with additional premises, some goods *simpliciter* also establish unconditional reasons.

[22] 'Unconditional goods' are defined by analogy with unconditional reasons, i.e. as those whose value does not depend on, and is not derived from, the value of something else.

requires only beliefs about one's opportunities and abilities. There is no way in which it can be necessary that to be rational these beliefs must bring any desire in their wake. Moreover, many of the options which are good for one are not ones which when the opportunity arises should be chosen. They may then be defeated by competing considerations (which establish that an alternative option is even better, or that one has an overriding moral duty to take another action, etc.). Something may be good for one and be such that one should never choose it. How can it be a condition of rationality that one should have a desire for it, a desire destined to be frustrated?

Belief that one has an adequate reason to do what is good for one requires also belief that competing reasons do not defeat that reason. If rational belief in sufficient reasons does not necessarily presuppose or otherwise require desires of any kind, nor does rational belief in adequate reasons since it requires nothing else beyond a view about the relative stringency of the sufficient reasons involved. Moreover, on many occasions people have many competing but adequate reasons to pursue any of a number of incompatible courses of action, each being, or leading to, goods for them.[23] There can be no necessary volitional impediment for many people who do not want—say—to take up skiing to realize rationally that they have an adequate reason to do so. They would know the value of skiing, know that they are able-bodied and not short of cash and therefore able to engage in it, and that they can learn to do it in the right spirit. They will know that on many occasions there are no pressing calls on their time or resources with a greater claim than skiing, and therefore that they have an adequate reason to take up skiing. But while there can be no volitional impediment to their coming to that conclusion, given the modest intellectual power it calls for, nor is there anything in the process which will guarantee that in coming to that conclusion the desire to ski (or to take up skiing) will rise in them.

This conclusion is innocent enough. After all, to be perfect conformers with reason we need not do everything we have adequate reason to do, so why should it be necessary that we should want to do it if we believe that we have adequate reason to do it? Here too, wanting to do everything we have adequate reason to do is a mark of avarice. After all we cannot do everything we have adequate reason to do, and we should learn to live within our means, that is, we should learn not to want too many things when it is impossible for us to get all of them.

The next stage of the argument applies these conclusions to type (4)

---

[23] Though poverty, ill health, overriding moral emergencies, etc. may greatly reduce the range of such opportunities.

propositions. One has a conclusive reason(s) to do something only if the reason for doing it defeats all competing reasons. To establish that one has a conclusive reason all one needs is knowledge and understanding of type (3) propositions, that is, propositions about adequate reasons. Since rationally believing type (3) propositions does not involve any desire, nor does rationally believing propositions about conclusive reasons, unless there is some reason to think that the process of reasoning from propositions about adequate reasons to propositions about conclusive reasons will inevitably excite a desire to do what one has a conclusive reason to do. There is no reason to think that that is so.

Weak-willed action is proof of the fact that it is not so. In acting out of weakness of the will one acts against one's better judgement, but one rarely acts against one's will. Weak-willed action consists in following the lesser reason, often because one wants to do so more than one wants any alternative supported by better reasons. But is it not the case that one must at least have some desire to do what one believes one has a conclusive reason to do, even if it is not as strong as some rival desire? The evidence suggests otherwise, as we are familiar with cases of weakness of the will where the agent did not want at all to do what he believed that he had conclusive reason to do.

Weak-willed action is irrational action, but the belief in conclusive reasons which it flouts need not be irrational. That is presupposed by the preceding argument from weak-willed action to the character of rational belief. Can one argue that unless we have a desire to act in accordance with our beliefs in conclusive reasons those beliefs themselves are irrational? No parallel argument could apply to beliefs in adequate reasons. We have too many adequate reasons for incompatible options for it to be rationally required that we desire to pursue all of them. It is therefore mysterious why a belief that there is only one acceptable option should be irrational just because the agent does not desire to perform that action. Still, the case will be strengthened if the third thesis, that appeal to desires is not necessary for the explanation of intentional action, is true.

5. WHAT CAN THE WILL EXPLAIN?

To some the justification for giving the will a special role in the account of practical thought lies in metaphysical considerations. Since nothing in the world constitutes reasons for action, what else can reasons be if not desires, or whatever acquires the status of a reason by its relation to a desire? Such considerations fall outside the ambit of this chapter. Two other clusters of considerations invoked to justify a special role for the will do require examination here. First, reasons are practical. They lead one to action. Second, reasons are explanatory. One can explain an action by citing the reasons for which it was taken. The two may be thought to be two sides of the same coin, but I will deny that they are. Both have led many to the conclusion that an account of reasons, of the facts which constitute them, or of belief in either of these or of action for reasons, requires allowing the will a special role.

The will plays two related roles in human life. A good deal of confusion is caused by confusing them. First and foremost, the will is the capacity for intentional action. Having a will is having the ability to act at will, that is the ability to direct one's actions in light of one's understanding of oneself and of one's situation. Some plants and many animal species have a capacity for action, but no will, for they cannot set themselves goals, chosen in light of a view of how things are around them. In some animal species, and in some human beings, the capacity is very limited, amounting, for example, to little more than the ability to control one's action at will, while the goals one has are not subject to one's decision. There is no point in trying to delineate the different forms that the capacity can take. For present purposes it is best characterized as it appears when fully developed in mature human beings, while allowing (*a*) that often it takes lesser forms, and (*b*) that the further boundaries of what counts as that capacity are blurred. In its full form the will is the capacity to take action at will, to choose what to do, to plan and decide on one's course of action, and to do all of that in light of one's view of oneself and one's situation and of what would be appropriate in the circumstances.

Since the will is the capacity for intentional action all intentional actions are manifestations of the will. This fact determines one sense of 'to want'. In this sense to say that I did something because I wanted to do it (or that I omitted to do something because I wanted to) is to mark the action as intentional, that is, as an act I did for a reason. As such, acts we do because we want to are contrasted with accidental acts, acts done by mistake, or acts which are unintended by-products of intentional acts, as well as with acts entirely out of our control, such as involuntary (knee jerks), or semi-voluntary acts (breathing), or those which are acts of the body but not of the person (digesting food, being bodily manipulated with strong overriding force). On the other hand, in this sense of 'want' (which I will call the 'thin' sense of 'desire' or 'want') coerced actions are actions we do because we want to (we hand over the money because we want to do so in order to stay alive).

The second role of the will is related but different. We are attached to different possibilities to different degrees, and our attachments can differ in quality. Expressions of degree or quality of attachment are expressions of the will. These manifestations of the will can have two effects. The will can determine our choice of action, our intentions, and aspirations. Even when it does not do or cannot do that, it can colour the way we do what we do, hope for what we hope, believe in what we believe,[24] etc. The second of these effects is manifested most clearly when the will determines our attitude to our actions (and to our intentional omissions). We can do what we do voluntarily or involuntarily (in the other sense of the word), willingly or reluctantly, enthusiastically or grudgingly, and so on. Sometimes we do what we do unwillingly (as when a child, when told to do so, unwillingly lets a sibling play with a toy). Sometimes we are forced to act against our will (e.g. when we act under duress, or when we are coerced, but more generally when we are forced to take an undesired action to avoid a greater evil). Sometimes we do things which we very much do not want to do but recognize an obligation to do. In this sense, not every intentional action is done because we want to do it. To say that we want it is to designate one possible attitude to an intentional action, rather than (as in the first sense of want) to designate it as intentional. To distinguish the two senses of 'want' or 'desire' I will call the second 'thick'.

The diverse attitudes of the will can be attached to other objects than the agents' actions. We can be happy or content with our emotions, or be unhappy with them, entertain them reluctantly or faint-heartedly. (We can be uneasy about them even while we think them to be justified.) Similarly we can entertain hopes and aspirations reluctantly, hesitatingly, or enthusiastically. And so on.

Finally, as mentioned above, the will (in the thick sense) can determine which actions, emotions, thoughts, etc. we have. Our hopes, aspirations, and thick-desires, or thick-wants, play a role in determining our actions, emotions, thoughts, and beliefs (though sometimes only by explaining their irrationality—as in cases of self-deception, repression, and weakness of the will). They do so in one of two sets of circumstances. First, when reason determines what we should do or feel, and we go against reason. I have already mentioned the case of irrational action when we act against our better judgement, that is, prefer the option supported by the lesser reason. Often, weak-willed action is action in pursuit of what we want most, in spite of knowing that it is not the best option. That is not always true: we can point to emotions, moods, personality disorders, and other factors as the explanation. They can lead us to do what we do not really want to do. But not infrequently weak-willed action is action motivated by a (thick-)desire for it or its object.

---

[24] Belief is a particularly difficult case in this context. We cannot choose what to believe, but we can believe reluctantly, or gladly, with relief, or with regret. See 'When We are Ourselves' (Ch. 1 above).

The second type of circumstances in which we do what we do because we want it is the standard situation for choice and action that I focused on before, that is, those cases in which, as we see it, several options are supported by incommensurate reasons which are not defeated by any competing reason. In these situations, as we see them, reason cannot determine what to do. Whatever we choose to do we will do for a reason, that is, for the reason which, as we see it, supports the option we pursue. But as we believe that other reasons, not defeated by it, support alternative options, that cannot be the full story of why we do what we do. To explain our choice we sometimes refer to our (thick-)desire. We realized that the reasons for the different options were all undefeated, but we wanted to do this rather than anything else, or we wanted to achieve what this action promised to achieve.

The view that I have outlined can be summarized by saying that the will is the capacity for intentional action, which is instantiated in every intentional action. This gives rise to the thin sense of 'want': I do what I want to do whenever I act intentionally. The will is also the ability to be attached to various options, actions, or objects, which expresses itself in the attitude with which we do what we do, and which enables us to choose, even when, as is normal, reason does not dictate a unique choice. This second power of the will gives rise to the thick sense of 'want', meaning an attachment not required by reason (though we can be attached in that way to an option prescribed by reason, as well as to one proscribed by it).

The two senses of 'want' identify two ways in which the fact that someone did something because he wanted to can explain the action. If the want is a thin-want the explanation is merely that the action was intentional. If it is a thick-want the explanation is that the action was intentional, and that the agent was not merely doing what reason required. He was following his desires either to do willingly what reason dictates, or to choose among rationally eligible options, or to go against reason.

As we know people most commonly answer requests for an explanation of an action with 'Because I wanted to', when they intend to rebuff the inquirer. In many contexts the very question 'Why did you do it?' implies belief that the act was intentional. Therefore, in that context, 'because I wanted to' does not explain anything. It rebuffs the question. The thick sense of 'want' can be used to give more informative answers, especially when the feature of the situation which attracted one's desire is spelt out (I went to Banbury because I wanted to see Jane).

These explanations help to clarify the relations between normative beliefs and the will. We can now see that the arguments of the previous section relate to thin-desires. Does the picture change when attention is turned to thick-desires? I do not believe that it does. There is no reason to think that having a normative belief of any of the four classes we enumerated necessarily involves thickly wanting anything. In this sense wanting something either colours our attitude to what we are going to do because we believe the best reason dictates that we should do it, or it facilitates choice among options rendered eligible by reason, or it may lead us to act against reason. Of the three only the first can plausibly be thought to support a thesis that desire is involved with normative beliefs, but as we saw generally conformity with normative beliefs does not require any special motive. Hence there is no case for thinking that normative beliefs require desire in its second sense.

Perhaps the following can be thought to support a connection between beliefs in conclusive reasons and thick-desires. If one has conclusive reason to do V then one has a conclusive reason to (thickly) want to do V. Believing that one has a conclusive reason to want something is the same as wanting it, or is otherwise a sufficient condition of wanting it.

There is something to this argument, but it is fallacious all the same. Having a reason (conclusive or otherwise) to do something provides one with a reason to want to do it. Some exceptional cases apart, all reasons to want anything are of this kind. They are conditional reasons: we have reason to want to do V because we have reason to do V and wanting to do V will tend to lead us to do what we have reason to do. Such reasons are rarely conclusive, not even when the reason for the act on which they are conditioned are conclusive. As we saw, if one is lucky one may do what one has reason to do without intending to do it for that reason. Similarly, one may do it without wanting to do it. One may do what one has conclusive reason to do even though one very much does not want to do it.[25]

6. ON WHAT ONE NEED NOT EXPLAIN ABOUT NORMATIVITY

It is time to turn to the third conclusion mentioned above: that belief can lead to action, and explain action without the mediation of desire. Theses postulating a necessary connection between normative beliefs and desires must have been partly motivated by a difficulty in accepting that beliefs can be practical, that is, that people may take action, and that they may come to want to act, because, as they see it, this is a good, or the best thing to do, or something they must do. I am not sure what these perceived difficulties are. I assume that it is not that such explanations are not supported by

[25] The rejection of this argument is in line with our common knowledge that one can believe that one has a reason, even a strong reason to want something, without wanting it.

exceptionless law-like generalizations, since no psychological explanations are so supported.

Perhaps one felt difficulty is that if normative beliefs can lead people to take action (and to conceive desires, form intentions, take decisions, etc.) they must be a funny sort of belief, since non-normative beliefs cannot do so. Without going into the question whether or not normative beliefs are special in this regard, we can safely say that this difficulty is illusory. If normative beliefs alone can lead people to action, etc., that is not because they are beliefs of a special kind (consisting in part of volitional states or dispositions) but because they are beliefs about a special aspect of the world, its normative aspect.[26]

The answer to the philosophical question: 'How is it that people can respond appropriately to the normative aspects of the world?' is bound to be disappointing: they can because they are rational, that is because they have the capacity to do so (as well as the ancillary capacities it presupposes). 'What sort of an answer is that?' you may say. It is totally uninformative. To which one must reply: 'What sort of a *philosophical* question was it in the first place?' There are of course non-philosophical questions to ask about the preconditions of the capacity to be rational. And there are philosophical questions about its contours and relations to other phenomena. But if one says: 'I did this because it was a good thing to do', we could ask for amplification, and verification. But once these are given can we respond 'That cannot explain your action for it merely expresses your beliefs, and does not show what you wanted to do'? That would show that we do not understand the nature of value and reason. They are such as to call for an appropriate response. Believing that there is a reason is believing that certain responses are appropriate and if that does not explain why one responds in those ways what does?

Some may object that I am mistaking the part for the whole. They will admit that having capacity-rationality is trivially part of what makes us capable of responding appropriately to reason. That, they claim, is only the uninteresting part of the answer. To be able to respond appropriately to reason we must also be *capable* of using our rationality appropriately. We know that we do not always do so. That is, we know that rational people sometimes fail to respond to reason properly. Such failures are often attributable to failures of other capacities. They are often due to failures of memory, or perception, mistakes of reasoning, and their like. But sometimes they appear to be due simply to the failure to be rational. Weakness of the will and impetuosity are the paradigm examples. It follows from the

---

[26] The attempt by some writers to regard desires or dispositions to have them as constituent parts of normative beliefs seems to show the hold that the Humean view of motivation has even on those who reject it.

fact that those who have capacity-rationality can fail to use it correctly that there is something more to explain: we require an explanation of what enables us to use the capacity in the right way, and what makes us so use it when we do.

Thus the objection so far. It is evident that as stated it is partly misconceived. The search for a capacity which enables us to use our capacities correctly is illusory, and can lead to infinite regress. There is no need for an additional capacity to be capable of using a capacity well. That is what perfect possession of the said capacity gives one in the first place. Having the capacity to walk is being able to walk well (without wobbling, etc.). Not every time we walk do we walk well, and there is room for an explanation of why the capacity failed us on this or that occasion, but no room for invoking a further capacity to use well the first capacity.

But the objection can be recast to avoid this unacceptable supposition. It amounts to no more than pointing out the need for an explanation for the fact that the capacity was exercised well, when it was so exercised, an explanation not offered by just pointing to the possession of capacity-rationality. It can be reinforced by drawing an analogy with other capacities. Some people can swim, drive a car, speak English, and solve mathematical problems. But noting that people can do these things does not explain when they do them and why. That they can do them means, in all such cases, that they can also not do them. They may keep out of the water, use public transport, speak only French, and avoid mathematics. We need an explanation of when and why we swim, drive, speak English, or solve mathematical problems. Pointing to the ability will not explain its use.

It now seems that I found myself giving an uninformative answer because I asked the wrong question. The question should be not what makes it possible for us to respond to the normative aspects of the world. To answer this question we may need do no more than point to the fact that we are rational. The real question is when and why do we use that capacity correctly, why do we sometimes react rationally, and sometimes not?

This is indeed a real, and a hard question. But it should not be conceived by way of analogy with questions like 'when and why do we swim or drive cars?' These are capacities which Kenny (adapting Aristotle) has aptly called 'two-way' capacities. They endow us with the ability to exercise them or not to exercise them at will. This is the mark of the higher, but also more superficial, of our abilities. Basic abilities are much closer to dispositions. 'This car is able to do 120 mph' means that 'it will do so if . . .'. 'People are able to survive without water for three days' means that they are likely to survive for three days even if they have no water. Interestingly our most fundamental abilities occupy a midway position between simple dispositions and two-way abilities. Our perceptual abilities are a typical example.

We are able to see because when in a lit environment we open our eyes we see what is in front of them. Recognitional abilities are similar: we are able to recognize people we have met before because when we see them again we know who they are; we can recognize a valid argument because when presented with one we realize that it is valid, or something like this.

Our basic abilities occupy a midway position between dispositional abilities, as we may call them, and two-way abilities, because on the one hand they resemble dispositional abilities in requiring neither a decision, nor an intention, nor a desire, for their exercise, but on the other hand they can fail to be properly or successfully exercised for a whole array of psychological reasons. Lack of attention, various moods, an *idée fixe*, and many other conditions can distort what we see, and the same goes, only even more so, for recognitional capacities, and our other basic capacities. This dependence on other psychological conditions may create the impression that these abilities resemble two-way abilities in requiring a decision or an intention for their exercise. This is a mistake. They are exercised automatically in the appropriate circumstances. No further explanation of their exercise is called for, other than pointing to the circumstances: 'Why did I see John last Thursday? Because he was sitting in full view when I came to the Common Room.' But in all these cases failure to exercise the ability is possible, and calls for an explanation: 'I was too distracted to notice him', etc.[27]

Rationality is one of these intermediate abilities. It is exercised in the right circumstances provided nothing interferes. Examining the role of the will in explanation of conduct shows this to be the case. We cannot appeal to people's thin-desires to explain why they act rationally. It is, of course, true that we can appropriately respond to reason because we have a will. In the thin sense of 'want', people want to do what they do intentionally, as well as what they intend to do. People can respond to reason because they are capable of having intentions, and engaging in intentional actions. So much is true, but nothing more follows from the fact that we possess a will regarding our ability to respond to reason. The preceding arguments have established that it is not the case that whenever we believe that we have a reason (or an adequate or a conclusive reason) to do something then, if we are rational, we want to do it. All that can be said is the truism that if we

---

[27] One may suspect that the distinction between explanation of successful exercise (none needed) and explanation of failure (required in the case of failure) is untenable. Is it not the case that absence of the conditions which generate failure is part of the explanation of successful exercise of these abilities? Yes, but this is not a contentful specification of all the conditions of success, and none is available. There is no complete listing of the possible conditions which could vitiate success. We can only say that none occurred, and therefore the ability was exercised. When it fails one can, of course, point to a concrete condition responsible for the failure.

do what we have reason to do for that reason then we do it because (in the thin sense) we want to do it. This is not more than saying that if we do it for that reason we do it intentionally. It is of course false that if we do it intentionally, that is for a reason, then we do it because we want, in the thick sense, to do it. We may very much not want to do it, and do it for the reason all the same.

Invoking the will is, therefore, no help with the question, 'How is it that sometimes we respond appropriately to reason?' Nor, I have suggested, is there anything here to explain. Our rational ability is an ability which expresses itself in action when the circumstances are right and nothing, including psychological factors, interferes. Of course, the question can be asked why people do not always want to do what they believe they have reason to do. That is a question about the conditions which interfere with the exercise of rationality. Such questions call for a theory of weakness of the will or impetuosity: conditions which philosophers, novelists, and psychologists have studied in their various ways. At the superficial level such explanations do invoke the will: we follow our will when we act against our better judgement, for even then we act for a reason, albeit for the lesser reason. The deeper explanations reveal a whole array of different conditions hidden behind that phrase. None of that raises doubts about the ability of beliefs to motivate. That follows from the nature of our rational capacity. Given that it is an ability which, barring interference, expresses itself in its exercise when conditions appear to be appropriate, it follows that, other things being equal, once we come to believe that we are presented with normative factors, we respond appropriately.

Does not the disanalogy between action and belief show up the inadequacy of my answer? The considerations just adumbrated explain how it is that we can respond appropriately to reasons for belief, that is, by forming beliefs which, as we see it, we have compelling reasons (i.e. reasons which, in the circumstances, it is irrational not to conform with) to adopt, and avoiding others. The answer is: because we are rational. Normally, coming to believe that there are compelling reasons to believe that such and such is coming to believe that such and such. There is no gap between (perceived) reason and response to it. This is indeed what the considerations I rehearsed above would lead one to expect. Things are somewhat more complex within the latitude of reasons. When one believes oneself to have an adequate (but not a compelling) reason to believe a proposition, one either comes to believe it or not. No decision, no intervention of the will, is in question, but the explanation of why one either did or did not form the belief will call on something more than the reason for it. It will invoke one's credulity, one's trust in government, etc.[28] Actions, the argument for the disanalogy proceeds, are different. Reason does not guarantee an appropriate response. It needs the mediation of the will to lead to action, and the will can also lead one to act against reason.

This asymmetry is real enough. The distinctions we drew between different types of ability explain and reinforce it. As I have suggested, we can appropriately respond to reason because we have the capacity to be rational, a capacity which, barring interference, is exercised when circumstances appear to be appropriate. But the capacity to act is a two-way capacity, its exercise calls for intention, that is, for an exercise of our will. Hence when the response to reason calls for action it involves the will, that is, it involves forming an intention to act.

The asymmetry does not affect the basic answer to the questions of how it is that people are able to respond to reason, and why they respond to reason, when they do. The answer is still because they are rational. Pointing to the mediation of the will does not alter the answer, for the will itself—just like belief—is guided by (perceived) reason. When, as we perceive it, we have a conclusive reason to do something, we form the intention to do it, unless we are irrational.[29] We do it because we are rational. These comments are directly relevant to thin-desires. But they apply to thick-desires as well. Once again much confusion is caused by failing to distinguish them properly. One such failure leads to the supposition that if we have conclusive reason to act then we have a conclusive reason to want (thickly) to act. That is not so. Regret, reluctance, etc. have their reasons as well. As novelists and writers on moral psychology pointed out, on occasion it is rational to do what we have conclusive reason to do reluctantly, and it may be immoral to do so enthusiastically.

Just as with belief, so with action, when no option is supported by conclusive reasons, when we face conflicting adequate reasons for action, the explanation of why we followed the reasons we did will involve more than the invocation of our rationality. It will allude to our tastes, predilections, and much else besides. But to the extent that the question is merely of why we followed reason the answer is simply that we are rational. The fact that action is a two-way capacity, and requires the mediation of the will does not alter matters. The mediation of the will helps explain how the two-way ability to act is governed by our rationality.

---

[28] They can play a role in explaining rational beliefs, as well as irrational ones.

[29] There are degrees of irrationality. The irrationality of weak-willed or of impetuous action is that we act on what we believe to be the lesser reason. It does not escape the governance of reason altogether.

6

Notes on Value and Objectivity

1. THE LONG ROUTE

(a) Introduction

It is natural that we should be interested in the nature of objectivity in general, and in the objectivity or otherwise of practical thought in particular. In one of its senses objectivity is a precondition of knowledge. It also demarcates a type of thought[1] which is importantly different from others.

In this chapter our interest is in one way in which various types of thought differ. They are subject to different disciplines. Suppose, for example, that I say 'I will be a good teacher' and you tell me: 'But you have tried and failed for years', I may reply by saying: 'So what? That does not stop me from daydreaming', a response which is inappropriate if the thought expresses a belief. This is but one example of one aspect of what I called the different 'disciplines' to which a thought or the holding of a thought can be subjected, a difference which marks the distinction between classes of thoughts and of ways of holding them. These disciplines determine whether my thought and yours, which have the same content, belong to the same type.

Of some thoughts, for example, it is possible to say, 'They were mistaken', whereas of others this is inappropriate. A closely connected mark is that having or holding some thoughts can constitute knowledge. I mean that the fact that I think that a general election was held in Italy yesterday is part of what makes it true that I know that a general election took place in Italy yesterday.

We mark this distinction between classes of thoughts that can constitute knowledge and can be mistaken and those which cannot by calling the first objective, and the others subjective. When we ask whether practical thought is objective or subjective we are asking whether it is subject to one type of

---

I am grateful to Peter Hacker and especially to Brian Leiter for comments on an earlier version.

[1] Unless otherwise indicated, when referring to what people think, I have in mind the thought (or thought-content) rather than the act or activity of thinking.

discipline or another. So the inquiry is natural and important. In the first part of the chapter ('The Long Route') I will say something in general about the way we can characterize and explain objectivity in abstract terms. Parts 2 and 3 attempt to allay certain doubts about the objectivity of practical thought. Part 2 deals with the fact that practical concepts are parochial, and not universally accessible to all. Part 3 deals with the social dependence of practical concepts.

(b) Some Senses of the Objective/Subjective Contrast

The objective/subjective distinction originates in philosophy. With time its uses multiplied. People, beliefs, sometimes even facts, are said to be objective or subjective, not only thoughts. And the suspicion is strong that more than one distinction is being drawn by the use of these words. Here, to illustrate the point, are a couple of senses of the objective/subjective contrast. In science it is sometimes said that an experiment is subjective if its results cannot be mechanically replicated. 'Objective', in this case, has something to do with inter-subjectivity, when the inter-subjective standard assumes the very strict form of a more or less mechanical process of experimentation whose results can be established by relying on little more than simple perception (assuming, of course, a rich background knowledge). A much more common use of the contrast, and a much less interesting one, is that by which any mental states are subjective, meaning belonging to a subject, and statements about mental states are subjective simply in virtue of being about mental states.

More relevant for our purpose is a third common sense in which the distinction is used. In what I will call *the epistemic sense* people are objective about certain matters if they are, in forming or holding opinions, judgements, and the like, about these matters, properly sensitive to factors which are epistemically relevant to the truth or correctness of their opinions or judgements, that is, if they respond to these factors as they should. Their views or beliefs may be wrong or mistaken, but there are no emotionally induced distortions in the way they were reached, or the conditions under which they are held. That means, for example, that people are objective in this sense if they form their opinions and judgements on the basis of the relevant evidence available to them, mindful of whether or not they were in circumstances which might affect the reliability of their perceptions or thought processes, and when their selection of information as relevant and their evaluation of it are sensible, and are not affected by such emotional or other psychological distortions. Opinions and beliefs are objective if they are reached or held in an objective manner. Sometimes people are said to be objective if they are capable of being objective in the sense just explained.

A related sense is that of objectivity as *impartiality*. People are impartial if and only if, in matters affecting others as well as possibly themselves, they act on relevant reasons and shun irrelevant ones, in particular if they shun irrelevant considerations which favour themselves or people or causes dear to their heart, and if their evaluation of the situation is not distorted by the fact that such people or causes are dear to them.[2] Epistemic objectivity as a capacity to avoid bias, or other emotional distortions, requires impartiality as one of its constituent conditions, and this condition by itself is sometimes taken to make a person an objective judge of a certain matter. But the impartiality sense of objectivity reaches beyond these cases. It is the most important sense of objectivity in practical matters, objectivity in action (e.g. when the objectivity of judges or of officials is in question usually impartiality is meant). Not infrequently official action is based in part not on the beliefs of the officials concerned, but on propositions which are accepted by them as a reasonable basis for action in the circumstances of the case. Objectivity as impartiality can also characterize deliberation and decision-making based on accepted—rather than believed—premises. This requirement of objectivity is a requirement of impartiality in all the stages of the decision-making process.

Our interest is in a different distinction drawn by the objective-subjective contrast. I identified it at the outset as the sense of objectivity in which it is a condition of the possibility or perhaps of the conceivability of knowledge, and a condition for the applicability of the notions of mistaken or correct (true) thoughts. Inter-subjectivity, albeit in a weaker sense than that required by the scientific usage that I mentioned, and the possibility of holding views which are not influenced by bias, or by similar cognitive distortions, are among the general conditions for the possibility of knowledge. But equally clearly we have not yet identified the core sense which is relevant for our purpose. For lack of a better word, I will sometimes refer to *domain-objectivity* when wishing to distinguish this sense of objectivity from others. Primarily it is domains of thoughts, propositions, or statements that are objective in that sense.[3] By natural extension the single propositions, statements, and thoughts are objective if they belong to an objective domain, and so is whatever they are about.

It is not easy to describe what makes domains of thought objective. The

---

[2] Bear in mind that it would be odd actually to talk of people's impartiality unless someone challenged it or unless the circumstances of the action invited doubts about it. At the hands of some contractarian or constructivist philosophers impartiality extends in another direction as well: in matters of ethics what impartial judges accept is thereby made true. But I will not explore the contractarian uses of the notion.

[3] Though nothing much depends on the way domains are demarcated. The criteria of objectivity determine whether a domain is objective or not, whichever way it is carved.

difficulty is that in trying to do so one enters disputes about the nature of what there is, the nature of reality, and about the structure of thoughts or of propositions about how things are. A proposition is objective if it is about an object of a non-empty kind, that is such that there are objects belonging to it, some writers suggest.[4] But what counts as an object and how do we determine what kind it belongs to? Worse still, how do we determine what propositions are about? Consider, for example, propositions like, 'The African Lion lives to be 23 years old, and fathers 3.7 cubs'; 'There are two types of energy, static and kinetic'. Both are objective propositions. That is not in dispute. But is it because they are about objects such as the African Lion, and Energy? Or are they about lions, or about all the lions bred in Africa, or about all the objects in the world? To resolve these questions we need to come to a view regarding the status of universals, of dummy-objects, and of the conditions for the existence of objects in general. We may also have to enter into the morass of determining what propositions are *about*. And there are further difficulties in store.

David Wiggins seems to side-step these problems when he says that 'A subject matter is objective (or relates to an objective reality) if and only if there are questions about it (and enough questions about it) that admit of answers that are substantially true—simply and plainly true'.[5] The qualification 'substantially' true puts us on our guard, however. It would seem that in order to gain an understanding of objectivity we need to resolve issues concerning various kinds of truths.[6]

Trying to side-step these issues as well I suggested at the beginning of this chapter that a domain is objective if propositions which belong to it can state what one knows, if thoughts which belong to it can manifest what one knows. If only true propositions can be known, and only true thoughts can express one's knowledge, domains are objective in this sense only if thoughts, propositions, and statements which belong to them can be true or false. But problems are to be found here too. If there can be aspects of reality which it is logically impossible for us (but who are we? The human race? Or all agents capable of knowing something? Or each one of us?) to know anything about then, while the objectivity of a domain is a precondition of knowledge, the reverse is not the case. We cannot say that a domain is objective only if it can express knowledge, that is, express what is know-

---

[4] For example, A. Marmor, 'Three Concepts of Objectivity', in A. Marmor (ed.), *Law and Interpretation* (Oxford: OUP, 1996).

[5] D. Wiggins, 'Objectivity and Subjectivity in Ethics, with Two Postscripts about Truth', in B. Hooker (ed.), *Truth in Ethics* (Oxford: Blackwells, 1996).

[6] Wiggins's own view is explained in 'What would be a Substantive Theory of Truth?', in Z. van Straaten (ed.), *Philosophical Subjects: Essays presented to P. F. Strawson* (Oxford: OUP, 1980).

able. There may be (objective domains of) propositions which state how things are regarding matters of which it is impossible to have any knowledge. This is one reason why I will not try to define domain-objectivity, or to give necessary and sufficient conditions for the objectivity of domains. Rather I will attempt to elucidate the notion by considering a number of conditions which partially characterize it.

While the epistemic and domain senses of objectivity are obviously interrelated they differ in important respects. When judging someone or some opinions to be epistemically objective (or lacking objectivity) one presupposes that the matter which is so judged is domain objective. In other words, domain objectivity marks the fact that we are dealing with a domain about which one can be objective in the epistemic sense, and statements which are domain objective are those which *can* also be epistemically objective.

One way in which the two clusters of senses differ is in the responsibility[7] of people who are or are not, or whose opinions are or are not, objective in the various senses. People should be epistemically objective and their opinions should not be epistemically subjective. They are responsible for failing to be as they should, for such failures are due to biases and other distortions of their cognitive functioning for which people are held responsible. Their responsibility for their failures of epistemic objectivity does not assume that knowledge is a good that they should pursue. It only means that they should not form judgements which are tainted by bias. Even though in some of its variants noted above epistemic responsibility is a matter of ability rather than performance, it is an ability the presence or lack of which can only be established by performance. Hence those who lack it are those who are lacking in performance.[8]

The only responsibility that can arise if an area of inquiry or judgements about it are domain subjective is responsibility for failure to realize that the domain is subjective. There can be, of course, no responsibility for these matters or judgements being subjective. This is just how things are. Nor for that matter can people be responsible for treating matters subjectively in these cases, for there is nothing else they can properly do.

It is crucial to notice that in no sense is objectivity identified with truth, though in all of them it is related more or less indirectly to truth. Thoughts which are objective can be the subject of knowledge, and they are expressed

---

[7] Responsibility, rather than more narrowly moral responsibility.

[8] Whether this applies to epistemic objectivity in all its variants is open to doubt. Perhaps the capacity to be epistemically objective (one version of epistemic objectivity noted above) is an exception. The question whether or not one is responsible for not being objective in that sense involves considerations of aspects of responsibility which cannot be pursued here.

Notes on Value and Objectivity 123

in propositions which can be true or false (or correct or incorrect). People who are epistemically objective judges of certain matters are not free from error in those matters. They are merely free from errors arising out of biases and an emotionally blinkered inability to respond to the evidence and evaluate it. Statements and opinions which are epistemically objective are those which are neither reached nor sustained through biases of this kind. But obviously they can be false or mistaken for other reasons. Epistemic objectivity is closely associated with rationality. It is a condition of being a rational judge of certain matters that one is epistemically objective regarding them. Being objective is not, however, sufficient to make one a rational judge. Various inabilities may undermine one's rationality which do not arise out of bias, but are a result of cognitive incompetence,[9] hastiness, and like defects which do not undermine one's objectivity.

(c) Some Conditions of Domain-Objectivity

Given our interest in the objectivity of practical thought we can leave the epistemic sense on one side, and concentrate on the question of the objectivity of the domain of practical or evaluative thought. What exactly is domain-objectivity? How is it to be explained?

Possibly there is no short answer to the question. A domain of thought is objective if and only if thoughts belonging to it satisfy a whole range of criteria. They define the discipline to which objective thoughts are subject. We have already encountered a few of them:

(1) The possibility of knowledge condition: only if a domain is objective can it express knowledge, or be said to be about something that one can have knowledge of.

(2) The possibility of error condition: a domain is objective only if thoughts which belong to it obey the distinction between seeming and being, that is, only if the fact that I think that things are so and so does not constitute their being so and so (some self-referential thoughts are the exception[10]).

(3) The possibility of epistemic objectivity: only if a domain is objective can one be an objective or a subjective judge of matters in this domain. Similarly, only then can one's opinions about it or the way one forms them be objective, etc. This last condition is in some sense a subsidiary of the first two. But another condition central to our understanding of the objective is:

[9] Except where the cognitive incompetence manifests itself in failure to realize or respond to factors which independently may affect one's objectivity. People's objectivity may be undermined by their incompetence in realizing that they are biased, etc.

[10] And this may account for the tendency to classify them as subjective.

(4) The relevance condition: a domain is objective only if thoughts which belong to it are such that there can be facts or other considerations which are reasons for believing that they are or are likely to be true or correct.

The second conditions allows us

(i) to talk of thoughts as being correct, true, or as being errors and mistakes;[11]
(ii) to admit that two views are contradictory, and therefore that there are logical relations among thoughts;
(iii) to talk of changing one's mind (with the implication that one was in error then, not only that one now wants something different), etc.

The fourth condition allows us to apply the distinction between what is relevant to the truth of a thought and what is not, and the whole terminology of support and confirmation. The reasons for holding a thought to be true are of a large variety of kinds. They may be evidential (there are heavy clouds, therefore it will rain) or legal (it has been approved by the Queen in Parliament, therefore it is a valid law) or moral (it shows disrespect therefore it is wrong) or semantic (he is your uncle's son therefore he is your cousin), and many others. Reasons for believing that a thought is true need not be available to the person who has it, or at least need not be available to him as reasons for the thought. This caveat covers, among other cases, the case where belief is direct and not based on reasons. A person looking at a red bus and thinking 'this is a red bus', does not have reasons for his belief. But there are reasons to think his belief correct, for example, that he was in an advantageous position to judge the character and colour of the object he saw.

The objectivity of a domain does not presuppose that anyone can have either a priori or self-evident or incorrigible understanding of what relevant reasons are like or of the rules of reasoning in this domain. It only presupposes that the thoughts belonging to an objective domain (*a*) allow for the application of judgements based on reasons. Schematically, it allows for beliefs of the kind 'This thought is unjustified for the reason that . . .', where the reason adduced—even if it is a bad reason, and even if it is of a

---

[11] Some would make this the first and most important condition of objectivity. One way of formulating it is: a domain is objective if thoughts belonging to it deal with matters about which there are propositions which are true or false (or correct or incorrect, or more or less correct or incorrect). I state the condition in this way, rather than by saying that those thoughts express propositions which are true or false, in order to allow for the possibility of thoughts which are objective, and belong to an objective domain, but which express propositions which are neither true nor false.

type which cannot but be a bad reason—is one which can intelligibly be thought of as a reason in this context. And (*b*) they allow that there can be reasons of an appropriate kind, that is, reasons whose existence tends to make such beliefs true.

Two further important conditions derive from Williams's discussion of the absolute conception of reality (about which more will be said below). In advancing the absolute conception Williams was concerned with the conditions for the possibility of knowledge. His discussion is therefore relevant to objectivity understood as a mark of domains of thoughts which could constitute knowledge. Williams introduces the discussion by saying: 'If knowledge is what it claims to be, then it is knowledge of a reality which exists independently of that knowledge, ... Knowledge is of what is there *anyway*.'[12] This thought yields the condition of objectivity which can be formulated as follows:

(5) The independence condition: thoughts are objective only if they are about a reality[13] which exists independently of them, that is, whose truth is independent of the fact that those thoughts are entertained.[14]

If there are exceptions to this condition they are marginal and degenerate cases. Trying to refine the condition to accommodate them need not detain us. Williams follows the above quotation with a complex statement introducing several ideas, one of which can be called the single reality condition.

(6) The single reality condition: the domain of objective thoughts is subject to the constraint that thoughts constitute knowledge only if they can all be explained as being about a single reality.[15]

---

[12] B. Williams, *Descartes* (London: Penguin Books, 1978), 64.

[13] I am using a realist mode of expression ('about a reality') in a weak sense, in which we could say of arithmetical propositions that they are about numbers and their relations, without being committed to Platonism about numbers. This weak sense is explained in the second half of the independence condition.

[14] In 'What would a Substantive Theory of Truth be Like?' Wiggins suggests as a mark of truth that a statement's being true or not is independent of any particular subject's means of appraising its truth value. This goes beyond the independence condition. Practical or evaluative thought does not conform with this condition under some natural interpretations of it, but is objective. Some of the discussion which follows bears on the reasons for rejecting Wiggins's condition.

[15] 'Many would claim'—Williams observes—'that we are now familiar with the situation of doing with less than an absolute conception, and can, as modern persons and unlike the ambitious or complacent thinkers of earlier centuries, operate with a picture of the world which at the reflexive level we can recognize to be thoroughly relative to our language, our conceptual scheme—most generally, to our situation. But it is doubtful to what extent we really can operate with such a picture, and doubtful whether such views do not implicitly rely, in their self-understanding, on some presumed absolute conception, a framework within which our situation can be comprehensively related to other possible situations.'

The condition is intended by Williams to allow for the acceptance of apparently conflicting claims of knowledge, provided they can be reconciled as claims about a single reality (e.g. by representing it in different but inter-translatable schemes of representations), but to exclude claims whose apparent conflict cannot be thus reconciled. In particular he is keen to rule out suggested reconciliations which relativize claims of knowledge: 'p is true from my perspective, or relative to me, or from point of view x, even while not-p is true from your perspective', etc. It is a rejection of isolationism, of claims that every domain of thought must be judged by its own standards of truth, knowledge, and objectivity, which may be very different from those of any other domain.[16] The single reality condition, while allowing for different perspectives, and different domains of thoughts, each with its own standards of evidence, insists that they must all be reconcilable within one conception of reality. They must be shown to be not only consistent with each other, but also perspectives or domains which can be seen as being about different aspects of one world—not an easy condition to spell out,[17] but one which is worth retaining, as it bears on a variety of subjectivist and relativist claims.

We could go on drawing out the implications of these conditions, and adding others to them. I call this approach the 'long route' to an explanation of objectivity for it does not yield a comprehensive set of conditions satisfaction of which is necessary and sufficient for a domain to be objective, and which provides an adequate explanation of objectivity beyond the need for further refinement and adjustment. Any set of conditions, however successful it may be in answering the questions and concerns which led to its formulation, will need to be refined as new problems emerge. It is in principle impossible to circumvent the long route by providing a set of necessary and sufficient conditions which will never call for revision and refinement, and from which all the other necessary features of objectivity can be deduced. It is not possible to argue for this impossibility here. It depends, first, on the fact that propositions are open to somewhat different interpretations, that they are all inherently vague, and therefore even if true may call for further refinement to meet the needs of new puzzles and

---

(*Descartes*, 68). We should agree that the notion of 'relative reality' does not make much sense. There is no interesting sense in which something can be the case relative to us, but not be the case relative to others, unless, as Williams observes, such claims presuppose a common frame of reference.

[16] Such an isolationist position seems to be endorsed by Dworkin in 'Objectivity and Truth: You'd Better Believe It', *Philosophy and Public Affairs*, 25 (1996), 87.

[17] It is not clear whether, as formulated by Williams, the condition would rule out perspectivalist accounts of truth or of reality which are not self-contradictory. For a claim that there can be coherent perspectivalism see S. D. Hales, 'A Consistent Relativism', *Mind*, 106 (1997), 33.

hitherto unexplored questions.[18] It depends, second, on the ever present possibility that new questions will emerge forcing us to notice and articulate new conditions of objectivity. Perhaps the following could serve as an example of another condition which does not follow from the above, and which may illustrate how more and more may emerge with emerging reasons to think of them:

(7) *The possibility of irrationality condition*, that is, that it is possible to endorse propositions belonging to the domain out of wishful thinking, self-deception, etc.[19]

Even if the 'additional conditions' which may emerge with time apply to the same domain already delineated by previously spelt out conditions they are not redundant. An explanation of objectivity aims to do more than mark the boundaries of objective domains. It aims to explain puzzles about objectivity. The point I am pressing home here is that, as new puzzles arise, new conditions may be noticed which help to explain them away.

(d) Defending the Approach

Is this 'long' route to explaining objectivity adequate? Some may say that while it brings out necessary conditions of objectivity it is never going to get to the real hard questions: are there really things or properties like 'rights', 'tastefulness', or 'beauty'? Is it in principle possible for them to exist?

The problem with the approach I outlined, these people might say, is that it considers only internal criteria of objectivity. Basically it regards thoughts as objective if we treat them as objective or if the concepts and sentences employed to express them meet certain conditions, which show that they are treated as expressing thoughts which can be true or false, etc. But we cannot, so the objection goes, make a thought objective just by treating it as objective. Whether or not it is objective is not up to us. It depends

---

[18] This also explains why there is safety in numbers. The more criteria we have the firmer our grasp of the concept, for cumulatively they eliminate the possibility of misunderstandings relative to known questions. On the other hand they open up more possibilities of hitherto unthought of questions regarding which they are vague and need refinement.

[19] Cf. B. Williams, 'Truth in Ethics', in Hooker (ed.), *Truth in Ethics*, 25. (Note that this example merely illustrates the possibility of additional, logically independent, conditions. It does not illustrate any puzzles they may be called to dispel.)

My espousal of the long route is in line with Dworkin's position in 'Objectivity and Truth'. There he warns against taking it for granted that conditions for the objectivity of one domain (say relating material objects) apply also to all other domains (say that which relates to mathematics or to values).

on how things are in the world.[20] In classifying thoughts as objective we are saying that they constitute beliefs, that to hold such thoughts is to have certain beliefs, and that means that these thoughts can be true or false and that holding them can in principle amount to knowledge. This shows, the argument proceeds, that whether they are objective cannot just be a matter of how we treat them. It is a question of what the world really is like, a question about how things are in the world.

Here is my problem. Domains of thought are objective, I suggested at the outset, only if they are subject to disciplines which make them capable of constituting knowledge, and so on. The charge against the way I explained this route to an explanation of objectivity was that it led to an articulation of what we take to be the conditions of knowledge, rather than what the conditions of knowledge really are. It may seem that the only way to justify my position is to deny that the two can differ. But that would imply that we cannot be wrong about the conditions of knowledge, which seems too strong a claim. In fact it is not needed. All I need to argue for is that, necessarily, our knowledge or understanding of the conditions of objectivity depends on our knowledge or understanding of the conditions of knowledge. If our knowledge or understanding of one of these concepts is imperfect so is our knowledge or understanding of the other.

Whether our thoughts are true or not is immaterial to their objective character, but they must, among other things, be capable of being true or false, of bearing a truth value. Therefore, they cannot amount to knowledge unless they are about how things are anyway, about the world as it is independently of these thoughts. That means (given that the character of domains of thought depends on the disciplines to which *we* subject them) that they cannot be about reality unless we treat them as about how things are independently of thought about them.

As so far stated these considerations do not show more than that satisfying the conditions spelt out above, and others derived in like manner, are necessary for a domain of thought to be objective. But their implications reach further:

1. It is not the case that this approach allows that what is objective is 'up to us'. That would mean that we can choose whether to regard matters of taste or morality as objective. But the account I suggested has no such consequence.

2. Notice that these conditions do more than point to surface syntactical features, for example, that the thoughts are expressed in indicative

---

[20] This objection is based on claims endorsed by several philosophers. See e.g. Dummett on abstract objects in Frege, *Philosophy of Language* (London: Duckworth, 1973), 505; Wiggins, 'What would a Substantive Theory of Truth be Like?'; C. Wright, *Truth and Objectivity* (Oxford: OUP, 1992), ch. 1; Williams, 'Truth in Ethics'.

sentences, allow embedding, etc. They assume the practices which Wright regards as underlying what he calls 'the minimalist' account of truth.[21] Wright's account has convinced some writers that nothing of substance depends on allowing that propositions and utterances can be true or false, given the minimalist account of truth.[22] The condition of relevance, however, takes my explanation of objectivity beyond the conditions which, according to Wright, have to be satisfied for a truth predicate to apply to a domain.

3. The condition of relevance makes the objectivity of a domain dependent on the existence of criteria which support or undermine beliefs within that domain. These criteria could in appropriate circumstances warrant the conclusion that all beliefs within the domain are false or lacking in truth value (because a presupposition of their having truth value fails). Thus this approach allows in principle for an error theory[23] which, while admitting that a domain is the subject of objective thought, establishes that there can be nothing in it, that there can be no rights, no tasteful or beautiful objects, etc.

4. The approach allows for the possibility that a domain which appears objective is not in fact objective, even though it is taken by everyone to be objective. This can happen if discourse involving it collapses into contradiction or incoherence, or if it fails to cohere with other established beliefs.

5. The approach allows that our concepts of knowledge, truth, and objectivity may themselves be defective, and in need of revision (more on this in section 2(e) below).

6. Externalist accounts are the better accounts of knowledge. According to them, whether or not one's belief is justified depends, in part, on how things turn out in the world, and not merely on satisfying criteria which the agent is aware of.

The third, fourth, and fifth points establish that the approach I delineated is not essentially a conservative one, that it is open to challenges which can force revisions in, or even the abandonment of, established aspects of common discourse and thought. The last point is but one additional way in which the criteria of objectivity, derived from the essential properties of knowledge, are not 'too internal'.

This six-point reply to the objection may only prompt some of those who suspect the long route of being too internal to raise another charge. I seem to have an answer, they would say, because I conflate and confuse a

---

[21] *Truth and Objectivity*, chs. 1 and 2.
[22] Cf. e.g. B. Williams, 'Truth in Ethics', in Hooker (ed.), *Truth in Ethics*, 19–20 and elsewhere.
[23] In the sense with which the phrase was introduced by J. Mackie in *Ethics* (London: Penguin Books, 1977) ch. 1.

number of different issues: metaphysical, epistemic, and semantic. The possibility of error condition concerns semantics, the relevance and the possibility of irrationality conditions are explicitly epistemic, and the independence and single reality conditions are metaphysical.

At one level I have no defence against this charge. The list of criteria of objectivity does include criteria which can readily be classified as semantic, metaphysical, and epistemic, as well as some which may defy such a classification. Nor do I wish to raise any doubts about the legitimacy of separating issues into semantic, metaphysical, and epistemic. In many cases such a separation is useful, and in some it is essential. But not all concepts can be readily separated in this way, and to my mind the attempts by some writers[24] to define separate semantic and metaphysical senses of objectivity miss the point that the two are interdependent, and that at the most fundamental level these stipulated concepts are not useful.

Take the relevance condition. It is epistemic in nature, but not exclusively so. Someone who does not know anything at all about what may count as evidence in favour of the proposition that Gubaidulina is a great composer, or that this chair is not comfortable, or that Everest is the highest mountain on earth, does not really know what it is to be a composer or a mountain, etc. If upon hearing the claim that Gubaidulina is a great composer someone replies: 'Oh yes? Does she eat fish?' then, barring a peculiar sense of humour, his remarks reveal that he has not understood what he was told. Such misunderstandings are often used in popular humour to expose the ignorance and pretence of social climbers. Examples like this would show that part of understanding any concept is having some grasp of what counts as relevant evidence showing that it applies or does not apply.

At the same time, the fact that one thing or another is evidence for the existence of something, or for its possession of some property, tells us something about the nature of these existences: material things are those whose existence and properties can be established one way, mathematical objects and properties are those which are established in very different ways, etc. In sum, the relevance condition straddles the divide between the semantic, epistemic, and metaphysical. It requires more than knowledge of connections among concepts. It requires knowledge of how the way things are in the world is relevant to the application of concepts.

The interdependence of the different aspects (semantic, metaphysical, and epistemic) reveals itself in the way arguments regarding problem cases proceed. There is a striking correlation between those philosophers who

---

[24] e.g. Marmor, 'Three Concepts of Objectivity', and Pettit and Leiter in their contributions to Leiter (ed.), *Objectivity in Law and Morals* (Cambridge: Cambridge University Press, forthcoming).

think that there are 'non-naturalistic' moral properties and those who believe that moral predicates refer to such properties. John Mackie,[25] is among few philosophers who believe that moral predicates refer to non-natural properties, but that there are no such properties, nor can there be. Apart from him, those who believe that moral statements are 'semantically objective' also believe that there are moral properties, and—some argue—since there are no non-natural properties, moral properties must be natural properties. Those who believe that there are no moral properties opt for a non-cognitive interpretation of moral utterances and so on. The same is true regarding secondary qualities. Even Mackie does not offer an error theory of secondary qualities, or of mathematical properties. In all these cases one's view of the nature of the properties which exist and one's view of the semantics of the relevant range of predicates go hand in hand. They are interdependent, and needless to say so are the relevant evidential criteria.

The interdependence of the semantic and metaphysical is recognized and explained by Crispin Wright. He argues that, if one believes, as error theorists like Mackie and Field do, that even though propositions asserting the existence of ethical (or mathematical or other) properties are false, we need not radically change our use of them for they serve some other valid purpose, then one has to explain why one should not accept that truth in that domain is constituted by serving that purpose. In his words: 'Why insist on construing *truth* for moral discourse in terms which motivate a charge of global error, rather than explicate it in terms of the satisfaction of the putative subsidiary norm {what I called 'the valuable purpose'}, whatever it is? The question may have a good answer. . . . But I do not know of a promising argument in that direction.'[26] That is the sort of consideration which led me to claim that domain-objectivity combines semantic, epistemic, and metaphysical criteria.

In spite of these points doubts are likely to linger. While not being conservative, the criteria I mentioned are all in some sense internal to the ways we treat thoughts in the domain in question. Is there no possibility that a domain will meet these criteria and yet fail to be objective simply because of how things are? In principle the answer is affirmative. Since the long route deals with problems as they are encountered, and denies the feasibility of producing a definitive list of necessary and sufficient conditions for objectivity, the (epistemic) possibility that factors may emerge which defeat

---

[25] *Ethics*, ch. 1. Hartry Field is among the few who endorse an error theory of mathematical propositions. See e.g. his *Science without Numbers* (Oxford: Blackwell, 1980) and *Realism, Mathematics and Modality* (Oxford: Blackwell, 1989).

[26] 'Truth in Ethics', in Hooker (ed.), *Truth in Ethics*, 3. It may well be that Wright's argument here is the argument which Dworkin tries to make in his 'Truth and Objectivity'.

the objectivity of domains of thought which meet the above conditions cannot be ruled out. All we can do is examine specific doubts regarding the objectivity of practical thought. The rest of this chapter consists in dispelling two specific sources of such doubt which have attracted considerable attention.

2. THE ROLE OF PAROCHIAL CONCEPTS

(a) Is Parochial Knowledge Possible?

A couple of terminological stipulations will help us along. 'Perspectival knowledge' is knowledge which can only be expressed with the use of parochial concepts. 'Parochial concepts' are concepts which cannot be mastered by all, not even by everyone capable of knowledge. 'Non-parochial' concepts can be mastered by anyone capable of knowing anything at all. Any concepts possession of which requires having particular perceptual capacities (such as colour concepts), and not merely the possession of some perceptual capacity or other, are parochial concepts. For different reasons, concepts whose mastery presupposes interests or imaginative or emotive capacities which are not shared, nor can be shared, by all creatures capable of possessing knowledge are parochial concepts. We come to understand interests we do not share by relating them to interests we do share. If an interest is remote from any of ours, and if its role in the life of the people who have it is ramified and unlike the role of any interests we have, or know about, then explanation has to be supplemented with simulation or real habituation before we can understand it, or the concepts which presuppose its understanding. But our capacity for simulation or habituation is limited. Interests which will evolve only in the future, for example, cannot be understood in that way, and often they are interests which it is in principle impossible for us to understand. By the same token, many of our interests were beyond the reach of people in previous generations, and so were the concepts mastery of which depends on understanding these interests.

The impossibility of acquiring concepts which presuppose interests remote from those we have and which do not yet exist (and therefore cannot be mastered or discovered by simulation) is sufficient to show that practically all concepts which can be acquired only by people who understand some non-universal interests are parochial concepts. Regarding all of them there was a time when they were beyond the reach of people living at that time. There is, however, yet another type of limitation on people's ability in principle to master such concepts: habituation and simulation are demanding and relatively slow processes. You often have to immerse yourself in an alien culture, understand its concerns, religious and other beliefs, come to understand how people normally react in many to them normal situations, share—at least in imagination—their hopes, fears, and aspirations. All these factors mean that, even if there is no interest-dependent concept one cannot acquire, it is in principle possible for any person to master only a relatively small number of such concepts, and hence, given the length and diversity of human history, impossible in principle for anyone living today to master more than a fraction of the interest-dependent concepts which pertained to different human societies now or in the past, even if we leave aside the future.[27]

If interest-related concepts are parochial so are evaluative or normative concepts, for they are all interest-related (not, of course, in 'serving' the interests of the agent, but in the fact that mastery of the concept requires understanding some interests or others). This is evident when we consider relatively specific, so called thick, concepts, like the excellence of an opera, or a novel. But the same is true of our abstract normative concepts such as those designated by the terms 'duty', 'obligation', 'ought', 'a right', 'valuable', 'good', 'beautiful', 'person', 'happiness', 'pleasure'. The history of these terms and the attempt to find terms of comparable meaning in other languages show how their meaning mutated over time, and how different languages differ in their abstract normative vocabulary. It is reasonable to conclude that abstract normative concepts too are parochial.

Doubts have been cast on the objectivity of parochial concepts, on the possibility of knowledge that depends on their possession, and cannot be reformulated without their use. I will examine some grounds for such doubts.

(b) Nagel on the Objective and the Subjective

Nagel regards parochial concepts as subjective but does not deny that they enable us to acquire knowledge which cannot be obtained without them. In most respects my views are consonant with his. The most striking apparent difference is due to the special sense in which he uses the objective/subjective distinction, which differs from any we have mentioned so far: 'A view or form of thought is more objective than another if it relies less on the specifics of the individual's makeup and position in the world, or on

---

[27] Given that mastery of concepts is a matter of degree everything I say in the text has to be modulated to allow e.g. for a more imperfect mastery of a greater number of concepts. The fact that no one can master all interest-related concepts does not show that there are concepts that cannot be acquired by everyone. It establishes only a weaker parochiality, if you like collective parochiality, of interest-dependent concepts.

the character of the particular type of creature he is.'[28] In other words, Nagel calls a view or thought subjective if it essentially depends on employing parochial concepts for its expression. The greater its dependence on parochial concepts the more subjective it is.

For Nagel 'objectivity is a method of understanding'.[29] It seems to be a method of understanding reality, with different aspects of reality being understood depending on the degree of objectivity attained in the method of understanding them: 'We may think of reality as a set of concentric spheres, progressively revealed as we detach gradually from the contingencies of the self' (p. 5). This sentence may suggest that the more objective our method of understanding the more of reality we come to know and understand. But this is not Nagel's meaning, or at least it is only part of his meaning. While some aspects of reality reveal themselves only as they are objectively investigated, others are lost except when understood through subjective methods. 'The attempt to give a complete account of the world in objective terms ... inevitably leads to false reductions or to outright denial that certain patently real phenomena exist at all' (p. 7). In particular, 'The subjectivity of consciousness is an irreducible feature of reality' (p. 7), which presumably means that it can only be fully known and understood with the use of subjective methods, including the use of parochial concepts.

Nagel seems to think that only the mental requires parochial concepts for its understanding.

Although there is a connection between objectivity and reality—only the supposition that we and our appearances [*this seems to mean how things appear to us, not how we appear to others* (JR)] are part of a larger reality makes it reasonable to seek understanding by stepping back from the appearances in this way—still not all reality is better understood the more objectively it is viewed. Appearance and perspective are essential parts of what there is, and in some respects they are best understood from a less detached standpoint. Realism underlines the claims of objectivity and detachment, but it supports them only up to a point. (p. 4)

But how can we know that no other aspect of reality requires parochial concepts for its understanding? Perhaps the thought is that since the mental

---

[28] *The View from Nowhere* (New York: OUP, 1986), 5. He also says: 'To acquire a more objective understanding of some aspect of life or the world, we step back from our initial view of it and form a new conception which has that view and its relation to the world as its object. In other words we place ourselves in the world that is to be understood.' (Ibid. 4.) Here Nagel seems to be saying that a belief about the world is more subjective than a belief about my having a belief about the world. But my beliefs about the content of the theory of quantum mechanics are not more subjective than my belief that I have certain beliefs about quantum mechanics. They are simply different. I will assume that the quotation above is simply an unhappy formulation of the idea quoted in the main text.

[29] Ibid. 4.

is subjective it requires subjective concepts for its understanding. But that thought is guilty of the fallacy of equivocation: thought is subjective in the psychological sense which means simply that it is mental. The 'method of subjectivity' as a method of knowledge does not mean knowing in a way which involves mental states, dispositions, or capacities. All knowing involves the mental in these ways, be it knowledge obtained by more or less objective methods. 'The method of subjectivity' means knowledge which can only be obtained by the use of parochial concepts. To avoid equivocation the thought should be: parochial concepts, and thoughts involving them, can only be understood with the use of parochial concepts. That amounts to claiming that parochial concepts cannot be eliminated. If they are necessary for knowledge of certain matters, then those matters cannot be known 'objectively'. *That* would not justify the conclusion that only the mental can be understood by the use of parochial concepts.

Perhaps I am wrong to identify Nagel's understanding of the objective/subjective distinction with reliance on and the use of concepts which are more or less parochial? Perhaps all he means is that the mental can be understood only with the use of psychological concepts? He certainly believes the latter, but that is not all he is claiming.

The more objective our understanding the more detached it is from our specific situation, specific capacities, etc. To quote Nagel again: the more objective the thought the less it relies 'on the specifics of the individual's makeup and position in the world, or on the character of the particular type of creature he is'. These specifics constitute what he calls the special perspective of that creature. Objective knowledge, like any other knowledge, is obtained within that perspective, but it does not rely on it. It can be shared by people whose perspectives are different. Subjective knowledge cannot be shared in this way. It is available only to those who share the same perspective.

My suggestion is that perspectives can be identified by the range of concepts which those who inhabit them can possess. This does not exhaust the differences between perspectives, but the others follow from the inability of those who inhabit a perspective to possess certain concepts. The possession of concepts, let us remind ourselves, involves certain mental abilities, certain perceptual abilities, and certain experiences. For example, inability to master mathematical concepts makes one incapable of possessing a whole range of scientific concepts, the lack of sight makes the understanding of colour concepts incomplete, and those who never desired anything cannot understand what it is to want something.

So the more objective knowledge is the less does its possession presuppose. It presupposes fewer common mental abilities, fewer common perceptual abilities, and fewer common experiences. If that is so we can understand why knowledge of the nature of thought is more objective than the knowledge of the nature of Christianity. To understand the nature of thought one needs to have the capacity for thought, but other things being equal, this capacity is available to anyone capable of thinking. These may include Martians, automata, and others, beside humans. Knowledge of Christianity requires concepts such as salvation, redemption, and love which need not be available to all who are capable of knowledge. Hence it is more subjective.

This line of thought can explain some aspects of Nagel's position. But it does not seem to explain some of its basic tenets. First, it does not explain why all knowledge of the mental is more subjective. Since only people with a mental life are capable of knowledge none is excluded from the perspective which involves at least some mental concepts. Second, it does not explain why only the mental defies complete objectivity. It does not answer the question why we should assume that there are no aspects of reality which can be known or understood only by creatures with specific capacities and experiences, which are incompatible with the capacities needed to understand other aspects of reality. Nagel seems bereft of an argument which will limit his 'subjective method' of knowledge to the mental only.[30]

(c) Williams and the Priority of Non-Parochial Concepts

Williams in discussing secondary qualities introduces the requirement that all knowledge must be capable of being expressed without the use of parochial concepts. I will call this the *priority condition*, meaning the condition that a thought is objective only if it can be expressed without the use of parochial concepts. Here is his argument:

Can we really distinguish between some concepts or propositions which figure in the conception of the world without observers, and others that do not? Are not all our concepts ours . . . ? Of course; but there is no suggestion that we should try to describe a world without ourselves using any concepts, or without using concepts which we, human beings, can understand. The suggestion is that there are possible descriptions of the world using concepts which are not peculiarly ours, and not peculiarly relative to our experience. Such a description would be that which would be arrived at, as C.S. Peirce put it, if scientific enquiry continued long enough; it is the content of that 'final opinion' which Peirce believed that enquiry would inevitably converge upon, a final opinion . . . inde-

---

[30] This issue is relevant to the standing of perceptually dependent properties, e.g. colour properties, and I will not pursue it here.

pendent not indeed of thought in general, but of all that is arbitrary and individual in thought.[31]

> The scientific representation of the material world can be the point of convergence of the Peircean enquirer precisely because it does not have among its concepts any which reflect merely a local interest, taste or sensory peculiarity.... This extended conception would then be that absolute conception of reality.[32]

And Williams contrasts this view with that of a critic who maintains that 'scientific theories are a cultural product which it would be senseless to suppose could be freed from local relativities'.[33]

The motivating concern leading to the priority condition seems to be the need to establish the credentials of our knowledge claims, and of our concepts. We need to know that through our concepts we can understand the world as it is independently of us, that our thoughts are no mere shadows cast by our own concepts. Therefore, any view or thought which claims to be knowledge must meet a test which is concept-independent, or—given the impossibility of thought without concepts—which is at least independent of any concepts which are not accessible to everyone. That test is the Peirceian convergence of all those who are engaged in pure inquiry. In the nature of things if the convergence is to encompass all those capable of knowledge then it must exclude thoughts which essentially depend on parochial concepts for their expression. Such parochial thoughts will not be available to all inquirers and therefore will not be able to be subjected to the test of convergence.

The priority condition has been criticized as incoherent and inconsistent with its aim of establishing some limited credentials of knowledge which relies on parochial concepts.[34] In later writings Williams abandons it, and concedes that the understanding, as well as the explanation, of knowledge relying on parochial concepts, cannot be accomplished without such concepts.[35] This entails also abandoning the ideal convergence condition in Peirce's version which Williams endorsed earlier. There is knowledge regarding which no convergence of all competent inquirers is possible. 'Alien investigators', to use his phrase, may be unable to understand our

---

[31] *Descartes*, 244. Peirce's reference is from 'A Critical Review of Berkeley's Idealism', in Charles S. Peirce, *Selected Writings (Values in a World of Chance)*, ed. Philip P. Wiener (New York: Dover, 1966), 82.

[32] *Descartes*, 245.   [33] Ibid. 248.

[34] See H. Putnam, 'Bernard Williams and the Absolute Conception of the World', in *Renewing Philosophy* (Cambridge, Mass.: Harvard University Press, 1992), 80, and J. McDowell, 'Aesthetic Value, Objectivity, and the Fabric of the World', in Eva Schaper (ed.) *Pleasure, Preference and Value* (Cambridge: Cambridge University Press, 1983), 1.

[35] *Ethics and the Limits of Philosophy* (London: Fontana Press/Collins, 1985), 140.

perspective, even those aspects of it which yield knowledge, if that knowledge is dependent on parochial concepts.[36]

Convergence is in any case a suspect condition.[37] A degree of convergence is entailed by the fact that agreement in meaning presupposes a degree of agreement in judgement. This does indeed vindicate testing agreement in meaning by looking for agreement in judgement. But the convergence that test entails is limited to those who share the same meanings. This cannot be a requirement of a Peirceian convergence of all competent inquirers, since, by definition, they do not share understanding of parochial concepts. Within local communities who share parochial concepts, such as 'inflation', 'chivalry', and their like, there will indeed be a degree of convergence in judgement. But not enough to eliminate disagreements and disputes. In particular, beliefs whose justification typically involves complex reasoning regarding a diverse range of considerations will always be liable to disagreement even among those who share the same meaning and a similar environment (and therefore a similar evidential starting-point).

Most theorists who recommend convergence as a criterion of objectivity emphasize that it is the convergence of competent inquirers which is achieved when they follow the relevant reasons. The required convergence can never be the convergence of all. But who is competent is not a neutral question, independent of one's other epistemic claims. Rather, it is defined by competence to understand and apply the criteria of objectivity, and in particular the condition of relevance. Therefore, if parochial concepts are essential to some knowledge then convergence may possibly be attainable, but it will be confined to those who can master these concepts, not the Peirceian convergence of all competent inquirers. Ideal convergence cannot be a requirement which rules out parochial concepts, or removes them to a lesser status. Rather, settling the question of the status of parochial concepts is necessary before one can establish what sort of convergence is necessary.

There is another, perhaps more radical, limitation on any convergence requirement. Would the criterion of relevance meet a convergence requirement limited to those who master the relevant concepts? Not quite; it would have met the requirement but for the fact that it allows for indeterminacy of reasons which may lead rational inquirers, even when they share the same premises, to diverge in their conclusions on those occasions where it would be rational to believe a certain proposition and also rational to doubt it. The manifestations of the underdetermination of reasons are wide-

---

[36] *Ethics and the Limits of Philosophy*, 140.
[37] It is illuminatingly discussed by Wright in *Truth and Objectivity*, e.g. pp. 88–94.

spread and familiar. For example, two people hear the same testimony and one believes it while the other does not. In many (though not in all) everyday situations like this both have to admit that the other is not irrational, while insisting, of course, on the rationality of their own stance. Common as underdetermination by reason is it has not received adequate attention in epistemology. This is not the occasion to discuss it in detail,[38] though I will return to the point later.

(d) The Siren Call of Epistemic Absolutes

Why does Williams think that parochial concepts are more suspect than non-parochial ones? They are concepts 'which reflect merely a local interest, taste or sensory peculiarity'. What is it for a concept to reflect merely a local interest? It has become an oft-repeated philosophical example that the Inuits have more terms designating types of snow than are known to any other language. Are their concepts of types of snow an example of concepts of a 'mere local interest'? This is how Putnam understands Williams, for he thinks that 'grass' is similarly a local concept.[39] They may well be concepts which not every inquirer can master. Their mastery may well presuppose familiarity with some minutiae of Inuit life, which give their ways of distinguishing types of snow their point, and which are beyond the comprehension of Martians. As mentioned earlier, perceptual concepts are another class of parochial concepts. Since not all people possess the same sense organs not all of them can master the concepts possession of which requires perceiving the world though particular senses.

It is not my purpose to argue that scientific theories are likely to find concepts like 'grass' or 'sweet' particularly useful.[40] Suppose that they do not. Is that relevant to the preconditions of knowledge or to the nature of reality or the world? Accountants have no more use for the notion of quarks than physicists for the notion of inflation. Does it follow that inflation is a mere illusion? Clearly not. The interest of Inuits in snow may lead to the emergence of a range of parochial concepts, which are no use to the rest

---

[38] C. Wright's condition of cognitive command (*Truth and Objectivity*, 92–3) disregards the existence of rational underdetermination in its assertion that a discourse exhibits cognitive command only if all disagreements can be explained by 'divergent input'. On pp. 95 ff. Wright has an interesting discussion of the related topic of the degree to which reason can be permissive only, but he does not fully adjust his conclusions to allow for its insights.

[39] 'Objectivity and the Science/Ethics Distinction', in *Realism with a Human Face* (Cambridge, Mass.: Harvard University Press, 1990).

[40] For a critique of the absolute conception which argues that science too needs perspectival concepts see Putnam, 'Objectivity and the Science/Ethics Distinction'. Note that to establish his case Putnam has to show not only that different systems of representations can be used in science, but also that they employ what I call parochial concepts.

of the world. But *that* does not show that they do not pick out real features of the real world. In fact it is hardly conceivable that they could express local, or indeed any, tastes or interests if they did not. The same considerations apply to perceptual concepts. That certain creatures lack a certain perceptual capacity may prevent them from becoming aware of certain aspects of the world which can be known only by those who have it. It does not show that those who have those senses are not able through them to perceive how things really are, thus acquiring (perceptual) knowledge the others lack.[41]

Clearly some concepts have no use in formulating any true thoughts about how things are (other than about what use people made of those concepts). The credentials of concepts are not beyond question. But I doubt that parochial concepts need more defence than non-parochial ones. 'Ether', 'alkahest', and other scientific or pseudo-scientific concepts, non-parochial if any are, fail the test. They are no help in acquiring knowledge. Some of these concepts are empirically empty. Others are conceptually incoherent or inconsistent with basic scientific laws.

Non-parochial concepts, because they are in principle accessible to all, have one obvious advantage. When they can be used to test parochial concepts and parochial epistemic principles, then they can be used to test whether those parochial concepts and principles are free of local biases. Such taints will be exposed once the concepts and principles which incorporate them are judged by principles which are accessible to people not blinkered by those interests, and whose vision is not distorted by the peculiarities of any specific perceptual capacity, or alleged capacity.

It does not follow that all parochial concepts or principles can be thoroughly tested in this way. Moreover, pointing out this advantage is very different from giving non-parochial concepts and principles special priority, a special status among the conditions for the possibility of knowledge.[42]

It seems to me that the thought that they could play such a criterial role is a mutation of a Cartesian ideal. Not that Williams's absolute conception involves a commitment to self-evident knowledge, but it is committed to the thesis that the objectivity of thought is underpinned by an epistemic

---

[41] There may or may not be reasons to think that some perceptual concepts, those designating the so-called secondary qualities, designate relational properties of things. For example, there may or may not be reason to think that they designate how things when observed strike the observer, rather than how they are when not observed. Williams advances some arguments to that effect, and their examination is irrelevant to my argument here. The only relevant point is that the fact that perceptual concepts are local is not such an argument.   [42] This is one of the points made by McDowell, 'Aesthetic Value'.

principle stating that under ideal conditions knowledge is undisputed and clear for all to see. Two ideas combine here, one explicit and one implicit. The first is that under ideal conditions there will not be any deep disagreement. (If a disagreement occurs it will be quickly resolved—by looking at the evidence as it were.) The second is that in the ideal conditions epistemic tests will not lead us astray. In the real world, it is acknowledged, we are at the mercy of epistemic luck. We may often be epistemically justified, indeed required, to accept beliefs which are in fact false. But under ideal conditions this will not happen.

These ideal conditions may never be realized, but only an epistemology which subjects itself to this test, which accepts that what is true will be recognized as such under ideal conditions, can underpin a claim to objectivity. Only domains of thought which can stand this test (i.e. that of the thoughts which belong to them, under ideal conditions competent inquirers will necessarily converge and accept the same thoughts, and reject the same thoughts) are domains of objective thought. While we acknowledge, the thought is, that in real life we are at the mercy of epistemic luck since we may be rationally justified in accepting false propositions as true, no domain of thought is objective if it is necessarily always subject to epistemic luck, if there are no circumstances in which the gap between justified belief and true belief is closed.

There is no cogent reason to accept this yearning for freedom from epistemic luck. In all areas of knowledge there are limits—imposed by conditions of intelligibility—to the possibility of error. But beyond that we are at the mercy of epistemic luck. This is an inevitable result of the fact that (again with the same exception already mentioned) epistemic justification is path-dependent. This means that what is rational for one person to accept (given his situation and history) it may well be rational for another person to reject (given his situation and history). It follows that whether or not they have knowledge depends, for both of them, on the luck of their situation. There is no reason to think that this path-dependence can be overcome by everyone occupying the same starting-point. There are good reasons to think that it is not possible for everyone to occupy the same starting-point (this would involve e.g. time travel, changes in perceptual organs, as well as complete change of culture). There are also good reasons to think that there is no starting-point such that those who can occupy it can know everything that can be known. If some knowledge is parochial then that possibility is ruled out. If people must diverge in their epistemic baggage then path-dependence is a necessary feature of human existence, one which cannot be overcome under any conditions, however ideal. There is therefore no reason to make submission to a luckfree ideal test a condition of objectivity.

(e) Epistemic Anxieties and the Long Route

I suggested that domains of thought are objective if they meet conditions like the possibility of error, the relevance condition, the possibility of irrationality, the independence condition, and the single reality condition. The list can be extended indefinitely. The method of 'the long route' consists in tracing various truisms associated with the logic of truth and knowledge. We seek them out as the need arises, that is, as we encounter questions and doubts which they help to answer.

I raised a doubt about this method, namely that it is 'too exclusively internal'. We can agree that whatever meets its conditions is *thought by us* to be objective, but is it necessarily so in reality? The thought that this method is 'too internal' is the thought that there are, or at least that there could be, preconditions for anything being capable of being true or false which are due to how things are, and are not reflected in the logic of our concepts.

The quest for ideal convergence, or for the testing of parochial concepts by non-parochial ones, which are available to all, are manifestations of the same anxiety. They are attempts to break out of the inner and to connect with how things really are in the world. They do so by claiming that knowledge must be anchored in the universal, in those concepts which all can have, and those claims of knowledge round which all competent inquirers will converge in ideal conditions. By replying that the worry is illusory, that by exploring the preconditions of our concepts of knowledge and truth we are willy-nilly exploring features of reality, I was navigating a middle course. On the one hand is the Scylla of denying that the nature of reality, knowledge, truth, and objectivity is just what is revealed through use of the concepts we happen to have of them, and requiring some absolute test, satisfaction of which by a concept or a principle guarantees that they reach to reality 'as it really is'.[43] Against this is the Charybdis which denies that we can ever have any concepts of reality, knowledge, or truth different from those we happen to have, or that the nature of reality or knowledge can be different from what these concepts (our concepts of them) reveal. Our concepts are what we measure by. A thought which is not a thought (i.e. does not conform to our concept of a thought) is not a thought. Knowledge which is not knowledge (i.e. not an instance of our concept of knowledge) is not knowledge.

The middle road allows that our concepts can be subjected to rational

---

[43] It may be worth noting that the rejection of this option is not just an endorsement of the 'Neurath's boat' understanding of the pursuit of knowledge. Those who accept that we must start from here, i.e. from the beliefs we happen to have, can be wedded to an ideal convergence test or some other test of the kind here rejected.

evaluation, which may lead to revision. But it denies that the evaluation is in the light of any absolute test, like the tests of convergence. We judge our concepts in light of our concepts and beliefs. While it is necessary that in general they will be vindicated, some of them, some aspects of even the most basic of them, may turn out to be incoherent or unsustainable, given whatever else we know. If we are lucky we improve our understanding of reality, and of knowledge. But we do not do so by satisfying one or several master tests. Similarly some of our epistemic procedures may be misguided. What is taken to be good or adequate evidence for a class of conclusions may turn out to be inadequate. Considerations taken to be good reasons for certain positions may be irrelevant, or confused, or just insufficient to justify them.

The history of the practice of science provides examples of how epistemic standards change, often in the light of rational reflection and criticism, but without any master test which is held constant and governs the changes. Various people have suspected that concepts such as the divine, the supernatural, time travel, miracle, action at a distance, beauty, are not all that they seem to be. Arguments have been put forward to show that their use has to be abandoned because they are incoherent, or that they have to be reformed in some fundamental ways.

If that is so then even the necessary features of our concepts of objectivity and knowledge may stand in need of revision and can be revised through reasoning which follows the long route. To deny that is to assume that while the use of these concepts can reveal difficulties with concepts like 'beauty', that pressure is one-sided: our concept of 'beauty' comes under pressure for being in tension with the presuppositions of knowledge, but our concept of knowledge is not under pressure for being in conflict with necessary features of 'beauty'. But there is no reason to think that. So long as we remain holistic in our approach to the clarification of the structures of thought the possibility of a need to revise our notions of knowledge and truth remains.[44] I am not saying that they need revising, only that it is possible that they do.

To acknowledge this possibility is to acknowledge the possibility that there are preconditions for anything being true or false, or capable of being known, which are not reflected in our concepts, that is, our concepts as they are. Therefore, the long route is not 'purely internal' and self-vindicating. I conclude that it may be that the long route is all we need. As doubts about the objectivity of this or that domain arise we inquire and—if successful—

[44] Perhaps it is helpful to warn here that this reference to a holistic approach is not an endorsement of an epistemic approach based on coherence in any shape or form. I have explained some of the reasons for this in *Ethics in the Public Domain* (rev. edn. 1995), essay 13: 'The Relevance of Coherence'.

we establish conditions which settle the issue one way or another. In other words we need a focus for an inquiry. The focus establishes which results might be relevant and helpful. There is no way of producing an exhaustive list of such conditions, for we can never anticipate all the doubts which can arise concerning the objectivity of this or that domain. Put another way: there is no interesting comprehensive theory of objectivity. But there can be fruitful inquiries into the objectivity of one area or another when specific doubts arise regarding their status.

3. THE ILLUSION OF THE AUTHORITY OF THE SOCIAL

(a) Thick Concepts and the Social Connection

In elaborating on his absolute conception Williams adds another condition to those mentioned so far. It is set out in the words I italicize below: 'If knowledge is what it claims to be, then it is knowledge of a reality which exists independently of that knowledge, *and indeed (except for the special case where the reality known happens itself to be some psychological item) independently of any thought or experience.* Knowledge is of what is there anyway.'[45] So far as I know Williams does not develop this extension of his idea, but in one form or another it is a common condition in many discussions of realism. It is often set out in its strong form: knowledge must be of what is there anyway, independently not only of the thoughts and experiences of the agent, but of any thought or experience of anyone. This condition would rule out the possibility of knowledge of many properties of artefacts and of many socially constituted persons (organizations, cities, etc.), facts, and events.

Think of an existing chess club,[46] with its rules and customs. They are not merely created through acts involving thoughts and experiences, they are also maintained in existence through the continued intentions of the club's members to carry on with their participation in the club. To be sure, some people would want to say that such clubs or their rules and customs do not form a part of what is really real. But if they are right there must be other reasons for that view. It does not follow from the idea that knowledge is of what is there anyway.

Williams's condition fares no better if it is narrowed down to saying that knowledge must be of a reality which exists independently of any thoughts or beliefs about its existence. The example of the chess club refutes this

---

[45] Williams, *Descartes*, 64.
[46] I am assuming a club which is not legally incorporated.

condition as well since the existence of the club depends on some people believing (or having believed) that it exists.

Objects of knowledge can sometimes even depend on the agent's own prior thoughts and experiences. The motivation for the condition of independence, namely that knowledge is of what is there anyway, does not justify the blanket exclusion of all cases of this kind. For example, yesterday the chairperson of the chess club may have passed a regulation binding on the club. Its existence and content depend on his intentions in passing it. They also depend on his beliefs about what he was doing, that is, his belief that he is making a rule for the club. There is nothing in that to disqualify him from having knowledge of the existence or content of rules he made, any more than there is reason to deny that other people can have that knowledge. Moreover, his knowledge of the regulation is not knowledge of his own thoughts and intentions. It is knowledge of a rule of the club. Nor need it derive from his memory of his own thoughts. He may have forgotten that it is his regulation, and learn about it from colleagues. He, like anyone else, can have knowledge of the regulations of the club. The underlying rationale of the independence condition does not warrant Williams's claim that if knowledge is to be of what is there anyway it must be independent of what is there in virtue of people's or the agent's own thoughts and experiences. The objectivity of no domain of thought depends on this condition.

But is not that conclusion premature? It may be thought that, while in general views and thoughts about matters whose existence depends on psychological or social facts are objective, there is a special case against the objectivity of evaluative thought arising out of its possible dependence on social facts. If it turns out—it may be argued—that if value propositions are capable of being true or false then their truth value depends on social facts then normative or evaluative thought cannot be objective.

This particular objection to the objectivity of practical thought concentrates on what I called the relevance condition. Practical thought appears to meet the other conditions we canvassed. The real doubt about its objectivity is: does it meet the relevance condition? Are there grounds which are not merely persuasive, but logically relevant to the confirmation or disconfirmation of any practical thought? The most promising attempt to provide an affirmative answer relies on the use of thick concepts. But thick concepts seem to depend on a shared culture with its shared acceptance of various values. Hence it seems that the thick-concept solution to the problem of the relevance condition makes the truth of evaluative propositions depend on the social facts of shared views. This is where the objection is directed: if it turns out that, if practical propositions are true or false they are so in virtue of social facts, then they are not capable of being either true or false.

The objection is a serious one. Thick concepts are indeed crucial to any attempt to establish the objectivity of practical thought, and its conformity with the relevance condition. Consider the sort of reasons people give in support of such propositions. Simon should be respected because he acted with great dignity. Sarah deserves promotion for she solved a complicated problem with subtlety and ingenuity. Robin acted well; he kept his head under pressure, and showed cool judgement and discrimination in handling his boss. This is a great film: it is easy to understand without being trivial, and it combines humour and wisdom. Typically, just about all our evaluative reasoning is saturated with thick concepts of a variety of kinds. Both conclusions and reasons for them are typically expressed by the use of thick evaluative concepts. An account of the relevant reasons which support or undermine evaluative or normative propositions will largely consist in an explanation of the relations between thick concepts. But, and that is where the objection starts, mastery of thick concepts depends on shared understandings and shared judgements. These shared judgements both enable us to understand the meaning of thick evaluative terms, *and incline us to accept the legitimacy of their use.* There is no independent way of validating the legitimacy of the use of thick concepts. Hence, the validity of evaluative propositions, if it depends on thick concepts, depends on shared understandings and judgements, that is, on social facts. The truth or correctness of value propositions cannot, however, depend on social facts. Such dependence will make value judgements contingent, for the facts they depend on are contingent, and arbitrary—whether or not one has cogent reasons to accept them will depend on the evaluatively arbitrary fact of one's membership in one culture or another. Worst of all, if the truth conditions of evaluative propositions are contingent social facts then they cannot be normative, they are merely statements of those facts whose existence renders them true.

Since the normative cannot depend on social facts it cannot depend on thick concepts and, given the absence of any other plausible account of the way practical thought meets the relevance condition, we must conclude that it lacks objectivity.

(b) Types of Social Dependence

To evaluate the objection we need to investigate the ways, if any, in which value judgements depend on shared understandings and judgements. This requires relying on assumptions which cannot be explored here. The observations that follow will, therefore, be tentative, and subject to much further clarification and further supporting arguments.[47] I will be relying on one crucial distinction, the distinction between practices which create or sustain the existence of goods and values, and practices which are conditions for access to such goods or values. On the one hand, it is possible that values and goods are created or maintained in existence by social practices, and the shared beliefs and understandings which are part of them. I will call practices which bring into existence goods or values, or sustain them in existence, sustaining practices. On the other hand, it is possible that shared understandings affect not the existence of values and goods, but our ability to learn of them, and perhaps to benefit from them. Such practices control access to the values and goods concerned. Quite likely the social dependence of values and goods takes many and varied forms. I will briefly delineate four fairly typical types of case, starting with the closest to dependence of value on practice.

(i) 'Socially Created' Goods: Local Goods

The existence of some goods seems to be clearly socially dependent. It used to be important for young women, of a certain class, to walk only with short and measured steps, or for men to wear wigs when outside their homes. There were social advantages to behaving in accordance with conventions of manners, and disadvantages attached to flouting them. Conventions of manner, fashion, and deportment vary over time and space. A particular form of manner or dress can lose the meaning it has and acquire a different, even contradictory, meaning. It can have different, even mutually exclusive meanings in different places at the same time. Moreover, within a single country it can have one meaning in one subculture, and another, even incompatible meaning, in another subculture. In the same place and at the same time, what earns kudos in one class may earn the disrespect of another, etc.

In matters of fashion and manners what is valuable depends on what people do, that is, on conventional conduct, but also on shared attitudes and reactions, on a shared meaning associated with different modes of conduct, deportment, or dress. The dependence is multifaceted. There is

---

[47] They will also be crude in not drawing some elementary distinctions. I will refer to goods, values, valuables, norms, considerations which determine that an action is right or wrong, etc. without trying to distinguish between them. For present purposes such distinctions are immaterial. Furthermore, I will use examples, implying that they are examples of genuine goods, or values. Their purpose is to illustrate abstract general points. It is not my suggestion that everything which is endorsed by a local culture is good for that reason, and the examples can be substituted with others by those who doubt their credentials. Finally, I will consider only beliefs about intrinsic goods, and will avoid any reference to instrumental goods.

more than one value to be realized. In matters of fashion, for example, there are the values, say, of being at the cutting edge of advanced fashion, of keeping up with new fashions, of merging in the crowd, of being thoroughly conventional and non-distinctive, of being charmingly old-fashioned, of emphatically asserting one's indifference to fashion, of being assertively non-conventional, and many more. When we come to manners the number of different meanings different modes of conduct and address can display is much greater.

The practices and shared meanings of a society determine not only the benchmark of the normal, relative to which the conventional, defiant, cutting edge, etc. are defined. They also determine which meanings or values (e.g. that of conventionality, defiance, cutting edge) exist relative to the benchmark. Some cultures multiply meanings which turn on subtle distinctions. In others only a few distinctions determine different meanings. In some societies meanings are fixed and rigid, attached to easily identifiable external cues, in others they are more flexible, more complex in manifestation, allowing for more individual variations, and for easier mutation over time.

(ii) 'Socially Created Goods': The Temporally Unbound Variety

The type of good or social meaning I have in mind here may differ from local goods in degree only, but a difference there is. Take a game, for example chess, with the goods which playing it makes possible (being good at chess, being a good chess tactician, ingenious at the endgame, etc.). Chess was created at a particular time. It makes no sense to think of it as having existed from the creation of the world and only discovered at a certain time. It was invented, created, and developed, not discovered. So it too is socially created or socially constituted and like all socially created goods and meanings it has an origin in time, and its existence is contingent rather than necessary. It could have not been invented. But in one respect chess is unlike manners. Once invented it is with us forever. Of course it can be forgotten. Times may come when no one will know what chess is, no one will know how to play it. Some games which used to be played by people during the flowering of Maya civilization in the Yucatan, for example, are lost to us. But that is mere loss of knowledge, loss of access to a good. We can rediscover how to play these games. There is a sense in which once the game is invented it remains in existence for ever, or at least for as long as it is logically possible for it to be (if lost) rediscovered.[48]

---

[48] It is true that chess may be forgotten and then reinvented, rather than rediscovered. That would be the case if its re-emergence were independent of knowledge of its previous existence. But this seems to be consistent with my claim: so long as it can be rediscovered there is something to rediscover.

Many other goods belong to this kind. Think of New York Jewish humour. Enjoying it, being good at telling good New York Jewish jokes and witticisms, or being able to display that sense of humour in one's conversation is valuable and admirable. Like chess, New York Jewish humour and other goods of this kind are generated by a particular culture and did not exist beforehand. This sense of humour developed and emerged during a particular period in the history of New York. It did not exist as a timeless form of humour to be discovered by New York Jews in the nineteenth or twentieth century. Like all socially constituted goods New York Jewish humour enjoys a contingent existence. It might have not come into existence. But, unlike fashion and like chess, once it has been developed it remains in existence forever (or for as long as it can be—should it be lost—rediscovered). It is quite likely that times will come when people will not understand this form of humour. It is also likely that a time will come when there will be no one around capable of understanding it. But these are contingent facts, which do not limit the possibility that it will be rediscovered. What goes for New York Jewish humour goes for classical ballet, the novel, opera, and a large number of other goods which are culturally constituted in similar ways.

Wherein lies the difference between the two categories of socially created goods? In the possibility of enjoying them outside the cultures which bred and sustained them. Suppose you discover a game which has long been forgotten, or a form of music no longer practised in your culture. It is in principle possible to discover what they were, to come to understand them and the cultures which sustained them. That would involve understanding what was good in them. Once one understands those goods one can enjoy them, one can engage in them in the right way, bringing one the intrinsic benefits which they brought people in the cultures where they were practised. Naturally this requires further conditions, one needs to be good at games, have willing partners to play with, be musical, etc. But in principle those goods, though created and practised in one culture, can be enjoyed by people in other cultures, even by individuals who live in cultures where the game or form of music did not take root. Not so with regard to local goods. While we can learn and appreciate the fashions or manners of previous times, or far-away places, we cannot enjoy their benefits unless they become the fashions and manners of our society.[49]

---

[49] Two qualifications do not erode the contrast I draw in the text. First, there are 'deviant' ways of enjoying local goods in alien cultures: it could e.g. mark one as an eccentric. Similarly, there is usually a whole network of meaning associated with all goods—socially constituted or not—which is lost when they are moved from one context to another. Playing chess in 17th-cent. Paris invokes different meanings than playing in Washington Sq. in New York today.

(iii) Goods which are Not Socially Created[50] with Limited, Culturally Conditioned Accessibility

Sunsets are not constituted by social practices and shared meanings, nor are beautiful sunsets, nor the beauty of beautiful sunsets. There were beautiful sunsets on earth at least since its atmosphere acquired its present constitution. There probably were beautiful sunsets before the emergence of animal life on the earth. It is possible, however, that there were periods when people did not enjoy beautiful sunsets, and did not find them attractive in any aesthetic way at all. It is also likely that after people developed an aesthetic response to natural phenomena they differed in what they found valuable in nature, and in the values they found in what was valuable. Possibly there are psychological universals which determine a degree of similarity in sensitivity across cultures. But perusal of works of art suggests that, whatever the similarities, the differences in aesthetic responses to, and appreciation of, nature among cultures are considerable. Moreover, the responses to, and appreciation of, the same natural phenomenon (e.g. sunsets) may be incompatible, in that no person can appreciate all aspects of the beauty of a sunset at the same time, without being ambivalent about the phenomena he is reacting to. For example, the beauty of the sea, the same sea in the same conditions, can be perceived as due to its tranquil and harmonious character by a holiday-maker on an afternoon walk, and due to its hidden awesome power by a fisherman who knows its fickleness.

It is possible that the sea has all these qualities. This is easy to explain if these are relational qualities, for example. If anything is beautiful if and only if it looks beautiful, beauty is a property of appearance, a matter of how things appear. The appearance of things is an objective matter about which mistakes can be made.[51] One may, for example, mistakenly think that a good-looking person is rather plain. Yet some properties of the appearance of things are relational or confined to certain circumstances: some may relate to how they appear in daytime, and others to their nocturnal appearance, etc.

Objective though they are, not everyone can perceive the way things appear. To be capable of perceiving the appearance of things one may need to be acculturated in suitable ways. Let us think of the values which became prevalent with the Romantic Movement in the eighteenth century. We can understand them and relate to them, as we are the children of the Romantic Movement. They are easier to appreciate for some than for

---

[50] I will call any good, norm, or value which is not socially constituted 'universal', even though it may not be strictly universal, as its existence may be conditioned by other factors.

[51] See generally, P. M. S. Hacker, *Appearance and Reality* (Oxford: Blackwell, 1987).

others, and perhaps no one can appreciate all of them any more. But since Romanticism they have become in principle available to people. Romanticism made forms of appreciation of nature possible which were not possible before. But Romanticism no more changed nature, or the appearance of nature, by creating new valuable features in it than the development of humans or other animals with colour vision added colour to objects in the world. Red is not made red by the existence of people who can perceive it as red, and beautiful sunsets are not made beautiful by the existence of people who can appreciate their beauty. Culture does not create the beauty of nature. It merely enables us to become aware of it, to come to understand and enjoy it.

(iv) Goods with Universal, Culturally Conditioned Access

Some goods may be even more independent of social practices: not only are they not created by social practices, access to them is not restricted by social practices either. Even though sunsets are not man-made, nor is their beauty, the appreciation of their beauty is made possible by culture. One may feel that they are as local and time-bound as all the socially created goods briefly discussed above. Whether culture determines access rather than existence can be felt to be of little significance. What matters is accessibility. Consider the relation of value to personhood. Persons are rational beings, that is, they possess the ability to perceive that some things are good or bad in various ways, and to respond appropriately. They should find out enough about value to enable them to conduct themselves sensibly. They bear responsibility to find out enough about value, but that responsibility is limited by accessibility. They cannot come to appreciate normative aspects of the world which are not accessible to them. Three points seem to bear this out:

1. People cannot be blamed for not being guided by values they could not know about.

2. People's conduct cannot be morally wrong for disregarding or violating values or rules which they could not in principle know.

3. It is, of course, possible that lack of access to values will impoverish a person's life, and will render it less rich and admirable, etc. than it could have been had that person the ability in principle to understand and engage in more valuable activities. Similarly, lack of access to values may coarsen a person's character.

Access to a value, rather than its existence, is decisive in evaluations which presuppose responsibility, be they evaluations of people's actions, life, or character. Furthermore, for evaluations of life and character which do not presuppose responsibility, evaluations of them as limited, or coarse, or rich and refined, it does not matter whether the absence of a good from a person's life was due its non-existence or to its inaccessibility. Either way, the absence of the good from a person's life may be coarsening or impoverishing. These observations would justify the view that, as regards the kinds of values and goods considered so far, there is no significant normative difference between socially created values and those which are not so created, but whose accessibility is socially dependent. If this is all there is to say on the subject then a fairly strong form of social relativism might be vindicated. Are there any normative considerations which are universally accessible, that is, which are within the reach of all people, of whatever time or place, at least in principle?

A full answer to the question is beyond the scope of the present discussion.[52] For our purposes suffice it to say that one objection to the possibility of universally accessible normative considerations is mistaken. Consider the sort of normative considerations often advanced as universal and timeless. For example: it is always wrong to murder an innocent person.[53] If we can judge people to have acted wrongly in having committed murder we must assume that it was possible for them to know that they should not perform the actions which are the murder of innocent people. But we need not assume that they must have been able to understand the concept 'murder', 'person', 'innocent', 'intention', and 'killing', which we use to articulate and explain this rule. Arguably, even before these concepts were available to people they had other ways of categorizing mental states, other ways of marking transgressions, other ways of marking animals which as we now known belong to the species *Homo sapiens*. Their concepts and generalizations may have been based on false beliefs, and we may find them inadequate in many ways. But they may have enabled them to know that the acts which in fact constitute murder of innocent people are wrong. That is enough to establish that they had the access to the norm which is a precondition of being able to blame them for its violation. If people at all times had access to the norms, in one form or another, then we have here an example of a consideration, to which there is universal access, though that access is culturally determined.

---

[52] See my discussion of the universality of value in 'Moral Change and Social Relativism', in E. F. Paul, F. D. Miller, and J. Paul (eds.), *Cultural Pluralism and Moral Knowledge* (Cambridge: CUP, 1994) which is Ch. 7 below. Among other things I discuss there the possibility of applying judgements which presuppose responsibility, to people, their life, character, or actions, by values which were not created until a later time. In the present discussion I ignore that possibility.

[53] I present a simplified and inaccurate norm, to avoid complicated substantive moral issues.

(c) Social Dependence and Objectivity

What conclusions regarding the objectivity of value can be drawn from this fourfold classification, assuming that it is basically sound? First, we need to distinguish the social dependence of values from the social dependence of access to them. Second, while all but the most abstract values, goods, and other normative considerations are referred to by the use of thick terms, only some of them are socially created.

My observations at the beginning of Part 3 showed that social dependence does not necessarily pose a threat to objectivity. I believe that most people worry less about the objectivity of local goods, as I called them, than about the objectivity of socially created goods which are not local, or those which are not socially created at all. The doubt about the objectivity of value does not arise from the contingency of the social on which all value allegedly depends, but from the suspicion that, since knowledge of what is valuable depends on mastery of 'thick' concepts, it is suspect.

One additional source of suspicion that values which are socially constructed cannot be objective should be mentioned. It is sometimes assumed that if some good or value is socially created and sustained then the reason for its being good is that it is accepted as good, that people think that it is good, or variants on these. This is not so at all. Consider chess: neither the reasons for making one move rather than another in the course of the game, nor the reasons for playing the game, involve any appeal to the social practice which created the game. Similarly, we can give reasons for thinking one joke better than another, or one piano sonata better than another, but they will not and should not include an appeal to the fact that these goods are socially created. A joke is good because it is funny, because it has more than one sting, because it takes the mickey out of the pompous, who deserve the treatment, because it points out human foibles, etc. A piano sonata is good because it is full of musical ideas, ingenious variations, suspense and surprise, tension and its resolution, because it mixes moods, and speaks to the emotions, etc. The fact that a good is socially constituted is no more reason for its value than the fact that a chair is a product of human design is a reason for thinking it a good chair. The same goes for all artefacts, and for all socially constituted goods (see the qualification in the next paragraph). It must be so, for otherwise it would not be possible to distinguish good social creations, or artefacts, from bad ones.

It is true that practices and shared beliefs are (part of the) means by which we identify goods which are socially created or maintained. But identifying what is the good is not the same as explaining what it is which makes it good, or why it is good rather than bad.

Local goods may be thought to be a special case since they tend to be conventional goods. That is why some feel less suspicious of them. They feel that we understand the nature of conventions. After all they have received the seal of approval of game theory. Moreover, it may be thought that with conventional goods the explanation for what is good about this mode of conduct, or dress, etc. is clear: it is good because that is how people generally behave, how they dress, etc. This is, however, at best only part of the explanation.[54] The rest has to account for the reason for conforming to the conventional norm. We understand conventions only when we understand the good they are thought to achieve, and whether they in fact lead to good or ill.

The values served by conventional goods explain what, if anything, is good in the conventions, and enable us to distinguish between good and bad conventions. I emphasize this point for it shows that the explanation of the goodness of any good or valuable thing or option has to be relatively independent of the social practices which create that good. Only thus can we acknowledge that social conditions can also lead to bad practices, which will be mistakenly taken by their participants as good ones. In 'Moral Change and Social Relativism'[55] I suggested a different argument to the same effect, namely that the inherent intelligibility of values means that they have to be somewhat independent of social practices. The two arguments are two aspects of the same thought.

These arguments do not show that normative properties are not socially created. They show that they are not all conventional, and that their normative nature must be explained normatively, and cannot be explained in non-normative terms. But there can be social practices or other social phenomena which can only be identified in normative terms, and such social practices can be said to give rise to new normative properties consistently with the arguments above. We learn that not all goods are socially created, not from the argument above but by examining the nature of the various goods (as was sketched in the previous section). The preceding argument is meant to show that, even if all goods are socially created (and they are not), it does not follow that the explanation of why they are good, what makes them good, consists in an appeal to the fact that the relevant social practices exist. They must consist in pointing to good-making properties of the social practices concerned.

These remarks may lead to the opposite objection, namely that socially

---

[54] At best for, as was noted in discussing local goods, typically a single conventional standard provides an opportunity for a variety of goods, some of which depend not on conformity but on deviation from it (e.g. the good of being an unconventional person, or one with strong individual tastes).

[55] In Ch. 7 below.

created goods are not socially created at all. The goods involved in them are timeless, only the way they are realized is local. But while that may be true of some instances it is not generally true. For example, observing rules of polite behaviour tends to make one feel comfortable in social situations and facilitates interaction with others. That good is neither conventional, nor socially created. It is timeless. But to say this is to abstract from the differences between different societies and different codes of good behaviour. The abstract value of facilitating interactions may be the correct value to apply to the situation, yet it leaves out information which only a concrete and localized description of the good of polite behaviour in one or another social setting can convey. Concrete socially created values must be subsumed under abstract universal values, or they will be unintelligible. But they are no 'mere' instantiations of universal values. They are distinctive specific goods, which can be enjoyed only if created by social practices.[56]

(d) Objectivity and Thick Concepts

Can the objectivity of 'thick' concepts be defended? Suspicion of their use can now be seen to be independent of any doubts arising from the alleged social dependence of all value. But suspect they remain. I have already dismissed some of these suspicions. It is true that what we believe may well depend on which evaluative concepts we became familiar with first, and which evaluative beliefs we acquired first. That is a result of the path-dependence of epistemic justification, a feature of epistemic justification in all fields of knowledge. Furthermore, it is true that there is no hope of a Peirceian convergence regarding evaluative beliefs. There is no reason to think that there is a meaningful ideal situation in which the views of all competent believers will converge. Yet again, we saw reason to doubt the cogency of the requirement of such convergence as a precondition of the possibility of knowledge. Both these observations mean that there is an inevitable contingency not only about our evaluative beliefs, but also in the account of their epistemic justification. What we know and what we do not know is partly a matter of the accident of our circumstances, and even the best epistemic justification possible cannot rid our beliefs of an element of luck. But epistemic luck is a feature of the conditions of knowledge in general. It is not a circumstance special to evaluative beliefs, and it does not negate the possibility of knowledge.

There remains, however, another, though related, source of doubt about

---

[56] I have argued this and some other points made in the current section and the next one in 'Moral Change and Social Relativism'.

the objectivity of evaluative beliefs, if that objectivity depends on deploying 'thick' concepts. There is the familiar charge that the thick concepts of different cultures, or of different moral or religious outlooks, are incommensurate. Concepts which belong to one of these systems of thought cannot be explained in terms of concepts belonging to another. These thick concepts, the argument proceeds, are essential for the expression of the systems of thought to which they belong. The views of each system cannot, therefore, be expressed or explained using the concepts of another system. This leads the objector to the conclusion that, even when one can be confident that one's evaluative beliefs are justified from within one's own system of thought, one has to acknowledge that that is only a relative justification. Incompatible beliefs enjoy equally cogent justification within other systems of thought. Furthermore, the arguments refuting the other system of thought as a whole to one's own satisfaction are themselves relative to one's own system of thought. The rival system is not only impregnable in its own terms, but quite likely contains within itself cogent arguments refuting one's own system of thought.

According to the objector it follows that there is no rational way to adjudicate between different systems of thought.[57] This would seem inconsistent with the objectivity of evaluative thought. For, the objector points out, many conflicting evaluative thoughts have equal credentials. Therefore, none of them can be correct or true. The argument is not merely that they cannot be known to be correct or true. That would have been the case had there been non-relational grounds establishing one rather than the other which people cannot, not even in principle, come to know.[58] But, according to the objector's argument, the failure is not of ability to know. There are no such grounds, therefore there is nothing to know.

Much has been written about the coherence of the incommensurability claim which underlies the objection. I will put such doubts to one side. The objection is also vulnerable on other grounds. It relies heavily on the inability to explain the concepts of one culture, or system of thought, using those of another. But how important is this limitation? The argument is often discussed as revolving not around the relations between concepts belong-

---

[57] My formulation of the objection is not meant to capture the precise argument of any writer, though it borrows from points advanced by a number of philosophers. For example, some aspects of such a view were elaborated by A. MacIntyre in *Three Rival Versions of Moral Inquiry* (London: Duckworth, 1990). Davidson's 'On the Very Idea of a Conceptual Scheme', in his *Truth and Interpretation* (Oxford: Oxford University Press, 1984), is the best known attempt to refute such views. But see Hacker, 'On Davidson's Idea of a Conceptual Scheme', *Philosophical Quarterly*, 46 (1996), 289.

[58] The argument presupposes, correctly, that evaluative beliefs are not about brute facts. What value things have is an intelligible matter. Necessarily if something has a value in one way or another then there are reasons which explain this fact.

ing to two different systems of thought, but around the relation between the meanings of terms in two languages. In the development of languages, however, new terms are often added whose meaning cannot be precisely explained using the other terms of the language. We learn their meaning in part through use, and by ostension, and only in part by locating their meaning relative to that of other words.[59] We do the same when we encounter concepts in a foreign culture. Words are added to our language, often borrowed from the other language, whose meaning is learnt not exclusively through explanation, but by ostension, and through habituation to aspects of the alien culture which they signify.

There is little doubt that often we fail to understand concepts embedded in a culture or system of thought which is alien to us. But is there any reason to think that even given favourable conditions we could not master them? That they cannot be exhaustively or satisfactorily explained using our concepts does not establish that conclusion, for we can learn them directly, by being exposed to their use, rather than through translation. Sometimes we could do so by actually living in the alien society, at other times it is possible to learn their meaning by learning about that society and reconstructing in imagination, or simulation, its ways and beliefs.

To claim that members of one culture cannot in any way come to understand the concepts of another amounts to the implausible claim that people have the capacity to acquire the concepts of one culture only. Once they have done so their conceptual capacity is exhausted or perhaps blocked. This seems an implausible supposition.

I can think of only one possible reason for it. Complete understanding of a concept—and it is important to remember that understanding is a matter of degree—involves knowing its relations with all the concepts one understands. Take, for example, the relation 'being incompatible with'. One does not understand what it is to be blue if one does not know that it excludes being red, nor what it is to be just if one does not know that it excludes being unfair. It follows that in a way the more concepts one has already acquired the more difficult it is for one to acquire new ones, for one would have to understand whether they are or are not compatible with those one has already mastered. Could it not therefore be the case that for this reason those who have mastered the concepts of our culture cannot understand those of ancient alien civilizations? Our inability to understand their

---

[59] The *Oxford English Dictionary* defines 'nerd' as 'An insignificant or contemptible person, one who is conventional, affected, or studious; a "square", a "swot".' Surely this misses out a lot which is essential to the understanding of the term in contemporary, especially American culture. The *OED* instances the following (from an ad in the New York Times, 1978): 'The nerdiest nerds on TV are really smart cookies.' This is made mysterious rather than explained by their definition.

concepts is no sign of reduced mental ability. Rather, to understand their concepts we have to know the degree to which they are compatible with ours. Members of those ancient civilizations themselves did not have that knowledge. Since they did not know our concepts they did not have to know how our concepts relate to theirs in order to understand theirs. We do, and this is why we cannot understand their concepts.

At this point the argument that systems of thought are incommensurate because their concepts are not mutually translatable has been abandoned in favour of the assertion that systems of thought are incommensurate, because no one can master the concepts of more than one of them. The new contention is, however, implausible. It flies in the face of the evidence. There were and are people who inhabited more than one culture, and understood both. It also overlooks the fact that our own culture contains concepts derived from different systems of thought, which have not merged together. While some of us do not have use for concepts such as grace, sacred, blessed, prayer, and others, for the most part we manage to understand them, when we try. Finally, the conclusion exaggerates the conceptual insularity of different cultures. To be sure there are many culture-specific concepts, concepts which evolved in one culture and have no parallels in others. But they are embedded in a conceptual framework which includes many concepts bridging the cultural gap, or which have at least near relatives in other cultures. It seems safe to dismiss the thesis than no person can master concepts of more than one culture, and with it the thesis that there are past or present cultures whose concepts cannot in principle be understood by us.[60]

It may be worth pointing out that the considerations I have advanced here are consistent with the view expressed in Part 2 about the essentially local character of evaluative concepts, or of many of them, and of the non-existence of a Peirceian ideal condition from which everything can be known. There I was arguing that it is impossible, even if only because of the impossibility of knowing the future, for anyone to master all the evaluative concepts. Here, I have argued that there is no general reason to think that no one can come to know and understand more than one of the existing systems of thought. This conclusion can be reinforced to the effect that no past or present human culture and its concepts are beyond the comprehension of people for whom it is an alien culture. There are no human cultural islands which cannot be understood by anyone other than their members.

At this point one may be tempted to resuscitate the challenge to the

---

[60] This remark is confined to cultures of creatures who share our perceptual capacities, and emotional make-up.

objectivity of evaluative thought, while abandoning the conceptual incommensurability thesis. One may argue that (1) all justification is internal to a system of thought, and that (2) there is no way of adjudicating between beliefs belonging to different systems of thought, and since (3) some beliefs belonging to different systems of thought are incompatible and cannot both be true, on pain of contradiction, it follows that no beliefs are true. As before this argument presupposes (i) that evaluative beliefs are true only if there are reasons which explain how it is that they are true, and (ii) that evaluative reasons are in principle available to people, though not necessarily to everyone. For reasons we cannot explore here these seem reasonable assumptions.

This challenge to the objectivity of evaluative thought is ill founded. It is true that all justifications are relative: they are all addressed to an actual or potential audience, addressing the doubts of *that* audience, and relying on what *that* audience accepts. The relativity of justifications is itself a result both of the parochial character of (many) evaluative concepts, and of the path-dependence of epistemic justifications. So long as all the different justifications are consistent, that relativity does not undermine the objectivity of evaluative thought. Nor does it follow from the relativity of justification that there is no way of adjudicating between incompatible thoughts or beliefs.

More generally I suspect that not infrequently the sense that incompatible evaluative propositions have equal credentials and therefore neither can be true results from a failure to distinguish two types of incompatibility. Two evaluative propositions can be (1) inconsistent with each other, or they can (2) express values, virtues, or ideals which cannot be all realized in the life of a single person. The second kind of incompatibility does not undermine the objectivity of evaluative thought. It merely leads to value pluralism.

The first kind of incompatibility is relevant to the debate on objectivity. Given the two presuppositions I accepted it must be the case that only one of two inconsistent propositions can be adequately supported by reasons. But we have to distinguish epistemic from constitutive reasons (though they may overlap). Two people can have adequate epistemic reasons for accepting each of two inconsistent propositions. These could be as banal as that different people, whose judgement they have good reason to trust but whose beliefs are inconsistent with each other, have advised them. Even constitutive reasons can conflict as there may be something to be said for both sides of an evaluative dispute (constitutive reasons are often prima facie). But evaluative propositions and their negations cannot both enjoy adequate or completely vindicatory support by reason. None of the considerations I have canvassed in this chapter suggest that inconsistent evaluative propositions do enjoy adequate or vindicatory support by reasons.

This has been a long and mostly negative discussion. There may be reasons for rejecting the objectivity of evaluative thought. I offered various considerations to show that many arguments offered as justifying such rejection do not succeed in doing so. The constructive contribution of my arguments is in showing how doubts about objectivity can arise out of a misunderstanding of objectivity and of justification. If you set us an unachievable target you will be able to show that we fail to achieve it. It is instructive to see how we were victims of an over-demanding and over-rigid conception of justification and objectivity. But the misguided allure of these 'high ideals' is not confined to evaluative thought. Those who succumb to them are entrapped by confusions in other areas of thought as well.

7

Moral Change and Social Relativism

1. THE STRUCTURE OF THE ARGUMENT

(a) Multiculturalism, Moral Knowledge, and Relativism

I could not write the essay I hoped to write. I hoped to write about cultural pluralism and moral epistemology by assuming that the first is the case and exploring what implications this may have for the second. But I soon realized that I do not know what cultural pluralism is. I do not mean that I have just belatedly discovered that the phrase 'cultural pluralism' is used in different ways on different occasions. I mean that I realized that I myself did not know in what sense the phrase may be used which makes it relevant to the inquiry suggested by the general topic of this volume. So the following reflections are based on one assumption: *the fact of multiculturalism cannot have much bearing on moral epistemology unless it bears on moral truths.*

One can, for example, imagine that membership in a cultural group is either essential or helpful to knowledge of certain moral matters. If so, then multiculturalism creates a rupture in moral knowledge in multicultural societies, with members of different cultural groups having partial moral knowledge, some of it never, or much less frequently, reached by members of other groups.

That something like this is indeed the case would not surprise me. I doubt whether the rupture is absolute, but it is not surprising if the moral significance of certain modes of conduct, individual or institutional, is easily perceived by members of cultural groups which are morally directly affected by it, whereas the access of most other people to it is rather like that of a blind person to the colours of objects in his immediate vicinity. Those who are not members of directly affected groups, or those who are not familiar with their life and problems at close quarters, may be unable to perceive the moral significance of the conduct I have in mind, but they

I am grateful to Andrei Marmor, John Hyman, and Carl Wellman for challenging and helpful comments on an earlier draft.

may come to learn how to tell what it is by indirect signs, or by the testimony of others who are directly affected by it.

For multiculturalism to have such significance for moral knowledge it is not enough to establish that members of different cultural groups differ in their moral opinions regarding the same phenomena. We are not interested in the phenomenology of moral error, but in differential access to moral truths. So the epistemic implications of multiculturalism presuppose that members of different cultural groups find that ease of access to at least some moral truths varies with one's cultural group. One—though not the only—plausible explanation of such differential access is that membership in cultural groups has moral implications—that is, that the moral significance of actions, attitudes, and their like differs in different cultural communities. There is a sense in which this is trivially true. We need only think of the fact that the same form of address may be polite in one cultural group, and rude in another. The question is: is there a more interesting way in which the moral significance of acts or facts depends on the cultural groups in which they take place?

I should hasten to say that the supposition that close familiarity with a cultural group gives one easy access to some moral knowledge does not require that the variability of moral meaning of acts and attitudes be philosophically deep or interesting. Even simple moral/cultural variation gives rise to some epistemic consequences. However, if multiculturalism has more profound implications for moral truths, its epistemic implications are correspondingly more far-reaching.

The question we face is whether social/cultural practices affect morality. The stumbling block in coming to grips with the question is that we seem to lack an adequate model for a plausible explanation of such dependence. In this chapter I will explore one oft-refuted, oft-revived explanation—social relativism. The verdict will be a mixed one. Radical social relativism, I will follow many in arguing, fails. But constrained social relativism is plausible.

Social relativism is, though not among philosophers, a popular view. Belief in the possibility of moral change is, on the other hand, rarer. Yet the two seem to be analogous, the one seeming to be the temporal reflection, even consequence, of the other. Can we learn any lessons from the analogy? Or is it merely deceptive? This will be the route followed in this chapter. I will explore the limits of the possibility of moral change, and explore the analogy between it and the limits on plausible versions of social relativism. To begin with, some preliminary ground clearing and terminological clarification is offered, followed by a brief argument to show that social relativism presupposes the possibility of moral change. Section 2 explains the meaning of 'moral change' and argues that if radical moral change is possible it must remain unintelligible. Section 3 contains a brief argument to the effect that morality is inherently intelligible. It follows that radical moral change is impossible. Does it also follow that there are eternal moral verities? This is the question undertaken in Section 4. Its tentative conclusion is that it is likely that there are no eternal moral verities. Rather, morality should be thought of as evolving toward greater abstractedness and comprehensiveness, as human history evolves. This means, of course, that morality is in a significant way conditioned by social practices. My argument for that depends on the assumption that social conditions set limits to the possibilities of human understanding. However, in the final section, Section 5, I argue that this degree of social dependence is not sufficient to vindicate the social relativism identified at the outset, which is social relativism as popularly conceived. That form of the social relativism of morality stands refuted by the argument about the impossibility of a radical moral change in Section 2.

(b) Defining Social Relativism and Moral Change

By 'social relativism' I mean the view that

(A) the morality (the moral doctrines and principles) which is binding or valid for a person is a function of the moral practices[1] of his or her society.

The simplest form of social relativism holds that

(A1) each person is morally subject to (and only to) the morality practised in his or her society.

The truth of social relativism, if it is true, is not relativistic in any sense. That is, it is presented as a thesis which is true for all people at all times. Presumably, it is also a thesis whose truth is, in principle, available, that is, discoverable, by all people at all times.[2] This makes it difficult to espouse social relativism as a moral principle. If (A) is a moral principle, then it can be true only if

---

[1] When referring to 'the moral practices' of a society, I wish to imply neither that members of that society never fail to conform to the standards generally endorsed in that society, nor that mere lip service paid to a standard which is systematically disregarded in action is enough to make that standard part of the practice of the society. Rather, the phrase refers, as it commonly does, to a general but unspecified degree of endorsement coupled with a similarly general and unspecified degree of compliance in action. When referring to morality being a function of moral practices, I mean 'function' in its natural signification—i.e. a thing that depends on and varies with something else—which includes the idea that morality is a function sensitive to variations in moral practices. Functions which yield the same morality for all societies regardless of variations in their moral practices are excluded.

[2] This condition will be examined below.

(C) the practices of all societies (past, present, and future) are such that given the correct function by which their practices determine the moral principles which are binding or valid on their members, (A) is a valid principle in their societies.

If the function is identity and the correct version of social relativism is (A1), then (A)—and (A1)—is true only if

(C1) the practices of all societies require all people to be guided by (and only by) the practices of their society.

If this condition is met, then (A) is a self-verifying moral principle. That it is self-verifying does not of course show that it is true. Conflicting principles can be self-verifying. But the fact that it is self-verifying, if it is a fact, may be thought to give it some weight. If, however, the condition is not met, then (A) is false by its own terms. That is, given—as (A) says—that every person is morally subject to the practices of his society and to them alone, it follows that it is not the case that all are morally bound by the practices of their own society, unless the practices of their society say so.

We known that if this is how (A) is to be understood, that is, if it is to be seen as a moral principle, and therefore subject to condition (C), then it is false. Many of us live in societies whose practices do not support such a conclusion, and we all know of such societies. It is true that the practices of most societies require their own members to abide by the practices of their own societies. There are ways of understanding this statement which render it tautological (and by most other interpretations it is probably false).[3] Not many societies, however, recognize that the same holds for members of other societies regarding their practices. They tend to judge others by the standards by which they judge themselves.

This refutes (A1) as a moral principle. Similar considerations tell against (A) in all its forms. It is difficult to present them in anything like a conclusive form with complete generality. Broadly speaking, they consist in pointing out that the morality practised in various societies does not take any notice of the moral practices of other societies when judging some actions of their members.[4]

There is another, independent, reason for rejecting (A), or at least (A1),[5]

---

[3] It is tautological if it is read as saying: 'The moral rules practised in this society which apply to its members, apply to its members'; i.e. the rules require conformity from those they apply to. It is false if it means: 'The moral rules practised in this society stipulate that the fact that they are practised is a reason for members of the society in which they are practised to follow them.'

[4] Though quite often we invoke the practices of other societies to excuse or mitigate our judgement of actions of their members.

[5] I do not know whether the argument applies to other, yet to be specified, versions of (A). The following remarks constitute a prima-facie case for thinking that it does.

if it is taken as a moral principle. It imposes a conventionalist interpretation on morality. According to it, one's rights and duties are those one enjoys by the practices of one's society. The principle makes this coincidence necessary. This poses a problem to anyone who accepts (A1) when facing questions about the justification of having a duty or a right, or regarding the justification of any other aspect of morality. Of course, the practices of his society will include principles and considerations which can be adduced as a justification of the rights or duties he is concerned to justify. But he has to face the question of whether (A1) itself is irrelevant to such justification. Since it is assumed to be a moral principle, and since it directly bears on the question of what rights and duties people have, it is difficult to avoid regarding it as (at least one) justification for them. That justification, however, turns all morality into a matter of convention: this is how one ought to behave because this is how people generally behave, and how they think they ought to behave, and so on.

It hardly needs arguing that thoroughgoing justificatory conventionalism is a travesty of morality. While people may sometimes appeal to what everyone believes, and to how people act, as evidence for accepting that their views are correct, only in special cases do they regard such facts as (non-epistemic) justificatory reasons. As a moral principle, (A) must be rejected.

But (A) can be understood not as a moral principle but as something else. I will consider the possibility that it is a result of the meaning, or essence, of morality. Whatever moral principles are valid, they will be of a different order from an explanation of what morality is. Such an explanation may include claims like 'Moral statements are statements about one person's duties to his fellow beings.' These need not be statements of moral principle to be true. They can include a thesis like (A). This would be a statement that, of the different rules which apply to a person, the moral rules which apply to him are those which are practised in his society. This 'meta-ethical' statement is not a piece of verbal legislation. It is a thesis about what morality really is. But it is not a moral view about what moral duties people have. It is a 'meta-ethical' view, on a par with the thesis that, of the duties which a person is subject to, his duties to others are his moral duties. On this understanding, the primary import of the social relativistic thesis is not to argue which rights, duties, etc. people have but to classify and clarify the nature of rights and duties, etc., which people do have.

This understanding of the social relativistic thesis is compatible with the possibility that the thesis bears on the question 'Which rights and duties do people have?' as well. No independence or priority of the theory of morality relative to morality, or vice versa, is assumed. This may raise some people's eyebrows regarding the very distinction between morality and the theory of morality. But such suspicions are misplaced. The distinction is present in our common reflections on morality and the concepts we employ in it. It is not meant to do much heavy duty. It is pointless to try a general characterization. For present purposes, suffice it to emphasize that moral principles are reason-giving or explanatory. That means that a principle of the form 'If C, then one has a right to A' states more than a juxtaposition of C and a right to A. It states that C is (at least a part of) a reason for, or an explanation or justification of, such a right. It follows that not all statements of this form are statements of moral principles. Some of them may be true theoretical statements about morality.

While I have treated 'social relativism' as a term of art, 'moral change' is meant to be understood in its ordinary meaning—except that usually when we think of moral change we think of a person or a society changing their moral views or practices. The moral change we will be concerned with is that of morality itself. Can morality change? In a minimal sense, morality changes when a moral statement which is true at one point is no longer true. It is necessary, however, to distinguish between a change in the rights, duties, etc., which are the consequences of applying (possibly an unchanged) morality to changing circumstances, and a change in morality itself. As a partial first step in that direction,[6] let me say that a moral change occurs when a moral statement which does not refer to any particular individual is true at one time and false at another. Thus, that JR now has a duty he did not have yesterday is not sufficient to establish that a moral change has occurred (though a change in JR's duties may be due to a moral change). But that it was true yesterday and is no longer true that those who promise have a duty to do as they promised does establish, if true, the occurrence of a moral change.

(c) Social Relativism Presupposes Moral Change

Social relativism can be sustained only if moral change is possible. We know that social practices can (and do) change. If, as social relativism claims, morality is a function of social practices, then morality can (and does) change as well. To assume that it is a function of social practices which is indifferent to changes in such practices would be to run against the very idea of social relativism. It is true, for example, that by pegging the function to some primordial stage of development, even an unvarying function can preserve something of the intuitions behind social relativism, namely that members of different societies are subject to different moral principles

---

[6] The distinction is discussed again in the next section. No final and comprehensive criteria for drawing it are needed for the purposes of this chapter.

(members of each society being subject to a morality fixed once and for all for members of that society as a function of their social condition at a specified time). But this is achieved at the cost of abandoning the other, and central, intuition which makes social relativism attractive, that is, that the moral principles which apply to a person reflect his social environment (this may be thought necessary e.g., to show that it is possible for people to come to know the moral principles which apply to them—or, according to other views, to show that they can always be motivated by those principles, that such a motivation is available to them).

This suggests a simple refutation of social relativism: since social relativism presupposes the possibility of moral change, and since moral change is impossible, social relativism is false. This is the argument to be explored below. We need to inquire into the possibility of moral change and into the reasons for rejecting it in order to establish that the moral change social relativism presupposes is in fact impossible. The conclusions will be far less clear-cut than the argument assumes. Some moral change is possible. Therefore, so far as this argument goes there is room for some forms of social relativism. Whether the constrained social relativism one ends up with satisfies the intuitions of real hard-boiled social relativists is a question I will only be able to touch on in concluding this chapter.

2. THE INTELLIGIBILITY OF MORAL CHANGE

(a) Narrowing the Issue

A common view has it that there can be no moral change. Morality (i.e. all true moral propositions) is, according to this view, universal and, in some sense, necessary. Hence, it cannot be contingent on facts which may change over time. But why should this be so? Moreover, can this view be consistently sustained? It seems impossible to deny that some moral change occurs. For example, the duties of charity depend on the political situation in one's country. The introduction of a just tax law, and of adequate and efficient welfare services radically changes one's duty to give to charity. The nature of the change depends on the circumstances before and after the change. But the following, for example, may be true of some hypothetical situation: until the change in the law, one had a duty to give one-tenth of one's income to charity, but after that the duty is to give only half as much.

Some may say that this is not really moral change. It is merely a change in the application of a moral principle at a fairly low level of generalization. Notice though that the change can occur at any level of generality.

According to common rule-utilitarian moralities, all moral principles barring one—that is, barring the principle of utility itself—are subject to change. Why must the principle of utility itself be an exception? It seems that the underlying idea is that there cannot be a complete moral change; not everything can change, at least not at once. Belief in the impossibility of total moral change is, however, but a special case of the underlying thesis that any change must be an application of an unchanging principle to changing circumstances. The only moral change which is impossible is one which does not presuppose this combination of unchanging principle and changing circumstances.

(b) The Basic Argument

Why must all moral change presuppose an unchanging moral background? It is not as if a presupposed unchanging moral background is necessary for us to be able to distinguish between continuity and change. All we need for this is the ability to distinguish between different moral principles, and to be able to establish whether they are true or not. If we can tell that proposition P expresses a moral principle, and that it was true at t_0 and false at t_1, we know that a moral change has occurred.

There is, however, a powerful argument against the possibility of moral change. While conceding that moral change can be detected even when it is not merely a change in the application of the same principle to changing circumstances, the argument claims that if such change is possible it is bound to remain unintelligible. The reason, according to the argument, is that to explain any moral change we need a backdrop of an unchanging principle. Here is one way of spelling out the argument. Suppose that the moral change we have in mind entails that from today I may not do something which I was allowed to do until now. If I inquire why I may not do it, the answer is that it is prohibited by a principle. If so, why was it permissible until now? Because, the answer goes, the principle is a new one. But this is puzzling. What could explain how a principle which was not valid until now has become a binding moral principle? Perhaps things have changed, and this explains its becoming binding. In that case there is a complete statement of the change, call it P, such that there is a valid universal principle which has not changed on the relevant occasion:

(D) If P, then acts of the relevant kind are forbidden.

The consequent of (D) ('acts of the relevant kind are forbidden') is the new principle. (D) itself, however, is an unchanging principle, and one which explains the validity of the new principle.

This, you may say, is cheating. Conditionals such as (D) are not really moral principles. Rather, they are statements that the antecedent brings about a moral change. What else could count as a moral change? That is, the objection goes, when people say that morality cannot change, they say that something which is imaginable (moral change) cannot happen. But if (D) counts as a moral principle, then there is nothing which could be imagined as a moral change, for it follows from the supervenience of the moral on the non-moral[7] that there cannot be any moral change without a change describable in non-moral terms.[8] There are problems here which cannot be fully explored now. Surely some universal statements with non-moral antecedents and moral consequents are statements of moral principles. Take, for example,

(D1) When you knowingly cause another person to rely on you to act in a certain way, and when, because of his reliance, failing to so act will be to his detriment, you have an obligation to act in that way.

We need, therefore, an account of when statements like (D) state a principle and when they state the conditions which will bring about the coming into force of the principle stated in the consequent. Whatever it may be (and I will give a partial elucidation of the distinction below), let us agree that such an account can be given. Is it possible that some non-moral change will make a moral change intelligible? But what change could explain a change in the validity of a moral principle?

Suppose that the alleged new principle is that women should have the same employment opportunities as men. What sort of change can explain the principle's newly acquired validity? Perhaps the change is in the domestic technologies which mean that housekeeping and child-rearing are no longer a full-time job (clothes and bread and the like are bought rather than made at home; cleaning, washing, and cooking are easier with the new implements available; and if only there were child-minding facilities, neither parent would need to spend a whole day at home). But why should these changes make a moral difference? Why should the fact that housekeeping and child-rearing are a full-time job mean that women need not have equal job opportunities? Should it not be their choice which parent stays at home and which one goes on the job market? The story is

---

[7] 'The supervenience of the moral on the non-moral' refers to a familiar philosophical doctrine according to which two things can vary in their moral properties only if they vary in their non-moral properties.

[8] Can it be otherwise? Perhaps if the moral change is not merely in one principle, but if the whole of morality valid at one point is replaced by a different morality at a later time. Perhaps then the new morality can still supervene on the same non-moral facts, only in a different configuration. But if such a change were to happen, its occurrence would surely be unintelligible. The possibility of moral change through conceptual change will be separately considered below.

familiar. Any factual narrative either will require moral assumptions to explain why it leads to a change of moral principle or will itself incorporate moral factors (which have not changed) which will explain how the moral change has come about. Either way, a moral change cannot be intelligible except through an unchanging moral background which explains why changing circumstances brought it about.

We can now better see when conditionals such as (D) state moral principles and when they do not. The requirement that moral predicates supervene on non-moral ones implies no more than that some such conditional is true whenever a new moral principle, that is, the one stated by the consequent, becomes valid. But it does not imply that these conditionals are themselves moral principles. It is satisfied, for example, by

(D2) If a star has collapsed, smoking is wrong.

This is not a moral principle, for the fact that a star has collapsed is not a reason why smoking is prohibited. That smoking damages the health of those who inhale tobacco smoke is—perhaps—a reason why smoking, or smoking in public, is wrong. If so, then the statement

(D3) If inhaling tobacco smoke damages one's health, then smoking in public is wrong

is a statement of moral principle. Conditionals of the (D) form in which the antecedent specifies the reason for the validity of the consequent are statements of moral principles. But if so, it follows that the coming into effect of a new moral principle is explicable only if there is another (D)-type principle specifying the reasons for it and thus explaining why it came into effect. If there is no such explanatory principle already in force, then the coming into effect of the new principle is unintelligible.

The question of the boundary of morality may pose another difficulty here. Is it unintelligible for evaluative/normative principles which are not moral ones to explain a moral change? Must it be made explicable by reference to other specifically moral considerations? I do not mean to suggest that it must. The argument is really about the conditions for the intelligibility of change of normative/evaluative principles of any kind, be they moral or not. It claims that for such change to be intelligible there must be an unchanging evaluative/normative principle, whether classified as moral or not, which explains the change. I will continue to discuss the problem in terms of the relations between moral principles. But everything I say should be understood as subject to this explanation.

(c) Apropos Supervenience

The basic argument took us into a consideration of supervenience and justifies a brief detour to comment on the relation between the requirement of supervenience and that of moral intelligibility. They show that supervenience does not guarantee intelligibility. It can be satisfied by the truth of propositions such as (D2) which leave the moral principle concerned entirely unintelligible. I believe that the requirement of supervenience owes its appeal to the thought that without it morality is unintelligible. If so, then it may be tempting to react to the above by saying that supervenience is a necessary but not a sufficient condition for the intelligibility of morality. But the condition of intelligibility we were exploring—that is, that there be a background normative/evaluative principle which states a reason for the principle to be explained, even if it is only a sufficient and not a necessary condition of intelligibility (and I wish to express no opinion on this point)—does not itself presuppose supervenience. It can be satisfied by an antecedent which includes reference to other evaluative/normative considerations. Intelligibility, in other words, can be achieved through a series of ultimately circular explanations. This does not mean that morality can be made intelligible without any reference to non-moral facts. But it does mean that if there are reasons for accepting the requirement of supervenience, then they must be independent of the claim that without it morality cannot be intelligible.

(d) The Case of Conceptual Change

We can now return to our main topic. Moral change can be intelligible only if we assume a currently unchanging principle which states the reasons for the change. This view may be too simplistic. Possibly, radical moral change, that is, that which does not presuppose a continuing background, requires conceptual change. Our moral concepts are not constant. See, for example, the vying for centre-stage position of the concepts 'happiness', 'eudaimonia', 'well-being', 'individual welfare', and 'flourishing'. They all aim at roughly the same role in moral thought, and while being similar they clearly differ. Similarly, it makes a difference whether souls, human beings, rational beings, persons, or members of some other category are thought to be the primary moral subjects. 'Treat every soul as an end in itself' differs from 'Treat every rational being as an end in itself'. These are examples of rival concepts which are part of our conceptual armoury. We are aware, however, that over the years moral principles have 'changed their meaning' through conceptual changes in which similar but not identical concepts succeeded each other in the moral principles in which they are embedded. Imagine such a change in a fundamental principle. Imagine a change which may happen through a subtle change which is not even echoed in a terminological change: the principle may be stated using the same words, but the meaning of the words may have shifted, so that they now state a different, and therefore new, principle. Is it not true that these cases exemplify moral changes which are intelligible, but do not presuppose a continuing moral principle to make them intelligible?

These cases are far from clear. When it is possible for people to realize that a conceptual change has occurred, they are likely to be aware that it accompanied a change of their moral views. In that case they may well regard the previous, unmodified principle as inferior to the new one, that is, as having been mistaken. If so, then there is no evidence here that morality has changed; so far as we know, only people's views on morality have changed. Alternatively, it may be a case of a moral change subsumed under and explained by some unchanging principle. These are the only ways in which the situation can be viewed. Suppose, however, that people cannot establish that a conceptual change has occurred. It may be in principle imperceptible from the new vantage point. Would that warrant saying that there has been a moral change (through the change in the meaning of the principle embodying the concept which changed its meaning) which need not be subsumed under any unchanging principle to be intelligible? I do not believe so. The people whose concept it is do not believe that there was a moral change, since they are unaware of the conceptual shift which led to it. So far as they are concerned, the principle they now believe to be valid has always been valid, and any principle inconsistent with it—as we assume the old one to be—was always, in their eyes, invalid. For anyone who is aware of the change, and who regards it as a moral change rather than as a change in people's moral views, it will not be intelligible unless it can be accounted for in the ordinary way, that is, as an application of an unchanging principle. So this is not an example of the intelligibility of radical moral change.

3. MUST MORALITY BE INTELLIGIBLE?

Accepting that to be intelligible a moral change must assume an unchanging moral principle(s) which explains how changing circumstances brought into effect a new moral principle, or led to the lapse of an old one, the question remains: must morality be intelligible? Can we not say that the fact that an action is morally required or morally prohibited, or that a character trait is virtuous or evil, is a matter of how the world is, and there is no a priori reason to believe that the world must be intelligible? It is what it is. We may or may not find out how it is, and we are lucky if we ever understand why it is as it is.

An oversimple, yet fundamentally correct, answer to this question is that morality *is* intelligible, for its role is to enable people to comprehend themselves and their world. This answer may be disputed in various ways. First, it is true that we explain how people ought to behave, and also how they actually conduct themselves and society, by reference to moral facts (e.g. the broadening of the scope of moral sensitivity led to a decline in the spirit of community, and to a growth in selfishness, which itself accounts for the decline in the fortunes of elderly people). But this does not mean that morality must be intelligible through and through. It may explain what it explains in so far as it is itself intelligible, and not beyond. Second, it is wrong, some may say, to suggest that it is 'the role' of morality to make things intelligible. To say so is to suggest that it is the nature of morality to be instrumental to some purpose external to it. In fact, morality is, to repeat the previous point, simply part of the world. Moral principles just happen to be valid in this world. This is just how the world is. Like other facts about the world, morality helps explain people and society to the extent that it is itself understood. But we cannot assume that it is altogether intelligible any more than we can assume this about other aspects of the world. Moreover, morality must be conceived in this way, for it could not explain anything if it were not an aspect of reality. Whatever it explains, it explains by reference to this aspect of the world. How else could it explain either how people should behave or how they do?

The second objection is beside the point. No one is denying (nor is it affirmed) that moral discourse is about an aspect of the world. All that is asserted is that moral statements are essentially explicable, intelligible. It is not consistent with our idea of morality, with the nature of our moral discourse, that what is morally permissible or forbidden, etc., is so for no reason or for mysterious reasons. If moral discourse is about a part of reality, then it is an inherently intelligible part of reality. That is all. Herein lies one of the differences between morality and taboo, magical instructions, etc.: that the former is necessarily intelligible, whereas the latter are not necessarily so. Moral facts are in order, but they are not like facts about the weather. Besides reasons for believing that something is morally so and so, there are reasons which justify its being so and so, and they are non-contingently related to what they are reasons for.[9] Likewise, moral facts are non-contingently related to the conclusions they support, including conclusions about the appropriateness of certain actions or evaluations.

Part of the opposition to the thought that morality is inherently intelligible results from an incorrect understanding of the implications of that thought. For example, the claim that morality is intelligible may be thought to assign morality an excessively rationalistic character. But this is not so.

---

[9] The justifying reasons may also be one's epistemic reasons. But one may have other epistemic reasons e.g. reliable advice.

There is no implication here that people who make moral statements must fully understand their implication or be fully cognizant of their justification, or that they are at fault to some degree if this is not so. With moral as with other knowledge, possessing it does not presuppose full understanding of its grounds and justification.[10] Nor should we think of intelligibility as involving a rationalistic view. It is intelligible to people that hunger makes concentration difficult, and slows down mental processes. There is nothing rationalistic about this. To be intelligible, such connections require appropriate experience, or learning from (or about) those who have such experience. Finally, to repeat the obvious, intelligibility does not depend on showing that morality serves a purpose external to itself.[11] Intelligibility may consist in explaining the point of a rule or a goal rather than its external purpose.

But, another objector may say, is a moral change less intelligible than its absence? Do we not need an explanation for why moral changes do not occur? That is a misunderstanding. We explain why morality is as it is by giving reasons for the moral doctrines and principles which are valid. This explains why they are as they are, that is, why they are not different, why they do not change. It is change that, to be intelligible, requires additional explanation, not its absence. Nor can one object that it is impossible on pain of infinite regress to explain why morality is as it is. Every 'why' question can receive an answer. Infinite regress or (wide) circles are no objection to intelligibility. What is intelligible is a self-supporting whole (including its potential for infinite expansion).

These comments are meant to remove objections to the claim that morality is inherently intelligible. The argument for the claim proceeds from the basic features of moral discourse and its presuppositions. That discourse is explanatory and clarifying, or it assumes that all moral statements can be justified, and their justification can be understood. Hence the claim about the essential intelligibility of morality. This way of proceeding from discourse to aspects of the world will strike some as odd. But I believe that it is sound and not unique to morality. To the extent that our discourse clarifies aspects of the world, we can learn from the nature of the discourse which aspects of the world it is about. It is possible that the discourse as a whole is incoherent. But barring that possibility it follows that the world

---

[10] A closely related point is discussed in some detail in the appendix to Joseph Raz, *Practical Reason and Norms*, 2nd edn. (Oxford: Oxford University Press, 1999), as well as by Samuel Scheffler in *Human Morality* (New York: OUP, 1992).

[11] The view that it does is a legacy of the instrumental conception of reason. Unfortunately, many who reject it do accept instrumental rationality as the clearest and safest form of practical rationality. See, however, Jean Hampton, 'Rethinking Reason', *American Philosophical Quarterly*, 29/3 (July 1992), 219–36, for arguments that, far from being so instrumental, rationality presupposes noninstrumental practical rationality. Arguments to the same effect were pressed by Warren Quinn. See *Morality and Action*, Cambridge, 1993.

Moral Change and Social Relativism

has aspects which display the attributes ascribed to them by the essential features of that discourse. In other words, assuming that the discourse is not incoherent as a whole, its essential features are reflected in reality. Any assumption of a stronger independence of thought and reality is itself incoherent.

4. ARE THERE ETERNAL MORAL VERITIES?

(a) An Argument for Timeless Moral Verities

Does the argument advanced show that there are timeless valid moral[12] principles? The issue is far from clear. On its face it only shows that no change is intelligible except against the background of a (then) unchanging principle, which may itself have come into force, or which may lose validity, at some time or another—a change which will itself become intelligible because of yet another principle. One may think that this leaves the door open to the possibility that all moral principles are valid only for a limited time.[13]

The requirement of intelligibility seems, however, to be the basis of a stronger conclusion. It means not only that a moral change is intelligible when it occurs but that it remains intelligible. If the only principles which explain the change at the time are then superseded, the change they explained is no longer explicable.

In some cases, the explaining principles (i.e. the ones explaining the original change) are not the only ones to explain that change. Commonly, there may be more abstract principles which explain the explaining principles. These more abstract principles will explain the conditions under which the explaining principles may themselves change, but they also—perhaps indirectly—explain the original change. In that case, there is no difficulty in imagining that the explaining principles themselves change at some later date. But their change is possible only because of the persistence of more abstract principles which remain unchanged.

The process here envisaged is one of continuing ascent towards more abstract and more permanent principles. We can readily imagine that more and more abstract principles emerge with time. As history unfolds we are

---

[12] Or at least timeless normative/evaluative principles?

[13] It may be that morality itself makes sense or is in force only under certain conditions, e.g. only while moral agents exist. The discussion of the temporal boundaries of moral principles is not meant to reflect this fact but to assume it. That is, the question under consideration is whether there must be one or more moral principles which must be valid for as long as morality is in force or makes sense, or whether this is not so and it is possible that no single moral principle is valid throughout the period during which morality is in force.

continuously forced to conclude that principles which appeared immutable are in fact valid only under specific social, economic, or cultural conditions. As those conditions change, the principles lose their validity. But the realization that this is so is made possible by the emergence of those more abstract principles we talked about which explain that change. The more abstract principles are taken to apply to the old as well as to the new conditions. They can explain the change because they span the periods, old and new, and provide the background continuity necessary for the intelligibility of moral change. This is why their emergence is itself a discovery of principles which were valid all along, rather than an emergence of new principles. Were they new, they would not be able to explain why the old explaining principles lapsed.

This story is schematic and 'cleansed' of any suggestion that previous generations were in part mistaken in their moral beliefs. Typically, as the conditions of life change we come to discover new, more abstract principles which explain the limited durability of moral verities hitherto believed to be eternal, and, at the same time, we come to believe that the previous generations were in part mistaken about morality, and that what we now see as the lapsed principles were not exactly as people then believed them to be.

(b) A Counter Argument

If I am right so far, morality does contain unchanging principles. But there is a powerful objection to this line of argument. Why should the fact that the explaining principle lapses make the change that it explained inexplicable? It remains intelligible by reference to the lapsed principle which was valid at the time. The fact that the principle is no longer valid does not matter to the intelligibility of a moral change which it explained and justified when it was in force. In this respect, the case of moral change is like that of any action or anything else subject to moral judgement on the basis of the now-lapsed, but at the time valid, principle. Action taken at the time the principle was in force, which the principle showed to be right, remains right even though the principle lapsed. It does not lapse retroactively. Its moral significance at the time it was valid is not annulled.

How convincing is the counter argument? It is surely sound in its implications for the assessment of actions, emotions, character, institutions, and other subjects of moral evaluation. But does it also apply to the assessment of morality itself? This seems to me far from clear. One may hold that if the counter argument succeeds then it may be the case that our morality, that is, the morality which is currently in force, contains no explanation for the past change in moral principle. This, one may hold, is impossible. It is,

Moral Change and Social Relativism

of course, true that we know today of a moral explanation for the moral change, that is, its explanation by the then-valid, now-lapsed principle. But since we do not now hold that explaining principle to be valid, our current morality does not contain an explanation for the change.

This attempted rebuttal depends on a subtle distinction: the distinction between (1) an explanation provided by the morality currently in force, and (2) an explanation which relies on principles no longer in force, but an explanation which is still true today. The rebuttal claims that morality must be intelligible and that it is intelligible only if, for any given time t, a moral change which occurred at any time is intelligible only if a moral explanation of it is available in terms of principles valid at t.

The claim does not seem implausible, but I can think of no argument to support it. Even if we grant it, we are still short of an argument for the existence of timeless moral truths. There can be more than one explanation of a single moral change. It may be possible for a moral change to be explicable by reference to one explaining principle at the time that it occurred, and to become additionally explicable in terms of another principle which comes into force at a later time. If so, then if the first, original explaining principle lapses some time after the new explanation becomes available, the condition of intelligibility stated in the attempted rebuttal is met, and yet there may be no timeless moral truths.

To succeed, the rebuttal has to be reinforced by another claim. One way of doing so is to claim that to be good an explanation of a moral change has to be available at the time of the change. An explanation cannot be retroactive, relying on principles which were not valid at the time the change occurred. If morality has to be intelligible, and if moral change is intelligible only if it is explicable in terms of principles valid both at the time of the change and at the time of the explanation, then there are timeless moral truths.

(c) Moral Progress Towards Unchanging Principles

The second condition for the success of the rebuttal seems more intuitively obvious than the first. How can a change be explained by a principle not valid at the time it occurred? Nevertheless it admits of an exception. Admittedly, the exception I have in mind is not only of limited scope, but is also not out of sympathy with the spirit of the requirement that the principle explaining a change be valid at the time of the change.

A simple case will illustrate how an exception can be sympathetic. Imagine that a law is replaced with another law similar in its general character but correcting certain anomalies due to overgeneralized application of the original law. The old law is no longer in force, and the new one was not in force until now. But we could still admit that a legal change explicable at the time by an aspect of the old law which has not changed, an aspect which remained unaffected by the difference between the old and the new law, is now explicable on the basis of the new law. Even though the new law was not valid at the time, its spirit—incorporated in the old law—was. Of course, this case is not directly relevant to morality. The old law is replaced because it was defective all along. The case of moral change is not like that. Morality cannot be defective. Moral change, we are assuming, follows change in the circumstances of the life of the people to whom the morality applies. I mention the legal case only as an analogy. For I believe that it finds analogy in morality.

If the analogy can be sustained, then we have two rival views of how to understand a moral change which happens when a moral principle believed at the time to be ultimate and universal changes. Both views assume that while the lapsed principle was valid at the time, belief in its timeless validity was mistaken. One view discussed earlier assumes unchanging, universal moral principles which are discovered (often roughly at the time when some of the known principles lapse) as a result of changes in the circumstances of people's lives, and which explain the moral change.

The legal analogy suggests a different way of understanding roughly the same story. It too allows for a change in circumstances which leads to principles hitherto in force losing their point and validity. It too regards this change as explicable by more abstract principles which were not previously accepted or known, and which vindicate the old principles as valid in the past, while explaining why they are valid no more.[14] But now we are invited to conceive of these more abstract principles, not as unchanging principles recently discovered, but as new principles which have recently emerged. Even though they are new—the legal analogy suggests—since they are in keeping with the spirit of the old principles (as is witnessed by the fact that they vindicate their validity for their time, and that they are, broadly speaking, generalizations of the earlier principles which are now a special case of the new principles), they can explain why the old principles lapsed.

How are we to judge between the picture of morality as resting on eternal verities and the one which sees it as perpetually evolving towards more general principles? Oddly enough, the very argument—that morality is inherently intelligible—which I have used to set limits to the possibility of moral change provides a reason for preferring the view which allows for the possibility that some changes are made intelligible only through new emerging principles. For the intelligibility of morality requires that morality should be in principle accessible to the people to whom it applies. Again

---

[14] Some changes are explained by principles which were known and understood all along. I am simply interested in the case where this is not so.

the argument for this thesis cannot be examined here. It turns once more on the point I have relied upon earlier, that morality has a role which it ought to play in people's lives, the role of making intelligible, giving meaning to, various aspects of their lives, and the possibilities open to them in life, and thus also providing guidance in their lives. The argument relies on the contention that principles which in principle cannot fulfil that role cannot be valid moral principles.

Arguably, moral principles can be conceived, understood, and believed only by people who either share a culture or know or could find out about a culture which makes the principles conceivable. Arguably, people who lived long before the rise of the great monotheistic religions and in conditions which made their rise impossible to envisage could not have understood moral notions and moral principles which those religions brought in their wake (such as the universal moral standing of all persons). If so—and the argument cannot be examined here—then there is substantive bite to the thesis that moral principles cannot be valid at a time when they cannot be conceived, or when it is impossible for people to come to know them.

For current purposes I will simply accept these contentions. In particular, I will accept the exception to the rule that a moral change is intelligible only by reference to principles valid both at the time the change occurred and at the time of the explanation. The exception allows that a change is intelligible if explained by principles which, though not valid at the time it occurred because at that time they were beyond people's grasp, vindicate the principles then valid. This exception disproves the claim that there must be timeless moral verities. There may be no timeless moral principles after all. Morality may be essentially temporal. This type of change, consisting as it does of ever-increasing generality of scope, is not disruptive change. It does not turn morality into disjointed temporal segments. At any given time, the whole of morality, past and present, is comprehensible in the light of currently valid moral principles. Morality may be pluralistic, but its pluralism does not comprise distinct and unconnected temporal segments. This view of the limits to moral change, while allowing that there may be no eternal moral verities, justifies the claim that morality continuously and endlessly develops towards unchanging moral principles, since every change is subsumed under a principle, old or new, which is of greater scope and generality.

5. FROM CHANGE TO SOCIAL RELATIVISM

The impossibility of radical moral change, that is, one which does not presuppose a continuing moral principle, does not establish that there cannot be any moral change. As we saw, it does not even establish that there is a moral principle which cannot change. Moreover, someone may say that everything but one principle can change all at once. This is in principle so, if one believes in a monolithic ethic. Not so for moral pluralists. For pluralists, the message is that many principles must persist through any moral change, however far-reaching. For present purposes, however, the main importance of the impossibility of radical moral change is that it provides strong reasons for suspecting that social relativism is untenable.

How so? The argument is simple. The very idea of social relativism implies that a change in social practice is sufficient for a change of moral principle; that is, what is asserted is precisely that no continuing moral principle is necessary. If the function from social practices to moral principles presupposes some moral principles—that is, if it is a function from social practices and moral principles to moral principles—there would be no guarantee that social practices condition morality until some continuing principles were known, and by definition these could not be a function of social practices themselves.

Another way of arguing for the same conclusion is this. If the morality valid for a person is a function of the moral practices of that person's society, then it changes as the moral practices of that society change. Moral practices can change completely. Since morality in its entirety is supposed by social relativists to be a function of social practices, it follows that morality, too, must be capable of changing completely. Hence, again, the possibility of radical moral change is a consequence of social relativism. Since we have just seen that radical moral change is impossible, it follows that social relativism is untenable. Can the argument be avoided by assuming that social change is gradual? After all, if social change is gradual, every change in a social practice occurs against a backdrop of continuing social practices. That appears to satisfy the limit on change which our argument imposed, so that while every moral principle may change, every change occurs against a backdrop of continuing moral principles. But this reconciliation is illusory. The argument against radical moral change establishes more than that every change happens against a backdrop of continuing principles, so that morality cannot change all at once. It establishes also that it cannot change completely. At any time, the principle which explains change is either one which has always been valid or one which embraces and explains principles which were valid prior to its emergence. Since morality cannot change completely and social practices can, social relativism is untenable.

I believe that one of the main attractions of social relativism is the thought that morality must be accessible to the people whom it binds. I have argued that that very thought derives from the fact that morality is inherently intelligible, and that the inherent intelligibility of morality is inconsistent with its being a function of the social practices of the society which it binds. The requirement of the intelligibility of morality means that morality is constrained by the culture of the people whom it binds. It cannot contain principles inaccessible to their understanding, and their culture sets boundaries to their understanding. But this constraint is satisfied by much which is unrelated to their own practices, and which history, travel, writing, or human imagination make comprehensible to them.

Some moral philosophers regard ethics as limited by tradition, with the conversation of the deaf being conducted across the boundaries of traditions. If so, and if the different cultures in a multicultural society stand for different traditions, then multiculturalism imports the existence of a moral chasm between the different traditions and communities in society. The argument of this chapter suggests that this thought is incompatible with an understanding of the nature of morality. Multiculturalism gives rise to problems of communication and of comprehension. But there is something to communicate and something to comprehend. There is a morality which applies to all the traditions and all the cultures, a morality which bridges the divide between them.

We can now see that the impossibility of radical moral change is a stronger thesis than may appear at first sight. It denies the compartmentalization of morality into a changing and an unchanging part. In other words, morality cannot be partly universal and partly socially relative, unless the socially relative part is a mere application of the universal part. So it is not merely that every morality must contain a universal part, principles such as 'Do not torture' and 'Do not intentionally kill the innocent'. Its universal part must explain why the contingent part is cogent, why it is as it is. This universal part explains how social practices and other circumstances can make a moral difference. This means that social relativism is untenable even in the modest form which says that part of morality is socially relative, and is not subsumed under (is not mere application of) non-socially relative moral principles.

8

Mixing Values

I want to explore, in a tentative way, one aspect of a familiar question. Under what conditions can one compare the strength or stringency of conflicting reasons for and against an action where they are a function of irreducibly different values that its performance manifests, contributes to, or detracts from?[1] When of two sets of conflicting reasons neither is at least as weighty as the other they are incommensurable, and so are the actions they are the only reasons for.

The question applies both to individual actions and to types of actions. When considering types of actions the question refers to the reasons for actions which exist in virtue of those actions being of that type. The values of actions or objects are irreducibly different if they are not due to or are not exhausted by the consequences the actions (or possession or use of the objects) will or may have, and the actions or objects do not possess a third value of which the different values are instances.

Since reasons for action often depend on the value of objects I will often refer to the value of objects to illustrate points about reasons for action. The value of objects affects reasons for the actions which produce them (e.g. the value of refrigerators affects the value of making them) as well as, in many cases, the reasons for or against using (or engaging with) them (e.g. the value of a piano sonata reflects on the reasons for listening to it, playing it, composing it, conversing about it, etc.).

Notice that the question I will explore concerns only reasons for actions based on the value of actions or their consequences. Some reasons for actions do not derive from any value considerations. The fact that I like (i.e. enjoy) bananas better than pears is a reason for me to choose a banana rather than a pear, when offered both. But this does not show that bananas are more valuable than pears.[2] Only if there are value-based reasons for an action do they reflect on the value of the action. My choosing a banana does

---

[1] I will normally refer to options, i.e. alternative actions an agent has the ability and opportunity to perform. Reasons against an option are reasons for the option of omitting to perform the first.

[2] Does it show that bananas are more valuable to me? Possibly, but I will not be concerned with values which are essentially relative to the agent. My interest is in goods the value of which is a reason for developing a liking for them, rather than with goods whose value derives from an unreasoned, brute, though possibly acquired, taste for them.

Mixing Values

not have greater value than if I chose otherwise. Possibly, however, when I perform or fail to perform an action for which there are value-related reasons (which I should have been able to know about) that fact reflects on the value of my action. If so, and if these considerations are the only ones which reflect on the value of actions, then our question can also be stated as whether one can compare the value of actions when it is due to different irreducible values.[3]

The following two propositions, among others, anchor our understanding of the discourse about the value of actions (and of value-based reasons for their performance):

(1) Other things being equal, an agent who could know that A is better than B and who could perform either, is doing the right (proper, correct, etc.) thing if he does A rather than B and the wrong (misguided, etc.) thing if he does B rather than A.

(2) Other things being equal, if the proposition that the feature F contributes to the value of actions which have it is intelligible then that an agent does A rather than B, because he believes that its possession of F makes it the better action, makes his action intelligible. It makes us understand (at least to a degree) his action (his acting as he did).

The first condition ties value to reasons for action. It takes it to be a conceptual truth that one has reason to realize value, and that the greater the value the more stringent the reason. The second condition ties value to explanation. Belief in value explains why the action was done, makes its performance intelligible.

1. THE ARGUMENT FROM COMMON MEASURE

A familiar argument proceeds as follows. One needs a common measure to show why one action or object is better than another. If the value of novels and poems is instrumental, for example, as means of entertaining people,

---

[3] The connection between the value of an action and reasons for it is less straightforward than this sentence implies. On some views one's reasons are determined by one's reasonable belief in the value of one's options, and not by their true value. Secondly, sometimes the value of an option (logically) cannot be a reason for performing it. For example, if a parent's sacrificing his annual holiday to be with his child during a period of stress is good because it encourages the child by expressing his parent's love for him, then it cannot have that value if performed to give encouragement, but only if performed out of love. However, these gaps between value and reasons are not significant for our purpose. If there is widespread and significant incommensurability of reasons there is nothing here to lead one to doubt that there is also widespread and significant incommensurability of the values of concrete options, and vice versa.

or of instructing them about the human condition, then we can judge whether poetry is better or less good than novels, or whether a particular novel is better or less good than a particular poem. Likewise if they are both valuable only in possessing some common property, for example, if the value of both novels and poems derives from the degree of creativity displayed in them. But if they have no common measure (in value) then, while we can say that this poem ranks higher among poems (being the best post-war poem, let us say) than this novel ranks among novels (since it is, let us assume, a mediocre novel), we cannot say that this poem is better than this novel.

It is no objection to this argument (which I will dub 'the common argument') that different options can be given a consistent transitive ranking even though they contain no common element which can be relied upon to calibrate their value. The formal possibility of such ranking does not help us understand what makes an option which is ranked in a certain way in terms of one value better or worse than (or as good as) another option whose value is different and distinct. But does one need such an explanation? Is not the answer that we just know that even the best detective story is not as good a work of fiction as William Golding's *Darkness Visible* (a very good, but not outstanding novel)? But do I know this? Before we can accept such judgements we should establish that they make sense. The fact that we often have knowledge the grounds for which we cannot articulate, or even knowledge the grounds of which cannot be exhaustively articulated, is not in question here. The question is: is there anything to know? Does a comparison of the value of options deriving their value from distinct goods make sense? If it does then it must be possible to explain how it makes sense. The question is not to explain the meaning of '*A* is better than *B*'. We understand this, but in a way which suggests (because of the common argument spelt out above) that its application may be limited to contexts in which the value is either instrumental or calibrated through a common value that *A* and *B* are instances of. If comparisons of value are not so restricted then there must be an explanation of the sense of such comparisons.

Nor can one rely on the fact that people make confident comparative judgements of this kind as the explanation. At most this would suggest that such judgements are not always mistaken. We would still need an explanation of how they work. What is the difference between a correct judgement and a mistaken one? Furthermore, the mere prevalence of such judgements is no guarantee that not all of them are mistaken. This is not a case of faulting a complete category of judgements. The common argument casts no doubt on value comparisons where there is a common measure. Comparisons of options of mixed values is not a distinct linguistic type of judgement. They may be a mere extension of familiar judgements beyond the area in which they make sense.

2. GOODS OF MIXED VALUE

A strong challenge to the common argument derives from the existence of many goods of mixed value. Most intrinsic goods do display a variety of distinct values. Think of playing football, going to the theatre, bell-ringing, writing an orchestral piece, having a party, and so on. They all combine one or more social goods (conducting relations with one or more people, displaying, expressing, reinforcing communal identification, etc.) with an exercise, or an enhancement of another good (physical, imaginative, creative, emotional, etc.). In all these cases we can distinguish degrees of success (and failure) of the activity.[4] This presupposes that we can compare different mixes of distinct goods as to their comparative value.

Must this be so? Do we understand what it means for items of one type of mixed-value goods to be compared in value? Here we may feel that the practice of making such comparisons (of different novels, different paintings, different parties, different hill-walking holidays) is too established to entertain doubts about its sense. Still, there is an apparent way of avoiding this conclusion. It relies on the fact that the ranking of different alternatives is incomplete. Consider a novel. Its merit depends on a combination of distinct goods. Its plotting, its linguistic skill, its humour, its insight, etc. But not all novels can be ranked as either better than or as good as each other. It would be false to say that *Darkness Visible* is just as good as *Thérèse Raquin*. Nor will it be true that the novels are roughly as good as each other.[5] This is so not because either is better or worse. They are just too unlike each other to admit of such a ranking. (Different people may, of course, prefer the one or the other, though if sensible they will admit that that is not because their favourite novel is the better one. People may even prefer a novel they realize to be less good than the alternative.) One suggestion might be that one novel is better than another only if it is what I shall call 'Pareto superior'[6] to it, and that novels are roughly equal in merit if each of their virtues roughly match. This makes sense of (limited) comparisons of goods of mixed value which do not assume

---

[4] I deliberately choose examples of activities which are predominantly of intrinsic value. Other activities, like practising medicine, could serve just as well, but their considerable instrumental value tends to complicate the picture.

[5] See my discussion of rough equality in *The Morality of Freedom* (Oxford: OUP, 1986).

[6] I trust that this natural extension of Pareto superiority is readily comprehensible. A good or option is Pareto superior to another, I shall say, if it is superior to it in respect of at least one value, and not inferior in any.

cross-value comparisons, and are therefore unproblematic. It is evident, however, that we commonly rank novels even when this condition is not met. We readily say that one novel is not as funny as the other but its power to enchant makes it superior.

There is a simple answer to the question of how we compare the value of options or objects which are mixed-value goods. The very nature of the good they exhibit includes a standard of its own excellence. Just as the essential properties of knives include that they are cutting instruments, thus establishing that ability to cut well is a standard of excellence for knives, so the essential qualities of novels include standards for excellence of novels by which we can rank different novels even if they are neither Pareto superior to each other nor roughly equal in all their good-making qualities. I will call this the inherent standard argument. It responds to a familiar picture or intuition which seems to explain it. It is the picture sometimes expressed by the elusive saying 'the whole is greater than the sum of its parts'. The whole (a novel, a holiday, a party, etc.) is a new good, not merely a 'mechanical aggregate' of its parts. The good of the whole (a novel, let us say) is not merely the mechanical aggregation of its parts (humour, fascination with strange goings-on, learning about other people's problems, etc.). It is a new independent good which is constituted by the constituent goods being present *in the right way and in the right proportions*. A combination of the goods in these proportions creates a new good, and allows one to compare different items of the new good; this implies comparison between the contributions of the constituent goods.[7]

The argument is not that every inherent standard determines a norm for comparing items of that good which display different mixtures of its constituent goods. The inherent standard may do no more than list the constituent goods, without affording a way of ranking them. The inherent standard argument merely claims that such ranking may be established by inherent standards, and when it is it allows for comparisons of such goods involving comparisons of different values.

The argument reflects two beliefs. First, it presupposes that we do not fully understand what a mixed-value type (novel, tragedy, an evening at the disco) is until we understand what makes for a good token of the type. (If we do not understand that a knife is an instrument and therefore should be handy to use we fail to understand fully what knives are.) Second is the basic intuition expressed above that how much of each good property an item of a mixed-value good should ideally have depends on the contribu-

---

[7] One may say that every good is made of various components, except that with simple goods they are not independently valuable. The simple good consists of the non-valuable components being present in the right proportions. The case of a mixed good is merely a special case of what is true of all goods.

tion of that property to an ideal whole, which being a composite is defined by the ideal proportion of its contributing parts. A slick style and a gripping plot while ideal for a whodunit are too much of a good thing for a psychological novel, which should lead the reader to reflect on non-trivial aspects of human character, and is therefore better if its style, while interesting, is not too gripping and slick. (As the example shows, the more concrete forms are likely to lead to more complete ranking than the more general ones.)

The inherent standard argument does not, of course, entitle one to conclude that a complete ranking is possible on the basis of the standards embedded in the essential qualities of goods. Nor do we assume that that is the only possibly ground for ranking instances of mixed-value goods. For our purpose it is enough that there should be some non-Pareto comparisons to refute completely the common argument. But assuming that the inherent standard argument is a good one, does it refute the common argument? Of course, in providing one class of counter examples it formally refutes it. But perhaps it merely establishes an exception to the general case. Is the inherent standard argument confined to mixed-value goods? They are characterized by inherent standards. By definition no such argument is available when comparing two disparate goods, such as a detective story with a war film. The force of this attempt to confine the scope of the inherent standard argument is far from self-evident. As will appear in what follows I regard the inherent standards of mixed-value goods as sustained by social practices. It is arguable that there are social practices which sustain generally accepted comparisons of different options whose value is determined by distinct values. To judge the soundness of using this similarity to extend the inherent standard arguments to comparisons of distinct goods not belonging to a common mixed-value good, we need to understand better why inherent standards for comparing different instances of the same mixed-value good make sense.

3. THE RELEVANCE OF SOCIAL PRACTICE

None of the goods of mixed value would have existed without sustaining social practices. Bell-ringing, symphonic music, football, marriage, dances, lyric poetry, are all contingent historical products. They are all associated with activities which are rule-governed within social practices. That is, in all these cases the normal cases of meaningfully engaging in the relevant behaviour in a rewarding way (playing football, going to a concert, writing a poem, going to a dance) are cases of people knowingly conforming with social practices and their standards. People think of their acts under these descriptions, they dress and conduct themselves as one should in the football ground, or the concert hall, etc.

Had the relevant social practices not existed all these activities, and the mixed-value goods they are associated with, would not have been possible.[8] This is not at all surprising given that all these activities are acquired tastes. To acquire the skills and discrimination that succeeding in them requires one has to be socialized, habituated in their ways. This requires a culture with practices which make transmission and habituation possible. But what has the dependence on social practices to do with the value of the activity? It is certainly wrong to say that in all these cases success consists in conforming with the social practice, or that the success depends on (or that it normally presupposes) acting, when engaging in the activities, in order to conform with the practice. Is it not the case that the existence of a social practice 'merely' provides the opportunity to pursue these mixed-value goods, but does not affect their value? We are unable to participate in the tragedy competitions during the ancient Greek festivals. But had we been able to do so without (assume *per impossible*) a supporting practice it would have been as valuable for us as it was for ancient Greek tragedians.

In the following comments I will suggest that while all this is true it is not the whole truth. That is, I will suggest that it is false that mixed-value goods are goods only for people who live in a society with practices which sustain these goods. They are good, period. But people may be unable to partake of them in the absence of a sustaining practice. It is also false that the proper or normal reason for acting while engaging in them is to conform with the social practice. Yet the sustaining practice does affect the existence of the mixed good.

Is the value of a mixed-value good independent of the contingent existence of a practice? I do not wish to suggest that what is a (non-mixed) value depends on nothing but a social practice. But given that there are several values is there anything other than social practice to make a particular mix of ingredients a distinctive mixed-value good? Once we identify a mixed-value good we are, as the inherent standard argument shows, in a position to compare the excellence, merit, or value of different goods of this kind even though this involves comparison across different distinct values. We can rank some mixes of value very low, as when we say that the author's desire for humour spoils any psychological insight the novel might have had, and gets in the way of the plot. *Ergo* it is a poor novel. But can we identify a mixed-value good which is not sustained by a social practice?

---

[8] Or would have been different. One needs to distinguish between the defining rules of football, say, and the social conventions of the football culture. Playing football would have been possible, and rewarding, so long as one plays by its constitutive rules in an environment in which there is some supportive football culture, which need not be ours. Different attending practices may lead to different goods.

Mixing Values

If the existence of a sustaining social practice merely provides the opportunity to engage in the valuable activity then the activity must have been valuable before the opportunity arose. If it is so, then, even though there was no opportunity for anyone to play cricket or watch others do so before the game developed and was established in a social practice, the game was valuable before that time. There was as it were the idea of cricket, complete with the proviso that it requires a social practice for anyone to be able to play with, train, watch, manage, etc. cricket teams.

This Platonist view conflicts with a fundamental aspect of our understanding of values. The conflict is manifested by its inability to account for our common ways of thinking and talking of mixed-value goods, which endow historical contingencies with a greater role. The Platonist cannot say that cricket or Commedia dell'arte and other mixed-value goods were developed or invented. According to him they were rather discovered, revealed, or unfolded. Similarly, the Platonist has some difficulty in explaining the fact that goods change over time, that they do not have a fixed form. It is enough to think of the changes in the institution of marriage in this country over the centuries.

The problem is that the Platonist is committed to belief in unknowable values. How do we know which mixed-value goods there are? Normally we cite such goods as are sustained by social practices existing or which existed somewhere at some time. Alternatively, as in the example of gay marriages, we imagine modifications to existing (now or of old) practices. Can we imagine other practices? Does not fiction provide illustrations of purely invented goods? I doubt it. It seems that even inventive utopian fiction consists of describing modifications of known practice-supported goods. But the idea of a totally unknowable good is suspect.[9] Human goods are for people, they are what can enrich their lives. Unknowable ones cannot, and are not goods.[10]

Finally, it seems that Platonism leads to the view that every mix of values, which can be supported by a social practice (and the limitations of people's faculties and abilities make this a substantive restriction[11]), and which does not have deleterious consequences, is a good. In other words, there is no

---

[9] Some of these goods are only unknowable for a person given his time in history. In time they will be revealed in some society or other. Other goods will remain unknowable for ever, as there will always remain unrealizable goods, sustainable by practices which were never adopted, and thus some goods remain unknowable for ever. It is not my claim that there are specific goods which must remain unknowable, but this does not weaken the force of the objection.

[10] A good we know of can enrich us even though we may not realize that it is a good. A good we cannot know of cannot.

[11] Though it merely restricts one sufficient condition for a mix to be a good. There could be mixed-value goods based on variants on social practices which, given human nature, cannot be endorsed by social practices, and are destined to remain marginal variants.

independent criterion determining what mix of values can constitute a mixed-value good. Anything (subject to the above restriction) goes, provided it is supported by a social practice. This is readily seen in our tolerant culture in the proliferation of literary forms. What is a bad novel too preoccupied with plot at the expense of character may be a good spy novel, or a detective story, or any of several other literary styles putting a premium on action and discounting character. A bad novel may be a good historical novel, and a bad historical novel may be a good historical romance. And who is to say that the species and subspecies we recognize exhaust possibilities? Is there anything to exclude the proliferation of more species and their subdivisions? It seems therefore that given a sustaining practice any mix of goods is a mixed-value good. Platonism means that they were such since the beginning of time. But as the only difference between any odd mix of goods and a mixed-value good is a sustaining practice it seems odd that its emergence has nothing to do with the coming into being of the good.

One version of Platonism, let's call it social Platonism, escapes these strictures. It holds that a form of marriage, for example, is good only for members of communities in which a sustaining social practice prevails. In turning towards social relativism the Platonist abandons the 'opportunity only' view of the relevance of social practice expressed above. We no longer regard social practices as mere opportunities for benefiting from certain goods. They are now conditions for the goodness of those goods.[12] But this relativist Platonism is wrong. It exaggerates the importance of social practices. It stops us from saying that it would have been good for us to be able to enjoy a certain good if only we could. For the relativist maintains that the good is no good at all for us in the absence of the appropriate sustaining social practice. For example, John and Jerry could not say that it would have been good for them to be able to get married (to each other). In the absence of a practice of gay marriages such marriage is not good for them, at least not for as long as they stay in their society. This seems wrong. We feel that it would have been good for them to be able to get married. The absence of a practice of gay marriages makes it impossible for them to do so, but it does not negate the value of doing so for gay people living in our society.

These considerations lead me to the supposition that only practice-supported mixed-value goods and their variants exist. This rejects both Platonism, which regards social practices as affecting opportunity but not existence, and social Platonism. For once a good exists it is true for all that

---

[12] This is the mark of social relativism. It is to be contrasted with moral relativism, which holds that the same propositions can be true for some people while false for others.

engaging with it is good or valuable, if only they had an opportunity to do so. This is then true even of people who existed before the sustaining practice emerged.

One objection to this conclusion is that I have been concentrating on trivial goods like novels and cricket. It is otherwise with moral goods, it will be said. But I doubt it. Moral goods are just goods which through their effects on people other than the agent acquire a moral label. Of course, no one would claim that any way of practising medicine would be acceptable. It must cure the ill. But that is because medicine is primarily instrumental in value. Nor would every practice of friendship be acceptable. Friendship is intrinsically valuable. But to be acceptable it must be good for both participants, and not only to one of them.

Another objection to the above conclusion sees the survival of the enjoyer of goods as a limiting condition of their acceptability. Various mixes which lead to death, or a high risk of death, at least if this affects young people, should be held unacceptable, they would say. I find it difficult to accept a transcendent value of survival. Life seems not so much intrinsically valuable as a precondition for doing anything valuable. But if so life should not be valued (except on instrumental grounds) except in as much as it is spent in valuable pursuits. There is no intrinsic value in vegetating life. If so then one cannot restrict forms of valuable activities by a requirement of survival. The boot is on the other foot. Survival is to be (intrinsically) valuable only if it is used to engage in valuable activities.

4. CONCERNING THE STRUCTURE OF VALUE

The argument so far raises as many questions as it answers. I was drawn towards two conclusions:

1. Mixed-value goods are practice-dependent and the supporting practice is normative. It fixes standards of success which enable one to rank goods of the relevant type, even though such ranking implies ranking between different mixes of distinct value which goes beyond relying on Pareto improvements.

2. Any mix of values could, if supported by a social practice (and if meeting one or two other conditions, like not having bad consequences) be a mixed-value good.

Does not the second conclusion undermine the first? If any mix will do, how can the inherent standards rank some combinations above others? The answer must be that the fact that there is a social practice sustaining one mix of values, whereas there is no practice sustaining another mix, accounts for this difference. But how can it? What is it about social practices which gives them this status? In answering this question we will also pick up and explore the earlier cryptic remarks about the ability to deviate from the standard supported by the social practice, and to generate variations on recognized goods.

The answer lies with the basic structure of value, a topic which cannot be rehearsed here beyond adverting to one familiar point. That something is of value must be so independently of the agent's will. Mixed-value goods may depend on social practices, but social practices, while the product of human actions, are not subject to the will of any individual. The reason for this condition[13] is well-known. We guide and judge ourselves by the value of our options, our actions, emotions, attitudes, and character. But the very idea of judging implies a standard by which one judges, which is independent of the judge. People do sometimes set targets to themselves in an arbitrary way and attempt to achieve them, but they do so only to the extent that they believe that testing their resolve to stick to targets and their ability to accomplish what they set out to do are valuable. And these values do not depend on their will. One basic function of social practices is to fix on particular value-mixes that people could aim at. This role is made necessary by a number of central features of value and of human nature, of which I will comment briefly on two.

First is the importance, given human nature, of normality. One of the central polarities in life is between routine and innovation. Normality provides the reassurance and security of being within well-established boundaries, on a familiar terrain, and normality is a condition of inter-generational transmission of cultural forms and of a sense of continuity with history. Innovation is necessary to accommodate the need for self-expression, for activities which manifest one's individuality, one's imagination and enterprise, and therefore mark one as different from others.[14] Most people require some balance between the two in their lives. Our concern is not with this balance and its precise role in life. Rather, we are concerned with the implications of this polarity for the nature of values. To provide an anchor for the distinction between normality and innovation, the fixing of targets noted above, that is, the fixing of particular mixes of values as good to aim at, has to be underpinned by social practices. They generate goods with a particular social profile (high-brow, trendy, for sporty types, etc.). They also generate goods pursuit of which is normal, and which can be

---

[13] Whose precise articulation with all the required qualifications need not concern us.

[14] See on the manifestation of the corresponding polarity of identification based on belonging v. achievement in A. Margalit and J. Raz, 'National Self-Determination', *Journal of Philosophy* (Sept. 1990), included in my *Ethics in the Public Domain*.

modified to make room for variations expressing the need for innovation. Since innovation depends on its contrast with normality it is impossible without fixed normal forms.

Second, there is the fact that values are an acquired taste. Again, the case should not be exaggerated. Basic values have roots in human nature (as do basic human vices). But there is no culture without acculturation, and values are creatures of culture. Acculturation presupposes social practices into which one grows, or which one acquires later by habituation.

As these comments make clear, the dependence of mixed-value goods on social practices has two aspects. Normality is confined to the goods sustained by practices in the agent's society. But acculturation includes, in many cultures, familiarizing people with alien cultures and their practices and they remain a source of innovation. The old is a source of the new. The birth of a mixed-value good requires the evolution of a supporting practice, but the demise of the practice, while it may deprive people of opportunities of enjoying that good, does not deprive it of value. This is but one reason for not identifying mixed-value goods with their sustaining practices. The relationship is not one of identity. And the existence of the social practice is not a 'reason' why this mix is the superior one. The standard which is sustained by the practice, and not the practice itself, is the ultimate direct justification for preferring this particular mix.[15] Perhaps even the phrase 'a sustaining practice' which I have used is misleading. But further exploration of the relation of the value and its sustaining practice cannot be undertaken here.

5. COMPARING DISTINCT VALUES

The examination of mixed-value goods was undertaken in pursuit of a refutation of the common argument according to which there is no value ranking of goods whose merit is due to different and distinct intrinsic values. The result must be declared a partial success. On the one hand, different instances of one mixed-value good (different detective stories, different mountain climbing expeditions) can be ranked where the inherent standard of that good warrants it, and inherent standards do allow us to rank across distinct values. On the other hand, in so far as this argument is concerned, the case of instances of one mixed-value good cannot be generalized. It does not extend to comparing instances of

---

[15] See below on direct and indirect justifications. We can of course justify the claim that the constituent goods are indeed good.

different (mixed-value or other) goods, nor to the comparison of different good (-types).

The ability to compare (some) instances of the same mixed-value good is a necessary corollary of its dependence on a sustaining social practice, and that is necessary for its existence (the constraint of acculturation) and for it to function as a normal paradigm. These considerations do not apply to comparing instances of different goods. Admittedly, we do find conventional views that opera is a higher good than football, etc. But whereas the inherent standards of mixed goods are necessary for their existence, and essential for the crucial tension between normality and innovation, conventional wisdom about the ranking of different goods does not serve a similar role which could legitimate their existence. A society with a more egalitarian culture in which goods are not ranked allows for acculturation and for both normality and innovation.

Am I selling my own argument short? Could it not be said that part and parcel of mixed-value goods is the practice which fixes their ranking among other goods? One misses, on this view, part of the meaning of opera if one does not realize that it is an elitist good. Part of the good of being an opera fan is belonging to a select minority. Anyone who is not aware of this is not aware of what kind of a good opera is. There is clearly some truth in these claims. It is true that opera and other goods have a conventional social profile. This leads to side benefits, or incidental drawbacks, of engaging with such goods. One may lose or gain friends, one may acquire a certain reputation for moving in certain circles, and one's own self-image may be affected. But all these are side-effects. They are not essential ingredients of the good itself, as is witnessed by the fact that it is not uncommon for the social profile of a good to differ between social circles, who all agree on the inherent standard of the good. The point should not be exaggerated. The inherent standard of a good may itself be subject to disagreement, due to the normality/innovation tension noted above.[16] But it remains the case that its conventionally accepted social profile is separable from the good, and is not essential for its survival or identity. The practice of viewing the good in this way is not one which can be justified by the considerations which were adduced above as justifying the inherent standard of the good.

Furthermore, the justification of the inherent standards of mixed-value goods which I have outlined in the previous section is indirect in the following sense. A direct justification is one which can answer the question 'Why is X good?' by mentioning good-making features of X. What makes something good are features of that thing or of its relations to other things.

---

[16] See also the comments on its fragile nature below.

The story of the previous section was different. It related not to the content of the good but to its mode of generation, that is, to the fact that mixed-value goods are created by a sustaining social practice. To use a phrase introduced by H. L. A. Hart, this is a content-independent justification. Social practice can be a source of a variety of mixed-value goods, including, as was noted above, of conflicting and inconsistent ones. That is why we could conduct our inquiry without looking in detail at any particular good. Finally, there is nothing intrinsically valuable about social practices as such (and there are many pernicious social practices); the justification of giving social practices this weight in our understanding of mixed-value goods depended on other considerations (acculturation and the normality/innovation distinction) which are the presupposition of the very existence of mixed-value goods in human societies. In that sense the justification offered in the previous section is indirect. But most people who argue that opera is a higher good than football have a much more direct consideration in mind. They regard it as a manifestation of a higher aspect of human abilities, or something like that. The inherent standard argument cannot be generalized to justify such conclusions.

In any case the ranking established by the inherent standard argument is of the wrong kind for those who look for a general ranking of goods. It is fragile ranking, continuously in tension and liable to be undermined at any time. The inherent standard sets standards of success, but also a standard to rebel against, a baseline for modifications and variations. The tensions between old and new, between conformity and individuality, between security and risk are ever present and they continuously challenge existing standards, threatening to turn what they dub vulgar, improper, inferior, kitsch, etc. into a new model for a transformed standard. After all 'from the outside', for one who does not accept the prevailing standard there is nothing to be said for the superiority of the mix of values it sanctions over those mixes it regards as inferior other than that it sets a standard to aim at; but standards can be aimed at in rebellion as well as in acceptance. The fact that the only ranking the inherent standard establishes is such a fragile one is important in understanding the nature of the mixed-value goods exception to the common argument that there is no way of ranking goods of distinct kinds. Such 'fragile' ranking is not the sort that those who wish to claim the superiority of high culture over low-brow goods aim at. Their arguments must derive from other sources.

This consideration militates against an otherwise appealing possibility of extending the mixed-value goods case to include well-being. If the good life is a mixed-value good then it has its own inherent standard of ranking and this provides, as such inherent standards can do, for the proper ranking of even distinct goods. This view requires careful examination. The fact that the inherent standard of normal goods is flexible in the sense described is a small consideration against it, given that the aspired-to inherent standard of well-being is meant to be inflexible. More persuasively, this flexibility shows that even if well-being is an independent mixed-value good with rigid standards,[17] the vindication of its internal standard must follow a different route from the one chartered here which can only establish flexible standards.[18]

Suppose for a moment that no other sources are available and that distinct goods cannot be ranked. What conclusions should one draw from this? This shows that value pluralism leads to value incommensurability. It does not, however, in itself establish incommensurability of reasons for concrete options. There are reasons which do not derive from the value of the options but from, for example, the personality of the agents, or their biography. These include their tastes, their ambitions for themselves, etc. Some writers try to reduce all of these to the value (and not merely value to the agent) of such options, and dealing properly with such views must remain a task for another occasion. Consider, however, the situation of opera lovers. Even on the supposition that opera is no better than football they are not unreasonable to prefer opera. Given that their preference is reasonable so is their wish (if they happen to have it) to live in an opera-loving society. I do not have to believe that what I have a taste for is better than all else to have a reasonable wish that others share my taste. I will find myself in a, for me, more congenial environment if others share my taste.[19] Given the reasonableness of this wish I am entitled to let it guide me in my actions and commitments, both private and public. None of this implies a judgement of superior value, and I am committed to the view that 'justice' is as much on the side of the football fan, who reciprocates my preferences. The just outcome in issues to do with allocation of public resources depends on the numbers who have one or the other reasonable view.[20]

---

[17] Which need not of course be complete. Just like other internal standards it may provide merely a partial ranking.

[18] Common philosophical views hold on to an inflexible standard as illustrated above by the example of higher v. lower activities (opera v. football, or perhaps I should have chosen opera against music hall). It is logically possible to develop a flexible view of human well-being. This will make the nature of well-being practice-dependent in ways which generate difficulties that cannot be explored here.

[19] I do not mean to suggest that I should prefer to live in a like-minded society. Some people prefer to have eccentric tastes, for they feel a need to be different. Others are just indifferent to their neighbours' tastes on such matters, etc.

[20] Which does not mean that winner takes all. There may be a case for an equitable compromise.

APPENDIX

This essay was presented to the joint session of the Aristotelian Society and Mind Association in 1991. It was followed by a paper by Professor. James Griffin,[21] criticizing some of my contentions, and presenting a different view about value incommensurability. What follows is an edited version of my reply to him given orally at the session:

In the background are two large problems. One concerns the way in which social practices are relevant to the existence or validity of at least some values. The second is the knotty problem of the role of reason in practical deliberation and in guiding action. As to the second, much attention has been focused on a wide variety of sceptical and nihilistic views about intrinsic values. Against them are ranged the rationalists who believe that there are adequate reasons to guide choices in all but trivial cases. But there is also a middle position according to which there are reasons to guide people's action towards valuable or right options and away from bad or wrong ones, but that quite commonly those underdetermine choices. Where they do people do what they want, pathological cases excepted. What they want they want for reasons. The will is intelligible. But the reasons which make the will intelligible do not determine it. Reasons would have justified and made intelligible a different want as well. There are, in other words, no reasons to want one rather than the other of the valuable options. How can reason so radically underdetermine choice? One straightforward explanation is that the different reasons for one action or another are incommensurate. One type of case in which reasons may be incommensurate is where they arise out of different values, assuming that different values are always incommensurate. Prof. Griffin rejects this explanation, and in a way so do I. My rejection is, however, more modest than his. My essay is concerned with the special case of mixed-value goods. We can compare two novels and judge one to be superior to the other on the ground that though it is not as good in one value (say not as funny) it is better in another (say in insight) in a way which more than compensates for this deficiency. I try to say something about what makes such cases possible and conclude that while they make sense, and are often true, they are made possible by conditions which are special to mixed-value goods and cannot be extended to other comparisons of value. I should clarify this point: I do not claim to have provided an explanation of all possible comparisons of value of two mixed-value goods of the same kind (say, two novels), only to have offered some reflections on such comparisons which derive from the fact that the compared items belong to one type of mixed-value good (two novels, two operas, etc.).

My explanation both of the possibility and of the limited scope of such comparisons is that they derive from the fact that each type of such goods is

[21] Published in the joint volume of the *Proceedings of the Aristotelian Society*, 85 (1991), under the same title as my paper.

constituted by standards which also determine what counts as good specimens of the type. *To understand what novels are is also to understand what good novels are.* One presupposition of this statement is that mixed-value goods provide one example of the much used, and abused, principle that the whole is larger than the sum of its parts. Think of three novels, one witty and insightful, the second witty but uninsightful, the third insightful but dead earnest. It is nonsense to suggest that since the first incorporates both insight and wit each of the others is half as good as the first (let us disregard other features, and assume that the first is the equal of the others in their respective qualities). It is precisely the combination of wit and insight in one novel which gives the first the advantage, and it is the interplay of the two, the way they are mixed or separated, feed off each other, or bounce off each other, which accounts for whatever is good in it. The whole is greater than the sum of the parts because it is in the nature of novels to generate such combinations of interacting goods. To understand this is part of what it takes to understand what novels are.

Mixed-value goods are constituted by standards, and one thing that those standards do is indicate the way different component goods interact. Because of this they provide a way of ranking different items of the type, including some rankings which allow for trade-offs between different goods.

Griffin rejects all this. 'My main doubt', he says, 'is that novels (and most mixed-value goods) are not like knives in the important respect. Knives do a job ... But novels ... do many jobs' (p. 105). Granted, but is that 'the important respect'? Some may even say that novels do no job in the sense that knives do. All this is immaterial. The point of referring to knives was to bring another example (i.e. of a tool which is not a mixed-value good) where the standards which determine what items belong to the kind also determine which of them are good items of the kind.

Griffin's discussion of C. P. Snow and Wodehouse illustrates the pitfalls of incautious comparisons. His purpose is to show that, since Wodehouse is better than Snow, a fact which does not derive from the inherent standards of the type, there must be other grounds for that fact. His reason for believing that Wodehouse is the better novelist is that 'Wodehouse's strengths are great and Snow's slight' (p. 105). This can mean one of two things. He may mean that Wodehouse is strong in a dimension more important than the one in which Snow excels. But given that Griffin regards Snow as giving more understanding of our life and times than Wodehouse and Wodehouse as being a better stylist and giving more entertainment than Snow, we can I think dismiss this possibility. Griffin must therefore mean his observation in the other sense, that is he must mean that Wodehouse's strength in the dimension he is good at is great while Snow is only moderately strong in the dimension he is good at. This is rather like saying that Mickey Mouse is bigger than Pooh Bear because Mickey is a big mouse, while Pooh is a small bear. To justify Griffin's judgement on Snow and Wodehouse one needs to calibrate the dimensions they are good at—one cannot rely as Griffin does on their relative situation within the two distinct dimensions.

Is Wodehouse the better novelist? It is interesting that, while this is clearly the view which Griffin needs to defend, he never asserts it outright. Instead he repeatedly says, 'I myself rank the novels', or 'I rank them as I do'. You may say that this comes to the same thing when said by a modest man. But I am not sure. When I say I rank Dostoevsky above Tolstoy I do not mean to say that he is the better novelist, only that he is more to my taste, that I get more out of him, that I am more susceptible to his charms than to those of Tolstoy, etc. In fact I do not believe that they are rankable, or that *The Brothers Karamazov* and *War and Peace* are rankable. If my use of 'I rank them' is not idiosyncratic, if its normal use does not always mean 'I believe in the following objective, impersonal ranking', then Griffin is allowing himself to draw from the uncontroversial fact that I can have reasonable, not just brute, but reasoned, preferences the unwarranted conclusion that in such cases an impersonal ranking of values exists.

As I said the gist of my suggestion is that mixed-value goods are constituted by inherent standards, which provide for some modest ranking possibilities. This is not quite the way Griffin understands me. He says that I think that the standards of correctness for judgements of comparative value come from social practices. This may give a slightly distorted idea of my view for two reasons. First, I took pains to emphasize that I am not claiming that there are no other grounds for comparison of values. I remain an agnostic on that. Second, the comparisons are based on reason-giving standards. I did say, but this is a separate, detachable point, that I believe that such standards can exist only if underpinned by social practices. But it is not my view that such social practices have 'authority' over us in the sense that their existence is a reason for accepting the standards. Rather their existence is a necessary presupposition for the existence of the standards, including for their rejection, for innovative experimentation with them, etc. My belief in the necessity of an underlying social practice (perhaps it is better to speak of a shared understanding, for a practice may suggest reasoned regularities such as brushing one's teeth before one goes to bed), my belief in the necessity of an underlying common understanding, derives from two beliefs: (1) that any combination of *goods* can be an independent good, that is, that while there may be basic primary goods, what combination of goods constitutes a whole which is larger than the sum of its parts is largely a matter of social practice; (2) that reference to normality is crucial to those goods: they must be capable of being aimed at, recognized, talked about, followed, deviated from, capable of forming a basis for improvisation, a standard by which to distinguish the routine from the innovative, etc., to be what they are, that is, to be independent mixed-value goods.

Let me turn to Griffin's paper to explain my doubts, and this may help me in explaining the way I understand the problem. Griffin's paper ranges over more problems than I have time to mention. My comments will be confined to pp. 106–10. These are the pages in which he explains the comparability of what he calls the prudential values. In saying this I do not mean to agree that the examples considered in those pages are of prudential values. But let this be as it may.

I will comment briefly on two of Griffin's main theses:

(1) 'Belief that something is important runs into belief about why it is important, which runs into belief about how important it is' (p. 108).
(2) 'the comparisons that I have mentioned (e.g. of Dostoyevski and Proust) all turn on the extent to which human interests are satisfied'.

I have my doubts about Griffin's second contention, that comparing the value of novels, for example, is judging which meets human interests to a higher degree. Griffin remarks that this is to assume a controversial view about the assessment of novels. Perhaps. But what worries me is that it seems to be misguided about the nature of human interest. Why should the interests of one who reads Proust be served better than the interests of one who reads Agatha Christie (since we both agree that these two are comparable)? Two difficulties come to mind. The first has to do with the reckoning. At any given time I may have better reason to read Christie than Proust. It all depends on the time available, my mood, concentration, and so on. Over a lifetime it may turn out that there were more occasions in which Christie trumped Proust, it may also turn out that I had reason to spend more time reading her than Proust. I do not know whether this is so, my point is simply that were it so it would not have affected my judgement of their relative value. Moreover to think that judgement of Proust's value depends on the degree to which reading him serves the interests of people on average seems somehow off the mark. Did the value of Senecan tragedies decline in the Middle Ages because given the circumstances of the time they were of little service to people's interests? Did it then grow in the Jacobean period only to decline later? Would people who, though psychologically acute and insightful, are unaware of the psychological needs of the bulk of the population, be bad literary critics? These doubts have to do with the directness of the relationship between goods and interests. My second difficulty with Griffin's suggestion goes further and questions the direction of that relationship. I believe that the reason we think—to the extent we do—that a person who spends his time with Proust is better off than one who spends it with Christie is that we think Proust's the better novel. That is, we have no independent conception of well-being which enables us to judge what is good for people, and therefore what is good. We know what is good and conclude that that is good for people, that it is in their interest to spend time with the good. This is obviously far too simple a statement. To the extent that the good and interests are interconnected there is some truth on both sides—at least to the degree that people's interests are the product of nature rather than nurture they determine what is good rather than are determined by it. But to a large degree people's well-being is determined by nurture, by culture. Here mixed-value goods are particularly prominent, and here I come back to my claim that their standards of excellence are at least in part internal to the 'artificial' genre they belong to. Here rather than learning what is valuable by reference to human interest we learn what is good for people by learning what is valuable. I have to admit that this point seems to be basic to the very idea of culture.

Finally, let me come to Griffin's first thesis, namely that knowing that something is valuable and why tells you how valuable it is and enables you to compare it with other valuables. Knowing how important an object or a skill, etc., is may mean no more than that one knows what one loses by lacking it: I cannot play Beethoven piano music, cannot use it to express my feelings and musical sensibility; I am confined to records and concerts. It tells us when the use of the skill or the object is important (important to read not to display on shelves). But none of these will enable us to compare it with other values. To know how important it is in the relevant sense is to know how important it is in relation to other values. In that sense to say that one cannot know that understanding is important without knowing how important it is is to say that one cannot know that understanding is important without knowing that humour is as well, and without knowing about their relative importance. This I see no reason to accept. If one can understand one value without knowing of some others it should not be difficult to establish that even when one knows of both one need not know how they rank relative to each other. In truth these points do not matter for Griffin's first thesis must be judged a *petitio principi*. The most he could argue is that if one understands two values one understands which is more important, if they are capable of being ranked in importance, or knows that they are incommensurate, if they are incommensurate.

9

The Value of Practice

Why is the thought that values, at least some values, are 'socially constituted', that is created and maintained by social practices, so appealing? One reason is that if true it could pave the way to a rebuttal of one of the persistent doubts about the possibility of knowledge about values. It would seem that the evaluative beliefs shared in a society or a culture are a major factor in explaining why members of a society have the evaluative views they do. This may shake our confidence in the objectivity of such beliefs. If they track not the values things actually have, but the value people around believe them to have, then what ground do we have to trust people's evaluative judgements? Or their ability to form sound evaluative judgements? It might seem that at best we should conclude that if there are truths about matters of value they are unknowable. We may stumble upon them occasionally, but we never have reason to trust our judgement or that of others. If, however, value is socially constituted then the fact that our judgements track common views may show that they track value which is itself not independent of those views.

As stated, both the sceptical argument and its suggested rebuttal are feeble caricatures. Many people have views which differ significantly from those common in their social group. Moreover, just about all contemporary societies lack social cohesion, and enjoy a degree of open communications across groups and a degree of social and cultural mobility, which defy any simple explanation of people's views by reference to the views common in their social group(s). The sceptical argument must allow for these complexities. So must any account of values which regards them as socially constituted. It must allow for the fact that not only the good, but also the bad is socially constituted, and that some societies may be led astray, and take good for bad and bad for good. An account which has the consequence that people whose evaluative views differ from those around them must be wrong is a non-starter, if only because of the impossibility, in many cases, of providing a value-independent fix on what are the views around people. The complexities which render the caricatures so inadequate complement each other, and may allow for developments which will render the view that values are socially constituted attractive for the reason that it provides the best answer to the epistemic doubts indicated above.

I do not propose to pursue this line of thought, beyond adding one observation. Given that the connection between people's evaluative views and those of their society is loose, it is possible that in some cases it testifies to no more than the fact that access to values, that is the ability to become aware of their existence, and the ability to engage with what is valuable, is socially limited. That is, in many cases it may be that the social dependence of evaluative beliefs testifies not to the social constitution of value but to the social dependence of access to value.

It is not difficult to think of other reasons for suspecting that at least some values are socially constituted. If they are, a ready explanation for some of the diversity of value practices and in evaluative beliefs is readily available, or at least so it seems. But neither the epistemic argument nor the argument from diversity is a strong argument for the social constitution of (some) values. They are just as likely to be seen as arguments against the knowability of values, or against their objectivity. This is because the thought that values are socially constituted brings with it puzzles and paradoxes. I have dismissed some of them in previous chapters. But others remain.

Yet that some values are socially constituted seems to be an inescapable conclusion of additional arguments. In this chapter I examine one such argument, and some additional puzzles and contradictions which bedevil some theses affirming the social constitution of value.

1. SOCIALLY CREATED GOODS

I will refer blandly to engaging with value to cover the multitude of ways in which intrinsic value can feature in our life to our advantage: it includes reading a good novel, or writing one, or discussing it, etc.; playing the piano, composing for it, listening to it (with attention and comprehension), talking about it, etc.; being at a party, hill walking, and so on and so forth. The expression conveys the point that engaging with intrinsic value is something active, in that it requires intention and attention. Needless to say the same is not true of instrumental value, which can benefit us without our awareness of the fact. The active aspect of engagement with (intrinsic) value does not always mean that the engagement begins intentionally. I can lie down to rest and only gradually become aware of a sense of well-being spreading through my aching body as my muscles relax, and my skin responds to the heat of the day. The instrumental benefits of the event do not depend on my awareness of it, but it features as an intrinsically valuable episode of pleasure only to the extent that I am aware of it.

The intentionality of engagement with value means that engagement with value presupposes, with few exceptions, that what is valuable is recognized as valuable under some concept or another. The example of resting in the sun illustrates the sort of case which may be the exception to this rule: cases where recognition of the good may be preconceptual. It is likely that pure hedonic pleasures, the enjoyment of sensations in themselves, are the main exception.[1]

That the intentionality of engagement with value means that such engagement depends on the availability of concepts through which the nature of the good is understood is shown by the fact that engagement with value depends on knowing the difference between successful and failed engagement. Understanding the nature of a good or of a valuable kind of activity or experience involves understanding what it is to be a successful instance of that activity or experience, and of being able to distinguish better from less good instances of the good. To understand the contemporary idea of a holiday one needs to be able to tell a successful holiday from a less successful one. To understand poetry requires being able to tell a good poem from a not so good one. All goods are identified by standards of excellence. Understanding the type involves mastering the standards of excellence which constitute it and being able to apply them. Such an understanding constitutes mastering the concept of the type of good or value involved.

Concepts being historical products, access to value, where it depends on possession of concepts, is historically or culturally regulated. Access to certain values may be denied people altogether, when no appropriate concepts exist, and it may be directed, filtered, through different concepts in different cultures, depending on the concepts available to their members.[2]

The social dependence of access to value does not in itself establish the social dependence of value. Are any values created? Some are inclined to deny that possibility. 'People can create or make objects of value, but not values.' But things are not that straightforward, partly because the way we identify and individuate values is far from clear. Take a common case. Every year toy and games manufacturers bring out a number of new games. Imagine a person who invents a new board game. I will assume that it is a good. It is an invented, a newly created good. It differs from existing games, and it is not a discovery of an ideal of a game, which has been there all along waiting to be discovered. Does the new game bring a new value into existence? If the paradigms for values are 'life, liberty, and (the pursuit of) happiness', or 'liberty, equality, and fraternity' then clearly no new value is

---

[1] Though some pleasurable perceptions, e.g. the enjoyable perception of a colour one likes, which do not require any recognition of objects, or any other point of reference beyond the perceiving subject, are another exception.

[2] These matters are discussed in 'Notes on the Objectivity of Value', and in 'Moral Change and Social Relativism', Chs. 5 and 6 above.

brought into the world by the new game. But, following an established tradition, I will use the term in a sense in which it is true, say, that opera embodies a distinctive value, that is, that there is a value which good operas but nothing else can fully realize.

Does the creation, or invention, of a new game amount to the creation of a new value, understanding value in this broad sense? It creates not only a new good, a new object of value (in the way in which a new good piano and a new good painting are new objects of value). It creates a new form of the good. There is a new activity which is good or of value, of playing the game, and a new desirable goal, of winning the game, which did not exist before. Are values correlated with distinctive forms of the good? Does the creation of a new form of good amount to the creation of a new value? Before we face this question let me repeat a couple of familiar points about the emergence and continued existence of new forms of goods.

The game in the example starts life as a private game. If its promoter is successful it will catch on and will be played by many. But unless it is spectacularly successful that will not bring a major change to its status and meaning. Those who play it might just as well be playing a game they or their grandfather invented.[3] But most forms of good we know of in our lives, whether or not they or their ancestors were invented by an individual, are transmitted to us socially, that is they are sustained, and sometimes are created, by social practices based on common understandings of their meaning.

Social practices, and I refer to them as sustaining practices, do more than preserve and facilitate the transmission of knowledge about forms of good which could be created by individuals. They usually thicken the texture of goods, allowing them to develop greater subtlety and nuance. The thick texture of most forms of good makes it impossible to learn them by description. They have to be absorbed by assimilation, by habituation. The ability to engage with them presupposes implicit knowledge and understanding which one acquires through habituation, and cannot acquire by description. Consider an example. Think of Javanese humour. We cannot expect to understand Javanese jokes just upon being told them. We need to live among Javanese people, preferably in normal conditions, but if that is impossible then among an immigrant community in another country, and get the hang of Javanese humour by osmosis. Learning about Javanese humour from books about humour is a very inferior way,

---

[3] In fact very little need happen for a game to acquire additional, external, meanings. The fact that it is commercially marketed, rather than invented by me yesterday afternoon, gives it a certain appearance of legitimacy (i.e. that it is not too silly, etc.), but denies it a certain excitement and freshness. If it descends from grandfather it is likely to have acquired a family-related aura of tradition and respect.

affording only a very partial understanding, though seeing humour displayed in films, stories, and other records may come closer to living among the Javanese.

The thick texture of many created forms of the good shows that they are created by sustaining practices. No human culture can exist without such socially sustained forms of the good. I will not further refer to the distinction between forms of goods which are invented by individuals, and those which are created by social practices. I will refer to both as socially created (forms of the) good. Our interest is in the question whether some values are created by people, and to that purpose the distinction between individual and social creation is immaterial. The conclusion established by our consideration of the invented game is that at least some forms of the good are socially created. It does not follow from the considerations adduced here that the forms of the good die when the sustaining practices lapse. Once created they remain in existence. They may be forgotten, but they can always be rediscovered, and regain their popularity. Some socially created goods can only be engaged with in a society where there are practices sustaining them. When discussing such goods, which I call local goods, I gave good manners and goods of fashion as examples of local goods.[4] But for the main part our concern is with the general category of socially created goods.

Let us return to consider whether different forms of the good import different values by posing this question: what difference can it make whether one engages with one form of good or another? Why does it matter whether one plays chess or monopoly, whether one listens to a symphony or a string quartet? Chances of success and desire for variety are obvious reasons for choosing one over the other, reasons which do not imply anything about the value of the competing goods. I may be good at monopoly and very bad at chess. The good of engaging with value is conditional on doing so well, that is well enough. But there is less of a point in playing chess if one does it badly.[5] Similarly, if I played lots of monopoly recently I have a reason to turn to chess now just to have a refreshing change. But such reasons do not tell the full story. Even disregarding the impact of playing one game better than the other and of diversity, I may enjoy one more than the other. Since the pleasures involved are not purely sensual they are pleasures in successfully engaging with different goods, that is, different values. The same point is expressed when I observe, correctly, that 'I do not get the same thing out of the two games'. While they may both involve planning, caution and daring, foresight and imagination, etc. they

---

[4] See Ch. 6 above.

[5] Of course there may be instrumental reasons to play chess even if one does so badly. One may do so e.g. to improve one's game or to please one's partner.

differ in important respects. Even if they do not differ in the mental powers they engage they differ in the way these powers relate to one another in the pursuit of victory in the game. Even if they do not differ in their component goods they differ in the way they combine to set the standard of excellence for playing the game.

The example of board games does not transfer without modification to other goods (e.g. different musical or different literary forms). But the lesson is the same: each form of the good has its own standard of excellence, which is a distinct value for it can be realized only through engaging with that form of the good. These values are humble values, for they are relatively concrete. We understand them by seeing how they incorporate more abstract values, in a unique combination(s). That is, we understand a concrete value, like the value of chess, when we understand how playing well engages one with other more abstract values, and does so in the way which is appropriate to chess.

In a way concrete values like the value of a particular game, the value of a particular, socially conditioned, form of friendship, the value of a literary form, such as the sonnet, are continuous with the value of some objects, like works of art. Good paintings, and other good works of art,[6] are uniquely valuable. They instantiate in a unique way a number of valuable characteristics. Unlike uniquely valuable objects, however, distinct forms of the good set standards for excellence which apply to an open class of activities and objects.

2. SUBSUMPTION THROUGH THICK AND THIN

Let us make a short detour, and divert our attention from values to the concepts through which we conceive them. It is a general feature of concepts that they do not provide recipes for the generation of their own instantiations. Mastering the concept of a table may enable one to identify tables when coming across them. But it is not much help in designing new types or styles of tables. Understanding what birds are enables one to identify a bird when encountering one. But it is not much use in discovering which birds exist in which habitats. One has to wait until one encounters them, or is informed by those who have. True, some of their general characteristics can be inferred from the nature of the habitat. But for that one needs more than mastery of the notion of a bird, one needs knowledge of zoology.

---

[6] This statement needs qualification to apply to mechanically reproducible works of art.

In moral and evaluative matters we expect otherwise. We expect that mastery of moral principles and knowledge of what is valuable will enable us to determine what is morally right, or what is valuable in particular circumstances. By reference to general principles applied to the circumstances of any society we expect to be able to establish what would be a just rate of tax in that society. Indeed we must be able to do so if morality and values generally are to guide our lives. If they are to affect our decisions, judgements, attitudes, and imaginings we must be able to reason from the general to the particular, and not merely recognize the general in the particular when we encounter it. Can the social dependence of some values, that is, the fact that they are created and sustained by social practices, be compatible with the universality of value? While values do indeed guide one and enable one to form attitudes and plans of action ahead of the events to which they apply that ability is circumscribed. It exists within social contexts one has sufficient familiarity with, either through socialization or through learning about them. Beyond them the concepts one mastered cannot be relied upon to apply unmodified. Moreover, when we talk of future societies and cultures there is in principle a limit to what can be said about the values which apply to them.

How can these points be reconciled with the requirement of intelligibility which leads to the irresistible attraction of universality of value? Nothing in the examples I gave and the general lessons drawn from them should be allowed to justify the conclusion that our concepts apply only to familiar cultures. Javanese humour is humour. Their jokes, if they have jokes, are jokes. Granted that we cannot have a thick understanding of the concept 'Javanese humour' without familiarity with their society and with instances of their humour, still we cannot recognize their humour for what it is unless we can subsume it under a more general concept, and recognize theirs as an instance of humour.

I feel that we are walking on a knife edge. On the one hand, the requirement of intelligibility abhors a vacuum. It seems to imply that there is no room for new values, except in as much as they can be subsumed under existing ones in the way that changing circumstances yield a new just rate of tax. On the other hand, the argument that some values are socially created suggests that new values arise as cultures and societies evolve and change. The resolution of the tension between the two poles lies in the reciprocal relationship between evolving practices and new values on the one hand and explaining concepts on the other hand. Described with extreme schematic oversimplification this is how it works.[7]

Evolving practices give rise to new values. Commonly their emergence

---

[7] These matters are discussed in Ch. 7 above.

is recognized by subsuming them under familiar values.[8] Thus existing values make possible the recognition of new values when encountered, but they do not allow either prescribing or designing them, in the sense of saying 'these are the values one should have in these cultural conditions', nor do existing values provide a base for predicting which new values would evolve. New values emerge with evolving social practices and cultural developments. Once new subsumed values emerge reflection on them leads to a reinterpretation and a change of understanding of the more universal value concepts under which they were subsumed, thus leading to the emergence of new abstract value concepts to cover both new and old concrete values. In this way the intelligibility and the social dependence of values are reconciled. They are reconciled through the fact that intelligibility does not mean a permanent frame of reference. It allows a constantly shifting perspective. It does entail that there is no value vacuum at any given moment, without endowing this moment with permanence. It is a separate question whether the new abstract value concepts enable us to gain a better understanding of previously existing more abstract values, or whether the emergence of these concepts is also the emergence of new abstract values, in the same way that the emergence of new concepts such as 'abstract expressionism', 'gay marriages', 'surrogate mothers' accompanies the creation of new values.

I know of no general answer to this ontological question. But in general it seems that the emergence of abstract value concepts merely improves the understanding of previously existing values. As we saw earlier[9] when the value is instantiated by natural phenomena, for example landscapes, the value cannot be new, only access to it through the new concept is new. Similarly, if there is a right not to be tortured that right predates the concept of a right. The emergence of the concept merely enables us to understand that the right exists. The same goes for other abstract value concepts, such as the value of self-expression or of autonomy. The reason is that in these cases the value can be enjoyed by people who do not have the abstract concept. They cannot enjoy it without some concepts, but it is enough for them to have more concrete concepts, which are appropriately related to the right against torture, or to the state of expressing oneself, or of being autonomous.

[8] This description is greatly oversimplified. It attempts to establish dualities where often only continuities of tension exist. The new values do not emerge in discrete steps, they grow out of the old ones, often through conflicts of rejection and resistance. Anyone who ever thought of customs and social practices knows that every act of following a practice is also a small step towards its reinforcement. Every deviation from it is both an offence and a step towards its modification. The interpretation and justification of a practice are often indistinguishable from its reinterpretation, revision, and transformation.
[9] In Ch. 6 above.

Among those moral philosophers who distinguish between thick and thin evaluative concepts a trend has evolved to object to the tendency of non-cognitivist philosophers to assume that thin evaluative concepts can be understood independently of thick ones. Some of them argue that the relationship is the reverse one. Thin concepts can only be understood and explained through thick ones, which in turn are independent of their thin brothers. The view that I have been urging rejects both extremes. The thin and thick concepts are interdependent. Thick concepts have to be explained by reference to thinner ones in order to satisfy the requirement of intelligibility. The thin concepts, on the other hand, while explained by reference to thicker ones, also have an open-ended aspect: new thick concepts subject to them can always emerge. This makes them relatively independent of the thick concepts currently subsumed under them.

3. DOES PRACTICE MAKE GOOD?

This reconciliation of continuity through change, of the interdependence of thick and thin concepts, and of the intelligibility and the social dependence of values, may raise again the spectre of conventionalism. It is useful to restate why the social dependence espoused here is not conventionalist. A mark of conventions is that the reason for following them is that this is how things are done, this is how people generally behave. To non-Romans the injunction 'When in Rome do as the Romans do' is conventionalist advice. The Romans will—typically—have other reasons for doing as they do.

The social dependence of value has nothing to do with the affirmation of social practices as reasons for their own validity. I referred to the relevant social practices as sustaining practices. They are necessary for the existence of values. But they are not their justification. They are part of a sustaining background. They play a crucial role in the explanation of the reality of values, but that role is to be distinguished from that of justifying the values. Justification proceeds in terms of other values, and the way they are to be realized in particular circumstances. The social basis of value drops out of sight when justification is concerned and plays no role in it at all.

Concrete values are not determined by universal values any more than Chippendale chairs are made necessary by the concept of a chair. Once Chippendale chairs were invented it was possible to debate whether or not they were good chairs. Here the concept of a chair does include a standard of excellence which when applied to the conditions of the time and place can assist towards a verdict. Aesthetic, economic, and other standards may also apply. Likewise, the fact that the social basis of value plays no part in their justification leaves room for the examination of the value of different social practices. Some may be found to be debased, corrupt, or evil. Conventionalism is essentially conservative. The social dependence of value is not. It allows for a radical criticism of social practices.

We can therefore reply with a firm 'No' to the question whether this form of the social dependence of value is excessively conservative, running the danger of approving of all forms of locally approved atrocities. The social dependence explored here applies equally to goods and bads. It was not part of the thesis that being sustained by a social practice is itself either a good or a component of a good. It is neither. It is merely a precondition of being either a good or a bad, of the socially dependent kind. Regarding both goods and bads there is the exception of conventional goods and bads regarding which the existence of a practice is a component of the good or bad. For all other socially created goods and bads having been practised at one time is merely a precondition of their existence. It does not establish that they are good, bad, or indifferent. That is the role of the usual kind of arguments showing how they instantiate values (or evils), arguments to which the existence of the sustaining practice is immaterial (or plays the subsidiary role of showing that in the social conditions prevailing this is the way to instantiate this value).

None of this succeeds altogether in disposing of the role of practices in fashioning (some) goods. The doubt arises in the following way. Consider the way we normally explain what is good or of value in various types of good or valuable goods or activities. We should concentrate on examples which are normally without instrumental value, so that only their intrinsic value is being explained. When explaining the good of bell-ringing, or of celebrating May morning near Magdalen bridge, or of playing bridge, or of reading the novels of Ivan Klima, or of going to the opera, we would normally list and relate various goods which are integral to the activity under consideration. Valuable activities may combine sociability with being in beautiful locations; cleverness with stretching one's memory and with strategic thinking; the pleasure of suspense or of anticipation may be combined with humour and psychological insight, and so on. This is a crude illustration. A good explanation will be extended and sensitive to details and nuance. Nor will it relate different goods like so many items of merchandise in a shop. Rather it will emphasize their integration, inter-relations, and proportions. Still one way or another a common way of explaining what is good in valuable activities consists in showing how the good explained is a complex good combining a mix of valuable components which one proceeds to detail and to set out their ideal or proper inter-relations.

Most goods, and all socially created goods, are mixed-value goods. Their goodness consists in their special combination of constituent goods. Understanding the nature of opera, bridge (the game), bell-ringing, sonnets, novels, etc. consists in part in understanding what makes for a good game of bridge, good opera performance, good bell-ringing evening, and so on. Understanding the type of good each of these activities is includes understanding their specific standards of excellence and that means understanding which combinations of component goods, and in what proportions and relations, make for a good instance of the kind. These defining standards of excellence of mixed-value goods are socially determined, and learnt by habituation, as well as by secondary means presupposing habituation. Their mastery constitutes a skill, rather than a body of articulated knowledge. There is, of course, nothing in that knowledge which cannot be articulated. It is only the task of giving it complete and exhaustive articulation which necessarily eludes us.

No one doubts that humour, ingenuity, imagination, companionship, and so on are good. But can we give a complete account of why they must combine in that particular way to make for a good dance, or a good party, or a good night at the opera, etc.? Yes we can, for the combination is dictated by the constitution of the good. Here, however, we come across an element of pure contingency. For while this good could not have been different, on pain of not being this good, there could have been a different good constituted by a different combination of goods, in different proportions. There could have been even a different good whose standards of excellence make what is a poor specimen of one good a good specimen of the other.

While only goods can account for the value of anything of value, the combination of values which is part of what determines its nature is determined by the historical circumstances which explain the growth of one form of good in one culture or subculture and of another form of good in another culture. If we recognize that both a Byzantine iconic painting and a painting in the style of Fuseli can be beautiful, that both the formal style of a sonnet, and the free conversational verse of C. K. Williams are good poetry, then we must recognize that the existence of any one form of mixed good is not exclusive. Its opposite—as it were—may also be good.

Is there any limit to which combinations of values can be constitutive types, or genres of mixed goods when enshrined in common practices defining such genres and types? I cannot think of any, nor can I see what evaluative resources there are which can set such limits. There is an element of contingency at the root of mixed-value goods.

While these comments apply only to mixed-value goods, the distinction between the simple and the mixed is not ontological or absolute. What is simple for the purpose of one explanation may well turn complex if further explanations are required. This invites a further consideration of the nature and scope of the views expressed above, but they will have to await another occasion.

4. CAN ONE WRITE A NOVEL WHICH IS BOTH GOOD AND BAD ALL OVER?

We have to keep exorcising ghosts. They keep coming back to haunt us. One of the simple howlers committed by many (non-philosophical) social relativists is that of asserting that the same thing can be both good and bad at the same time. Some sustaining social practices make it good, others make it bad. Is not my version of the social dependence of value guilty of the same howler? If early nineteenth-century Romantic paintings and thirteenth-century Byzantine iconic paintings represent traditions upholding inconsistent standards of excellence in paintings, is it not the case that one of them must be wrong on pain of contradiction? Not necessarily.

For one thing there is no doubt that there are good Romantic paintings and good Byzantine paintings. It would not do to say that when we recognize the excellence of a painting as an instance of a genre we do not judge it as a painting, that only its qualification as a Byzantine work is at issue and we merely apply Byzantine standards, whose validity we deny. We do not have any grounds for denying the validity of those standards. We may not like Byzantine paintings much. But that does not mean that they are not good paintings. We need not like every beautiful object. We need no reason for not liking them. They may simply not be our cup of tea. But if they are not beautiful then there must be a reason why. You may say that the standards of early nineteenth-century Romantic paintings are good enough reason for condemning Byzantine paintings. But there is an incongruity in even trying to do so. Byzantine paintings are not meant to be judged by those standards. They are not Romantic paintings. They are Byzantine icons. To judge them by early nineteenth-century Romantic standards is to miss the point.

Our Romantic friend may reply that he is judging them by the standards of good paintings, which happen to be those of early nineteenth-century Romantic paintings. But that claim is precisely what is at issue. The alternative position allows that the very notion of a painting imports some criteria of excellence, but denies that they are sufficient to judge how good a painting is except if it is a good painting because it is a good Dutch genre painting, or a good Impressionist painting, or a good Cubist one, etc. The standards of beauty[10] in painting *tout court* need concretizing through being supplemented by those of different periods, styles, etc. Can our Romantic friend avoid this conclusion? He is in danger of contradicting himself unless he maintains that none but early nineteenth-century Romantic paintings are any good. This is absurd. But is it logically coherent? The crux is in the intelligibility of claiming—as our Romantic friend must—that Byzantine standards represent what Byzantines believed to be the correct standards of beauty in paintings, but that they were wrong. It is this claim which I find impossible to sustain when a coherent cultural practice is under consideration. The notion that they simply made a mistake about beauty which we can now correct seems incredible. How can we understand it? That they believed that the very notion of painting imports the standards of excellence displayed in good Byzantine paintings? This would merely show that they lacked the concept of painting, having 'instead', as it were, the notion of a Byzantine painting. If so they made no mistake. But nothing follows from that about the standards of excellence in paintings generally. I see no way in which we can make coherent sense of the claim by practitioners or admirers of different painting styles that their style is the only one to include good paintings.

Notice that I do not deny that we judge paintings as good or bad paintings, not merely as good or bad examples of this or that genre of painting. Take someone for whom painting stopped with the Impressionists. Such a person will say—as indeed will I—that Monet's Rouen Cathedral paintings are beautiful paintings. He would not be content to say that they are beautiful Impressionist paintings. And he is of course right. All I am saying is that they are beautiful paintings because they are beautiful Impressionist paintings, and a Rothko is also a beautiful painting, because it is a beautiful Abstract Expressionist painting. In that way paintings which meet contradictory criteria of beauty can all be good and beautiful paintings. What is true of paintings is true of all the arts, of games, sports, outdoor activities, parties and other social gatherings, friendships, and so on.

Does it follow that one and the same painting can be beautiful and ugly all over since it can meet the criteria of excellence of one style while qualifying as ugly by those of another style? Not so, for it cannot belong to more than one style, or—to be more accurate—it cannot belong to two conflicting styles at the same time.

---

[10] I use 'beauty' and 'excellence' as applied to paintings interchangeably. Arguably, 'beauty' is just one form of excellence in a painting, and paintings can excel without being beautiful. Possibly the term can be used either way. I use it as I do to avoid monotony in writing, and not to deny the existence of an alternative sense of the term.

5. NON-CONFORMITY: DEVIATIONS AND INTERPRETATIONS

There is, however, a puzzle here. Think of a person who has a very wide and fleshy face, and who, were he to be judged by—let us say—Inuit standards of good looks, would be good-looking. As it happens that person is not an Inuit, but a Caucasian American living in Beverly Hills, and by the standards which apply to him he is rather plain. Our normal way of understanding the situation is that he is plain, though had he lived among Inuits or had he been an Inuit he would have been good-looking. Their standards apply to them. Their writ does not run in Beverly Hills. Why not? After all, we can assume that our person is indistinguishable in his looks from some Inuit. How could two people looking exactly the same be one plain and the other good-looking? This seems both unjust and illogical a position to end up with.

All I can say is that I am not to blame. This is how things are. The beauty of a face is not only in the face. The type of face it is (human or dog, Inuit or Angelino, etc.) determines the standards by which it is judged, and those have a local bias in the sense that while a range of different standards are all valid they have a divided jurisdiction. Given that not all of them are compatible they must—on pain of contradiction—divide their jurisdiction. Consequently one is judged by the standards under the jurisdiction of which one falls.

This creates tensions, which we accommodate through nuance and flexibility which ease the tensions, but do not resolve them altogether. All I can do here is to mention a few such complications. First, and this is really an easy case, one culture can accommodate a variety of standards. Typically all cultures sustain different standards for the good looks of men and women. But similarly they can sustain standards which approve of rugged looks and also ones prizing gentle good looks. In this case there is one qualification. As a man, one excels by meeting a standard set as an alternative: one can excel either by being rugged or by being gentle. But there may also be different standards for different qualifiers: ideals of Chinese beauty may differ from ideals of black beauty, etc. In the same way our culture may sustain different genres of paintings or literature, and admire them simultaneously, in the sense that we can[11] regard works which excel in any of them as great art or literature. The nature of the genres of literature, or of the types of good looks, determines what they apply to, they fix their jurisdiction. In some cases a work belongs to the type within which it would

---

[11] Sometimes, of course, some genres are regarded as of lesser value so that even the best works of those genres cannot rank as great literature.

rank highest. In others such a principle of charity is supplemented or supplanted by other criteria.

Sometimes goods are, and not infrequently they are deliberately made, ambiguous, that is they belong to a domain in-between genres, fitting and not fitting two or more genres. Some cultures evolve genres of ambiguity, that is standards which regard certain types of ambiguity as forms of excellence. Other cultures regard all ambiguity as a failure, and have no genre to which the ambiguous object or activity belongs. Needless to say, talking of 'genres of ambiguity' smacks of formalizing the very genre-breaking spirit of the age. There is nothing wrong with this, so long as it is recognized that genres may differ in the degree of formalization of their standards. Some allow for great fluidity, and for the easy generation of new, sometimes evanescent and ephemeral, genres. Others do not.

Where multiple genres and criteria apply within a culture matters are on the whole more straightforward. Tensions arise when they do not, when one culture recognizes the standards of another, and admits them to be valid for that other culture, but does not adopt them as its own. This very notion is mysterious. If they are valid for them why are they not valid for us? Furthermore, my plain-looking Beverly Hills friend has what could be described as a beautiful Inuit face. Nevertheless he is not an Inuit therefore he is neither a good-looking Inuit nor a good-looking person.

There is no way of dissolving these puzzles. All one can do is to point to instances of their existence, and to their inevitability. But first note that there is a way of trying to understand them which leads directly to contradiction. If you say that each genre-based standard sets presumptively sufficient conditions for counting as a good painting or as good-looking, or as good poetry, etc. then there is no way of denying that those which are bad by the standards of one subgenre may be good by those of another. The way to avoid a contradiction is to insist on a separation between the test for belonging to a genre and those of excelling within it. For any person or any poem the route to good looks or to greatness goes through admission to a subgenre and excellence within it. This is so whether or not multiple genres are current within one culture. The puzzle of my plain-looking Beverly Hills friend is that just because certain types are not current within his culture he is denied access to a standard at which, had he been allowed to be judged by it, he would have excelled.

That that is indeed how things are can be seen from various examples. Take just one. Imagine that you find a painting which looks like a Dutch genre painting. Is it a good painting? Everything may depend on whether it is a Dutch genre painting. If it is then it is also a good painting (I assume that it is good by the standards of Dutch genre paintings). It is a good painting because it is a good Dutch genre painting. If, on the other hand, it was painted early this century by a Royal Academician whose work is derivative and imitative then it is not a good painting. It is certainly not a good Dutch genre painting since it is not a Dutch genre painting at all. Rather it is in the style of a Dutch genre painting. Just as good looks depend not only on the looks of the person, so the beauty of a painting does not depend only on what it looks like. To be a good painting it has to be good of a kind and to belong to the kind it needs qualifications which are not exhausted by the way it looks.

Why should this be so? It is not clear what sort of explanation is asked for. It is, as we saw, a result of the contingent element of mixed-value goods, of their social dependence. We are dealing with the contingent undergrowth of evaluative phenomena. It is as it is. It is outside the realm of reason and justification. It is part of the conditions which determine the shape of values, but are not themselves values or evaluations. There may be causal explanations of why our practices which underpin values and evaluative discourse have this shape. But if there are such causal explanations I do not know what they are. What form of explanation can we furnish from inside the evaluative domain of its dependence on contingent facts? We can point out that it is inevitable if we are to have socially created goods, and mixed-value goods more generally. We can then point out the impoverishment which we would suffer were there no mixed-value goods. Such an explanation would show how the puzzles have their sources in features of value which fulfil crucial roles in our lives, without which life would be drastically impoverished. This form of explanation does not justify them in the ordinary sense. It does not show that the puzzling features of local values are valuable, or good to have. But it explains them in explaining how they are integral to central aspects of the value system.

10

The Truth in Particularism

When reflecting on the way we come to do what we do, or to refrain from what we refrain from doing, it is natural to be torn between a particularist and a generalist tendency. We tend towards a generalist view when we feel that at least sometimes we are guided by general precepts and are inclined to believe that it is always possible to be so guided. 'I must do this'—I may say—'My son is relying on me.' Or, 'I cannot do this. It would be cheating.' I am, and am conscious of being, guided in my decision by general precepts: 'One should not cheat.' 'One should not let one's children down.' These principles may be too simple. They may have to be refined and qualified to be exceptionlessly true. But surely such refinements are forthcoming if we are minded to look for them. How else can we tell what to do and what not to do?

But sometimes such reflection seems out of place. I do what I do because I know (or believe I know) that that is what should be done in the circumstances. I see a toddler about to step into the road and I stop him. I have no general principle in mind. Indeed, the moment I think of any general principle examples which refute it come to mind (the adult accompanying the toddler is keeping a close eye on him, etc.). No generalization free from exceptions, however complex, seems possible. Moreover, I do not and should not consult any such generalization before acting. I spot a mistake in a student's essay and I remark on it. I do not think: 'I should correct all the mistakes I spot, and therefore, having spotted this mistake, I should correct it.' It would be absurd to let such a generalization mediate between my perception of the situation and my action, or intention to act. In any case I do not believe in this generalization, nor in any other. Sometimes it would be better not to correct this or that mistake. To correct it would be to appear unduly severe, or critical, would be beyond the student's ability to understand, or to remember, etc. There is no exceptionless generalization about when to correct mistakes which I believe.

These are but examples of some of the kinds of contexts in which it would be natural to be drawn in a generalist or a particularist direction.[1]

I am grateful to Martin Stone, Ben Zipursky, John Hyman, and Anthony Kenny for comments which helped me improve this chapter.

[1] I tried to describe these examples as they may be described by people who are not committed to any theoretical account of these cases. They are meant to provide a non-

But where do these directions lead? Do they lead to two theoretical positions about the nature of reasons or of practical deliberation, between which one should adjudicate? Or do they remain, as above, vague generalizations each possibly expressing some partial truth? Would the appearance of conflict be dissolved once we carefully distinguish the question of how we (properly) deliberate about what to do from the question of the nature of the considerations which may be relevant to establish what we should or should not have done? My aim is not typological and I will not essay a characterization of 'ethical particularism'. My aim is to examine some of the thoughts which may tempt in one direction or another. In particular I will suggest that Dancy and Winch help us locate two problems in understanding reasons for actions, which I will describe, and to which I will offer a solution.

The first section examines the case for a generalist position as I understand it, and believe it to be true. Whatever is true in particularist claims has to be compatible with it. The following sections examine three particularistic tendencies: the case against principles (section 2), Dancy's thesis that what is a reason in one situation may be no reason in another (sections 3 and 4), and the argument, deriving from Winch, about the difference between the first- and the third-person perspective (section 5).

1. THE GENERALIST TENDENCY: INTELLIGIBILITY AND SUPERVENIENCE

Throughout the discussion I will hold to two considerations which any account has to accommodate. First, the (evaluative) properties of actions[2] which make them good or bad, right or wrong, and therefore ones which we have reason to perform or to avoid, serve both to judge the wisdom, morality, desirability, etc., of actions, and to guide agents in forming intentions, and in deciding what to do. I will refer to them as the evaluative and the guiding function of reasons and of evaluative properties.[3] I will assume

---

theoretical way of locating the whereabouts of the issues to be considered. I suspect that the expression 'ethical particularism' is used to refer to a whole family of views. I will continue to talk vaguely of 'particularist directions' to avoid singling out any one of them, or the implication that they constitute a family united by important theoretical common features.

[2] Including the properties of the context of the actions and of their relations to other acts or events.

[3] Some evaluative properties figure not so much in reasons for or against performing actions but in reasons for or against performing them in one manner or another: if you are to do *A* do so skilfully, courageously, etc. Some evaluative properties provide what I called 'conditional reasons', i.e. reasons which presuppose other reasons: if you have reason to sit down choose a comfortable chair to sit on (see Ch. 5 above).

that while possibly the two come apart in some cases, in general reasons and evaluative properties cannot serve one role unless they can serve the other. Second, the domain of evaluative properties and of reasons is intelligible. I can only give a very vague description of this point. Some of its more precise implications will emerge below. The intelligibility of the domain of value means that nothing in it is as it is just because that is how it is; there is nothing 'arbitrary'[4] in the domain of value. It is, after all, the domain of reason(s). There is an explanation for everything, an explanation for why what is good is good, what is bad is bad, etc.[5] The intelligibility of value exerts a strong pressure towards some sort of a generalist view. In particular, it implies that regarding any two situations such that some evaluative concept applies to one of them but not to the other there is some further difference between them which can be helpful in explaining why. How is this point to be understood?

One suggestion is that it reflects the supervenience of the evaluative on the non-evaluative. In any case, it may be argued, an examination of such supervenience claims holds the key to an understanding of the debate between generalists and particularists. I doubt, however, whether there is much we can learn from any general supervenience thesis we know of today. Before we proceed with the debate about particularism I will deviate to explain the irrelevance of supervenience to that debate.

To begin we should note that, as is generally agreed, there is no reason to think that the evaluative predicates of English (or of any other natural language) supervene on its non-evaluative predicates. Nor is there any reason to think that the evaluative concepts available to English speakers (or to members of any other group) today supervene on non-evaluative concepts available to them.[6] In fact my doubt is more general. It concerns the

---

The evaluative properties which feature in reasons for action are varied. They may show the action to be sensible, sensibly cautious, wise, generous, just, right, and so on. To simplify I will refer to reasons as showing actions to be good or right, and will disregard the wide range of dimensions in which they can be good. This may give a regrettably artificial air to some of the points below, but I believe that it does not affect any of the arguments.

[4] This is a rhetorical way of making the point. But be warned that it begs the question: something is arbitrary if it flouts reasons, or is brought about in disregard for reasons, where reasons apply. If a domain is not intelligible through and through then those aspects of it which escape reason are not arbitrary.

[5] Some people assume the intelligibility of the evaluative domain while denying that it follows that everything in it can be explained. If they are right, and something more will be said on the issue later on, that is enough for my purposes, provided that the dependence of intelligibility on conceptual thought is preserved.

[6] This is no surprise to philosophers upholding the supervenience of the evaluative on the non-evaluative. As will be seen in what follows their theses concern the supervenience of evaluative properties on non-evaluative ones.

truth of global evaluative supervenience theses in general.[7] Applied to predicates the general evaluative supervenience thesis says that evaluative predicates (of a given language at a given time) supervene on (its) non-evaluative ones if and only if necessarily[8] for any two situations, if there is an evaluative predicate which applies to one and not to the other then there is a non-evaluative predicate which applies to one and not to the other. An analogous thesis asserts the supervenience of evaluative concepts on non-evaluative ones. Which predicates belong to a language at any given time is a contingent matter, a product of its historical development to that time, and so is the number and identity of the concepts available to any person, or any cultural group. Hence if predicate or concept supervenience obtains at any given time that would be a surprising contingent matter, of no philosophical interest, unless there is some factor or mechanism which makes it necessary[9] that it should exist.

An argument which, if sound, would establish some[10] form of evaluative supervenience would show that one cannot master evaluative predicates or concepts, and cannot have the ability to use them correctly, unless one has command of non-evaluative predicates or concepts such that one's skill in correctly applying the evaluative predicates or concepts consists in establishing which of the non-evaluative ones apply and concluding on that basis whether the relevant evaluative predicates or concepts apply. This, however, is not so. We commonly learn to apply evaluative predicates and concepts by example, and through their association with other predicates or concepts, mostly with other evaluative predicates and concepts. Examining people's command of such predicates and concepts reveals that their ability to identify contexts to which they apply in evaluative terms far exceeds their ability to describe them in non-evaluative terms. Often there is no alternative way of determining the application of evaluative concepts, except by reference to other evaluative concepts. Supervenience, as McDowell pointed out, leaves this possibility open.[11] If evaluative predicates and

---

[7] Global because it refers to the supervenience of all evaluative predicates, concepts, or properties, on all the non-evaluative ones; specific supervenience theses relate to the supervenience of one evaluative predicate, concept, or property, or of a class of them, on some non-evaluative ones.

[8] A weaker form of supervenience will be confined to how things are rather than how they are necessarily. As our interest is in a claim that supervenience is of the essence of the evaluative the stronger form is relevant here.

[9] Even natural necessity may endow supervenience with a philosophical significance.

[10] Directly the argument shows the correctness of some specific, rather than global, supervenience theses. I will suggest below that in general explanatory needs call for specific rather than global supervenience theses, if any.

[11] 'It does not follow from the satisfaction of this requirement [i.e. that of supervenience] that the set of items to which the supervening term is correctly applied need constitute a

concepts supervene on non-evaluative ones that is not because people's understanding of them and their ability to apply them correctly presuppose knowledge of how they or the contexts of their application can be characterized or identified by non-evaluative predicates and concepts.

The alternative arguments I can think of, when given their strongest form, support a different thesis. Take for example an argument which says that since evaluative discourse is objective, admitting of the possibility of mistakes, and of criteria of correctness, evaluative predicates and concepts must supervene on non-evaluative ones, for ultimately only naturalistic discourse can be objective. Any other domain of discourse can be objective only to the extent that it depends on naturalistic discourse. As stated this suggestion for an argument flies in the face of the facts. A good deal of reasoning proceeds with the use of evaluative predicates and concepts. It presupposes an understanding of the implications of the applications of such predicates and concepts, but—to repeat the point made above—such understanding commonly expresses itself in terms which involve the use of other evaluative predicates and concepts.

To strengthen this argument it has to include claims about what are alleged to be more fundamental conditions of objectivity, for example, that without supervenience there will be no guarantee of convergence of inquirers under ideal conditions; or that without supervenience the existence of evaluative facts will not be the best explanation of any beliefs in evaluative propositions; and that these (i.e. convergence and the best explanation thesis) are preconditions of objectivity. I do not think that either of these is a condition of objectivity.[12] But this is beside the immediate point. What is relevant here is that even if they are based on sound premises such arguments cannot establish the supervenience thesis we are considering, for they do not address the difficulty for the thesis raised by the contingency of the range of available predicates and concepts. At best such arguments would establish supervenience in some ideal or extended languages, not in languages as we have them.

The same is true of other possible arguments. Some will argue that the understanding of predicates and concepts which I relied on above, while

---

kind recognisable as such at the level supervened upon. . . . Hence there need be no possibility of mastering, in a way that would enable one to go on to new cases, a term that is to function at the level supervened upon, but is to group together exactly the items to which competent users would apply the supervening term. Understanding why just those things belong together may essentially require understanding the supervening term.' 'Non-Cognitivism and Rule Following', in *Mind, Value and Reality* (Cambridge, Mass.: Harvard University Press, 1998), 202.

[12] See 'Notes on Value and Objectivity', in Brian Leiter (ed.), *Objectivity in Morality and in the Law* (Cambridge: CUP, 1999), which is Ch. 6 above.

real enough, is defective and incomplete. A complete understanding of evaluative concepts includes understanding how the evaluative properties they refer to supervene on non-evaluative properties. If sound such an argument will show that no one today has a complete understanding of many evaluative concepts. Some people would regard this as a *reductio ad absurdum* of the argument, and conclude that it cannot be sound. My point here is different. It is that if sound the argument establishes supervenience not under present conditions but under ideal conditions. Ideal conditions of what? A natural suggestion is to turn to extensions of English and other natural languages. For example, it may be claimed that at any time it is possible to enrich English with additional non-evaluative predicates so that the evaluative predicates English has at that time will turn out to supervene on its non-evaluative predicates. But this route does not seem very promising. For one thing it seems to be compatible with the reverse thesis. At any given time, the counter-thesis goes, if the evaluative predicates then in English supervene on its non-evaluative predicates it is possible to enrich English with additional evaluative predicates so that its evaluative predicates will no longer supervene on the non-evaluative ones.

You may well feel that I have been led up the garden path by approaching supervenience via a confused thesis about the intelligibility of the evaluative domain. The case for supervenience depends on metaphysical considerations about the nature of what can exist (and some would add epistemic considerations about what can be known).[13] The arguments sketched or hinted at in the preceding two paragraphs are metaphysical in character and therefore cannot be taken to establish supervenience of predicates or concepts. They are theses about the world, or more specifically about the properties which exist in the world. They are about the supervenience of evaluative properties on non-evaluative properties, not about predicates or concepts. Properties manifested in the world are, as the saying goes, part of the fabric of the world and their identity and number does not depend on the current state of this language or that, nor on that of any conceptual repertoire of any person or group.

The difference between concepts and properties can be exaggerated. While the criteria of identity of properties differ from those of concepts, they too depend, however indirectly, on our conceptual repertoire, actual or possible. This is consistent with several of the theses about the identification of properties. Suppose, for example, that they are identified by reference to the causal powers of things. Different conceptual schemes offer different ways of individuating the causal powers of things, and there-

---

[13] Relying e.g. on Benacerraf's 'Mathematical Truth', *The Journal of Philosophy*, 70 (1973), 661.

fore, according to that view of properties, different principles for the individuation of properties. This casts no doubt on the objectivity of properties (or of concepts), it merely reminds us that different aspects of reality are accessible to different creatures, and this depends on their conceptual reach as much as it does on their sense organs, intellectual ability, and other factors. Claims that evaluative properties supervene over non-evaluative ones have, therefore, either to be relativized to particular schemes for the individuation of properties, or to apply to all sets of properties according to all possible principles for their individuation.

It is tempting to think that if the global supervenience of the evaluative on the non-evaluative is a cogent thesis at all it must apply to the relations between evaluative and non-evaluative properties under any scheme for identifying them. However, the motivation either way seems unclear. My doubts stem from the fact that the explanatory advantages of the thesis of the supervenience of the evaluative on the non-evaluative seem to depend on the availability of more specific explanatory theses. We are in need of some understanding of which non-evaluative properties specific evaluative properties depend on, and why. We seek to understand how evaluative events (i.e. events in which evaluative properties figure, like murder, or the performance of kind acts) fit in our understanding of causal explanations of events, and with our tendency to regard causal explanations as the primary mode of explanations of events. The puzzles about the way evaluative facts and events fit in our scientific world-view are not solved by one global thesis of the supervenience of the evaluative but by specific theses which are not directly entailed by it.

The problem is not only that the specific theses we need to generate the explanations we are looking for are not entailed by a global evaluative supervenience thesis. The problem is that the global evaluative supervenience thesis does not even guarantee the possibility of these additional theses. Just as we have no reason to think that any set of concepts available to us at any time is such that its evaluative concepts supervene on the rest so we have no reason to think that in any set of properties we know of at any given time the evaluative ones supervene on the rest. If any such set can be expanded by adding non-evaluative properties so that in the expanded set the evaluative properties supervene on the rest then it may also be possible further to expand the expanded set by adding additional evaluative properties so that the new set will not meet the condition of the supervenience of the evaluative.[14] It is possible that the general evaluative supervenience thesis is true in virtue of properties we cannot in principle come to know, and that therefore cannot figure in any explanation of the properties we do

---

[14] I am assuming that the number of properties is infinite.

know. These remarks show how little the general thesis gives us. It does not have much, if any, explanatory power. But the less explanatory power it has the less reason we have to believe in it. If some form of evaluative supervenience obtains, then for it to serve a significant explanatory role we need specific rather than merely global evaluative supervenience theses, but no such theses are available. I will, therefore, disregard the question of supervenience for the remainder of this chapter.

Putting supervenience on one side, let us return to the thesis about the intelligibility of the evaluative. It implies that whenever two situations differ in some evaluative property there is an explanation of that difference. Inevitably such an explanation points to a difference (that is, another difference) between the situations which accounts for the fact that the evaluative property applies to one and not to the other. Typically explanations will be couched in evaluative terms. They will not all conform to one explanatory pattern. They will meet different puzzlements in different ways. Nor will they ever end, nor even strive to reach a bedrock of final indubitability and transparency. They will aim at answering present questions, not to put to rest all possible ones. Is there an interesting 'particularist' thesis compatible with the intelligibility of value? Does not the intelligibility of value compel the rejection of particularism?

The case for an affirmative answer to this second question may lie in the thought that since, regarding any evaluative concept and any two situations, if it applies to one and not to the other there is an explanation for this difference, it must be in principle possible to amass all the points which all these explanations may rely on and formulate one principle which sets a comprehensive and exceptionless rule for the use of that evaluative concept. That, the assumption is, is inconsistent with particularism. The discussion below will bear on the argument from the availability of explanations of differences in pair-wise comparisons to the existence of comprehensive and exceptionless principles. First, we may use the assumption that such principles are inconsistent with particularism to launch an examination of some specific claims advanced in the name of particularism.

2. PUTTING PRINCIPLES IN THEIR PLACE

Particularist tendencies are aroused by reflection on (some) examples of concrete situations in which it would be at best misleading, and possibly outright false, to say of people who acted well that they acted on the basis of a principle, even though they acted intentionally and for a reason. Writers on the topic concentrate on particularism regarding ethics. But as there are no context-independent nor theoretically significant boundaries between ethical matters and other evaluative or normative issues I will disregard this limitation on the particularist case.[15] Outside the domain of morality the temptation to think of intention or action as guided by principles almost disappears. Where the issue is essentially instrumental, that is, about the way to achieve a set goal, it seems that principles are out of place (though rules of thumb may be a great help).[16] They do not figure when deciding about a menu which will be tasty, varied, and low in fat content, nor in choosing the best investment, nor in deciding whether to fly or to take the train to one's destination, etc. Nor, however, do principles figure when the decision is based on the intrinsic value of different options, as when one chooses which novel to read, or where to take a holiday (among equally expensive options), and so on.

Many moral actions are no different. You see children torturing a cat and you stop them. No principle figures in your decision. In this just as in the non-moral cases the action is intentional and is taken for a reason. The reasons the agents would cite if asked (and the reasons which figure in their deliberations where their actions are preceded by deliberation) are some prominent aspect(s) of the situation, as they saw it: that the cat is being tortured, that Ibiza would afford a very relaxing holiday, that this novel is excellent in its portrayal of a doctor confronting moral dilemmas, etc. Were the reasons which figure in deliberation, or those cited by agents when they are asked, roughly at the time of action, why they do it, the only reasons for which they act, completely described, then we would be within sight of a particularist thesis: something about reasons for an action typically being capable of being also reasons against it. To quote Dancy:

> The fact that an action will give pleasure can be a reason for doing it or for approving of it when done. But it can also be a reason for disapproving of it. If I tread on a worm by mistake, my action is perhaps morally indifferent. But if I tread on it with pleasure or to give you pleasure, my action is the worse for it.[17]

Even before we examine such a thesis we can endorse a milder anti-principle thesis. Since explicit deliberation does not usually take the form of identifying and following a principle, there is no reason to think that an augmented account of being guided by reasons, one which takes note of the way we are guided by reasons which do not figure in deliberation, to the extent that we are so guided, would take the form of identifying

---

[15] For my reasons for doubting the significance of the boundary see 'On the Moral Point of View', in J. B. Schneewind (ed.), *Reason, Ethics and Society: Themes from Kurt Baier* (Chicago: Open Court, 1996), 58. This is Ch. 11 below.

[16] See on rules of thumb D. Regan, 'Law's Halo', *Social Philosophy and Policy*, 4 (1986), 15.

[17] Dancy, *Moral Reasons* (Oxford: Blackwell, 1993), 56.

principles and following them. Possibly, when rational one is guided by considerations which can be expressed as a principle. But it is hard to think of a reason for claiming that one's reasoning, explicit or implicit, conscious or subliminal, must consist in identifying principles, and following them. The natural assumption must be that it takes the form that it appears to take in much explicit deliberation, that is establishing the considerations for and against available options, and evaluating their relative merits.

This does not mean that principles do not play any role in guiding action. Rather, it would seem that they play the role which has often been assigned to them.[18] They may point out an important consideration to be taken into account, so that being guided by such a principle is the same as giving the reason to which it points due weight in one's reasoning. In this sense, 'Do not disappoint your friends' can be said to be a principle. Other principles do not mention any consideration to bear in mind. Instead they tell their subjects what to do (e.g. 'Do not be late for your appointments'). Such principles can be valid if they reflect what one has to do in the circumstances given all the conflicting reasons which apply. Roughly speaking they are valid if they represent the correct outcome of rational deliberation about the merit of the various reasons which bear on such decisions.[19] Some principles fall in between these two kinds. They indicate that the consideration they point to is conclusive, or just very stringent, in itself, so that even while they point to a single consideration they also point to a decisive reason. 'Always treat the humanity in others as an end in itself, and never as a means only' may be a principle whose supporters typically think of it in that way. This familiar view of principles can explain why they are important in moral education, as well as why they are more often mentioned in moral contexts than in others: many people believe that some moral considerations are in and of themselves conclusive reasons for action, regardless of what reasons point the other way, perhaps barring some exceptional circumstances.

If 'moral particularism is the view that general moral principles play less of a role in moral thought than has often been claimed'[20] then these con-

---

[18] The examples that follow assume that we are dealing with stand-alone principles, and disregard their role within inter-related and inter-dependent systems of rules and principles, such as the law.

[19] I have suggested that typically such principles function as mandatory norms which themselves constitute protected reasons for action, which while being dependent on, also displace the reasons whose verdict on the situation they reflect. See for the general analysis *Practical Reason and Norms* (Oxford: Oxford University Press, 1999), and for its application to the special context of norms set by authority *The Morality of Freedom* (Oxford: OUP, 1986).

[20] As per Roger Crisp in 'Moral Particularism', *Encyclopaedia of Philosophy*, ed. E. Craig (London: Routledge, 1998).

siderations are ample vindication of it.[21] However, as the quotation from Dancy makes clear, some understand particularism to endorse a much stronger thesis about the nature of moral reasons, and by implication of reasons generally. Is Dancy right in claiming that what is a reason in one context need not be a reason for the same action in another?

3. REASONS AND JUSTIFICATION

There is a superficial way of understanding Dancy's thesis. When so understood it is true but uninteresting. What people cite as their reason in a particular situation they may cite as a reason for another, even a contradictory action or behaviour on other occasions. That the action will give you pleasure may be cited by your friend as a reason to perform it. It may, however, be a reason not to perform it (e.g. for someone in charge of punishing you, or, as in Dancy's example, where the pleasure is unworthy). We do not regard this fact as remarkable for we assume that in both cases there is more to reasons for action than what people would typically cite as their reasons. Your friend mentions your pleasure as his reason for he assumes that the other factors which along with it make a reason are known, or could be learnt from the context, or are not of interest, to whoever he is addressing. When we think of his reason in its entirety we realize that it cannot be a reason for the opposing action.

Dancy does not have the superficial reading of his thesis in mind. His thesis applies not to what people would typically cite as a reason, but to reasons as they are. And it applies not to aspects of reasons taken in isolation, but to complete reasons.[22] Reasons, in his usage and mine, need not

---

[21] Another reason militates against assigning principles a major role in practical philosophy. The term covers distinct normative phenomena, and its philosophical use invites misunderstandings, and futile dispute about meaning. It can of course be given a technical meaning within this or that theory, but given its profligacy it is hard to avoid using it in its natural meaning even when that deviates from the technical definition.

[22] A terminological point is called for here. In part this chapter strives to contribute to the explanation of the concept of 'a reason'. The phrase 'a complete reason' is, however, given a somewhat stipulative definition, aimed at helping with the explanation of reasons. A complete reason consists of all the facts stated by the non-redundant premises of a sound, deductive argument entailing as its conclusion a proposition of the form 'There is a reason for P to V' (where P stands for an expression referring to an agent or a group of agents, and V for a description of an action, omission, or a mode of conduct). A similar definition can be provided for reasons for belief, emotions, etc. An examination of the use of expressions such as 'this is a different reason', 'this is the same reason', and similar expressions, will show that this notion of complete reason captures an important aspect of our understanding of reasons. It is partly stipulative in regimenting the use of expressions such as 'same reason' and 'different reason', which in their ordinary use often invoke differing, context-dependent, standards of completeness.

be conclusive. They are conclusive when they prevail over all conflicting reasons. Dancy's thesis is not that one and the same reason may be conclusive in one situation and defeated by other reasons in another. Rather it is that the very same features of a situation which are a reason in the context of that situation may not be a reason at all in another, or even be a reason for a conflicting action. Another of his examples illustrates the first possibility: that I borrowed a book from you is, often, a reason to return it to you. But if having borrowed it I discover that you stole it from the public library I have no reason to return it to you.

What would show him to be right or wrong? To refute him it is not enough to show that there is a difference between situations where the reason points one way and situations in which it points some other way. This is readily allowed by Dancy. His example of the way giving pleasure can be good or bad comes with an explanation of the difference. His thesis depends on the fact that the features in which the situations differ which provide the explanation are not parts of the reasons for action. Why not?

As was pointed out at the beginning of the chapter, the value of actions serves both an evaluative and a guiding function. It is the basis by which they are judged, as well as serving as a reason for their performance. While the two can come apart in certain cases, they cannot drift too far apart without conflicting with our understanding of the notions of guiding and of evaluating actions. A major weakness of Dancy's thesis is that it drives a wedge between reasons for action and the evaluation of those actions.[23] Here is one way of presenting the point. I have taken reasons to be features of the action they are reasons for. They are generic features of action-types capable of being instantiated on various occasions. That an action would be the returning of a borrowed book is such a feature. According to Dancy, the same feature can be a reason for the action of which it is a feature in

In another partly stipulative deviation from ordinary usage I refer to any fact stated by any proposition which can be a non-redundant premise in a sound argument of the kind just described as a reason (or as part of a (complete) reason). Some aspects of a complete reason are more readily perceived as reasons than others. Contrast 'I am thirsty' with 'this liquid will not harm me' as statements of reasons for drinking the liquid in front of me. Ordinary usage allows reference to many aspects of complete reasons as reasons when the context is appropriate (e.g. 'this is water' is often cited as a reason for drinking it). Appropriateness is a matter of sensible assumptions about what the addressees of various remarks know, and what they do not, what would puzzle them and what would be taken as self-evident, etc. Generally, any aspect of a complete reason can be cited as a reason in some circumstances, and I will use the term 'reason' to refer to any such aspect.

[23] It is not clear whether Dancy is fully aware of this. He says 'the fact that . . . can be a reason for doing it or for approving of it when done. But it can also be a reason for disapproving of it' (*Moral Reasons*, 56). He seems to apply his particularist thesis not only to reasons but also to values generally. To follow him would fly in the face of the intelligibility of value, to which, as his discussion of all his examples shows, he is committed.

one context and against it in another. How can that be? This cannot be an arbitrary brute fact. The intelligibility of value means that there must be a difference between the context of the two instantiations which explains why the same fact (e.g. that the action is a returning of a borrowed book) is a reason in one and not in the other. Yet, the difference will not figure as part of the reason. If it did then it would not be true that the same fact is a reason in one situation and not in the other. Therefore, according to Dancy, the considerations which determine what is right (or good, etc.) extend beyond that reason itself. It follows that not everything relevant for the evaluation of an action is part of the reasons for or against the action. We know that this is the case in some special contexts—for example, that some values can be achieved only by actions which are not taken in order to achieve them. But Dancy's thesis is meant to be a general thesis, arising out of the nature of practical rationality itself, and not limited to special types of reasons.

The question inevitably arises: if certain factors are relevant to the evaluation of an action why are they not also part of the reasons for or against it? Should we not do the right (wise, sensible, etc.) thing and avoid wrong (foolish, etc.) actions? Does that not mean that the factors which determine the rightness (or wisdom, etc.) of an action are the reasons for it? An affirmative answer refutes Dancy's thesis, for it denies (special cases aside) the general gap between reason and evaluation on which his thesis depends. One route for avoiding an affirmative answer is through raising the guiding problem. We can accept the principle that *in any given situation only what can be someone's reason in that situation* (i.e. can be a reason for which they then act) *can be a reason*. Only those evaluative considerations which can serve a guiding function are reasons for action. Relying on this principle it can be argued, in support of Dancy's thesis, that while most evaluatively relevant considerations can be (part of) someone's reason for action, in any given situation no one can be guided by all the evaluatively relevant factors present in it, or at least that that is not normally, or commonly possible.

4. THE GUIDING PROBLEM

The issue turns on whether there is more to people's reasons than those factors which figure in their deliberations, and which they cite as reasons when asked, and on how much more is part of their reasons. We can only judge the matter against a picture, however rough and sketchy, of the way we are normally guided by reasons. In outlining such a picture I will disregard the cases where we act out of a belief in a reason which is false, where the reason does not exist. I assume that such cases are to be analysed by reference to the normal case, the case in which no such mistake occurs. There are two ways in which the reasons we act for are not the reasons which figure in our deliberations, nor the ones we will avow when asked. We may be mistaken about the reasons for which we act. We may think we act for reasons which are not genuinely our reasons, while rejecting the thought that our reasons are what they really are. We also may simply be aware of only some or some aspects of our reasons while being unaware of others.

We act for reasons whenever we act intentionally, but only on some of these occasions do we deliberate shortly before acting.[24] What marks intentional action as guided by reasons is not that it follows deliberation, but that it is undertaken in light of an appreciation, accurate or faulty, of our situation in the world (an appreciation of ourselves as well as of our environment). That appreciation is embodied in beliefs formed over time, as well as in what we currently learn of our immediate circumstances at the time of action.

That action for reasons is action informed and shaped by our appreciation of ourselves and our circumstances allows both for mistakenly thinking that a certain reason exists when it does not, and for being ignorant of the fact that certain reasons exist. For our purpose here a third kind of mistake is pertinent: we may be mistaken about the reasons for which we act. We may believe that we act for reasons which we do not in fact act for, and we may be unaware of the reasons for which we do act. Action for reasons presupposes an appreciation of the situation we are in, but it does not presuppose self-knowledge. It does not presuppose knowledge of our own beliefs, and of which of them inform us of the reasons for which we act. But we have to tread carefully here. For creatures capable of self-knowledge, having beliefs involves having the capacity to be non-inferentially aware of them.[25] Mistakes and ignorance have to be explained. The onus in explaining mistakes is particularly severe. Ignorance can be due to no more than inattention, failure of recall, etc. Mistakes about what one believes, or desires, or feels call for stricter explanations, especially in the many cases in which they involve self-deception.

In acting for reasons we can be wrong not only about how things are in the world and about ourselves. We can also be mistaken about our reasons,

---

[24] Earlier deliberations and advanced planning and decisions are central to human rational capacity. I exclude them at this point because they do not pinpoint the time of action, and therefore do not lead to the formation of an intention which uniquely identifies the act performed.

[25] Such a capacity is consistent with externalism about mind and meaning. While creatures capable of self-knowledge are capable of being non-inferentially aware of their beliefs, that does not imply that they always have complete knowledge of the content of their beliefs. More needs to be said about externalism and self-knowledge.

i.e. the facets of ourselves and of our situation (of which we know), which guide our actions. Such mistakes would typically occur when we are affected by motivated irrationality, subject to wish-fulfilment, to the distorting effects of a sense of guilt or shame, or other factors which lead to self-deception. I mention these factors not because they are central to an evaluation of Dancy's thesis. They are not. I mention them because once we allow that we may be mistaken about the reasons for which we act we must allow that we can act for reasons which do not figure in our deliberation, and which we would not cite when asked (by ourselves or others) for our reasons. The centre of the argument about Dancy's thesis rests with the second way in which there is more to reasons than that: the case of ignorance of our reasons, rather than of mistakes about them.

We may be unaware of our own reasons. We act for reasons we know of, be it through our general stock of beliefs, or through what we come to believe about the situation we are in at the time of action. Either way we know more than we can articulate. No one can spell out all that he knows, and no one can detail all that he perceives, or even just sees at any moment. There may be nothing we know which cannot be stated, and nothing we see which cannot be described. But it does not follow that we can state all that we know, and all we see. While not all that we know, nor all of our perceptions, are tapped by us when they are relevant, while we may fail—as we say—fully to grasp the implications of some of our knowledge, our rational responsiveness to their implications does not require conscious reflection or deliberate articulation. We can rationally respond to what we see and act as we do because of what we know, without being aware of that knowledge at the time. Hence the reasons for which we act need not be reasons about which we deliberated prior to action.

There are various contexts in which we act for reasons without deliberation. There are the many actions we perform regularly which are embedded in automatic routines. Standing in the kitchen I decide to get something from the fridge. A whole series of actions follows as it were automatically. I am barely aware that I perform them. They are all done for reasons, but these have been instilled in me and I need not reflect on them or re-endorse them. The reason-guided character of the actions is manifest in the fact that I monitor them, and will abort them if the situation changes, or is revealed to have changed. Some rules, like 'wash your hands before eating', are internalized and lead to semi-automatic action similar to actions embedded in automatic routines. I will say nothing about these types of cases, nor several others. To the extent that they are relevant to our purpose they share the characteristics of the situations which more obviously serve in particularist arguments.

One kind of case is exemplified by the toddler example: you see a toddler about to step into the road and you reach out and stop him. Your action is swift. You do not stop to ask yourself what you should do. You react to the situation as you see it. I will refer to such actions as swift actions. The second type of situation I have in mind is very different. You agonize over a question for a long time. Let us suppose that I cannot decide whether to take up a job offer or not.[26] I do deliberate and survey all the reasons for and against that I can think of, but am unconvinced either way. I let the matter rest for a while, and a week later when I think of it again the decision is immediately clear: I should accept the offer. At that stage, the stage when I actually reach a decision, I do not deliberate. Nor am I able, once the decision is taken, to adduce any reasons to justify it that I did not have before. I have no new arguments. I just made up my mind, apparently on the basis of the old arguments. Let us call such cases opaque cases.

Action without deliberation is not action without awareness of its reasons. Self-conscious beings are capable of describing their intentional actions in one way or another (if only in their thoughts). They may act semi-automatically, or swiftly, or opaquely, but in all cases some description of their action, as intentional, is available to them at the time. If they do not actively think of what they are doing the thought can be triggered by questions. Moreover, whenever a self-conscious being acts intentionally a description of the action which, as he sees it, shows it to be desirable is available to him.[27] That means that people have citable reasons for their intentional actions, i.e. they act intentionally for reasons which are available to them if asked at the time.

This does not mean that the reasons for which people act are (identical with) the reasons available to them when they act. The case for mistakes was made above, and there are further reasons to doubt that identity. We have to rely on counterfactuals to establish people's citable reasons, that is the reasons available to them at the time of action. But what sort of counterfactual condition is relevant here? People will give different answers to different questions. Perhaps we should say that their reasons are the totality of the reasons they will mention in reply to all the (infinite number of) questions they can be asked. However problems remain. Once we move beyond the most obvious aspects of the situation people's claims about their reasons will depend on their frame of mind at the time. They may be more or less attuned to the significance of different aspects of their situation as

---

[26] For an analogous moral case think of a person agonizing whether to volunteer for a food convoy for the relief of starving people during the war in Bosnia. Matters may progress exactly as in the job example.

[27] All this is subject to the possibility of mistakes mentioned above, and to various pathologies we need not examine in this brief sketch.

they know it. You may say that that does not matter. Their reasons depend on their frame of mind at the time. If because of their mood at the time they do not then know of certain reasons, or if their knowledge remains untapped, if it does not influence their conduct, not even counterfactually, then they do not act for these reasons.

While true, when given as a reply to the objection this answer assumes without justification that people's frames of mind affect what reasons they act for, and does not affect their ability to articulate them or to become aware of them. Experience teaches us that that is not so. In certain moods our ability to acknowledge our concerns and to become aware of what we know is affected and no longer matches the reality of our concerns. Nor does it mean that we do not respond to the knowledge of which we remain unaware at the time. For example, we may avow willingness to act out of revenge when we are not actually willing to do so, and vice versa. One cannot escape the difficulty by making the counterfactual by which we identify the reasons for which we act relative to answers we would give when in a cognitively ideal frame of mind. To do so is to make the opposite mistake of thinking that our frame of mind affects only our ability to become aware of our reasons, but not our reasons themselves. It follows that sometimes what we would cite as reasons if asked are not our real reasons. Therefore, our reasons cannot be identified with our citable reasons.

While this argument relies on the possibility of making mistakes it does not assume that in the situations in which the counterfactual test will yield the wrong results we are actually making a mistake about our reasons. In most of those cases the reasons we would cite if we asked ourselves appropriate questions are not elicited and are not ones we have in mind when we think of our reasons for our actions. Hypothetical mistakes are not real mistakes.

The argument suggests, however, an approach to the identification of the reasons for which people act, namely they are the reasons they would avow if asked appropriate questions at the time, provided their answers are not distorted by mistakes. Where they are so distorted, understanding the mistakes and the reasons for them may lead to the real reasons for those actions. Needless to say, if this is a correct test for identifying the reasons for which self-conscious creatures acted then the notion is very vague. There are other reasons to think that it is vague so this should not be taken as an objection to the test.

Let us return to Dancy's thesis. According to it, the very facts which are a reason a person has for one act on one occasion may be, for the very same person, a reason for another, even conflicting action on another occasion. As we saw, this yields the result that reasons for people's actions do not determine whether their actions are right or wrong, wise or foolish, etc. To know that one needs more than the reasons people have.[28] Reasons, however, are general, according to Dancy. They are features of situations, or of actions, which can be instantiated on an indefinite number of occasions. His view is particularist in the sense that the rightness of an action is not determined by the reasons which apply to the agent. There can be a rival particularist thesis. It can be illustrated by thinking of both swift and opaque actions. In both cases it is natural, when asked for one's reasons, to point to the situation as a whole: 'in these circumstances that was the right thing to do'. The situation in all its concreteness is what one reacted to. That explains how swift intentional action is possible. The absence of deliberation shows, so the argument might go, that one reacted to the perceived situation as a whole, not to any part of it. The opaqueness of opaque cases shows that no feature of them satisfied the agent as decisive, or determinative. Rather the agent reacted to the situation as a whole.

In some ways this view that reasons are concrete is more attractively particularistic than Dancy's thesis. On this view reasons are particular, not general as per Dancy. Being particular they cannot justify any other action (assuming that they are conclusive reasons for the action taken). But, unlike Dancy's reasons, they justify the action they are reasons for. No gap is allowed between the evaluative and the guiding functions of evaluative considerations. These advantages notwithstanding, Dancy's thesis is the better one. The concrete reasons view appears to do justice to the fact that we can have the skill to discern reasons without analysis and reasoning. But in fact it goes overboard, and undermines its own case. It claims not that we can without deliberation distinguish relevant from irrelevant features in a concrete situation, as indeed we can, but that we do not need to discern any features of a situation to know that it is a reason for this action rather than that. That is to deny the intelligibility of reasons, for intelligibility depends on generality. Nor is it reasonable to deny the generality of reasons in the case of either swift or opaque actions. If we ask people who act swiftly and without deliberation they would still be able to distinguish relevant from irrelevant features of the situation: that the toddler (who was stopped from stepping into the road) was wearing green trousers was irrelevant. That the road was busy with traffic was relevant, and so on. There can be no general argument that people are always mistaken when they so identify the features which they took to be reasons.

---

[28] Two clarificatory reminders may be helpful here. First, in this chapter 'reason' refers to good or valid reasons. Second, when discussing the possibility that people's reasons, i.e. the reasons which apply to them, in any given situation determine whether what they do or may do in that situation is right or wrong, etc., I am referring to the totality of all the reasons applying to them in that situation, and not merely to a single reason.

Preserving the connection between reasons and intelligibility is an advantage of Dancy's thesis. Moreover, the approach delineated above for identifying the reasons which guide people's actions appears to support at least a weak form of Dancy's thesis. Is there any general reason to suppose that, if prompted by all the pertinent questions, every agent would cite enough features of his situation as his reason for the reason he cites to be incapable of being in different circumstances a good reason for a conflicting action?

Unfortunately for Dancy's thesis the answer is yes. Possibly whenever what people would cite as their reason (when duly prompted) can be a reason for a conflicting action then their understanding of their own reason is incomplete. If their understanding of their reasons were adequate they would not cite factors which can fail to be reasons for the same action in different circumstances. That is, whenever people act for a particular reason, and because they do so in those circumstances, their action is justified, their reason includes all the relevant evaluative factors which show their action to be justified.[29] That (sometimes) the factors people would cite if asked for their reason fail to meet this condition does not show anything about the nature of *reasons*. It shows that those people's *understanding* of their reasons is imperfect. If so then the gap between guidance and evaluation that Dancy's thesis assumes does not exist, and the thesis is mistaken. It gains an aura of plausibility because sometimes people's understanding of their own reasons is incomplete. If one identifies people's reasons too closely with their understanding of their reasons Dancy's thesis appears plausible.

This reply to Dancy is supported first by reflection on some of his examples, and secondly by a general consideration of the relation between one's reasons and one's statement of one's reasons. Some of Dancy's examples are problematic. Several involve the notoriously complex question about the nature of pleasure and pain. To the extent that his particularist thesis is made more plausible if one supposes, as Dancy does, that pleasure is not always a reason for, and pain not always a reason against, action, this may be an argument against the supposed view of pleasure and pain, rather than in favour of particularism. But take the book loan example mentioned above. Most likely when asked people would say their reason for returning

---

[29] This is true even when additional evaluative features of the situation were not part of their reason, but bear on the justification of the action. If these additional features tell against the action then the reason for which the agent acted will show them to be defeated in the circumstances. If the additional features tell in favour of the action they will be additional reasons for performing it which were not the agent's reasons, or evaluative features which cannot serve as reasons (they will be self-defeating if relied on, etc.). But the action is justified even without taking them into account.

the book was that they borrowed it, or promised to return it. But if asked at the time would the fact that the person from whom it was borrowed had the right to possess it, that he did not steal it, etc. be relevant to their reason (i.e. was their reason that they borrowed from someone entitled to lend them the book), most people would say yes. Regarding those people the example fails. Their reason was not one which applies in cases of a borrower who stole the book. If they are right it would follow that a more complete statement of the reason for which people who borrow a book should return it is that it was borrowed from someone entitled to have it. If so then those who would deny, when appropriately asked, that the fact that the book was not stolen was part of their reason would be under suspicion that they simply misunderstand the reason for which they act. They may have acted for a good reason, but they have only an incomplete understanding of it.

Dancy objects to counting the absence of conditions like the death of the promisee, which he calls defeaters, among the elements which make up a reason: 'there are just too many potential defeaters for the absence of each one to count among our original reasons'.[30] But this remark confuses articulation and knowledge. There are too many potential defeaters for us to be able to mention all of them or to think of all of them. But it does not follow that we cannot know all of them.[31] And those who know all of them may be guided by all of them (i.e. by their absence). That is, for those who know them all, their absence can be part of the reason.

Still, the reply to my promising story applies only to this example. For any statement of a reason, however expanded, an example can be found of a situation in which that reason is no reason (not, that is, unless expanded further). There is no general argument to show that any such new example can be countered by further aspects of their reasons elicited from those who acted for that reason where it was a good reason. So let us imagine a case. Suppose that John promises his neighbour to look after his cacti when he goes on holiday. When you ask John for his reason he would cite his promise. Suppose that as a matter of fact the promise remains binding even if the neighbour dies during his holiday, but only until an executor is appointed to deal with his property, whereupon it lapses. However, when we ask John whether his reason includes the fact that his neighbour is still alive, he does not give this answer. Imagine first that he gives no answer. He simply says that he does not know whether the promise remains binding after the death of his neighbour. The

---

[30] *Moral Reasons*, 81.

[31] There are other reasons to think that we cannot know all of them. The argument below allows for that possibility.

question is: what was John's reason for looking after the cacti? It seems to me that he acted for the right reason (that is because he promised, and the promisee has not died, etc.) though his understanding of it is incomplete.

There is no direct argument here against Dancy's suggestion that he acted for the reason that he promised *tout court*. It cannot be refuted by the fact that in pleading ignorance John denies that he takes a promise to be a reason regardless of whether the promisee is alive. To take this as an argument against Dancy is to beg the question against him. But that was not the purpose of the argument. Its purpose was to show that there is an acceptable alternative to Dancy's position. The reason for preferring it is that it avoids the gap between evaluative considerations and reasons which Dancy's position opens.

But there are additional reasons for preferring my suggestion. First, at the level of describing the phenomena, it is closer to the way we understand reasons. We may assume that people disagree about the precise conditions under which a promise expires, or about who can make promises, and in what ways and under what conditions binding promises are made, etc. Are we to say that people who disagree with each other do not act for the same reason when they keep a promise because they (rightly) believe that it was binding? In fact we regard all of them as having the same reason, though they differ in the way they understand it, and at least some of them understand it imperfectly.

At a more abstract level my suggestion relies on the fact that, since reasons are objective, one can refer to them without understanding them well, even while being mistaken about some of their aspects.[32] All these possibilities arise out of general features of reference, and there is no reason to think that reference to reasons is the exception. Indeed it cannot be a total exception or we will not be able to explain how it could be that one acts intentionally and for a reason, without knowing anything about it, except that one knows that it exists for one was assured of this by reliable people. It is not clear whether Dancy can account for the fact that our reasons need not be totally transparent to ourselves.

---

[32] As would be the case in our example were John of the view that the promise binds until his neighbour's heir releases him from it or that it lapses immediately upon the death of his neighbour. The relative opacity of reference throws up various intriguing questions in some problem cases. Some would be cases where people try to act for a reason and think they did, but through their misunderstanding of it they did not succeed. Another general result is that in explaining agent's actions one would sometimes need to refer not only to their reasons, but also to some aspect of the reasons which they knew and thought relevant.

5. THE PERSONAL PERSPECTIVE

The attractions and the interpretations of particularism are many. I will end by examining just one other claim, based on the distinction between first-person and third-person practical judgements. The claim I have in mind was put forward by Winch whose view 'puts a certain class of *first person* moral judgements in a special position as not subject to the universalisability principle'.[33] Winch uses Melville's *Billy Budd* to illustrate his view. In the story Vere finds himself confronting a conflict between his private conscience and the 'imperial one', embodied in the military code. He sees it as a moral conflict between two moral 'oughts', each of which is, in Winch's view, universalizable. In deciding to condemn Billy Budd and execute him Vere acts on a moral judgement as to what he should do, given his situation. This judgement, says Winch, is not universalizable. Winch finds that were he confronted with the same situation

I could not have acted as did Vere; . . . I should have found it morally impossible to condemn a man 'innocent before God' under such circumstances. In reaching this decision I do not think that I should appeal to any considerations over and above those to which Vere himself appeals. It is just that I think I should find the considerations connected with Billy Budd's peculiar innocence too powerful to be overridden by the appeal to military duty. (p. 163)

Nevertheless, Winch tells us, 'The story seems to me to show that Vere did what was, for him, the right thing to do' (pp. 163–4). It is merely that it would have been wrong for Winch to do the same.

This example illustrates Winch's general claim that

if A says 'X is the right thing for me to do' and if B, in a situation not relevantly different, says 'X is the wrong thing for me to do', it can be that both are correct. That is, it may be that neither what each says, nor anything entailed by what each says, contradicts anything said or implied by the other. (pp. 164–5)

Winch is at pains to emphasize that he is talking of genuine judgements, and that he, Vere, or anyone else making such judgements can be mistaken. Whether his account of the conditions under which we will be mistaken is adequate is immaterial to our purpose.[34] My discussion of the example assumes that all the normal ways in which people can make mistakes apply to such judgements as well. The crux of the matter is not in the ways the claim can be wrong, but in the factors which can make it right.

---

[33] 'The Universalisability of Moral Judgements', in his *Ethics and Action* (London: Routledge and Kegan Paul, 1972), 159.
[34] Wiggins in his illuminating discussion of Winch's article has shown them to be too narrow. See 'Truth, and Truth as Predicated of Moral Judgements', in his *Needs, Values, Truth*, 3rd edn. (Oxford: OUP, 1998), 166–84.

Winch explains that what is puzzling about the judgements he is concerned with is 'that they seem to span the gulf between propositions and expressions of decisions.... [T]he deciding what to do is, in a situation like this, itself a sort of finding out what is the right thing to do' (p. 165). This is the key to the explanation of the judgements under discussion. Two elements combine here. First, sometimes what makes an action right for me and wrong for you is something about me, and about you. Second, the process of discovery is the process of decision. They are inseparable. Both elements are problematical. What follows is my gloss on them. It does not necessarily coincide in all respects with Winch's view.

If what makes the action right for me is something about me, it is trivial that it is not necessarily right for everyone. This would show how it is possible that the two propositions (right for me and wrong for you, in the same situation) can both be true. But is this construal true to Winch's (and Melville's) description of Vere's and his own reasoning? Vere considered Budd's innocence, the situation of the navy, etc. He did not consider himself as a relevant factor. Winch, as we saw, tells us that 'I do not think that I should appeal to any considerations over and above those to which Vere himself appeals. It is just that I think I should find the considerations connected with Billy Budd's peculiar innocence too powerful to be overridden by the appeal to military duty.' If so then Winch does not rely on any consideration to do with who he is. But, if they are both right because they are different people does it not mean that they rely on different considerations: Vere on who he is, and Winch on who he is?

This reply misunderstands my first point. It was not that Vere's character or personality, or moral sensibilities, or anything like that figures among his reasons. At least it does not figure as such, under that description. It was merely that it is part of what makes the decision right for him. Sometimes people may rightly take their own personality as a reason: 'Given my nervous disposition', I may say, 'embarking on this course of action will cause me such anxiety that I had better avoid it.' But nothing of this kind is relevant to Winch's case. His case is that when faced 'with two conflicting sets of considerations, the one man was disposed to give precedence to the one, and acquit, the other to give precedence to the other, and convict' (p. 169). The fact that they had these dispositions makes their conflicting decisions right for them, but they are not among their reasons. How are we to understand this situation?

To make sense, and to avoid attributing a mistake to either of them, we must assume that Vere and the Captain of the Marines each takes his reason to be that, in the circumstances, one set of considerations is decisive for him, while conceding that if another person reaches a different decision they would not necessarily be wrong. Not every judgement of the relative stringency of different considerations is like that. Typically, cases like that of Winch and Vere occur when impersonally judged there is no answer to the question of which set of considerations must prevail.[35] Typically, that is, impersonally the conflicting considerations are incommensurate. In such cases the fact that the decision is Vere's or Winch's may make a difference. But if impersonally the conflicting reasons are incommensurate what is there for agents to discover through their decision? What was it that Winch discovered when he asked himself what he should have done in Vere's situation? Winch describes his own discovery: 'I could not have acted as did Vere; . . . I should have found it morally impossible . . .'. It is clear here that it is in a sense about himself. He still believes that Vere did no wrong. He simply discovered that he, Winch, *could not* do likewise, and that is the same as discovering that it is wrong for him, that for him one set of considerations (Budd's innocence) overrides the other. The impossibility is not a result of a belief that it is wrong. Nor is the belief that it is wrong a result of a feeling that one cannot perform the act. The two are one and the same. There is a belief about what is right for me which is an aspect of knowing what is normatively[36] possible or impossible for me to do. The two are one, or rather aspects of one phenomenon. It is significant that, as Winch points out, we tend to talk of impossibilities in these contexts. Impossibilities do not normally accompany judgements that of two conflicting reasons one is stricter than the other. Impossibility occurs in the context Winch discusses because one's judgement involves, in part, a discovery about oneself, about what one can or cannot do.

We are still dealing with the difficulty I started with: how can the decision be right, or even right for me, because of something about me, when my condition was not part of my reasons? Locating the phenomena among cases where of the conflicting considerations neither is superior to nor more stringent than the other, cases where reason underdetermines the result, where the two best options are incommensurate with each other, helps us towards a better understanding. It can explain, for example, how it could be that personal factors may matter, even though the choice is between life and death for another person. It cannot be that it was right to convict Billy Budd because Vere is such and such a person. But Winch does not say that it was right to convict Billy Budd (impersonally speaking, i.e. without regard to who is convicting him). He says that Vere's decision to convict

---

[35] It is not logically necessary that it be so. But this being the typical context we need not here consider others.

[36] Here too I do not believe that the impossibility need be moral. It could be an impossibility to allow that a pig's heart be transplanted to replace one's failing heart, or many others. They need not be irrational superstitious qualms. They may not be based on any false beliefs, nor need they display any other signs of irrationality.

was right for him. I added that this can only be if when impersonally judged neither course of action is dictated by reason, only if reason underdetermines the outcome. That is why it is impossible for Billy Budd, on Winch's analysis, to complain that he was wronged, though he was unlucky not to have Winch or the Captain of the Marines as his judge.

But if impersonally neither action was dictated by reason, how could one be *the* right action for one and the opposite action be *the* right action for the other? Winch does not mean that both courses of action were permissible. He is saying something quite different, which is captured by the invocation of impossibility: that it would have been impossible for him to convict (or for Vere to acquit), when the impossibility is not one of weakness of resolve. Winch's example is unusual. In most cases where the choice between options is underdetermined by reason people just follow their inclination, or follow a momentary desire, or just choose.[37] How can such cases, paradigmatic of unhindered choice, be determined by what it is not possible for one to do?

Whether people are aware of this or not, during their life, through myriad decisions and actions, people develop their personality, and create their own distinctive tastes and dispositions. Emphasizing that people's personality and some of their basic dispositions are self-determined is consistent with the fact that people's character is fundamentally affected by inherited characteristics, and by the impact of their environment on them. That goes without saying. Nor should we think of the self-determining aspect of character formation as intentional. It rarely is. We make our choices with an eye on the occasion. Yet such choices reveal aspects of ourselves to ourselves, and they create precedents, set and consolidate trends. The patterns of our lives help us make sense of our lives and of ourselves. We may fight them, and reverse them in future actions, accept them with pleasure, drift along with them without appreciating their significance, or follow some other course. One way or another our past actions and decisions form us. They make us into who we are. My purpose is not to explain this process, but merely to point to it. The point needed for understanding Winch's claim is the special importance of choices which are not determined by reason for the formation of our personality.

When we follow reason, or fail to follow it, we reveal and we mould our executive virtues or failings. It is, however, primarily where matters are underdetermined by reason that we reveal and mould our distinctive individuality, our tastes, our imagination, our sociability, and many of our other, including our moral, characteristics. Winch's claims concern the role of our moral character (though I would repeat again that similar considerations

[37] See my discussion in Ch. 3 above.

apply to various other aspects of character). Notoriously the morality of right and wrong is not exhaustive. Many moral acts are supererogatory. In these cases the demands of morality are incommensurate with some nonmoral reasons. When this is so regarding, say, charitable giving, or volunteering to help with various good causes, we are not rationally required to choose the moral option, but if we do we prove ourselves generous with our time or money. People's choices and their habits of giving determine how generous they are. Less often acknowledged by philosophers are the many occasions in which the demands of morality themselves are indeterminate (many cases of supererogation illustrate this indeterminacy as well). Often the demands of justice and of mercy are as we say 'finely balanced', that is incommensurate.[38] Some prove themselves, and make themselves, merciful by generally choosing the side of mercy. Others turn into stern and unforgiving people. These are crude and simple examples. The complexity of moral life defies such simple descriptions but confirms the general view they exemplify.

How do these features of moral psychology express themselves normatively? Impersonally judged since both options open to Vere are supported by incommensurate reasons neither is wrong.[39] It is possible that people when faced with such a decision would find that it is impossible for them to do anything but acquit (or convict). Does that impossibility have normative force? I think that it does. People do violence to themselves if they go against the grain, and act in a way which offends their moral character. Their integrity and self-respect are transgressed when they do so—unless, of course, they should do so. They may come to realize that their moral character is corrupt, or just that it leads them to the wrong option on a particular occasion. But we are assuming that that is not so, that impersonally the considerations which apply to the case underdetermine its outcome. In such a case it is right for people to act as their moral character tells them to act. But their reason is not that that is what they are disposed to do, or that that is more consistent with their past decisions. It is that they can do no other.[40] They cannot but prefer one set of considerations to the others; for them it is the more important or stringent set of considerations, even while knowing that impersonally speaking they are incommensurate.[41]

[38] For the reasons why cases like these are rarely cases in which the conflicting considerations are exactly equal in strength see Raz, *Morality of Freedom*, ch. 13.

[39] Those who think that there is a weak sense of 'right' in which it is synonymous with 'not wrong' would say that both options are right. It seems, however, that 'right' connotes more than that, so that saying that, impersonally judged, both convicting and acquitting Billy Budd would have been right is at least misleading.

[40] Even though, had they thought that their disposition led them to the wrong conclusion, they could have fought it and could have gone against it.

[41] These cases are interesting to compare with the normative effect of commitments:

So much for my attempt to make sense of the way in which an action may be right for me and wrong for you, in the circumstances Winch discusses. If these remarks are along the right lines they help with the second element in Winch's story: the reason the process of discovery is the process of decision, and the sense in which first-person judgements are different from third-person judgements. Note that Winch does not mean actual decision. He discovers what is right for him by imagining himself to be in Vere's shoes. Sometimes we may well feel that we cannot really know what we will do if faced with a decision until we are actually faced by it. The pressure of reality may prove our imagined response wrong. But this psychological possibility is beside Winch's point. His point is that we should think of the problem personally, rather than impersonally. Think not of what is right or wrong for one, but for us. The impersonal question engages our understanding of right and wrong. It should play a part in any decision-making. But in cases like Vere's decision we should also confront the personal question, imagine ourselves in the situation and ask what is right for us to do. Only thus do we let our moral character fully express itself. In what sense is a discovery involved? Suppose that I know myself well, suppose that I am a judge in a morally tainted system and not unfamiliar with ambiguous situations. Is there still something for me to discover? Do I not just know that the right thing for me is to decide this way? Note that what I know about myself may be known by others as well. If I can rely on that knowledge so can others. Will that not give the lie to the suggestion that first-person judgements are privileged?

The answer is that 'discovery', in the sense relevant here, need not be of something unknown or surprising. It can be no more than reaffirming what one thought to be the case any way. Indeed, many scientific discoveries are discoveries in that sense: experimental confirmation of a theoretically predicted result. In practical decision-making the element of discovery is in holding oneself open to what one may find, that is not prejudging the case.

people's personal commitments to various pursuits affect the reasons confronting them. After graduation when I considered becoming a teacher the merit of that activity, its impersonal importance, was an important consideration in my decision. A couple of years later, when I was a struggling beginner teacher, the value of teaching to me changed. It no longer was just the impersonal value of teaching. Now teaching is more valuable to me. Its value now is in part a product of my commitment to a teaching career. This 'extra' value is not merely the result of the economic or psychological investment. It is a result of the way my life became involved with teaching, the way success in teaching has become contributory to the success of my life, and walking away from it, or failing in it, a contribution towards the failure of my life.

So commitments are ways in which people's biography affects what is right or good for them, while not affecting the impersonal value of the options. Yet commitments need not affect people's character, and they are themselves additional reasons, reasons for the committed.

In some attenuated sense the same may be said of reflection on the merits of alternative options impersonally considered. But it is particularly important when the personal perspective predominates. The question is not, given my moral character what shall I do? To put it thus is to foreclose the possibility of a change in one's personal perspective, and to deny the self-determining, the self-creating aspect of decision and action. The question is, given these (impersonally valid) considerations what should *I* do? What is the right thing *for me* to do? This question allows my moral sensibilities to express themselves in evaluating the relative merits of the impersonally valid considerations. It also allows a continuous process of self-determination, for it leaves open the possibility, however unlikely, that my response will surprise me, that it will not confirm my own previously formed idea of myself.

Winch's example establishes the privileged standing of first-person judgement in this limited range of cases. This does not mean that only the people whose action it is can know what is right or wrong for them. The privilege has two aspects: first when Winch, as he does, asks what was right for Vere he is putting himself in Vere's shoes and asking the question as Vere would ask it, given his, i.e. Vere's, moral character. Winch may find the right answer, but he does it from Vere's point of view. Secondly, and this somewhat qualifies the first point, decision is part of discovery in the sense that it is open to development, and is part of the process in which we are part authors of our own character. In that sense but for the fact that Vere has already decided, Winch could not have known what was right for him. The answer must come from the person whose decision it is. Only they, by going through the process of confronting the issue in life or in their imagination, can discover/determine what is right for them.

6. HOW MUCH PARTICULARISM?

How much particularism do these reflections affirm? They reject the thought that morality or any other significant domain of practical rationality consists in principles, or that conformity to reason within it consists in following principles. Moreover, they suggest that our knowledge of reasons exceeds our ability to articulate them, and that to be guided by reasons we do not need to be good at articulating them. This conclusion is of great practical importance, though it is difficult to draw general operational instructions from it. It suggests that we know more than we know we know, and more than we can explain. Some of our knowledge can be brought to bear only in the concrete situation of decision and action. Any attempt to limit the freedom of judgement by restricting it to the application of general principles inevitably excludes our ability to tap the inarticulate fund of knowledge at our disposal. On the other hand, critical examination of our views requires (even if it is not exhausted by) articulation and explicit argument. When should we trust principles, which have been exposed to explicit rational scrutiny, and when our inarticulate knowledge, is not a question admitting of an easy general answer. Sometimes we can tell that we or others are good at judging matters of a certain kind by the results of our judgements. That would suggest that we, or they, should be trusted even when they cannot explain their judgements. This is especially so when understanding of matters in that area is slight. But often no easy guides like this one are available.

The most radically particularistic conclusion is indicated by the discussion of Winch's article. My conclusions apply in a restricted domain, typically where the impersonal reasons are incommensurate. But within this domain they are radical. As Winch indicates, they show that reasons for action are not universalizable. This is consistent with the intelligibility of reason, practical reason included. What makes it right for Vere to decide as he did, and for Winch to take the opposite decision, can be explained, and the explanation, relying on the difference in their moral character, and in the concrete fact that they did decide as they did, is universalizable. Whenever two situations are evaluatively different the difference can be explained in universalizable terms. But the explanations are not themselves reasons, and they need not refer to factors which are reasons. In this case they refer to the agents' moral character, and to the fact of their decisions, neither of which are reasons for these agents.

On the Moral Point of View

1. THE ISSUE

In the years since Kurt Baier made the notion of the moral point of view central to his moral philosophy[1] many moral philosophers have found the idea that morality consists of a set of considerations which form a point of view or which can be seen from a special point of view—not necessarily in the sense that Baier understood it to be so—fruitful and suggestive. This chapter offers some inconclusive reflections on the existence and nature of a moral point of view. In particular it argues against one way of conceiving it.

The moral point of view whose existence is my subject is not the common-or-garden point of view which is manifested whenever one says 'morally speaking what you did was not ideal', or 'morality demands very high standards of integrity', and the like. The use of such expressions indicates that the speaker believes that in the context of his utterance some considerations can usefully be marked off from others as being moral. Such a belief imports no commitment to the view that

(1) there is a philosophically deep way of dividing considerations into moral and non-moral such that even though other, context-dependent, uses of the terms are legitimate, it marks the correct, or the significant delineation of morality; or that
(2) moral considerations are a distinct type, distinct either in how we find out about them or in what makes them into considerations with a call on our attention.

The understanding of the moral point of view which I will challenge subscribes to both propositions. But right at the outset we can set aside one context of reference to points of view which, though presupposing the two propositions, is of no interest for the present inquiry. Quite often we refer to a point of view when we want to imply disbelief in the validity of the considerations encompassed by it, or when we wish to remain uncommitted to their validity. In this fashion an atheist may discuss how things are from a Christian point of view, meaning all those considerations that, in

[1] Kurt Baier, *The Moral Point of View* (Ithaca, NY: Cornell University Press, 1958).

virtue of their Christian beliefs, Christians believe to be valid. In a similar fashion the amoralist may talk of the moral point of view as encompassing those considerations that those who believe in morality believe to be valid. Adopting the common distinction between morality and beliefs about its content I will use 'morality' to refer only to valid considerations. People may have mistaken beliefs about morality. But it makes no sense to say that morality is mistaken.

Acceptance of the two propositions is common to all the philosophically significant reflections on the moral point of view. Kurt Baier and others who think of morality in that way usually add to the two propositions others relating to the comparative weight or stringency of moral considerations. These may be the assertion that:

(3') Whenever moral considerations apply one should follow (or comply with) them regardless of the countervailing non-moral considerations, unless the moral considerations themselves provide no definite guidance.[2]

An alternative principle which has found favour with some says

(3") Moral and non-moral considerations cannot be compared in stringency. When they conflict there is no true judgement of what one should do all things considered. One can only judge what one should do from a moral point of view and what one should do from some other point(s) of view.

Other philosophers have suggested various ways in which moral and non-moral considerations may be discounted against each other. I will discuss no such proposal in detail in this chapter. I am assuming, however, that all propositions which entail

(3) the moral character of a consideration affects the weight or stringency it has when it conflicts with the agent's desire or with other (non-moral) considerations affecting what the agent ought to do

presuppose that (1) and (2) are true. That is, I am assuming that if the moral character, rather than, or as well as, the specific content, of a consideration affects its weight or stringency, this is so because moral considerations belong to a special kind of consideration, whose nature affects their stringency.

Possibly, if propositions (1) and (2) are true, a decent argument can be put forward that typically the common use of expressions such as 'morally speaking' presupposes their truth. But no support for the truth of the two propositions can be derived from the use of these

---

[2] As might be the case if they are tied or incommensurate, or if they refer the agent to non-moral considerations.

expressions because they are readily explicable without presupposing the two propositions.

We are familiar with a variety of invocations of points of view. Consider but one example. 'As a teacher I have to condemn such conduct (say failing to complete your homework), but as a parent I fully understand it (the piano competition your boyfriend participated in yesterday was very important to you both).' In contexts like this, and arguably in all or most others, not much of general theoretical importance can be extracted from the fact that two points of view are contrasted. There is no assumption that they belong to different orders (ontic or metaphysical) of considerations, nor that they differ epistemically. Nor is it assumed that what counts as a parental consideration in this statement cannot consistently be counted as outside the parental perspective in some other context. On some other occasion the same parent can contrast her role as the daughter's mother with her role as her friend, both of which are subsumed under the same standpoint in the statement illustrated above.

Many philosophical discussions of ethics either argue for or simply proceed on the assumption that things are otherwise in ethics. They assume that the two propositions are true. There are a variety of reasons for which they may be thought to be true, and correspondingly a variety of ways of understanding what is the moral point of view and how it is constituted. I will examine only one way of understanding the moral point of view, an understanding which assumes something like the following. Every person has a non-moral reason to do whatever either best serves his interests, or contributes to achieving a goal he has, or contributes to making his life successful. Regarding any moral agent, the moral reasons which apply to him do not derive from his interest, goals, or well-being. Indeed they may conflict with them. The question of the binding force of morality is the question of how it is that people are bound by considerations which are independent of their goals, interests, or well-being.[3]

I will present what seems to me a powerful argument for the distinctness of the moral point of view and then proceed to examine its foundations. The results will be relevant to the assessment of other philosophical doctrines not directly connected with the examination of the issue of the nature of the moral standpoint. In particular they will be relevant to the thesis that there are internal and external reasons for action, and to forms of agent-relativism which depend on it.

---

[3] Moral considerations are independent of the interest of the agent when considered as the interest of this agent. They can be affected by it when it is taken to be the interest of one person among many.

2. PRELIMINARIES 1: CONTEXT-DEPENDENT STANDPOINTS

I will have little to say on the first of the two propositions which characterize belief in a distinctive moral point of view, namely the view that there is a coherent, context-independent way of separating the moral from the non-moral, on which a correct understanding of morality depends. Undermining the second proposition renders the first less secure. If there is no ontic, metaphysical, or epistemic significance to the distinction between moral and non-moral considerations, no difference between them which accounts for their call on our attention, then it is less likely that there is a context-independent distinction between them.

It is useful, however, to spend a few brief paragraphs in giving a concrete example of how the distinction between the moral and the non-moral could be context-dependent. Consider the observation: 'What I did may have been tactless, but it was not immoral. I'm not saying that it was a moral act. Rather that it was neither moral nor immoral, but merely tactless.' Contrast the case of a 'merely tactless' act and an action which humiliates. Both hurt others, and both may display an indifference or at least a careless disregard for the feelings of the hurt people. (One can be both tactless and humiliating deliberately. But one need not.) The claim that the tactless act escapes moral judgement depends on its relatively trivial consequences. It may have needlessly hurt other people, but it is not as grave a matter as humiliating them. (Notice that the gravity of humiliation is not in the degree of hurt to the feelings of the humiliated person. It is in the meaning, or symbolic significance of the act).

Contrast this case with the case of Peter and Butrus, who, being senior registrars in their respective hospitals, both apply for a position as consultant at a hospital in the capital of Somalia's most famine-stricken region. Peter has no previous connections with Somalia. His current job is at Guy's in London. He applies for the new job primarily because he wants to help with alleviating the suffering caused by the famine. He is aware that the work experience will help him in his future career. But he would not have taken his decision to go to Somalia for that reason. Butrus, who is currently serving in the same Somali hospital, is also motivated by a desire to alleviate the suffering caused by the famine. He too is aware that the new position will be a promotion and will advance his career. But he is young and relatively new in his current more junior position. Only his justified dissatisfaction with the incompetence of his superiors and its consequences for the victims of the famine makes him apply for promotion at the present time.

Unlike the example of tact and humiliation, in classifying Peter's and Butrus's actions as moral or non-moral their consequences or symbolic significance play a much lesser role. Peter's act is moral because of a combination of his motivation and of the disruption to his normal life that his action will—if successful—bring about. Had he gone to Somalia for career reasons his action would not have been regarded as moral, in spite of the fact that its consequences for the victims of the famine would have remained the same.[4] To the extent that we feel some ambivalence about calling Butrus's action moral that is because it involves no disruption to his normal life. If successful his life will remain the same, subject to the increased responsibilities he will assume and the greater rewards he will receive. His motivation is not in doubt, nor are the consequences of his actions to famine relief. They may affect our judgement of the morality of his character, but it is less clear that his action itself qualifies because of them as moral. I suppose that different people will feel differently regarding this case, and—more interestingly—that the same person may classify it differently on different occasions depending on the purpose and context of his remarks.

These illustrations do not prove that there is no common basis for all our (correct) classifications of actions or of considerations into moral and non-moral. That is not their point. Their point is to suggest that we are not compelled by the facts on the surface of our discourse to do so. Their point is to suggest that we are adept at interpreting such classifications as based on classifying principles in ways which change with the context. There may be a unified understanding of what is moral behind them, but on the other hand there may not. This matter cannot be taken for granted. Its outcome is determined by theoretical reflections on the nature of practical reason.

3. PRELIMINARIES 2: RELATIONAL GOODS

Moral considerations bear on the evaluation of character and character traits, emotions and attitudes, people and institutions, and many other factors. To simplify, and in the expectation that the arguments to be explored here are not affected by the simplification, I will proceed on the assumption that the respective natures of the good, values, and reasons for action are the backbone of the case for the existence of a moral point of

---

[4] Humiliating another person is a moral (as opposed to a non-moral) act regardless of one's motivation or of the impact of the action on the life of the humiliated.

view.[5] I will further proceed on the basis of a common though not unchallenged assumption about the dependence of reasons for action on values: Only if an action realizes or protects, or is likely to realize or protect, some good, or if it contributes to the realization or protection, or is likely to contribute to the realization or protection, of some good, can there be a reason for its performance, and the fact that it is so related to the good will be (part of) that reason.[6] The assumption is formulated to allow for the possibility of deontic requirements or prohibitions, that is, for the possibility that some actions are required or forbidden on grounds independent of how good they are, or of how much good or ill they will or are likely to bring about. I am assuming, however, that deontic requirements apply only to acts which are good,[7] and that deontic prohibitions apply only to actions which are bad. I believe that the conclusions of this paper are not affected by the existence of deontic requirements or prohibitions, even if that condition is rejected. To simplify the presentation of the argument of the essay I sometimes disregard the case of deontic considerations.

The assumption is of a one-way dependence. Reasons, it assumes, are rooted in values. It leaves untouched the question whether all values or goods provide reasons for action, as well as the question, some aspects of which will be at the centre of much of what follows, of which agents have reason to realize which values.

I will distinguish 'relational' and 'non-relational' judgements about goods or values. Non-relational judgements of value are judgements of the form 'X is good (or valuable)', or 'something is a good (or valuable) X'. Relational judgements of value have the form 'X is good (has value) for Y'. The variables X and Y can be replaced with the names or descriptions of objects, events, processes, actions, activities, institutions, animals, functions or roles, ideas, regimes, principles, and many others.

For some pairs, X and Y, the relation of X being good for Y holds true only if having X makes Y good, or better (than it would have been without X). If proportional representation is good for democracy then a democracy (any democratic regime) is a better democracy if it incorporates proportional representation. Similarly, if changing the engine oils every

---

[5] This means that I leave unexamined the possibility that moral musts and must nots are at the centre of the distinctness of the moral point of view. Such a view is inconsistent with our common understanding of morality which allows that some actions or consequences are morally desirable without being *musts*, and that some of them are supererogatory.

[6] In formulating claims and theses I will accentuate the positive. But they should be read to include the negative. That is, the fact that an action is necessary to avoid some ill is also a reason for its performance.

[7] This means that they have valuable qualities, though not necessarily that their performance is productive of more good on balance than the performance of any alternative option.

so often is good for the car this is only if a car which is so looked after is (or is likely to be) better (or in better condition) for being so looked after.[8] But this is not always the case. The fact that having a pay increase is good for teachers does not imply that having a pay increase makes teachers into better teachers. It need not even be likely that they will be better teachers (nor of course that they will be better people). Similarly, the fact that getting her much coveted delicacy is good for my cat is not conditional on it making her a better cat (nor on it making her a better pet).[9]

The question arises, what is the significance of this difference? I suggest, though I do not know whether this is a necessary as well as a sufficient condition, that if something can be good for X without making X better then X's good is not merely an instrumental good. It is good in itself. In other words, the fact that I claim that there are things which are good for my cat even though they do not make it into a better cat (nor a better pet, nor a better anything else[10]) indicates that I believe that the good of the cat matters in itself. But saying that the good of the cat matters in itself leaves open the question: matters to whom? Is it simply that it matters to the cat? Or does it matter in a non-relational way? Is the intrinsic good of the cat simply a good for the cat? Or is it good *tout court*, good *simpliciter*, or perhaps, as people sometimes say, the good of the cat contributes to the good of the world?

The issue concerning the separateness of the moral point of view may be thought to raise the question whether there are nonrelational goods, and of their relation to relational goods. But for this question to stand a chance of capturing the issue about the separateness of the moral point of view a non-relational good cannot just be a good described or asserted by a true non-relational value judgement. Clearly there are true non-relational value judgements. For example, 'the computer I am writing on is a good computer' is a true non-relational value judgement.

Perhaps something is a non-relational good if there is a true non-relational value judgement stating that it is a good, which neither presupposes nor entails the truth of a relational value judgement. Thus understood it could be argued that all goods are relational. Many non-relational judgements of value are either elliptical for relational judgements

---

[8] Notice here the various formulations which I allow as vindicating the same thesis. Throughout the chapter I will resort to simplified linguistic formulae, which have to be sensitively rendered in natural sentences in a context-dependent way.

[9] Is it true of all such cases that the fact that X is good for Y implies that X will, or is likely to, make Y's life better? Often, though not always, this is so, but my point here remains unaffected.

[10] Though sometimes they make the cat's life better.

of value or presuppose them. In those cases in which everything which is or can be good for X makes X better, how good X is matters because it matters to someone who has an interest in X. It also matters because there can be someone who could have or acquire an interest in X, and if he does, what is good for X would matter to him. This can be so either because X is useful to him (e.g. if it is his car) or because he has become fond of X and thus cares about its value or well-being (e.g. if X is his picture collection—which we can assume has no exchange value but is dear to his heart—or to give another example, if X is his cat). The case of beings of whom it is not true that necessarily what is good for them makes them better is even simpler. In their case what is good for them (or their well-being) matters in itself and not merely instrumentally or to those who are attached to them or who are fond of them, etc.; nevertheless what is good for them or for their well-being is, just by being good for them, essentially relational.

The reason this way of understanding relational and non-relational goods is unsatisfactory is that it always seems possible to invent a fictitious something or someone such that whatever is good is good for it or him, or alternatively to find a real someone or thing for whom whatever is good is good in a fictitious sense. For example, is it good for history if countries have good leaders? Is it good for humanity if the weather is good? Is it good for art if art education is good? Is the world a better world if it has more (morally) good people in it, or if more of the people in it are (morally) good? In some sense the answer to all these questions is in the affirmative. But the fact that we can say things like 'the world would be a better place if more people were good' may be a *façon de parler*, a mere way of saying that these things are good *tout court*, or that they are good for people, or for some other unstated subject.

This way of describing the difficulty is itself no more than a *façon de parler*. It merely shows that this way of drawing the distinction between a relational and a non-relational good does not capture the distinction I am after. Possibly everything which is good or valuable, including what is intrinsically good or valuable, is also good or valuable for someone or something, such that all non-relational goods are also relational ones. But this can be a merely grammatical fact. Views which regard all goods as relational should not gain plausibility by inventing empty relational judgements of value. 'If life is valuable then the world is better for the existence of life', etc.

To get closer to the underlying philosophical issues let me stipulate that a good is relational if and only if it is good solely because it is good for someone, that is, if it can be stated by a true relational value judgement the reason for which, or explanation of the truth of which, is exhausted on showing that it is good for someone. By way of contrast I will call a good or a value non-relational if what makes it good is (or depends in part on) something other than that it is good for someone. Naturally, since the same thing can be good in two ways, or for two reasons, the same good can be both a relational and a non-relational good. Promotion to managing director may be good both for Jane, since it serves her welfare, and for the company, which will get the benefit of her insight and initiative. So it is a relational good twice over. If anything can be non-relationally good at all then we must allow that it can also be relationally good, that is, good in a special way to some particular person.

Relational goods should not be confused with instrumental goods. The latter are relational goods, whose value resides in their having valuable consequences (or in the fact that they are likely to have such consequences). Relational goods can be intrinsically valuable. In many people's view a person's wisdom, for example, is intrinsically but relationally valuable. It is good because it makes one better, or makes one's life a better life. The relation of wisdom to its possessor is constitutive, not causal. Yet wisdom is often valued because of its contribution to the life or personality of its possessors, that is, relationally.

I have to admit that there is a certain awkwardness in the distinction, and in the way I will handle it in the next section. The awkwardness, I believe, is not accidental. Part of the purpose of this chapter is to show that the notions of being good *tout court* and of being good for someone are so closely connected that a systematic distinction between relational and non-relational goods is misleading. But as we are to examine a case for the moral point of view which depends on the distinction, the elucidation I have offered will be helpful in setting it out. A few examples will help in understanding the distinction. A good car is relationally good for its value derives from its value to potential users (and perhaps some others). A good holiday is likewise relationally good, for its goodness lies in its contribution to the well-being of those who have it. If I or my cat has a good life that good is, perhaps, non-relational. It is true that it is good for me and good for my cat to have a good life. But saying that does not illuminate the notion of a good life.[11] It is at best puzzling to say that the reason it is good to have a good life is that it is good for the person who has it. Clearly having a good life does not make the person whose life it is into a better person (though it may, and—more to the point—only people who are not bad in certain ways can have an altogether good life). What else can one mean by saying that the reason a good life is good is that it is good for those who enjoy it? These rephrasings of the near-tautology that a good life is good add very

---

[11] Other than negatively by excluding the thought that what is good about our life is that it is useful to someone else (though of course it may be that as well).

little to it, other than that in various contexts they can be used to dispel various possible misunderstandings.

Similarly, even those who believe that the world is a better world if the people in it are better people or if they have a better life do not normally regard this as a reason why a good life is valuable. A month's holiday in the mountains is a constitutive component of my life, and if it is good it makes my life better just by making part of it good. But I doubt whether we stand in the same relation to the world. While it makes sense[12] to say that someone wants a good holiday in order to have a good life it seems absurd to suggest that someone desires a good life, for himself or for another, *in order* to make the world into a better world. If this is absurd then the goodness of one's life or personality are non-relational.

4. THE THESIS AND ITS ARGUMENT

The conception of the moral point of view which is at the centre of the present inquiry turns on the way in which value relates to reasons for action. We can simplify the principle of the value-dependence of reasons by saying that, generally speaking, and subject to exceptions which need not concern us, we only have reason to perform actions which are likely to realize value. Talking of realizing value is jargon. I will use it as a shorthand for doing what is good for, or what prevents something bad happening to, someone whose good matters in itself. This formula requires sensitive unpacking. Take one example. Exercise is good for me. But I must take exercise (in the appropriate way) for it to do me any good. If something is valuable for me then there are various things which can happen or be brought about such that if they do happen I benefit from the good: this may be eating an apple, or listening to music, or watching a film, or repairing a roof, or keeping myself healthy. All such actions are covered by the jargon expression 'realizing value'. I will also talk of promoting value, or engaging in valuable activities, and use similar expressions all of which require sensitive translation into a range of ordinary verbs to make literal sense. Luckily, for present purposes the details of the unpacking do not matter.

What goods do we have reason to protect or promote, what good activities should we engage in? Is there any reason for anyone other than the being for whom the good is good to realize it? Clearly not everything which is good for someone or something gives rise to reasons for people other than those it is good for. Watering the flowers is sometimes good for them.

---

[12] However, see more on this below.

Having the car serviced every year is good for the engine. But not everyone has reason to water the flowers or to get the car serviced. Other things being equal only those who have an interest in the flowers or the car have a reason to look after their good. Does it follow that, other things being equal, only those with an interest in my well-being have a reason for doing what is good for me?

A simple consideration lends further support to the view that this is indeed so. What is good for one person may well be bad for another person. Assuming that the goods in question are relational goods, one of the people concerned has reason to bring that thing about (since it is good for him) and the other has reason to prevent its coming about (since it is bad for him). It would seem that other people whose interests are not involved have no reason either way. Some people, I believe, have been tempted by such considerations to embrace the view that all reasons are agent-relative, and that they all derive from what is good for the agent or for his life, or from goals which he happens to have. We need not consider that suggestion for the moment. Our immediate interest is in a much weaker, and therefore more plausible, thesis. All that the conception of the moral point of view investigated here has to establish is a certain difference between the way in which one's own good provides reasons for action for oneself and the way non-relational goods provide reasons for action. To establish that non-relational goods provide reasons (for everyone) is part of what is required to establish the validity of the moral point of view, as here envisaged. From the moral point of view, one may say, people have reason to protect and promote the good of all, because the good of people is good *simpliciter* and not only good for them. To establish the validity of the moral point of view is to show that people are permitted or required to adopt it either always or if certain conditions are met.

In setting out these points I have followed the common understanding that universal reasons arise either from what is good for everyone or from what is good *simpliciter*. Therefore, if everyone has reason to protect and promote what is good for John, regardless of whether what is good for John is good for everyone, then what is good for John is also good *simpliciter*.[13] Two obvious ways in which moral reasons can be distinct suggest themselves: the values (the moral goods) which give rise to moral reasons may be distinct, or they may be related to moral reasons in a way which is distinct and unlike the usual relations between goods and reasons. These two ways give rise to the two priority theses: the priority of relational goods over non-relational ones and the priority of relational reasons.

---

[13] For the present argument we need neither assent to nor dissent from the view that what is good for John cannot be good *simpliciter* unless everyone has reason to protect and promote it.

Let us turn first to the thesis of the priority of relational goods. For the purpose of the argument that follows it is convenient to proceed on the basis of a further assumption common to many writers about morality, namely that only considerations related to the character and the well-being of people are moral considerations. Most commonly it is assumed that morality regards the well-being of all human beings and the virtue of their characters as non-relationally valuable, and thus a source of reasons for action for all human beings.

If the well-being of people is a non-relational value, then, the claim is, it is also what I will call a *dependent* value. A value is dependent if it is valuable in a certain way, for someone or something, or for a certain reason, only because it is valuable in another way, or for another reason, or for something or someone else. The well-being of people is non-relationally valuable only because it is relationally valuable, only because it is, tautologically, good for the people whose well-being it is. Dependence can be reciprocal. But in the case of well-being the dependence is all one way. One's well-being is good for one independently of whether it is good for anyone else, or just good *simpliciter*. Individual well-being may be a special good. It is sometimes held to be the one ultimate or supreme good. But the same relationship of one-sided dependence, the claim is, applies to all goods. The normal way to show why it is good *simpliciter* that John shall not be homeless, is that it is good for John not to be homeless. But one can show that it is good for John without presupposing in anyway that it is good in a nonrelational way. It is morally good to assure John of adequate housing only because it is good for John to have adequate housing. It is good for John to have adequate housing not because it is morally important that he should have it. It is good for him since it is a precondition of his having a good life that he should be properly housed. When we think of that good not as a good for him but as a good *simpliciter*, and therefore as a moral good potentially determining moral reasons for everyone, we must acknowledge that the moral good depends on the, to use the common jargon, prudential good. Housing John is good morally only because it is good prudentially. If art is good, good *simpliciter*, that is only because it is good for people, but it is good for people independently of its being good *simpliciter*. If these assumptions are justified we could say that relational values have an ontic (as well as an epistemic) priority over moral ones. That is, moral values, which are non-relational, depend on relational values, whereas relational values do not (i.e. do not as such, not as a class) depend on moral values. The claim that there is such a one-sided dependence of non-relational goods on relational ones is the thesis of the priority of relational goods.

The second priority thesis, the priority of relational reasons, follows a parallel line of reasoning. Following the distinction between relational and nonrelational goods, a reason which one has to protect or promote a good because it is good for oneself will be called a relational reason. A reason one has to protect and promote what is good *simpliciter* is a non-relational reason. The thesis I will call 'the priority of relational reasons' holds:

(1) That something is good for the agent is a reason for him to protect or promote that good.
(2) The truth of (1) can be established without presupposing that people have reason to protect and promote non-relational goods.
(3) The moral point of view, or more generally, the view that people have reason to protect and promote non-relational goods, presupposes (1).

The vindication of the thesis seems to require no more than pointing out that the fact that something is good for John gives him a reason to bring it about which others do not have. Possibly what is good for John is also good non-relationally. Even if it is, however, the point that it is good for John stands. Therefore, he has a reason to realize it which is special to him, a reason separate and independent of any reason anybody else may have to realize that good. If owning a house is good for John then that is a reason for him to acquire a house. If his owning a house is a non-relational good then (from the moral point of view) everyone has a reason to see to it that he owns a house. But his reason differs from theirs, and would exist even if theirs did not. Moreover, given that, by our hypothesis, concern for him explains why other people have reason to provide him with housing it seems plausible that they can have such a reason only if he has an independent, relational reason to do so, for surely no one has reason to act for the good of a (competent) agent unless he has reason to do so himself. This is the thought behind the second priority thesis.

If the realm of morality is the realm of non-relational values and of the reasons for action they give rise to, the thesis of the priority of relational reasons constitutes an argument for the existence of a moral point of view. That is, it supports the conclusion that agents can recognize and pursue some values without recognizing or pursuing any moral values. This would show that moral values form either epistemically or metaphysically a separate range of considerations which can be validated or established only by special arguments, arguments which go beyond those which convince people of the existence of relational values.

It is implausible to suppose that if there are nonrelational values all of them are moral values. Beauty and understanding the nature of reality are often thought to be examples of non-relational values which are not moral. But while this may suggest that the considerations canvassed above should be supplemented with others to establish the distinctness of moral values when contrasted with other non-relational values, this need not concern us here. Believers in the moral point of view are normally concerned only with the contrast between it and relational values. This contrast will be the focus of our discussion. If it fails then one common and powerful case for a distinct moral point of view fails with it.

5. THE REFUTATION 1: THE PRIORITY OF RELATIONAL GOODS

The thesis of the priority of relational goods must be rejected if relational goods presuppose non-relational ones. The crucial case is of intrinsically valuable goods. The good of health, money, adequate temperature, etc. is that they enable people to have a better life. Reading poetry, climbing, skiing, disco-dancing, being with friends, and many other activities make the life of the person engaged in them better. They constitute his life and their goodness makes his life good.[14] These are good for the agent. They are also good *simpliciter* if we assume that everyone has reason to protect and promote whatever is good for any person. But are they good because they are good for their agents, or are they good for their agents because they are good? I will argue that both answers are correct, and therefore that the priority thesis is mistaken in that it denies this reciprocity.

Typical explanations of what is good for agents display a dual structure. It is good for Johnny to play the piano because engaging with music is good, and because he has enough of an ear and physical control to be able to do so by playing the piano. In other words in justifying that anything is good for any agent we show (*a*) that the thing is good, and (*b*) that the agent has the ability and the opportunity to have that good. I can think of no other way to account for why what is intrinsically good for some person or other (or for other things whose good matters in itself) is good for them. If this is so then relational goods presuppose non-relational goods.[15]

---

[14] Whereas doing a drab job to earn money, though also an activity which makes one's life what it is, is of no intrinsic value and thus does not make the life of the worker better, except that in earning money he obtains the opportunity to do something valuable at some future time.

[15] Possibly a third condition has to be met for something to be good for one: it may have to be consistent with one's existing valuable commitments and projects. I did not include it in my list above, for an alternative view is possible, i.e. that what is inconsistent with our current commitments and projects is good for us, other things being equal. But other things are not necessarily equal. This view has the advantage of explaining how one can rationally abandon some of one's current valuable projects and relationships for others. Either way my central claim in the text is unaffected.

The only alternative explanation I know of suggests that what is good for people is for them to have what they want, provided that their wants meet some conditions, a possible example of which is that having what one wants is not self-defeating.[16] This explanation fails because it does not take account of the fact that one can only want something because of a good one believes the thing to have.

Some people reject this point, believing that one can want anything, and not only what appears to one to be good or of value. This equates a desire for something with an urge for it which attacks one. Urges, impulses, cravings, passions, and their like are real enough, but it is wrong to take them as the basis for an analysis of wants and desires. (I am using 'desires' in the way customary in philosophical writings. Its common use makes it far closer to urges and passions. But when so understood its proper use is far too restricted for it to do its philosophical duty, that is, in its common use it is false that whenever one acts intentionally one acts because of a desire to do what one does.) Unlike urges, most ('philosophical') desires do not have a felt quality. My desire to get in time to a meeting on European democracy starting in an hour's time is typical of instrumental desires, and my desire to read Ivan Klima's new novel is typical of non-instrumental ones. Neither is a felt desire; they arose because of my belief that I have good reasons for both actions, and because something in me responded to these reasons and made me want to act on them.[17] If I do not get to act on them that is most likely to be either because the opportunity did not arise or because when it arose I preferred to act for another reason. Either way I am unlikely to feel frustration or any sense of loss. Of course if I tried to satisfy my desires and failed I may well feel frustrated. But that feeling of frustration is not a result of an unfulfilled desire but of a failed action, and is likely to be acute only if it is due to my clumsiness, thoughtlessness, incompetence, etc.

Of course, we do have urges, etc., to perform certain actions, but normally we do not endorse them, that is, they do not become our desires unless we find them (and it may be no more than a rationalization) to be backed by reasons. If a force beyond my control propels me to take an action which I see no reason to take, then, regardless of whether I actually take the action or not, it would be misleading to say that I want to take that

---

[16] i.e. provided that having what one wants does not make one regret having it and having wanted it.

[17] It could have been that I realized, or believed, that the reasons for the action are such that even when the reasons against performing it are taken into account it would be irrational not to perform it. At the other extreme I may conceive the desire to perform it because of its good points, even if, given the reasons against it, performing it would be irrational. But most commonly it is neither of these. The reasons which make me desire to perform an action are simply those reasons for it which I respond to, whereas others leave me relatively cold.

action. Not infrequently we prefer to satisfy an urge or a craving as a way of ridding ourselves of it. In those cases our reason is that the craving is troublesome and the action which satisfies it will rid us of it. Acting for such reasons is sometimes akratic, but it need not be. Either way it is action for a (good, albeit not necessarily sufficient) reason.[18]

So if I want to count the blades of grass in my garden I do so because I think that this will take my mind off some upsetting event, or because the action has some other good-making property. If I find myself drawn to count blades of grass, but cannot think of any reason for doing so, I would certainly deny that this is a desire of mine.[19] It is a force which seizes me in spite of myself. If I am overcome by it and perform the action, I would be right to say that I could not help it, though in a way it would be an intentional action. All I say is that anyone will recognize this as a pathological case.[20] Contrast it with many normal desires: if I want to have a drink because I think that it tastes good, and am then convinced that this is wrong, then I no longer want to have the drink. No loss, or regret, etc., is involved. The desire—as it were—disappears with the loss of belief in the reason.

The point is reinforced by the fact that there is always a reason for any desire. The statement that one wants to paint potatoes green is incomprehensible, not least to the agent himself, unless there is something in the action, his beliefs about it, or its circumstances and consequences, which appears to him to make the action sensible. Not everything can be desired. Only what is seen as in some way good can be.

Some people may concede that one can only desire what one believes one has reason to desire, while denying that the reason must be a good which what one desires is believed to possess. They may say that people's reasons for desiring whatever it is that they desire is that they believe that they would still have that desire even if they were completely rational and possessed all the information which might affect having such a desire. Such an attempt to reconcile the existence of reasons for all our desires with the primacy of relational goods fails for the simple reason that we need not desire what we believe to be good for us. I know that going to see good films would be (intrinsically) good for me. Yet I do not desire to see good films (nor bad ones either). I believe that it would be good for me to see good

---

[18] Some expressive actions are an interesting borderline case. I kick the table in frustration, or walk up and down. Do I do so to relieve tension (conforming to the pattern I described of satisfying an urge to get rid of it)? Perhaps, but I am also expressing my exasperation, anger, or what not, and the fact that an action has expressive meaning is a reason to perform it when such expression is appropriate.

[19] CISSY: What are you doing? SMUT: I am counting its (the sheep's) hairs. CISSY: Why? SMUT: To know how many it has. (Greenaway's film *Drowning by Numbers*.)

[20] The best analysis of such cases is provided by H. Frankfurt in *The Importance of What We Care About* (Cambridge CUP, 1988).

films because that is a valuable activity which it is within my imaginative, emotional, and intellectual capacity to benefit from, that is I am able to understand the films and react to them as one should. Yet I do not want to see films. I am too busy doing other things and have no regrets that films have to be left out of my life. I cannot have everything that it is good for me to have. There are just too many such things for me to have all of them. Therefore there is no point in wanting all of them.

Relational goods, I conclude, presuppose non-relational ones in that (*a*) understanding the concept of a relational good requires understanding the notion of non-relational goods, (*b*) there are no relational goods unless there are also non-relational ones, and (*c*) if anything is intrinsically good for a valuer (and I am assuming that the good of valuers is good in itself) then it is also good *simpliciter*. At the same time, as I indicated above, any intrinsic nonrelational good is also a relational one. Whatever is good *simpliciter* is at least potentially good for some valuer. That is, if it is intrinsically good then it is good for any valuer who can engage with it in the right way. Appreciating art is intrinsically good, and is good for those animals (so far as we know, all of them human) who can appreciate art. And what is instrumentally valuable can be valuable to anyone whose interests or worthwhile goals will be served by it.

For reasons already explained, the reciprocity of relational and non-relational goods is not to be confused with the priority of the non-relational goods. Nor does this reciprocity establish that values are anthropomorphic. Suppose that unbeknown to us there are Martian, nonhuman, persons who are valuers (in the sense in which we are). They, let us imagine, value many things we know nothing about, or that we do not value. The fact that their judgements of value differ from ours does not establish that they are false. They may be true and if they are true it follows that there are many things of whose value we are unaware. Perhaps we can learn about them and their value, perhaps we can even acquire the ability to engage in them in the right way, as one can be educated to appreciate the beauty of paintings. But even if we cannot, even if those goods are bound to remain beyond the reach of human valuers, we must concede that those things are good, even though not good for us. In relation to such goods our situation is that of a tone-deaf person with regard to music: he too must admit that music is valuable, even though he cannot relate to it.[21]

There remains the fact that, since whatever is good is (at least potentially) good for someone, there is a logical reciprocal relation between values

---

[21] Furthermore, just as the tone-deaf person has reasons to respect goods which he cannot engage with, because he has reason to respect other people, so do we have reason to respect 'Martian-only goods' to the extent that we have reasons to respect Martians. But this is a long and involved story.

and valuers, a relation which important though it is, and difficult to unpack and to state adequately as it is, is not one which lends any support to the view that moral value belongs to a special point of view.

6. THE REFUTATION 2: THE PRIORITY OF RELATIONAL REASONS

The argument of the previous section shows that the thesis of the priority of relational goods is mistaken, and therefore the conception of the moral point of view explained in section 4 above is mistaken as well. The distinctness of the moral point of view cannot rely on the contrast between relational and non-relational goods and reasons and on the priority of the first. The argument does not affect many of the other conceptions of the moral point of view which have been advanced by various writers on morality. For example it does not affect those,[22] like Nietzsche, who are primarily concerned to contrast the aesthetic with the moral point of view.[23] The argument does, of course, affect a whole family of conceptions of morality which directly or indirectly presuppose the primacy of relational goods. For different reasons it also affects most conceptions of morality which focus on a contrast between the moral point of view and that of self-interest. The argument of the previous section was that whatever is good for the agent (and thus in his interest) is also good *simpliciter*. The only condition for what is good to be good for a person is that he is able to take advantage of it, to engage with it in the right way. This suggests[24] that

---

[22] Given that clearly not all non-relational goods are moral ones, the argument of the previous section in itself does not establish that agents who act in pursuit of relational goods must be pursuing moral goods. That was not its aim. Its aim was to deny that the distinction serves to establish the existence of a special moral point of view. That aim should not be confused with the 'optimistic thesis' that all agents necessarily pursue moral goods, to which I do not subscribe, partly because I can see no great grounds for optimism, and partly because it itself presupposes the view here challenged, i.e. that the distinction between the moral and non-moral is of deep importance.

[23] Note, however, that the aesthetic may constitute a separate point of view even though morality does not. It is possible that aesthetic properties possess special features which mark them off from any other evaluative properties. That may show that they form a class on their own, and—depending on the nature of their separateness—that the aesthetic constitutes a distinctive point of view. That would leave morality indistinguishable from all other values, excepting aesthetic ones, and therefore would be consistent with the non-existence of a moral point of view.

[24] And I have argued to that effect in *The Morality of Freedom* (Oxford: OUP, 1986), ch. 12, and in 'Facing Up', *Southern California Law Review*, 62 (1989). My comments on self-interest (as well as on what is good for a person) are too brief to take account of nuance in our use of these concepts. My comments are true of a minimal use of these notions. But often they are used in a way that suggests not only that the good is within one's ability, but

self-interest does not constitute a distinct point of view in any 'deep' sense,[25] and that though a person's self-interest can conflict with moral considerations, there is no fundamental conflict between the two.

If the argument of the previous section disposes of the thesis of the priority of relational goods does it not also refute the priority of relational reasons? If what is good is good for any agent who can reach it then the very reason any agent has reason to pursue what is good for him is thereby also a reason to pursue what is good, and vice versa. But this thought leads to an objection to the priority of relational goods, based on the credentials of the priority of relational reasons. I will consider this objection by considering the case for the priority of relational reasons.

Typical examples of moral activities are: going to disaster areas to help victims, giving money to charity, offering shelter to homeless or stranded people, donating a kidney to save someone's life. They are, in other words, cases of providing people with the means or the preconditions for a decent life, rather than being involved with them in intrinsically valuable activities. Perhaps this reflection should be borne in mind when we consider below the claim that moral reasons always override conflicting non-moral ones. But for the moment the relevance of the point is that it reinforces the thought that typically moral reasons depend on prudential ones. The moral agent has reason to engage in moral activities because someone else—the intended beneficiary of his action—has such a reason. But the reason of the moral agent is problematical in the way that the reason the beneficiary has is not. For the moral action—so the argument goes—will (tautologically) benefit its beneficiary, but will not, except accidentally, benefit the moral agent.

It has to be admitted that many ways in which one person can contribute to the well-being of another do not conform to this pattern. People's lives are enriched by playing music together, by sailing together, by reciprocating the love of those who love them, by having parties together, etc. In some respects these are the most profound ways in which people affect each other's lives. In all these cases the goods they are pursuing are shared goods, rather than dependent ones. They are shared for they can only be enjoyed together. The sharing is an essential part of the good. Interestingly we do not tend to regard activities of the kind instanced by my list as moral; at

---

also that one has an opportunity to use it, that there is no greater good one can have, the having of which is inconsistent with having the good under consideration, and that having that good would fit well within the general pattern of one's life. More important is the fact that we say of things that they are in someone's self-interest almost entirely when they are instrumentally good for him. I am not discussing such additional features as they do not affect the argument of this chapter.

[25] Cf. my remarks on points of view at the beginning of the chapter.

least they are not typical of what we think of when we think of moral activities. So for the sake of the argument it is simplest to put them on one side and concentrate on the typical range of moral actions as illustrated above.

Proceeding, therefore, on the assumption that typical examples of moral action are instrumentally valuable to their intended beneficiaries (providing them with money, shelter, etc.) the question of the reasons the moral agent has to perform them may seem puzzling. Given my contention that what is good is also good for whoever realizes it I am committed to holding that since it is good for John to have housing it is also good for me to give him housing. In other words, I am committed to the view that it is good for anyone who can do so to realize any good *simpliciter*. But is it good for me to provide John with housing in the way it is good for him to have it or to provide it for himself, that is, instrumentally? Hardly. Special cases aside, doing the morally good thing is good for me in the same way that playing the piano or going to a dance is good for me, that is, because it is doing something intrinsically good, something worthwhile or worth doing. This makes it clear that such morally good actions are good for the agent in a different way from the way they are good for the recipient, for whom they are instrumentally good. Correspondingly, they furnish the moral agent with reasons which are different from those their beneficiaries may have in the same matter.

This may be the source of a doubt whether moral actions can really be good for the agent. Fundamentally, as we saw, they are actions which are good because they are instrumentally good for some beneficiary. How can that make them intrinsically good for the agent? Let us put on one side mixed cases like teaching. Only if being taught is instrumentally good for the taught, and only because of this, is teaching good for the teacher. But if this condition is satisfied then teaching can readily be understood to be intrinsically good for the teacher since teaching is a challenging, complex activity which can be fulfilling to those engaging in it.[26] Such cases are cases of ordinary valuable activities; teaching is not different in this regard from wind-surfing, except that given that serving another is the intrinsic purpose of the activity it cannot succeed, and therefore cannot be good for the agent, unless it is achieving its purpose, and that means that it cannot be intrinsically good for the teacher unless instrumentally good for the students. But how can the same be true of giving money to charity? Or donating blood? Where are the intrinsically good-

---

[26] It is also an occasion for establishing relationships with other people—other teachers and the pupils. But I am disregarding this aspect of the example as it merely brings out the fact that teaching is also a shared good. Perhaps surgery is a purer case here as in many hospitals surgeons have little to do with their patients—though they strike up relationships with other staff. It is important to remember that real-life examples are hardly ever pure.

making features of such acts which make them, like teaching, not only good for others but for the agent as well?

Maybe we can see here a way to justify the distinctness of the moral point of view. Moral actions are not, just by being morally good, good for their agents. If people have to abide by them this must be for different reasons or on different grounds from those which explain why they have reasons to engage in worthwhile actions which are such that engaging in them is good for the agents.

Promising as this line of thought may appear it leads nowhere. First, it is motivated by concentrating on a very narrow range of moral activities, the 'giving money to charity' type of examples. While these are among the typical examples we think of when thinking of moral actions, perhaps even the most typical, they cannot be regarded as exhausting the range of what is commonly believed to be central to morality. Cases of shared goods and mixed cases are regarded as having a moral bearing at least in some contexts. Moreover, according to all plausible accounts of their moral value, the fact that they are shared goods is essential to their moral character, and cannot be dismissed as a mere accidental concomitant of it.

The main reason why the priority of relational reasons is a blind alley is that the puzzle which created the temptation to go down that road in the narrow range of cases we concentrated on is not really a puzzle at all. The apparent puzzle arose by contrasting teaching with giving money to charity. Both are instrumentally valuable to the receiver, but while in the case of teaching we can understand both how it can be intrinsically valuable to the agent and why its value to the agent is conditional on its value to the intended beneficiaries, how could the same be true of giving to charity? What is intrinsically valuable about writing a cheque?

Thus drawn, the contrast between teaching and giving to charity is real enough, but it is not a contrast between the moral and the non-moral. It is a contrast between the intrinsic good of activities and the intrinsic good of acts, defined by their results,[27] whose value resides in the value of their results. Breaking the world 100-metre sprinting record is an example of such an act. Sprinters may enjoy the running, but they need not. Even if they do not the act of breaking the record is worthwhile. Its value is, however, in its result: setting a new world record. Those who achieve it cannot complain that they do not enjoy the activity of racing which led to the result as well. Their reward is in the result.[28] The same is true of giving to charity. There need be no intrinsic value in the activity which consti-

---

[27] I have in mind here the distinction between acts and activities drawn by G. H. von Wright in *Norm and Action* (London: Routledge & Kegan Paul, 1963). See also A. J. P. Kenny, *Action, Emotion, and Will* (London: Routledge & Kegan Paul, 1963).

[28] Since the result is intrinsic to the act (you cannot break the world record without setting a new one) the intrinsic value of the result makes the act itself intrinsically worthwhile.

tutes the giving. Writing a cheque need not be intrinsically rewarding. The value is in the giving to charity, in doing something which is morally good. That is the reward of the agent, just as setting a new record is the reward of the sprinter. The fact that the giving is not morally good unless it is instrumentally good to the needy endows giving to charity with a moral character that breaking the record does not have. But it does not help to show any respect in which moral considerations differ fundamentally from others.

7. THE QUESTION OF STRINGENCY

My refutation of the priority of relational goods consisted in showing that whatever is good for someone (whose good counts in itself) is also good *simpliciter*. The refutation of the priority of relational reasons consisted in showing that whatever is good *simpliciter* is also good to anyone who can realize it. Of course, 'good' here means 'good, other things being equal'. I am not trying to deny that pursuing a moral good may be against the interests of the agent. All I was arguing, all I had to establish to refute the priority of relational reasons, was that where that is so it is because of various side-effects of pursuing that moral good. In as much as it is a moral good it is in the interest of any agent capable of pursuing it to do so.[29] I will conclude by discussing briefly and in a preliminary way the contention that my argument in denying the special character of moral considerations makes their special stringency inexplicable.

Let it be granted that doing volunteer work at a hospital in one's free time can contribute as much to one's well-being as playing golf, or going to the beach. From this point of view moral and non-moral goods are on a par. But is not the claim that morality is special valid at least in that moral reasons are particularly stringent? Once we understand what it is that makes them so stringent we will understand what constitutes the moral point of view. Perhaps. The first difficulty is in articulating a sense in which moral considerations are more stringent. To start with we must put on one side the possibility that there are absolute moral injunctions (e.g. an absolute prohibition on torture). It is plausible to assume that in some sense of absolute there are such absolute moral prohibitions. But they do not constitute the whole of morality, nor are moral prohibitions the only absolute

---

[29] And—special cases aside—it does not matter whether the agent does so because he is aware of its 'moral character', though whether what is good is good for an agent only if he pursues the goal because he thinks it to be good is a separate issue. See my discussion of it in *Practical Reasons and Norms* (Oxford: Oxford University Press, 1999), 180–2. For a more extensive discussion see S. Scheffler, *Human Morality* (New York: OUP, 1992).

ones. Arguably there are also non-moral absolute prohibitions on sex between siblings or with corpses, or on eating human flesh. Some will classify some of these prohibitions as moral. Others will deny that they are absolute. Without full analysis of the notion of an absolute injunction, and of the reasons, if any, for them, all that can be said is that if there are such injunctions it is likely that some of them are non-moral, and that this is so for any account of morality other than one which stipulates that all absolute injunctions are moral injunctions just in virtue of being absolute. So absolute injunctions are irrelevant to the suggestion that moral considerations have a special kind of stringency. The same considerations show that concepts of guilt and of wrongdoing are not special to morality. They apply to all unjustified violations of absolute prohibitions.

Some people believe that all moral considerations override any and all non-moral considerations. This claim seems implausible. Assume that there are circumstances in which the only moral considerations which bear on the choice of action relate to human welfare. Assume that such was the case when Jane decided to have a baby. In doing so she changed her situation quite radically. As a lone parent bringing up a baby she had to give up her full-time work for the homeless in order to obtain a better paid and part-time job in the financial sector, and in order to spend the rest of her time with her baby. Her decision to have a baby was not motivated by any moral considerations. Nor were there any moral considerations in favour of having the baby, other than that as a healthy caring person she would not be acting irresponsibly in having it. At the time she made her decision there were no moral reasons for Jane to have a baby. On the other hand she had moral reasons to carry on with her work for the homeless, and having the baby put her in a situation in which it would have been immoral (because it would have involved neglecting her baby) to do so. Yet she did no wrong in deciding to have a baby and acting on her decision.

For the purpose of my argument it does not matter whether Jane's job in serving the homeless is morally supererogatory or whether she is discharging her moral duty to the poor in holding to that job. The question is whether moral considerations must be a special class, for otherwise one cannot explain their stringency. The answer is that they are not specially stringent, for example, some of them are supererogatory. To say that moral *duties* override non-moral considerations does not help support the suggestion that morality as a whole constitutes a special point of view. Furthermore, it is misleading to think of morality as consisting of either duties or of supererogation. Most moral considerations are in between. Jane's is a case in point. She has a job working for the homeless which she likes and which is well paid. She is making no sacrifice in doing it rather than working for a stockbroker. Other things being equal she would rather stay with that job. Other things are not equal. She wants a baby and therefore a part-time job which will pay as well as her full-time job. To achieve that she is willing to sacrifice some job satisfaction. There is nothing here to suggest that she is acting beyond the call of duty in working for the homeless.

The temptation to respond to her example by saying that it does not count for she is acting supererogatorily betrays the powerful grip of the confused picture of morality as particularly stringent that many of us succumb to. Being shown a moral consideration which is not stringent we want to consign it into a ghetto which does not count. In fact it does not belong to that ghetto. It is a typical case of moral consideration. Some will say that it is Jane's way of discharging her imperfect moral obligations to people in need. On that view it is a duty but an imperfect one for she could have discharged that duty some other way. There are, however, various obscurities in the notion of an imperfect duty which make it best to avoid it for the purpose of the present discussion. All that matters is that it exemplifies a moral consideration of a fairly common kind, which is overridden by a non-moral one, that is, the good of having a child.

There are countless examples of this kind, cases in which we make important decisions about our relations with other people which make us less able to conform to moral reasons which apply to us at the time, and where there is no moral reason to act as we do, but where we do no wrong is so doing. That last fact may be seized upon to show that morality permits us not to comply with moral reasons in the situations described, and therefore that they are not really cases of non-moral reasons overriding moral ones. Rather they are cases of morality overriding itself. But this is sheer confusion. There are no moral reasons which justify not acting on the moral reasons which apply to us at the time, and it is generally the case that we have reason not to put ourselves in a situation in which we will be unable to comply with reasons which apply to us. It follows that Jane has a moral reason not to have a baby. It is true that she is not acting wrongly, not even morally speaking, in deciding to have the baby. But to say this is to say that the moral reasons are overridden, or at least neutralized, by other considerations. And as the only other considerations are non-moral ones it is they which defeat, or neutralize, the moral reasons applying to her. One is not acting wrongly if one is acting on an undefeated reason, even if that reason is not a moral one, and even if it defeats or neutralizes conflicting moral reasons. Only those who have already established what is here denied, namely that there is an independent deep moral point of view, can expect that in such a situation one would be morally in the wrong, whatever is the true overall verdict about one's action, unless some special moral considerations provide dispensation from adhering to the moral reasons which apply to one.[30]

Accepting, then, that moral considerations are not always overriding, how is one to account for the general intuition that they possess special stringency? One suggestion might be that there is a positive/negative asymmetry in the case of non-moral reasons for action. Since playing golf is a good thing and since Jules likes playing he has a reason to spend Saturday afternoon playing golf. This means that if he decides to play golf for that reason his action will be intelligible and—assuming that, not unreasonably, he does not believe that he has overriding reasons not to play golf on Saturday—rational. But it does not follow that he has to explain why he did not play golf if he does not play golf. That he did not feel like doing so is a good enough explanation. He does not have to show that he did something at least as worthwhile instead. Moral reasons are not like that. They not only make actions in their pursuit intelligible, and, when they are reasonably not believed to be defeated, rational. They also make every failure to comply with them culpable, unless there is an appropriate justification or excuse, and 'I just did not feel like doing so' is neither. On this view the greater stringency of moral considerations lies in the fact that they are both reasons for an action and reasons against its omission, whereas non-moral reasons are subject to the negative/positive asymmetry, that is, they are reasons for an action but not against its omission.

The alleged negative/positive asymmetry is, however, no more than an illusion due to the other-regarding character of all or many typical moral considerations. In fact were Jules to spend the afternoon watching cartoons on TV rather than playing golf he would have shown himself to be a couch-potato. The reason to play golf is also a reason against omitting to play, in the sense that it reflects adversely on the character of the agent's actions if he does not follow it. He proves himself to be weak-willed, self-indulgent, etc. It is in precisely the same way that a failure to comply with moral reasons reflects on the agent, except that in the case of moral failure other people are typically affected, and therefore other people, not necessarily those affected, feel more of a right to pass judgement on the agent, and sometimes they do not stop there, and of course sometimes they are

---

[30] As Charles Larmore pointed out to me, my view denies the existence of justified immoralities, i.e. cases in which one takes the right or best (or at least a permissible) action which is none the less morally wrong for one to take. That is, on my view we may quite naturally say things like that in contexts in which the action taken is right because the non-moral reasons for it defeat the moral reasons against it. But 'moral' and 'non-moral' are used in a context-dependent way, without assuming any theoretical significance. What the position here advocated assumes is that there are no interesting dilemmas or difficult practical problems of this kind.

justified. But none of this establishes the special stringency of moral considerations, nor are these factors specific to morality. All we can say is that they are more typical of moral than of non-moral cases. But non-moral failures can also be failures towards friends, relations, or associates, triggering outside censure.

The question we are looking into is not whether many moral considerations are among the most weighty or stringent considerations which people face. We are looking for a reason to think that something which makes them moral also makes them weighty or stringent, that being moral gives them stringency, and this is the claim that we failed to substantiate. There could be other interpretations of the nature of moral considerations which will indeed show them to be more stringent than non-moral considerations. I have to admit that I know of none, and in their absence my tendency to believe that moral considerations do not form a special subclass of non-relational goods and values is strengthened.[31]

---

[31] I am grateful to Bonnie Kent, Charles Larmore, and Richard Moran for helpful comments on a draft of this essay.

12

The Amoralist

1. WHO IS HE?

Sometimes the amoralist is thought to present a problem for moral philosophy. If one can be an amoralist then the validity of morality is undermined unless one can be amoral only because of ignorance or irrationality. Morality, the underlying thought is, is rationally defensible only if it can marshal arguments in its support which an amoralist must rationally accept. My contention will be that the confrontation between the moralist and the amoralist is misconceived. Sections 5, 6, and 7 will explain my view by challenging the amoralist and the moralist in turn. I will argue that their confrontation is bogus for neither protagonist has a separate existence. But before coming to that I will, in section 2, challenge the way that Nagel has recently discussed the problem,[1] and will prepare, in sections 3 and 4, the ground for the main arguments. First of all (in the current section) I explain who the amoralist is.

I want to discuss one of the stock characters in moral philosophy's wax gallery. But as often more than one can claim the title. The amoralist is not, of course, the immoralist. He does not deliberately defy morality, that is, he is not a Miltonian Lucifer knowing the truth and rejecting it in his life. It is best to think of him as someone innocent of all knowledge of morality. Alternatively, if he was told about it he disbelieves it. He does not believe that it has any validity. He would accept it were he convinced of its validity but he is not convinced.

Nor is it essential that the amoralist be immoral. It is likely, perhaps inevitable, that during his life he will act morally wrongly as well as morally unwisely. But if this follows from his nature it does so only in combination with assumptions about common facts of human life. If he is lucky in his life (lucky not from his, but from the moral point of view) he may not act very immorally. He may not be guilty of more gross immoralities than many of us are.

The amoralist does not believe in morality, either because he doubts its

---

[1] Nagel's article 'The Value of Inviolability', *Revue de Métaphysique et de Morale*, 99 (1994), 149–66, not only led me to write this essay, but—in spite of my disagreement with it—greatly affected my own understanding of the problem.

validity, or because he is not aware of it, or does not comprehend it. This does not mean, of course, that he does not believe in any values, in anything being valuable. That would reduce the amoralist to the level of an animal able to pursue its bodily imperatives only, a creature driven by hunger for food or sex, by the need to discharge bodily functions, and to protect itself from extremes of heat or cold. Such creatures pose no challenge to moral philosophy.[2]

Elsewhere[3] I have cast doubt on the common assumption (among philosophers) that morality forms a distinct body of considerations which differs from that involved in other areas of practical thought. In a way the purpose of this chapter is to reinforce that doubt. To let the argument commence, however, we should suspend the doubt. I will return to it in the concluding section. An amoralist—I will say—is a person who denies that persons[4] are valuable in themselves.

This characterization of the amoralist is not without its problems. It implies an understanding of morality which may be challenged even by some people who believe themselves to uphold morality. True moral views, in their opinion, do not include endorsing that persons are valuable in themselves. As the persevering reader will discover at the end of this chapter, it is possible that I myself belong with those people. Yet my view is not that the divide between the moralist and the amoralist is to be drawn elsewhere, but that it is illusory. My argument to that effect applies directly only when the divide is defined by reference to the belief that people are valuable in themselves. Its lessons bear—I hope—on a wider family of ways of identifying the divide.

There is another difficulty with this way of characterizing the amoralist. The thought that people are valuable in themselves is a widely shared belief among moral philosophers, and though it is not often expressed by non-philosophers, moral philosophers usually think that it encapsulates the meaning of common beliefs. It is not, however, a belief which is easy to articulate or comprehend. That people have value in themselves means, one may say, that they are ends in themselves, though this piece of philosophical terminology is not much more perspicuous. Philosophers will generally agree that whatever else people having value in themselves, or being

---

[2] You may say that there is a problem if the creature who does not accept the existence of any values can do so—that is, if he has the mental capacity, the cognitive abilities, and the power of agency which enable one to recognize value—but the difficulties which this possibility gives rise to arise also in the case of the amoralist and will be examined below.

[3] In *The Morality of Freedom* (Oxford: OUP, 1986) and in 'On the Moral Point of View', in J. B. Schneewind (ed.), *Reason, Ethics, and Society* (Chicago: Open Court, 1996), 58–83, which is Ch. 11 above.

[4] Or other people or some other category deemed definitive of the class of those who are of value in themselves.

ends in themselves, means it means that, other things being equal, their interests should count. That is that, other things being equal, an action is (morally) justified only if it can be justified taking proper account of the interests of all those whose interests it affects. Again—the actual meaning and implication of this principle is much in dispute.

Many will say that an essential element of the idea that people have value in themselves is that they must be respected. This is certainly another philosophical platitude.[5] But it is an open question how much more this notion of respect involves beyond the requirement to take due notice of other people's interests in all actions which affect them, or at any rate not to act in ways which cannot be justified by an account which gives their interests their due recognition.

Notice that the amoralist is not to be equated with the egoist, or if he is an egoist he is only one of several distinct breeds of that character. He is not necessarily self-obsessed. He is not necessarily egocentric, that is, he need not be exclusively or predominantly concerned with himself, his own life or character. Nor need his activities and pursuits be self-regarding. He can take up causes. His life may revolve round a selfless dedication to restoring decaying or otherwise threatened works of art, or to solving the mystery of the basic laws of the universe, or to other (impersonal) ideals. At least if these avenues are not open to him it is not obvious on the surface of things why this is so. Such a conclusion requires a deeper argument.

Another respect in which the amoralist differs from some egoists is that at the basic level he is not partial to himself. He is not a person who believes that he or his life is valuable, but other people or their lives are not. He accepts that he and his life are—just like other people and their lives—devoid of all value. In this regard the amoralist resembles the moral egoist who believes that all life is of value but that only its possessor has any reason to do something about it.[6] Both are impartial at the most fundamental level in that neither claims to himself a value that is denied to others. Both are impartial in a way which leads to the conclusion that they have no reason to respect other people. The difference is that the amoralist, but not the moral egoist, denies that people are bearers of moral value.[7]

I hope that these remarks help in sketching the profile of the amoralist,

---

[5] A 'philosophical platitude' since 'respect' does not mean here what one means when talking of respecting the elderly, etc. For example, I may lose all my respect for a person upon discovering that he is mean and treacherous, without losing my 'philosophical respect' for him as a person.

[6] There are other versions of the moral egoist. Most importantly some maintain that while each person is valuable he is valuable to himself only. This view itself can bear several different interpretations. Nagel identifies his egoist with those who hold this view.

[7] Though I will not elaborate the point the argument of this essay undermines the moral egoist as well.

and in distinguishing between him and other characters familiar from the ethical Madame Tussaud's. Of course, much remains obscure. Some of the remaining unclarities will be dealt with in what follows. But some will remain, and I will return to this point in the final section. It is time to go back to the argument with which the chapter opened.

2. CHOOSING AGAINST THE AMORALIST: NAGEL'S ARGUMENT

If one can be an amoralist then the validity of morality is undermined unless one can be amoral only through ignorance or irrationality. Why should one think so? The simple argument runs somewhat as follows. If morality is valid, that is, if people are valuable in themselves, then it is possible for people to come to know that. Moreover, it is possible for people who are amoral to realize that there are rationally compelling reasons to accept that people are valuable in themselves. The amoralist who denies the validity of morality must, therefore, be blind to a valid argument available to him. Such blindness can be the result of ignorance of the factors relevant to the soundness of the argument, or sheer irrationality.

True, this argument is too simple. It disguises many ambiguities, and it begs many questions. I will not, however, try to challenge it directly. Rather I will undermine its most fundamental presupposition. It sees morality as a separate domain. The amoralist stands outside it and refuses to go in. The question is: is there anything outside morality which could rationally convince him to take the step of adopting the moral point of view.[8] This is the way Thomas Nagel understands the amoralist, and the way he confronts him. Nagel offers a consideration which purports to show that the amoralist has reason to become a moralist. 'Morality', he explains, 'is possible only for beings capable of seeing themselves as one individual among others more or less similar in general respects.'[9] Once people realize that fact they are said by Nagel to occupy not only their own individual point of view, but also an impersonal point of view which everyone can occupy. We need not be concerned here with the meaning of this statement. The important point is that people who grasp this fact face a choice:

---

[8] There are no metaphysical implications to my use of 'the moral point of view'. It means: accept the basic beliefs which mark one as a person with moral concerns and sensitivities, however mistaken one may be about various moral issues. The amoralist is not someone who makes moral mistakes (e.g. believing that abortion is wrong, or that it is not wrong, whichever happens to be the mistaken view). He is someone who declines to accept the basic moral beliefs, or who lacks basic comprehension of the nature of the moral. He stands outside morality altogether.   [9] Nagel, 'Value of Inviolability', 160.

This choice has to do with the relation between the value we naturally accord to ourselves and our fates from our own point of view, and the attitude we take toward these same things when viewed from the impersonal standpoint.... One alternative would be not to 'transfer' to the impersonal standpoint in any form those values which concern us from the personal standpoint. That would mean that the impersonal standpoint would remain purely descriptive, and our lives and what matters to us as we live them (including the lives of other people we care about) would not be regarded as mattering at all if considered apart from the fact that they are ours, or personally related to us. Each of us, then, would have a system of values centering on his own perspective, and would recognise that others were in exactly the same situation.

The other alternative would be to assign to one's life and what goes on in it some form of impersonal as well as purely perspectival value, not dependent on its being one's own. This would imply that everyone else was also the subject of impersonal value.... I believe, as did Kant, that what drives us in the direction of universalizability is the difficulty each person has in regarding himself as having value only *for himself*, but not *in himself*. If people are not ends in themselves—i.e. impersonally valuable—they have a much lower order of worth. Egoism amounts to a devaluation of oneself, along with everyone else.[10]

I will disregard certain aspects of Nagel's argument, including his controversial invocation of Kant, and his equally controversial use of 'universalizability', as well as the fact that he calls our amoralist 'the egoist'. My concern is with the fact that he thinks that people have a choice between amoralism and morality (i.e. holding that people do not have or that they do have 'impersonal' value), and that people's difficulty in not holding themselves to be impersonally valuable exerts a strong pressure for choosing morality.

It is not clear how Nagel means the choice to be understood. Cannot an amoralist accept Nagel's description as a description of the motives which lead people to escape the unflattering but true amoral view ('you do not have value in yourself, nor does anyone else') and find comfort in the delusion of morality's reassurance about our value and worth? Presumably it is not Nagel's view that moralists are deluding themselves. Therefore he must think that 'what drives us in the direction of' the moralist is a rational consideration capable of justifying our acceptance of the moralist's position. What is the rational reason Nagel is pointing to? The proposition that I (along with everyone else) have no value in myself is not self-refuting (or if it is then Nagel has not shown that it is), and the desire to be of value in myself is not a (valid) reason to believe that I have such value. It is difficult to read Nagel as pointing to the presence of any reason to believe the moralist. It seems that we have to take seriously the fact that the point

---

[10] Ibid. 160–1.

is made in terms of a choice: we are driven—says Nagel—to choose to reject the amoralist, and to join the moralist.[11]

What are we choosing, according to Nagel? We could of course choose to act as if the moralist is right. But why should we? There is no reason to do so if he is wrong, and doing so would not satisfy whatever it is that 'drives us' to choose as Nagel suggests, for it will not allay the fear that in ourselves we are of no value. Nagel cannot mean that we choose to believe that the moralist is right, that we are of value in ourselves, for we cannot choose to believe.[12] Besides, to avoid the charge that this is no more than an explanation of our self-deception the drive to embrace morality must make it justified for us to believe that people are of value in themselves, that is, it must bear on the credibility of that belief, on the likelihood that it is true. Wanting it to be true because otherwise we are of no value in ourselves cannot fulfil that role.

The most promising interpretation of Nagel's argument seems to be that the choice we have is neither a choice to believe or disbelieve the moralist nor a choice of acting as if we believe him. It is a choice *of accepting* the moralist's principle. I will also assume that the argument is that rationally choosing to accept the moralist's principle validates it, that is, renders it true[13] or makes it rational to believe that it is true.

The difference between believing a proposition and accepting it is meant to be fairly intuitive.[14] I accept a proposition if I use it as a premise in my deliberations, for any purpose other than in order to convince someone that I do believe it,[15] even though I do not believe it. I may indeed disbelieve it. Usually one accepts a proposition for a particular limited purpose. In all other matters one refrains from relying on the proposition, as one does not believe it. In principle, however, one can accept a proposition in all one's deliberations for which it is relevant. One difference between believing a proposition and accepting it which this characterization brings out is that accepted propositions feature only in one's deliberations. Beliefs affect one's imaginative life, one's subconscious thoughts, one's unarticulated reasons, and more.

---

[11] Indirectly, and as a consequence of this choice we may acquire a reason to believe the moralist. I will examine this possibility below.

[12] See my explanation of this fact in 'When We are Ourselves: The Active and the Passive', *Proceedings of the Aristotelian Society*, suppl. 71 (1997), which is Ch. 1 above.

[13] Since moral principles and moral propositions can be either true or false, and since Nagel takes them to be so I will not discuss variants of his arguments which reject that assumption.

[14] Cf. L. J. Cohen's description of the difference on pp. 4 ff. of *An Essay on Belief and Acceptance* (Oxford: OUP, 1992), though my views are not identical with his.

[15] This exception is necessary to distinguish accepting a belief from trying to deceive someone into believing that one believes it.

The Amoralist 279

Assuming that Nagel's argument is meant to show how it is rational to choose to accept the moralist's view, how are we to understand it? Two possibilities suggest themselves. According to the first, each one of us has a choice between accepting the amoralist's position and accepting some form of universal morality (as Nagel calls the alternative). Alternatively, it is not us but some idealized counterpart of us—for example, a rational and well-informed person, unencumbered by our beliefs and commitments—who has the choice.

At first blush we may find the second interpretation unattractive. Given that we are not in that situation doubts must arise as to why it matters what we would have chosen had we been in it. Of course the fact that under some hypothetical conditions I would have chosen not to enter into commitments which I have entered into does not in itself release me from those commitments, unless it can demonstrate one thing—unless it is a way of showing that those commitments were never binding as they rest on a false presupposition. The second reading, therefore, understands Nagel as providing a constructivist argument against the amoralist. It establishes that people are ends in themselves, by showing that our 'unencumbered selves' (if I may be allowed to borrow this jargon) would choose to accept that view rather than join the amoralist in its rejection.[16] Let me consider this second reading first.

Why should our 'unencumbered selves' be interested in the case for accepting the amoralist's position without believing it? Why should they not raise the question whether the amoralist is right, rather than whether his position should be accepted?

One type of case in which people accept propositions, when they do not believe in them, is temporary acceptance for some special purpose, paradigmatically in order to see what would follow from propositions or from their acceptance (as when a proposition is accepted 'for the sake of argument', or as a hypothesis in a *reductio ad absurdum* argument). Alternatively, propositions are accepted where action relying on the proposition or on its negation is required in circumstances in which no sufficient evidence to warrant belief in either is available, nor can it be obtained within the time constraints, and where there are some reasons to prefer the action based on the proposition to the action based on its negation, reasons which depend on the fact that the action is based on that proposition. (They may be that

---

[16] This would have been the natural way to understand Nagel's argument but for the fact that he does not claim that the choosers would be irrational to choose the amoralist's position. This fact makes one incline towards the first reading. However, the fact that on the first reading the argument is incapable of establishing the validity of the amoralist's claim, and can only establish a personal estoppel, suggests that the second reading should be considered in its own right.

the one is more likely to be true. But they can be other, for example ethical, reasons, as when the presumption of innocence may lead one to accept that Janet did not murder John.)

The second type of case in which people accept propositions that they do not believe in is irrelevant here. Given that our 'unencumbered selves' have all the time, rational capacity, and information that they need to find out whether to believe in the amoralist's view there seems no reason for them to accept it without believing in it.[17]

Could it be that our 'unencumbered selves' find themselves in the first type of situation? If so this is not part of Nagel's argument. He does not suggest accepting that the amoralist is wrong *arguendo* or as part of a *reductio*. Rather, according to this interpretation of his argument, he puts forward a reason for our unencumbered selves to accept that the amoralist is wrong as their conclusion. But that could never be justified except in the second type of situation, for a practical purpose when time, our resources, or our understanding are deficient. Since the reason given (that if the amoralist is wrong the chooser has greater value than if the amoralist is right) cannot possibly be a reason for believing that he is wrong, nor can it be a reason for accepting that he is wrong.

I have argued that the hypothetical choosers do not have reason to accept that the amoralist is wrong. By the same token Nagel does not provide us with a reason to believe that a hypothetical chooser has reason to accept morality as a principle of self-interest or in some other appropriately restricted way. This would not show the amoralist to be wrong, and there is little reason to think that Nagel understands his argument in this way.

So how does he understand it? Perhaps he has in mind choice not by our unencumbered selves, but by each of us as we are, as the first reading suggested. There is an initial difficulty with understanding Nagel in this way. On this reading he takes each one of us to be facing a choice. Though we are all under pressure to choose against the amoralist Nagel does not claim that we will be irrational to choose to join the amoralist. It follows that neither option is irrational, and therefore that choosing either of them cannot establish the truth of the option chosen.[18] If it could we might end with a contradiction if different people chose different options. One way of overcoming this difficulty is to understand the argument as giving rise

---

[17] In *Morality of Freedom*, 8–11, I argued for similar reasons that no presumptions of burden of proof have a place in philosophical arguments. It is possible that, these remarks notwithstanding, this is precisely the way in which Nagel understands his argument. He may be offering us a provisional morality—as Descartes once did—to serve us until our ability to understand ethics improves.

[18] This remark should not be taken to suggest that we cannot rationally believe what is false, only that if we can rationally believe (or accept) a proposition then our so accepting it cannot be used to show that it is false.

to a personal estoppel: since we would choose against the amoralist we cannot, in our practical thought, rely on the hypothesis that he may be right. He may be right, but we are estopped from relying on that possibility for we choose against him.

The estoppel interpretation is, however, unacceptable. Obviously those who choose against the amoralist, or who accept that he is wrong, should act in a way consistent with their choice. But there is nothing in the way they come to reject the amoralist to stop them from changing their mind, nor anything to stop them from raising doubts about the case, nothing which could constitute an estoppel.

Is there any other way of making good the argument on the assumption that it is addressed to us as we are? Perhaps Nagel does not mean to offer us an argument. I have already drawn attention to the fact that he does not say that those who choose the amoralist are irrational. His comments appear designed to show us that those who choose the moralist are rational in doing so, rather than to refute the amoralist. Perhaps he should be understood as follows. We—that is just about everyone reading him—do in fact believe that the amoralist is wrong, and the moralist right. While there is no compelling argument supporting these beliefs they can be rendered intelligible. They are intelligible as a response to the devaluation of people embedded in the amoralist position, a devaluation which drives us to embrace morality.

It may well be true that thus understood the consideration that Nagel relies on does render the choice of those who choose[19] against the amoralist intelligible. But that does not mean that it shows it to be a rationally defensible choice. If that is all we have to say about the amoralist Nagel's comments are liable to be understood as an explanation of how we come to have a wish-fulfilling false belief in morality.

To avoid the charge of self-deluding wish fulfilment Nagel has to mean his argument to show not only that the choice is intelligible in the sense of being understandable, but that it is intelligible in being a self-validating choice. He must mean either that the fact that people generally accept morality is evidence that they are right or that the fact that it seems to you, and to so many of us, obvious that we, each one thinking of him or herself, have value in ourselves is such evidence. But that form of presumptive intuitionism must be backed by an epistemic theory which explains when the obviousness of a belief can be evidence for its truth and when not. And that theory must then be applied to show why the amoralist's explanation of the belief as a result of wish fulfilment is not the right one.

---

[19] For this final reading of Nagel's argument, 'choose that so and so' is to be taken to mean 'come to believe that so and so.'

3. EXPANDING THE AMORALIST'S SYMPATHIES

Having explained why I find Nagel's argument against the amoralist wanting, I will consider the amoralist from a different perspective. In some ways Nagel's argument is attractively modest. But in one respect his modesty may be excessive. He allows for the intelligibility of the amoralist's view, and he allows that people can adopt his perspective. By implication he is suggesting that apart from being amoralist nothing much in their lives will be affected by such a stance. More specifically, and more accurately, he implies that their pursuit of their own self-interest need not be affected by being amoralists, at least that it need not be much affected. Is this true?

A familiar line of attack on the amoralist denies this assumption. If it can be shown that the value of people is presupposed by many goods that many people pursue, and the successful pursuit of which promotes the self-interest of those who pursue them, then an effective argument can be mustered against the amoralist. Some may try to show that since amoralists have to give up many goods which it is in their own interest to pursue, they can be true to their beliefs only at the cost of harming their self-interest. Perhaps it can even be shown that because of this anyone has a self-interested reason to believe in the value of people, though this step falls foul of my objection to Nagel. It does not prove the amoralist wrong. The argument I shall explore is different. It aims to show that there is no greater difficulty in persuading the amoralist of the value of other people than in persuading him of the value of many options whose pursuit is, or could be, in his own interest. It is not more difficult than recognizing the value of good wine. As will emerge I am far from sure, however, how far this argument can take us.

This line of reasoning once seemed sufficient, or almost so, to Bernard Williams. If the amoralist occasionally cares about other people, he pointed out, then

> He is still recognisably amoral, in the sense that no general considerations weigh with him, and he is extremely short on fairness and similar considerations. Although he acts for other people from time to time, it all depends on how he happens to feel. With this man, of course, in actual fact arguments of moral philosophy are not going to work . . . This is not the point. . . . The point is rather that he provides a model in terms of which we may glimpse what morality needs in order to get off the ground, even though it is unlikely in practice to get off the ground in a conversation with him. He gives us, I think, almost enough for he has the notion of doing something for somebody, because that person needs something. He operates with this notion only when he is so inclined; but it is not itself a notion of his being so inclined.[20]

[20] B. Williams, *Morality* (Harmondsworth: Penguin, 1973), 24–5.

Williams follows this passage with a description of how, given this base, one can try to extend the sympathies of the amoralist and motivate him to care about people's needs even when he does not feel like doing so at the time:

There are people who need help who are not people who at the moment he happens to want to help, or like; and there are other people who like and want to help other particular people in need. To get him to consider their situation seems rather an extension of his imagination and his understanding than a discontinuous step onto something quite different, the 'moral plane'. And if we could get him to consider their situation, in the sense of thinking about it and imagining it, he might conceivably start to show some consideration for it: we extend his sympathies.[21]

We must agree with Williams's central point: anyone who has any concern for other people, who has family attachments or friends, or just likes, is fond of, or loves some people is on the same plane as all people who accept moral considerations. There is no 'bottomless gulf' between them. But in elaborating the point I want to follow a line of thought somewhat different from Williams's.

With Williams we can leave on one side the amoralist who has no concern for people, no friendships,[22] no people he likes or is fond of, and who has no desire for such feelings, attitudes, and relationships. Such a person's well-being is drastically affected by these limitations. Not only relationships, but also all the activities which depend on them or which presuppose the appreciation of their value are denied him. This means, for example, that his ability to appreciate and benefit from literature and the arts, and from many social activities, is severely limited. There are things he can enjoy. But his life is so severely limited that—for reasons similar to those explained above concerning the person who denies any values—he poses no challenge to morality. The challenge is posed by an amoralist who can have a rich and rewarding life, while denying the value of people. Such an amoralist is like us in valuing friendship and companionship. He cares,

---

[21] Ibid. 25. In *Ethics and the Limits of Philosophy* (London: Collins, 1985) Williams seems more doubtful of this point. 'A limited benevolence or altruistic sentiment may move almost anyone to think that he should act in a certain way on a given occasion, but that fact does not present him with the ethical, as Moore's hand presented the sceptic with something material. The ethical involves more, a whole network of considerations, and the ethical sceptic could have a life that ignored such considerations altogether' (p. 25). But it is not clear whether Williams is here discussing the amoralist or someone who rejects all values.

[22] In talking of friendship I have in mind what one may call personal friendships. This excludes purely functional relationships, such as the distanced, though cordial relations which are bred by the need to co-operate to mutual advantage. I will, however, treat close relations between family relatives as a case of friendship.

however spasmodically, for some people.[23] Is it possible to be a consistent amoralist of this kind?

It would be a mistake, however, to focus on his limited motivation, as Williams does. The amoralist's refusal of morality is indeed accompanied by limited sympathies, and limited motivation. However, our sympathies and motivations are not brute facts about us. They are rational (in the sense of being responsive to reasons) attitudes and inclinations. A motivation can be acquired by rhetoric, but this would be rhetoric presenting or pretending to present the agent with reasons. The amoralist's motivation is limited because he does not believe that other people are valuable in themselves. Had he believed that they are ends in themselves we can expect that he would have been motivated to treat them as such. He would not be exceptionally consistent in giving due weight to this belief in his life. He would be just like many of us who are often unsure of the implications of the moralist's belief, and of whether we live up to them, and who are aware that at least some of the time we do not.

If, on the other hand, the amoralist does not come to believe in the value of people his sympathies could not possibly be extended to an adequate degree. He may come to care more often for more people. But so long as his sympathies are not guided by reasons it would be nothing short of miraculous for them to happen to coincide with the attitudes required by morality, assuming that it involves the proposition that all people are valuable in themselves. By examining the amoralist who has at his disposal the full range of goods by which his life can be enriched, and investigating the evaluative presuppositions of these goods we can—I will argue—demonstrate that there is no gulf between the moralist and the amoralist, and we can do so more securely and in a more far-reaching way than if we disregard these value-presuppositions in trying to extend the amoralist's sympathies and motivations.

This comment should not be read as an endorsement of some rationalistic view of how we form our view. When we are properly guided by reason we are not divorced from our emotions and feelings. Not only do they lead us to ideas which we can rationally examine in the light of reason, but reason itself involves an understanding which is informed by a sympathetic imagination. There are two ways in which we can readily imagine people whose reasoning leaves a lot to be desired extending their sympathies in line with moral concerns. First, if they live in a moral society and are merely

---

[23] Notice that I am less of a minimalist than Williams in the sort of concern for others my amoralist is assumed to have. The key is that he should be able to have a successful and rewarding personal life, and someone with very limited concern for others cannot have such a life. That said, it is entirely possible that the argument explored here would succeed equally well given more minimalist assumptions.

aping their neighbours for one reason or another. Second, if there is a biological correlation between what we are innately disposed to care about and what we morally should care about. I suspect that the second possibility is misconceived, but will not discuss it here. The aping hypothesis, while explaining why in particularly fortunate circumstances one individual or another may uncomprehendingly come to have appropriate sympathies, makes this explanation dependent on others being guided by reason.

4. UNDERMINING THE AMORALIST: FROM RELATIONAL TO NON-RELATIONAL VALUES

Is the amoralist committed to acknowledging the value of people just because he cares about some of them? Does his friendship with some of them commit him to admitting the value of all people?

He cannot say[24] that his reason for pleasing his friends, helping them in their need, and generally treating them decently is that he wants to do that. No doubt he does want to act as he does. But, as Williams has pointed out, that is not *his* reason, and in any case it is not the sort of thing that *can* be a reason.[25] But the amoralist can say that his reason is that they are his friends, or his colleagues at work, or his children or nephews, or that there is some other special relationship between him and them which makes them people whom he values, and that is his reason for treating them the way he does—not their intrinsic value as people.

This answer, however, will not do. We can start with the point made by Williams that the amoralist 'has the notion of doing something for somebody, because that person needs something'. Not only does he have the

---

[24] For presentational reasons I am using the amoralist not only as the topic of discussion, but also as his own advocate. This should not mislead. No assumption is made that the amoralist need be a sophisticated exponent and defender of his own position. The amoralist can be as inarticulate and as lacking in self-knowledge and in philosophical understanding as is consistent with his having friends. For ease of exposition I present his *amicus curiae*, who has all the arguments, as if he is an amoralist himself. He need not be, and as I said not every amoralist need be so well armed.

It follows that my argument is not *ad hominem*. I am not out to catch the amoralist admitting to views from which morality follows. I am trying to see how much of morality can be derived from the presuppositions of his life and of the options available to him, regardless of how he himself understands (or misunderstands) them.

[25] See generally on this point G. E. M. Anscombe, *Intention* (Oxford: Blackwell, 1957). For my attempt to explain why this is so see 'Incommensurability and Agency', in R. Chang (ed.), *Incommensurability, Incomparability and Practical Reason* (Cambridge, Mass.: Harvard Univ. Press, 1997), which is Ch. 3 above.

notion, he relies on it in his reasoning. That in itself shows no more than that the amoralist's reason for helping his friend may be a compound of (*a*) the fact that there is a person in need, and (*b*) the fact that that person is his friend. It does not show that he is committed to recognizing the value of people who are not friends, nor to recognizing a reason to help people just because they are in need. And I assume that Williams, with his sights firmly set on the restricted sympathies of the amoralist, did not mean to deny that.

We make some progress by introducing, for the purpose of this argument only, a distinction between behaviour which is specific to friendship, or more narrowly, specific to the type of friendship the amoralist has with the person in question, and behaviour which is not specific in that way. No claim is made that the distinction is either exhaustive or exclusive. The distinction is drawn from the point of view of the amoralist's friend. Behaviour[26] is specific to that type of friendship if it benefits the friend, or is agreeable to him, only because he is a friend, and it would not be beneficial or agreeable otherwise. Various displays of friendship are of this kind, for example, the marking of dates meaningful to the relationship, the display of various forms of familiarity and intimacy.

Of course much that goes on between friends is not specific in that sense. If one saves the friend's life this is, other things being equal, welcome to the friend, no matter who saved him. What matters to him most is being alive; whether he was saved by a friend, a stranger, or a natural event may matter, but comes a distant second. Many cases (e.g. being offered a loan to purchase a badly needed washing machine) include both specific and non-specific aspects. One may well be reluctant or unwilling to accept from a stranger what one accepts from a friend—to that extent offering or performing such services expresses the friendship. At the same time the act is beneficial or agreeable beyond the fact that it expresses the friendship. It also enables one to have a washing machine, etc., and that aspect of it is not specific in the sense explained.

To know how to conduct oneself with a friend one needs an understanding (inevitably mostly implicit) of what friendship is like.[27] The crucial point

---

[26] I am using 'behaviour' to include aspects of actions. That is, one action may exemplify two types of behaviour. For example, shaking someone's hand may be both greeting him, and being polite to him. It can be regarded as exemplifying both kinds of behaviour.

[27] If the point is in need of explanation see my discussion of it in *Morality of Freedom*. I explained there how our ability to have friends depends on knowledge of friendship (or of the relevant kind of friendship we have) and its normative implications. We must know— as must our friends—what is proper between friends, what duties they have to each other and what liberties they can take, etc. I then argued that to acquire this knowledge one has to be socialized into a society whose practices sustain such friendships. I am not, however, relying on this further point in the current argument. All that is assumed is that friendship

for my argument is that that will enable one not only to judge what friendship-specific conduct is appropriate and when. It will also enable one to know that one ought generally to behave in ways attuned to the interest of one's friends. That too is an aspect of friendship. It requires general concern for the friend as a person, not merely concern for his ability to act towards one as one's friend. That is, if I and my friend Jane spend our time together, discussing philosophy, going for walks in the hills, and confiding our marital difficulties to each other, then to continue to be Jane's friend I must not only be concerned with her willingness and ability to carry on with the activities which have come to give our friendship its special character. I must also be concerned with her well-being generally. (Other things being equal, I must be willing to help in other matters in her life, when help is needed, and so on). This general concern with the well-being of one's friends means that one is treating them as people who have value in themselves, and not merely as people who are valuable to one in one's own life.

All that may not worry the amoralist all that much. He may cheerfully admit that he has to treat his friends as friends are to be treated, that is as people who have intrinsic value, or he would not be their friend. He will remember that to have friends you must value them for what they are, value them in themselves, and not merely value them for what they mean to you, and for the benefit that you derive from their friendship. He will readily acknowledge that when he behaves towards them as a friend would, inevitably he is doing so because he values them in themselves. However, he values them in themselves not because they are people but because they are his friends. This is consistent—he will maintain—with his refusal to admit that people *qua* people have intrinsic value.

Think of the following case, the amoralist may say.[28] It shows that he does not value his friend as a person, but as a person who is his friend, a person from whom he derives the benefits of friendship. Suppose that what the amoralist values in the friendship is the wit of his friend, and that his friend's wit depends on the fact that he smokes. If so the amoralist would not want his friend to stop smoking, regardless of the damage smoking causes his health. This shows that he does not really care about the friend as a person, but only for what he gets out of him.

---

is a recognized form of relationship, or rather a range of such forms, knowledge of the nature of which is required in order to have friends. This depends on nothing more than the need to act properly towards one's friends, and the need—in some cases—to act from appropriate motives, which sometimes include recognition that some forms of conduct are appropriate whereas others are inappropriate between friends, depending on the circumstances.

[28] I owe this case and the argument for the amoralist which it yields to Penelope Bulloch.

There is no denying that such people exist. They may differ on one point. Some may say that other things being equal they would care about their friend, regardless of whether caring for him benefits them. In the imagined case, however, causing him to stop smoking would kill the friendship. That is why they would not get him to stop smoking. Such people recognize a conflict that any friend would recognize in the imagined situation, and solve it in the wrong way. They are friends—one may say—though not very good ones. They do not present a special problem for my argument, which turns on an other-things-being-equal recognition of the value of people as people. The more extreme amoralist may take a different tack. He may say that he cares about his friend, treats him as a person of value, only when doing so serves his own interest in the friendship. This amoralist simply is not a friend to this other person (though the other person may be a friend to him: their attitudes may diverge; this is common in practice, and need not delay us here).

Several people who heard earlier versions of my argument balked at points like this. Suppose, they said, that the amoralist has no friends in 'my' sense of friendship. Suppose he is simply someone who comes as close to friendship as is possible for a person who has the attitude described in the example. If my argument undermines the amoralist who has friends it would fail to undermine amoralists who have only this kind of limited friendships as we may call them. Indeed amoralists may well tend to have limited rather than full friendships, and would, therefore, be immune to my argument.

Remember, however, that I am not arguing that no amoralist can live without engaging in activities or relationships which commit him to views inconsistent with his amoralism. My argument is that there are activities, pursuits, relationships which though non-moral themselves commit anyone who regards them as valuable to the moralist's principle. Or at least this is the argument I am testing to see how far it will take us. Its aim is to show that those who accept *all* that life offers them, all that can enrich their own life, also accept the moralist principle. This, if successful, would show that there is no gulf between so-called prudence and morality, that the same arguments which would lead one to realize what is of value for his or her life, would also lead to the acceptance of morality.

So the objection must be understood to rely on the claim that limited friendships give one all that full friendships do. Naturally, that may be thought true of cases where attitudes are not reciprocal. Imagine a friendship in which John is a full friend of Jane, but she has only limited friendship for him.[29] She is his friend only in the limited sense. This may be the

---

[29] Since asymmetrical friendships are important to the objection I will refer to 'giving' and 'receiving' friendship, to indicate the presence of the difference in attitude between the friends.

case openly, and without deceit. John may wish that Jane reciprocated his attitude, but he may be willing to put up with what she is willing to give. Does not Jane, who has—let us assume—only limited friendships, and several of whose friends give her full friendship, does not she enjoy the best of both worlds? She both has the benefits of full friendship, she receives the care and respect that full friends give each other, but she does not give full friendship to her friends.

I take this to be the strongest form of the objection, for I assume that it will be generally recognized that most people crave, and for good reason, to have full friends. Being cared for and respected for one's own sake by a friend is one of the most valuable aspects of friendship. Jane would not pose a challenge to my argument should she need to accept the moralist's principle in order to have it. But, the objection runs, she has the benefit of full friendship, without being a full friend. Obviously the objection points to the possibility of another argument against the amoralist, slightly different from mine. It suggests that for the amoralist to have some of the benefits of a good life he must interact with moralists, and benefit from the fact that they are moralists. I think, however, that the objection fails for a separate reason, namely that to give full friendship is in itself a good of great importance in human life. Caring for and respecting others—not necessarily all others—is important to people's well-being, and it is doubly rewarding and valuable when it happens within a reciprocated relationship, that is, within a (full) friendship.

Having rejected the objection, I have to admit that whether my argument works still remains to be seen. The amoralist may while accepting the value of full friendship insist that his friends should be treated by him as people with value in themselves only because they are his friends. He should value them in themselves, and not just in friendship-specific ways. But other people may have no reason to value them at all. He may draw an analogy with trees. There is—let us imagine—an apple tree growing outside his window, providing fruit, shade, and improving the view from his window. He is very fond of the tree, and cares a great deal about it. He values the tree and treats it accordingly. To do that he must have a notion of the difference between a tree which is doing well and one which is ailing, or otherwise failing. Only thus can he effectively look after his tree. But it does not follow that he must treat all apple trees in the same way. He understands what it is for a tree to be respected and valued, what it is for a tree to be valuable. It does not follow from that that all trees are valuable. His tree has value for him. Some other trees may have value for other people. Some may have value to no one.

But possibly people are not like trees. I put it like that not because I doubt that people are ends in themselves, but because I want to leave open the possibility that trees are like people—that is, that they are intrinsically valuable, though not necessarily in the same way or to the same degree. It is important not to be diverted into an argument about the value of trees. So let us assume, for the sake of the argument, that trees are not intrinsically valuable. The amoralist is right to say that his apple tree may nevertheless have value for him. One way in which this is true is irrelevant to the argument. His apple tree is of value to him because it provides welcome shade and produces good apples. It is instrumentally good for him, for it has consequences which are themselves good for him. It is uncontroversial, but also irrelevant that instrumental goods can be good for one person and not for another. It is irrelevant because the case against the amoralist is that he is wrong about the intrinsic value of people, not about their instrumental value. Nor does the amoralist claim that his friends are merely of instrumental value to him. He values them in themselves and therefore in drawing the analogy with the tree he does not have in mind the instrumental value of the tree. Rather, his point is that the tree has more than mere instrumental value for him because he is attached to it, and that he can be attached to one tree without being attached to all trees.

I agree that being attached to an object, person, activity, or project can endow them with a value which they would not otherwise have. They will have that value for the people who are attached to them and not for others.[30] But one can only be attached to something if one believes it to be valuable, and the attachment endows the object with extra value only if that object is indeed valuable. I have discussed these matters at somewhat greater length elsewhere,[31] and will only gesture towards the three main points involved.

First, there is a reciprocal relationship between good (or valuable) and good (or valuable) for one. On the one hand, nothing can be good unless it is possible for it to be good for someone.[32] We can imagine goods which are not actually good for anyone at the moment, or even goods which are unlikely to be good for anyone in the foreseeable future. But it is unintelligible to say of something that it is good or valuable if it is impossible that it be of value to anyone. On the other hand, if anything is good and one can relate to it in 'the appropriate way' then other things being equal it is good for one. So if a novel is a good novel and I can read it with understanding then it is good for me to read it, other things being equal. There is no more to something being good for me than that it is a good which is

---

[30] We can here disregard the complications arising because some people may be attached to the person who is attached to the tree and because of that the tree may acquire enhanced value for them as well.

[31] See *Morality of Freedom*, 288–94; Chs. 11 and 3, above.

[32] I am assuming that sometimes being a good x is, or can be, good for that x (being a good person is or can be good for the person who is good).

within my reach (though of course other things may be better, or the cost of reaching it may be more than it is worth, etc.)

Second, all intentional action is undertaken for a reason. This implies that it is undertaken in the belief that it or some of its consequences are good. Some of our attachments were acquired by choice, and therefore in the belief that it is good to be so attached. Many, perhaps most, of people's attachments are not formed by choice. But they are sustained by our continuous engagement and involvement in them. Therefore, they too are accompanied by a belief in their value. The people who have those attachments would lose their will to be involved in them and would try to give them up were they to lose that belief.

Third, what is sometimes called the reality principle means that as our intentional actions (including those which manifest our attachments) are undertaken for what we believe to be good reasons,[33] they are worthwhile—unless accidentally—only if those reasons are sound. That implies that only if the objects of our attachments are of value is there any value in our attachments, or in the actions which manifest them. There may be exceptions to this rule, but they are, from the point of view of the current discussion, of minor importance.

In all but exceptional cases the value of an attachment depends on the value of what one is attached to. One's love of Beethoven's music can be valuable—exceptional circumstances excepted—only because Beethoven's music is valuable. In general the attachment will be manifested in a variety of ways, depending on its object, and it can be of value only if the way it manifests itself is suitable to the object towards which it is manifested. One's affection, admiration, respect, etc. are of value only if they are bestowed on objects which merit them.

The upshot of this discussion is that whatever is intrinsically good for a person is so only if it is good in a non-relativized way, only if it is valuable *tout court*. A person may become attached to something which is instrumentally valuable and which thereby acquires non-instrumental value for him. Alternatively people become attached to what they take to be intrinsically valuable. Believing that these valuable goods, relationships, or activities are within their reach they may make their enjoyment or pursuit one of their goals, and by thus becoming attached to them they endow them with greater value for themselves. But these activities and the like have value for them only if they are good and worthwhile independently of being embraced by them.

It is easy to misunderstand this point, and to think that I am presenting

---

[33] Though when we display weakness of will we believe that other things make them insufficient to justify the action we are taking.

some sort of desert account of attachment and relationships. As if I am saying that it is appropriate to admire only music which deserves admiration, or to love only people who deserve to be loved. My claim was different, though related. For our attachment to something to be of value, and for it to make its object of value to us, its object must have a value independently of it. Moreover it must have value of a kind which is appropriate for that attachment, which makes the attachment appropriate. So that if it involves admiring something or someone it should be admirable, if we love someone he or she must be worthy of love, if we are devoted to someone he or she must be worthy of devotion, and so on. This does not mean that the person or object must deserve the attachment. The notion of desert is more specific. When speaking of people deserving something the idea of desert imports, for example, the thought that the deserving people have accomplished something of value through their well-motivated endeavours. That accomplishment is the basis of their desert. Some forms of caring about things or people or of being attached to them may require that their objects deserve the attitude for the attitude to be valuable. But that is not generally the case. The tree in my example need not deserve the fond devotion its owner has for it. Attachment to trees does not demand that. It is appropriate if the tree is a good specimen of its kind, or if it played a significant role in the life of the person attached to it (even, for example, by bringing him useful income). Similarly in the case of friendship the argument is not that only some people are good enough to be my friends, that only some deserve to be my friends. On the contrary. After all, its purpose is to show that all people, some exceptions aside, are appropriate friends, for its purpose is to show that all people have the value which qualifies them as possible friends, and which is the value the moralist asserts in his basic principle.

5. THE AMORALIST'S MISTAKE

This then is where the amoralist goes wrong. He claims that his friends are valuable to him, but not valuable in themselves, independently of the value with which the friendship endows them. Their value depends on the fact that he is attached to them, that they are his friends. But that cannot be. Admittedly having become a friend of theirs means that in a sense they are valuable to him more than to other people: they mean to him more than they need mean to other people. But their value to him depends on the fact that the friendship is a valuable attachment or relationship. In its turn the value of the friendship depends on it being with people who are worthy of being his friends.

The Amoralist

The amoralist is still unimpressed. He will acknowledge—let us assume—that he was too hasty in claiming that it was just his attachment to his friends which endows them with value, and makes them worthy of his respect and concern. He will allow that they had to be independently valuable for his attachment to them to enhance their value for him. But, he will point out, by my own argument the same is true of his attachment to his tree. For as long as the argument does not distinguish people from trees there is nothing for him to worry about. His amorality remains intact.

In one respect the amoralist attitude to the tree of our example is like people's attitude to their friends: the reasons we come to be attached to them are biographical. I can cherish an object which saved my life, or a piece of music which I got to know when depressed, and which played a role in sustaining my spirits, a tree which I admired through the seasons, and I can acquire a friend because he saved my life, or because I got to know him when depressed and he used to cheer me up; and so on. But turn your attention not to why Hilary is Robin's friend, but to what is involved in that state of affairs, to the reasons which guide Robin's conduct towards Hilary, while he is his friend.

The reasons people have for being friends with each other can be—and often are—asymmetrical. Robin's reasons for being Hilary's friend need not be Hilary's reasons for being Robin's friend. Friendship is, however, a reciprocal relationship, in a way in which one's attachment to a tree is not. Within the relationship Robin and Hilary have to treat each other as in some sense equal. That does not mean that they are equal in strength, physical or emotional, or in wisdom or in any other way. It means that to be friends each must care for the other for the sake of the other, and not only for what he gets out of him. And they must recognize that the other merits such an attitude, and that they merit it in themselves, and not merely for their role in each other's biography.

This is where friendships differ from attachments to trees: friends are not merely people who care for each other, who care about the interest of the other as one cares about the well-being of one's tree. Friends are people who share intimacy, who treat each other as people, as persons with emotions, thoughts, and so on and so forth. Friends not only recognize that their friends are such people, and therefore have interests which trees do not have. They recognize that the fact that people can reciprocate each other's attachment, that they are capable of understanding and empathizing with each other, is essential to making people appropriate partners in friendships. And these features of people are drawn upon in the friendship, and valued by the friends in each other. This point is briefly summarized when we say that friendship requires that friends should treat each other with respect, that they should treat each other as ends in themselves, and not merely as people whose friendship is valuable.

Friendship requires respecting the friends in themselves, and not only for any instrumental value they may have, nor merely for their role in one's biography. As I explained, this does not mean that Robin need deny that he needs Hilary, that Hilary's support, his interest in Robin, and so on, are valued by Robin, that but for them Robin would not continue with the friendship. Nor need he deny that circumstances may change and he will lose his interest in the friendship and—quite legitimately—let it lapse. It does mean, however, that Robin must acknowledge that, while he is Hilary's friend, he cares about Hilary for what he is, and not merely for what he is to Robin. But then Hilary must merit that treatment. There must be a reason which makes him an appropriate object of such an attitude, and that reason cannot be that he is useful to Robin, nor that he features in a certain way in his life (e.g. reminds him of his much missed dead mother). To do that is to deny his independent value, to deny that the relationship is reciprocal between two people each recognizing that the other matters in himself, independently of the relationship.

For Robin to say that Hilary is not of value in his own right, that his value derives entirely from Robin's attachment to him, or from his role in Robin's life, is to reveal the friendship as a sham, as self-serving and egotistical. To care for someone for their own sake requires recognizing merit in them independently of their role in our life. Hence friendships are of value only if they are with people who are worthy of friendship, and of being the object of care and concern. Being worthy of such attitudes means having value in themselves.

Some would object to this argument. They would say that while some friendships are like that others are not. Moreover, they would insist, people may have quite a decent life without enjoying or seeking friendships of this kind. They take a mild interest in people from time to time, seek their company for what they can get out of it, and no more. I acknowledge both points, but they do not affect my case.

First, I should point out that I am using 'friend' in its primary sense, meaning 'one joined to another in mutual benevolence and intimacy' (*Oxford English Dictionary*). Most other uses of 'friend' derive from and retain elements of this meaning. The description of the reciprocal aspect of friendship sketched above, and the way it involves the recognition of the independent worth of the other are meant to be no more than an elaboration on the notion of joining together in mutual intimacy. So while it is true that 'lesser' friendships are common, the friendship I described is not some remote and demanding ideal. It is a common experience.

Second, having such friendships is of value to those who have them.

Friendships enrich the life of the friends. Indeed it is a common experience that friendship can play a central role in the life of people, that it is among the most significant factors which make many people's lives good and fulfilling. Moreover, and that is crucial for my case, it is not good for them because it is morally good. Volunteering to work for Oxfam in one's spare time may be good for one because it is a morally good thing to do. But there is nothing specifically morally good about having friends. People bereft of friends may have a lonely and impoverished life, but they are not morally at fault. Therefore one need not be a moralist to recognize the value of friendship, not even of full friendship as I described it.

Third, it may be that one's life can be fulfilling and rich enough without having friends of that kind. My amoralist may say: I do not actually want to have such friends, and I do not believe in them. They are based on the falsehood that people are of value in themselves. And living up to that view my amoralist may yet have a decent and successful life without friends of this kind. But you will remember my warning earlier that my argument is not *ad hominem*. Nor is it an argument that one has a so-called prudential reason to be moral for without morality one cannot have a good and fulfilling life. My argument is theoretical in aim: its goal is to deny that there is a divide—epistemological or metaphysical—between moral considerations and values and non-moral ones. That argument is unaffected by the stance I imagine here that the amoralist may adopt: his refusal to have friends does not matter. What matters is that he refuses to acknowledge that friendships are of value to the friends, for he realizes that that would lead to the endorsement of the value of people independently of one's attachment to them. In that refusal he concedes that he cannot sustain the argument that only his attachment to people endows them with value.

6. THE MORALIST'S DISAPPOINTMENT

The preceding argument exposes a mistake the amoralist is guilty of. But it is unlikely to give much comfort to the moralist. It seems to leave us in some sort of no man's land. The amoralist has been shown to be wrong in claiming that the people who are his friends are of value only because of his attachment to them. But the argument has not established that they are of value as people. The amoralist can therefore modify the position we ascribed to him. He can say that his friends are people who are valuable in themselves because they are funny, or loving, or wise, or whatever other property he values in them. He is still an amoralist because he denies that all people are of value.

A second feature of the preceding argument may worry the moralist. Allowing that the argument shows that some people are of value, what sort of value is it? I have argued that if they are of value to a person who is their friend, a person who is attached to them, then they must be of value also independently of that attachment. The same can be said about anything which is of value in a person's life. If collecting medieval musical instruments is an activity which contributes to the life of keen collectors, making their life better, then collecting medieval musical instruments must be a valuable activity in itself, regardless of whether or not one is keen on it. If this is all the argument established does it not equate people with medieval musical instruments, or with tennis, paintings, etc.? Surely the moralist's claim is that people are of value in a different way from the value, even the intrinsic value, of the objects, activities, relationships, and the rest which can make people's life better.

I am uncertain in what way the value of people, as understood by moralists, is special. But the following may at least be part of what is meant. Playing tennis is intrinsically good. It can also be good instrumentally, as a way of keeping fit, making friends or money, or gaining prestige. But apart from any beneficial consequences playing tennis may or may not have it is a valuable activity; it is an activity with intrinsic value. People too have intrinsic value. But that does not mean that they are equal in value to tennis. Think of a person, let us call her Julia, playing tennis. Other things being equal, playing tennis is good for Julia. It is a good thing for her to do. But is the fact that Julia plays tennis good for tennis? Under special circumstances this may be the case. It may be good for the game that Julia plays it if it is in danger of being forgotten, and her playing it helps keep it alive, or if she is such an outstanding and famous player that her example raises the level of the game generally. Even so the asymmetry I am pointing to is intact. In the ordinary case, that a person plays tennis is, other things being equal, good for him, and a good thing for him to do, but it is neither good nor bad for tennis.

We can terminologically mark this asymmetry by saying that whereas playing tennis is an intrinsically good or valuable activity, people are of value in themselves (and not merely intrinsically). Above[34] I referred to a condition for anything being good *tout court*, that is that it be possible for it to be good for someone. The terminological distinction just introduced is meant to chime with that condition: whatever is intrinsically good is capable of being good for something or someone which is good in itself.

---

[34] And remember that in section 4 the term 'intrinsically valuable' is used indiscriminately to cover both what I call intrinsically valuable and what has just been dubbed valuable in itself. In common and philosophical usage 'intrinsic value' is often used inclusively to cover both categories.

Being of value in oneself, or an end in oneself, marks one as one who counts, whose good matters because one counts, apart from any other reason why the good may count.

The pursuit of what is intrinsically valuable makes sense only to the extent that it is of value to those who are valuable in themselves. This condition is usually satisfied by the fact that the pursuit of what is intrinsically valuable is good for the person engaged in it (dancing, painting, etc. are good for those who dance or paint). Sometimes the activity is good for the actor (a good thing for him to do) only if it is good for someone else, or at least only if it could be good for someone else. Teaching and practising medicine are obvious examples. Painting and composing music are less obvious examples. They conform to this precept because the standards of excellence in these activities are essentially such that other people can have the benefit of successful creations as spectators, performers, or listeners.

The asymmetry between things which are intrinsically valuable and those which are of value in themselves is central to evaluative thought. The moralist claims not (or not merely) that people are intrinsically valuable but that they are valuable in themselves. That is—as we saw—one reason why the moralist is disappointed in the conclusion of the argument so far. It has not, he feels, shown that people are of value in themselves, only that they are intrinsically valuable, as tennis is.

If that is the source of the moralist's disappointment then it is unjustified. It overlooks the fact—just alluded to—that many intrinsically valuable activities presuppose that other people besides the agent are of value in themselves. To repeat, to teach is or can be intrinsically good to the teacher but only if he treats his students as of value in themselves; to compose good music can also be intrinsically valuable to the composer but only if it is music which can be and deserves to be meaningful and rewarding to other people. In brief, the value (to the agent) of many intrinsic goods depends on the fact that they are or can be good for people, and that means that it depends on the fact that people are of value in themselves. In friendship—which we assume that even the amoralist seeks—the treating of friends as of value in themselves is central to the relationship. Hence in being committed to the value of his friends, in being committed to their value as creatures worthy of being friends and of being treated as friends should be—the amoralist is committed to their value in themselves.

But—to return to the first objection—is he committed to holding that just being people makes them valuable? Perhaps it is being witty, warm, or generous people, for example, which endows them with value in themselves? If all we have to go on is that a would-be amoralist has John as his friend we will not be able to rebut his claim, should he be disposed to explain himself in this way, that it is John's generous nature which endows him with value in himself. Even so the amoralist's concession is not to be belittled. It reaches beyond the actual friends he has to all those who possess the value-endowing qualities he recognizes.

Yet without doubt one would want to go beyond the amoralist's friendship with John to look at other friendships that he has, or wishes to have, or about which he recognizes that they would be of value if he had them. We would want to explore his relations with his parents, or with his children. In these cases too it may be claimed that his well-being is greatly diminished if he has such relatives, or had them, but is not a friend of theirs, nor wishes to be, nor recognizes the value to his life had he been a friend of his parents or of his children. In these cases it is more difficult for the amoralist to say that his parents are people of value in themselves only because they are witty or generous, or have similar qualities.

Two further important steps in the argument should be noted. To simplify their presentation let us call relationships in which people are duty bound to treat each other as ends in themselves (or as having value in themselves) 'personal relationships'. First, the amoralist has, of course, to acknowledge that all people who possess the qualities which his friends have, and which make his friendships with them reasonable, are also of value in themselves. He has, however, to go one step further. He has to admit that all the people with whom it would be reasonable for him to have a personal relationship are also of value in themselves. This is the case even though at present he has no desire to become their friend, nor does he think he is even likely to be their friend. None of this matters. As we saw, should he be their friend they would be of value in themselves, and that would not be a result of the fact that he cares for them or is attached to them: his friendship is of value only if they are of value in themselves independently of it. Hence the conclusion that all those with whom it would be OK to have a personal relationship are of value in themselves regardless of how unlikely it is that one would want to have such a relationship with them.

Second, by parity of reasoning the same goes for those with whom it is reasonable for others to have a personal relationship. If the amoralist believes that it is reasonable that Rachel and Robert are friends then he must concede that both of them are of value in themselves.

7. DOUBTS ABOUT THE MORALIST

I will not pursue these reflections in detail. It is not my claim that there is a single knock-down argument which shows that the amoralist in recognizing values which can enrich his own life is committed to recognizing the value of all people. My suggestion was that there is enough in what he is committed to to advance the argument and narrow the gap between the amoralist and the moralist. How has it been narrowed? It is true that they are still separated by the moralist endorsing and the amoralist rejecting the proposition that all people are of value in and of themselves, or that just in virtue of being people they are ends in themselves. But now the amoralist no longer denies that people can be of value in themselves, and that some have such value. He merely insists that those who are of value in themselves are so in virtue of the possession of properties such as being witty, or wise, or good-looking. Moreover, there is no closed list of such properties that the amoralist who has been persuaded by my argument so far is limited to. Anything which could justify a personal relationship between any two or more people shows that they are ends in themselves. The amoralist has to concede that anyone with whom it is reasonable for anyone to have a personal relationship is of value in him- or herself.

The same is true of my response to the second objection—to the effect that the amoralist does not recognize the special value of people which the moralist has in mind. Here too the moralist may feel that the argument I relied on does not go all the way. It may show that people are of value in themselves rather than (just) intrinsically valuable, in terms of the stipulated distinction I introduced. But that does not show that one may never torture an innocent person, nor that the right action is the one which contributes most to the greatest happiness of the greatest number, nor even that all people are in themselves of equal value. The moralist may feel that that shows that I understand 'being of value in oneself' in a thin sense which differs from what he had in mind. For him it follows from the fact the people are of value in themselves that they should not be tortured, or that the right action is the one which contributes most to the greatest happiness of the greatest number, or which treats all people as equal. At this point I am reminded of the fact that I never did understand what the moralist's belief (that all people are of value in themselves) meant.

It is reasonable to understand the difference between those who, say, believe that it is never justified to torture the innocent and those who reject this, those who believe that the right action is the one which more than any other option open to the agent contributes to the greatest good of the greatest number and those who deny that, it is reasonable to understand such debates as disagreements within morality, disagreements about its content and implications among those who in principle recognize its binding force. We regard neither side to such disputes as an amoralist, but rather both as having different views of morality. So the fact that the amoralist rejects such views is not what makes him into an amoralist. What does? We can repeat the principle we assumed to unite them: that people are in and of themselves of value in themselves. I have just acknowledged that the amoralist is still refusing to acknowledge this principle and that we found no argument why he should.

The amoralist who followed us so far will agree that it is possible for all people to possess the qualities which make people valuable in themselves (being witty, wise, good-looking, etc.), when that is understood to mean that they belong to a species of animal which can, consistently with their nature as members of that species, possess these qualities. But that is not the same as holding them actually to be valuable in themselves. Though the two are sufficiently close that it is worth wondering whether the moralist actually means more, that is, whether all moralists must just in virtue of being moralists be committed to more than to the potentiality principle, as we may call it. It is clear that some of them do have more in mind, but is it of the essence of morality that one should?

In fact it is not even clear that it makes sense to say that believing that people are of value in themselves is the mark of the moral position (unless that is an inaccurate way of saying that people have the potential to possess the qualities which endow them with value in themselves). Try it whichever way you want: does it mean that no other quality (other than being human, or a person) is of moral relevance? This is hardly possible. Surely people's actual actions and intentions, virtues and vices are also of moral consequence.

Does it mean that no other quality is of moral consequence unless it is a quality of a human being? Some people believe that. They believe that even if there are non-human creatures who are witty, affectionate, wise, attractive, and so on and so forth, they have no value in themselves. Therefore, personal relationships with them are of no value, etc. But this is an implausible position, and not one shared by all moralists.

Does it mean that there are minimum requirements of conduct towards and entitlements of people just in virtue of being people, though a richer morality applies to those who possess other qualities beside mere humanity? Again many people believe that to be the case, and even more people think that they do. But not all moralists do. It is disputable whether membership in a species *Homo sapiens* endows a creature with value in itself. People who are born in irreversible coma, or without a brain apart from the brain stem are considered by many as having no value in themselves. This does not mean that we do not have any obligations regarding the way they are treated. But we may have such obligations regarding works of art, or features of the natural environment, even though they are not of value in themselves.

This is one reason why many prefer to talk of the value of persons, rather than people, understood as members of the species *Homo sapiens*. We may suspect, however, that unless persons are defined as being those creatures who are of value in themselves the same problems will arise. Neither I nor the amoralist who modified his position as a result of the previous arguments is denying that possession of some quality or other endows its possessors with value in themselves. Since the moralist is now supposed to agree that not all people possess such qualities, and therefore that not all people are of value in themselves, what is distinctive about his position? Perhaps that whatever the qualities are they endow all those who have them with the same value, with value to the same degree. The kingdom of ends in themselves is, he might say, a kingdom of the morally equal.

This, however, is yet another controversial claim, and it is controverted within morality. Utilitarians, for example, do not normally accept it. The question is whether there is only one quality which endows its possessors with value in themselves, and whether if there is more than one possession of several of them can endow some with greater value than others who possess one but not the others. Similarly, even if there is only one property which endows its possessors with value in themselves it may be that it can be exhibited by various creatures to various degrees in a way that will justify regarding some of them as having greater value than others. We need not express any view on these matters here. For our purpose the relevant conclusion is that the argument about these possibilities is an argument between different views of morality rather than an argument between the moralist and the amoralist.

The failure to identify a position which marks the moralist off from the (reformed) amoralist was a failure to find a way of reading 'people have value in themselves' which renders it both true and appropriate to be the mark of morality. But while the arguments that lead to that failure bear on some other ways of identifying morality, they do not apply to all of the ways by which philosophers have tried to mark the moral. For example, they do not apply to the view that there is an argument or a method of argument which can establish the truth of moral principles, whatever they are, and which is specific to moral issues. Such argument or method of argument will be different from the way we argue about the value of wine, or tennis, or the arts. It is a specifically moral form of argument. According to this view, the amoralist's mistake is that he denies the validity of that form of argument.

This is a very different way of identifying morality from the one I have been pursuing so far. It does not claim that morality is distinctive by its content. Rather it is distinctive by its employment of a special argument or by its method of argumentation. If such a form of argument exists then it is very different from the type of argument which, following Williams, I have explored in the previous section, for my arguments looked for the presupposition of ordinary beliefs about familiar values. This is but one reason to suspect the thesis that there is a distinctive form of moral reasoning: so much moral reasoning seems to be nothing but ordinary reasoning about what it is reasonable or unreasonable to do. I believe, though the matter cannot be gone into here, that no attempt to produce such a specifically 'moral' form of argument has been successful. I believe that evaluative arguments, moral and otherwise, are like all arguments, a matter of tracing the implications of the structures of our beliefs, in all the ways we know.

What is common to the view that the mark of morality is acceptance of the principle that people are of value in themselves and to the suggestion that it is marked by the deployment of a special method of argument is a conception of morality as an autonomous area, distinct from other practical concerns. This assumption, seen in operation in Nagel's argument, and essential to all contractarian approaches to morality, though not only to them, explains how the amoralist is possible: he is someone standing outside morality and denying that there is a route, a rationally compelling route, which could lead him in.

The direction of the arguments of this section and of the previous one was not to adjudicate between the moralist and the amoralist, but to deny the existence of the two characters by undermining that assumption. This does not mean rejecting the moralist's belief that people are valuable in themselves as false. It means, however, demoting it from its status as a foundational moral principle, or as the mark of morality. Principles like the moralist's principle are no more than a convenient—though inaccurate—summary or reminder of the conclusions of arguments like the arguments about the value of people explored in the course of this discussion. They are ordinary arguments employing no special method, and they arise out of and are part of our general understanding of value, reason, and norms, and of the meaning of human life. Neither the arguments nor their conclusions form a distinct realm, the moral realm, in any interesting sense. Moreover, the precise conclusions of the arguments are complex and nuanced. The moralist's principle, while an approximation that has its uses, is of little relevance in a discussion of the nature of morality.[35]

---

[35] I am grateful to Gerry Cohen, John Cottingham, Peter Hacker, Oswald Hanfling, Susan Hurley, John Hyman, Anthony Kenny, Derek Parfit, and Bede Rundle, for many helpful comments on an earlier draft of this essay. I am particularly grateful to Tom Nagel for trying patiently to explain his argument to me. I am also indebted to comments and suggestions by the participants of the St Andrews Conference on Practical Reason in March 1995, and especially to the editors of the volume in which this essay appeared, Garrett Cullity and Berys Gaut.

13

The Central Conflict: Morality and Self-Interest

[T]he most important point to make about the putative dualism of practical reason is that deliberation of a sufficiently global scope is not conducted in terms of 'prudence', 'self-interest' or 'flourishing' on the one side and 'morality' on the other. It is conducted in terms of strength of practical reasons.... [V]alues, neither expressly prudential nor expressly moral but values... are what we appeal to.[1]

Reflection on the nature of morality, the sources of its normativity, and the motivation people have, or should have, to abide by it, often centres on the problems posed by the possibility of conflict between morality and self-interest. It is sometimes said that the central question of morality is: why is it that we must conform with morality even when doing so involves significant sacrifice of our own interests?[2] The answer, it is thought, would explain the normativity of morality. It would explain why it is binding, and why every person has reason to conform with it. I will follow the same route. I too will use reflection on the nature of the conflict between morality and self-interest, but my goal is different. I aim to draw certain lessons about the nature of well-being.[3]

Various earlier versions of this chapter were presented at a seminar at NYU, at the Scots Philosophical Club, and at a one-day conference on well-being at University College, London. I have learnt much from questions and comments by participants on these occasions. I am particularly grateful for written comments or long conversations on the paper to Roger Crisp, Jonathan Dancy, Anthony Duff, Ronald Dworkin, Brad Hooker, and Tom Nagel.

[1] J. Griffin, *Well-Being* (Oxford: OUP, 1996), 161.
[2] To simplify I will consider only cases in which the sacrifice morality calls for falls short of sacrificing one's life, or putting it in grave danger. I will consider only the case of sacrifices of interests which one has while alive, not interest, if any, to remain alive. The latter case presents complications affecting not so much the central conflict as the peculiar nature of one's interest in remaining alive.
[3] To facilitate presentation and avoid monotony I will use 'in one's interest', 'self-interest', and 'well-being' interchangeably. The expressions diverge in meaning. 'Self-interest' is often used to refer to a kind of motive, and I will have nothing to say about the nature of that motive. When talking of a person's interest one commonly refers to the means which facilitate pursuance of that person's well-being or goals. It is in one's interest to be in good health and to have lots of money. On the other hand it is odd to say that it is in the interest of a Baroque music lover to listen to a good concert of Baroque music. This would indicate a reason for listening other than the beauty of the music (e.g. that it will correct

The key to my reflection is in Griffin's statement quoted above, which forms the backbone for all that follows, though my understanding of it and of the issues it raises is not entirely the same as his. I believe that this statement, in the interpretation that I give it, is true only if a common view about the relations between morality and self-interest is mistaken. But my purpose is not to establish that. Rather it is to explore difficulties, apparent or real, in the alternative which I favour, which I will call the classical view, for while not faithful in detail to Plato's or Aristotle's writings it derives from them, and from the philosophical tradition which their writings informed.

I will outline the classical view, contrasting it with some variants of one alternative, a common view about the relations between morality and well-being. I will then turn to the difficulties the classical approach has to face. I will take it for granted (*a*) that morality can call upon one to make sacrifices, and (*b*) that moral requirements can conflict with the well-being of the agent to whom they are addressed. The difficulty is that neither seems possible according to the classical view. All this will take up the first two sections.

The third section will start unravelling the mystery. It explains the character of a central case of self-sacrifice, showing (*a*) that self-sacrifice does not necessarily involve conflict of morality and self-interest, and (*b*) that when making sacrifices we do not necessarily harm our self-interest (or set back our well-being). This will lead to section 4 and to the central claim of the chapter, namely that while people may reasonably care about their own well-being, a person's well-being is not, for that person, a source of reasons for action. Section 5 will explain how it is that reason may require people to act against their own self-interest, while the final two sections reflect on the character of people's concern for their own well-being.

1. MUST MORALITY CONFLICT WITH SELF-INTEREST?

A common view of the nature of the conflict between morality and the agent's well-being sees the conflict as a natural result of the fact that morality and well-being are two separate, independent (though not entirely unrelated) domains. Each has an internal structure which secures the absence of internal conflicts (at least the absence of serious conflicts), but their independence of each other makes them liable to conflict with each other.

---

some mistaken view he holds, or introduce him to new people). These are just two examples of the many nuances in the language used in this domain. I will ignore all of them and will take well-being in its philosophical sense as my subject.

Reasons are either prudential or moral (or belonging to some other kind). Prudential reasons have a weight or stringency which is determined by the degree to which they serve the agent's well-being. The stringency of moral reasons is determined from the moral point of view, independently of their contribution to the well-being of the agent. It is not surprising that prudential and moral reasons often conflict. The hard question is what to do when they do, and how to understand the fact that moral reasons have normative force even though they do not serve the agent's well-being.

I have challenged this view elsewhere.[4] But it is necessary to recapitulate in order to launch the discussion and locate some of the views which separate this approach from others. Whenever we act intentionally we act for a reason or for reasons. That means that we do what we do because, as we see it, the action we perform is more attractive than its alternatives, that is, it appears to possesses some characteristic or other which makes it worthwhile, or better than the alternatives. This is where I am in total agreement with Griffin's statement. When we think about what to do we simply think of the options available and of which of them—if any—is best, and which—if any—is required.

That, understood in a way which is perhaps more radical than Griffin's, has major implications both for morality and for well-being. Regarding morality it means that moral values and moral requirements may differ in content from other values and requirements, but they do not differ fundamentally in the source of their normativity. I do not mean by this that there is just one explanation, or one master argument, which establishes all values and requirements. Far from it, I believe that many diverse arguments are required, for there are many diverse values and requirements. I mean rather that the diversity affects moral values and requirements as much as non-moral ones, and that there is nothing very special about the moral arguments, which sets them apart from the others. Were moral considerations a class apart, were they derived—as Kant, for example, thought—from a master argument which determines not only their content, but their

---

[4] Both issues are discussed in *The Morality of Freedom* (Oxford: OUP, 1986). More recently I addressed the first in 'On the Moral Point of View', in J. B. Schneewind (ed.), *Reason, Ethics, and Society* (Chicago: Open Court, 1996) and 'The Amoralist', in G. Cullity and B. Gaut (eds.), *Practical Reason and Ethics* (Oxford: OUP, 1997), which are Chs. 11 and 12 above. The second is challenged more indirectly. I argued—both in *Morality of Freedom* and in 'Duties of Well-Being' in my *Ethics in the Public Domain*, rev. edn. (Oxford: OUP, 1995)—that the reason for promoting one's own well-being is a formal reason, in itself without content, and that desires are not reasons—especially in 'Incommensurability and Agency', in Ruth Chang (ed.), *Incommensurability, Incomparability, and Practical Reason* (Cambridge: Harvard University Press, 1997), which is Ch. 3 above. On the second point see also W. Quinn, *Morality and Action*, essay 11. Griffin shares the first of the assumptions I challenge and, though his position on the second is more nuanced, our views on it are fairly close.

character and their stringency, we would not have been able, in practical deliberation, to take our eyes off this fact. It would have determined the outcome of our deliberation. For example, had Griffin, and others, been right in thinking that moral considerations always trump all others, their presence would have put an end to any consideration of any other factor.

I am not making this point as an argument against the special character of morality, or against its special stringency. For one thing, Griffin's statement quoted at the outset can have a sparer meaning which does not carry this implication. I am simply explaining the sense in which, as I see it, it is true that when we deliberate we consider which reasons are most pressing in a way which transcends and defies the common division of practical thought into moral and self-interested (and other) considerations. The implications of this view for well-being are equally far-reaching. If when we deliberate, reasons and values feature in our thoughts regardless of their relation to our well-being, then considerations which advance our well-being need not be undertaken with that as our end. How can that be?

Like others I take the notion of a person's well-being as the notion we use in general judgements about how well people's lives went for them, that is, excluding any consideration of their contribution to the well-being of others, or to culture, etc., except in as much as such contributions affected the quality of the life judged from the point of view of the person whose life it was. These are judgements of how good someone's life was, how good it was for the person whose life it was. Clearly this is not the only way in which the concept is used. The following example from an in-flight magazine is probably more typical of its common use: 'You will find Well-being located on Channel 3 . . . This is specifically designed to help you wind down . . . freeing both mind and body of tension and creating a sense of inner calm.' The philosophical use I am following is none the worse for deviating from other ordinary uses. But as we will see it is not without problems of its own.

The more successful a person is in his life the better is his life, other things being equal. Other things need not be equal for there are other factors which affect the quality of a person's life. One's attitude to oneself and to one's life is one of them. The life of people who are consumed by self-doubt, or self-hate, or suffer from very low self-esteem is diminished by these factors. Similarly, success in relationships or enterprises which are demeaning, worthless, or evil does not contribute to one's well-being. But provided one's success is in something worthwhile, and that one is at peace with oneself and wholehearted about one's life then well-being depends on the degree to which one is successful in one's relationships and goals.

Both goals and relationships are subject to people's voluntary control in the sense that they maintain and develop or pursue them at will. They can decide to abandon them or let them decline, or decide to let them assume a more or less prominent role in their lives. So people's well-being depends, up to a point, on themselves—on their wisdom and judgement in choosing goals and relationships, and in pursuing them.

As was noted, only the pursuit of worthwhile goals and relationships contributes to a person's well-being (though they may be goals which the person pursues only incidentally to the pursuit of another goal which may be worthless in itself). But are there any other restrictions on the sort of ends which could further a person's well-being? This question brings us to the heart of our subject. If the demands of morality and people's concern for their own well-being are often, perhaps even normally or necessarily, in conflict then perhaps all possible considerations, all possible goals, etc., divide into at least two distinct classes: one including those pursuit of which advances the agent's well-being and the other consisting of those pursuit of which is morally required, but which by their nature cannot advance the agent's well-being, and sometimes, or often, conflict with the agent's well-being. There may, of course, be other categories. Moreover, the first category may include moral requirements conformity to which (or attempts to conform) necessarily advances the agent's well-being.

Such division of considerations would offer a ready explanation of conflicts between morality and self-interest (or at least of one type of such conflicts). They occur when a moral consideration which is essentially unhelpful to one's well-being conflicts with considerations of one's well-being. I think that many believe this to be if not the only then the typical case of conflict between morality and self-interest. However, is there any general theoretical reason to think that such a division exists? One simple thought is that the goods which can be realized in or through action divide into two classes, those which are good for the agents, and those which are good for the recipient(s), for others affected by the action (or at least some of them). I do not wish to endorse the thought that moral considerations include only those which concern the well-being of others. But let us, for the sake of argument, follow the implications of this thought. Everyone would agree, of course, that many acts are good in both ways. They are, when successfully performed, good for those who perform them, and also for others. I have, morally have, to look after my ailing mother. I have to visit her, look to her needs, and give her strength and support. But doing all this also cements our relationship, and enhances the quality of my life. Arguably all actions which are intrinsically good or worthwhile, other than some of those whose *sole* intrinsic merit is that they give the agent hedonic pleasure (sun-bathing, eating, etc.), are also at least potentially beneficial to others, either instrumentally (as is the case with many economic activities, such as the work of a bank clerk, a plumber, a nurse, or a production worker), or intrinsically (as with creating or performing works of art or entertainment).

So the question is whether there are classes of action which are morally good, but which by their nature cannot contribute to the well-being of those who perform them. There are beyond doubt some cases which suggest this. For example, possibly one is morally required to kill or harm in some other way very wicked people (e.g. brutal dictators set on genocide). Is it plausible to think that one's well-being is served by killing another human being, even such a human being? Are we not inclined to think that we ought to kill while feeling personal discomfort with the act, regret that we have to perform it, and even distress at having to do so? That is indeed so, but it does not support the existence of moral requirements which do not serve the agent's well-being, unless one thinks, erroneously, that only what one takes pleasure in can contribute (non-instrumentally) to one's well-being. Many artists, writers, and others do not enjoy the process of creation, but the fact that they successfully engage in it contributes to their well-being.[5] Regarding the morally required killing it is arguable that thus proving oneself in action does, other things being equal, contribute to the goodness of one's life.[6]

Another type of moral requirements which seem to be inherently opposed to one's interest consists of some requirements of toleration, and of respect for the rights of opponents. Some people, pursuing their own interests, propose public measures which are harmful to my interests. I have a moral reason to let them present their case and argue for it within fair democratic procedures even though their doing so is against my interests. Here we need to distinguish two aspects of the situation. We are required to respect the democratic rights of others, regardless of the way their proposals bear on ours. Doing so is, I would claim, other things being equal, a good to the agent. What is against his interest is the use made on some occasions of the rights he protects. I do not have reason to support people's democratic rights because they conflict with my interest, only to support

---

[5] Whether or not they would have been better off had they enjoyed it is irrelevant to our purpose. Note that their creative activity is part of what makes their life go well for them. It is not (or not merely) a cause of some good.

[6] Moral tragedies are different. A person faces a moral tragedy if all the options open to him, at least all those which are not inferior to some others of those open to him, are morally wrong. Sophie's Choice is a well-known example. In this case doing what one is required to do cannot advance the agent's well-being. But that is because doing what is morally wrong cannot advance an agent's well-being, not because there are actions which are morally right which cannot advance his well-being. (Some people deny that it possible for an act which is morally required to be also morally wrong. We need not consider the matter here.)

them regardless of whether they conflict with my interest. It is accidental to the moral requirement that it happens on occasion to lead to consequences which put my interest at risk, or which harm it. I will consider such cases below.

A final example is a requirement, should there be one, to give, let us say, a tenth of my income to charity. Surely, here there can be no doubt that the moral requirement is essentially against my interest. It is a requirement to reduce my resources in favour of others, and reducing my resources is against my interest. Indeed so, unless what I do with my resources is not reduce them but use them. I am not acting against my interest when I go to see a film, even though I have to buy a ticket to do so. This is not simply 'reducing' my resources. It is using them. So the description of my tithe example is already loaded. If giving (that sum of) money to charity is an act that benefits me then the fact that it depletes my resources does not show that it is against my interest. It is just an ordinary case of using my resources.

But how can just signing a cheque, or handing over banknotes, to charity be in my interest? Looking after the poor, teaching, tending the ill, and so on are all activities which can benefit agents. They can give valuable content to their lives and bring satisfaction. But how can a momentary act be good for the agent? I have suggested that the difficulty presented in this case is the difficulty we generally have in understanding how acts, as against activities, can be intrinsically good.[7]

Breaking the world 100-metre sprinting record is an example of such an act. Sprinters may enjoy the running, but they need not. Even if they do not the act of breaking the record is worthwhile. Its value is, however, in its result: setting a new world record. Those who achieve it cannot complain that they do not enjoy the activity of racing which led to the result as well. Their reward is in the result.[8] The same is true of giving to charity. There need be no intrinsic value in the activity which constitutes the giving. Writing a cheque need not be intrinsically rewarding. The value is in the giving to charity, in doing something which is morally good. That is the reward of the agent, just as setting a new record is the reward of the sprinter.[9]

So giving to charity is good for the giver, or at least we have no reason to think otherwise.

Some people may object that, by removing the requirement that only

---

[7] I have in mind here the distinction between acts and activities as drawn by von Wright in *Norm and Action* (1963), see also A. J. P. Kenny, *Action, Emotion and Will* (London: Routledge & Kegan Paul, 1963).

[8] Since the result is intrinsic to the act (you cannot break the world record without setting a new one) the intrinsic value of the result makes the act itself intrinsically worthwhile.

[9] Quoted from Ch. 11 above.

what gives pleasure can be good for the agent, I removed the subjective element in the notion of well-being. And this, they will say, is inconsistent with the thought that the notion designates the goodness of the life *from the point of view of the person whose life it is*. If well-being is having a life full of good actions and activities then it is indistinguishable from the morally good life. But we know that people can have a good life even though their lives are not free from moral blemish. Moreover, we know that moral considerations can conflict with a person's self-interest. Hence, well-being must be connected to pleasure. This is its connection to the person's own point of view.

The objection is based on a misconception. The notion of well-being does indeed have a strong subjective element. It simply need not be through taking pleasure. People's lives go well for them only if, as we saw, they are at peace with themselves, and to the extent that they are wholeheartedly engaged in their relationships and in the pursuit of their goals. Moreover, pleasure is often no more than the satisfaction which is, or is inseparable from, the recognition of one's success in accomplishing what one wholeheartedly wanted to do. In that sense giving money to charity can give pleasure, and does not contribute to one's well-being unless it does.[10]

Henceforth I will proceed on the assumption that there are no moral considerations pursuit of which cannot serve the agent's own well-being (at least so long as we exclude consideration of the value of one's continued existence, and the possibility that there are moral requirements which necessarily include a requirement to sacrifice one's life). One can profit from, one's well-being can be served by, compliance with, or the attempt to comply with, any moral consideration. There is no conclusive argument to that effect that I know of. But considerations like those recited above, and the absence of successful counter arguments, give some support to this conclusion. One counter argument has already been intimated. It informed the objection which I have just dismissed. According to it, there is no way of distinguishing the moral life from the life which is good for the agent. Without this distinction it is impossible for morality to conflict with the agent's well-being. That objection lies at the core of the argument of this chapter.

---

[10] Recognition of success is not generally a necessary condition of the act, or activity, contributing to one's well-being. In particular, it is not generally the case that one needs to know that one's action had its hoped for (causal) consequences for the action to contribute to one's well-being. In the example of giving to charity, however, the success involved amounts to no more than realization that the act has been accomplished as intended (that one really did give to charity). One's pleasure in the act is no more than one's wholehearted commitment to it.

2. CAN MORALITY CONFLICT WITH SELF-INTEREST?

The direct implication of the discussion so far is that it is plausible to think that there is no inherent conflict between morality and self-interest. It does not follow that they do not conflict. Whether or not they do may depend on the circumstances, and on the choices people make during their lives. If an earthquake strikes it may become one's moral duty to abandon everything and dedicate oneself to helping the injured. This may set back one's career, or call for other major sacrifices. But if one strikes it lucky one can continue with normal life and never be called upon to make any sacrifice in the name of morality. Perhaps this picture is too optimistic. Perhaps morality is such that in the circumstances of life today all conscientious people have to make sacrifices all the time. I will avoid such issues as they take us into controversial questions about the nature and scope of moral reasons that do not belong to the present topic. The point which matters is that conflict, more or less likely, is contingent, not necessary.

But as noted above we are in danger not only of rightly denying that morality and self-interest inherently conflict, we are in danger of denying that morality and self-interest can ever conflict. How can such conflicts arise? If our well-being is determined, other things being equal, by success in our goals, which we can adopt, maintain or abandon, as well as upgrade or downgrade in importance relative to other goals, and since our well-being can be served by doing what we have moral reason to do, does it not follow that so long as we choose wisely we choose in ways that serve both morality and our well-being?

The difficulty results from the combination of the following propositions:
(1) Our well-being depends on success in pursuing worthwhile options. It does not matter whether they are worthwhile for moral or other reasons.
(2) When faced with conflicting considerations we should conform with those which are more important or more stringent. Doing what we have most reason to do is the rational course of action, and it is also the one which serves our well-being.
(3) When we have most reason to do what moral considerations indicate, that is when moral considerations outweigh or are more stringent than other considerations, then what we are morally required to do is also what we are rationally required to do, and thus it is what will serve our well-being.[11]

---

[11] To simplify presentation I write as if there is only one moral consideration present in each choice situation. It can be understood as the moral reason (or combination of reasons) which outweighs all the conflicting moral considerations which apply to the situation.

(4) When we have most reason to do what non-moral considerations suggest, even though moral considerations alone indicate a different action, then the moral considerations are overridden, and we are not doing anything morally wrong in not conforming to them.[12] Again, so long as we deliberate and act rationally and succeed in conforming to the best reason we are serving our well-being, and doing what we are morally required to do at the same time.

There is a second, closely related difficulty: the classical conception of well-being makes self-sacrifice impossible. We often feel that moral considerations force us to do what we do not want to do, and that is what is meant by saying that we have to make sacrifices if we are to be moral. But, and this is the difficulty, according to the classical view *so long as we are wholeheartedly rational* morality can never be rightly said to impose requirements which force us to do what we do not want to do. What we want we want for reasons, and we choose to do that which we believe is supported by the best reasons. If moral considerations require us to give up something we cherish we may regret the circumstances which made it so, and we may feel emotional difficulty in adjusting to them, in wholeheartedly endorsing our decision to do the right thing. But if we overcome them then in doing the moral thing we do what we want to do and we are making no sacrifices.

To illustrate the difficulty consider two pairs of cases, one involving a small the other a big decision. I can either use my car to go on a pleasant day trip this weekend or give it to someone—known through friends to be reliable, etc.—who needs it to go to the nearby town to visit his young son who is in hospital seriously ill. Usually in such cases there are questions about the other person's ability to get a car from other sources, or his ability to travel by bus, etc. So assume that it is known that there is no other way he can get to the hospital, and that that is nobody's fault. According to the classical view it is a straightforward comparison of the strength or stringency of the reasons for and against either option. It does not matter that one of them is a moral reason. If on reflection it turns out to be the strongest reason then I should lend the car to that person. My action will be a good action and therefore one which makes my life a little better. It is true that I am also denied a pleasant day in the country (we assume, of

---

[12] I am assuming here what I denied earlier, namely that moral considerations constitute a class apart, because I am presenting a view which I do not in fact share. The best exploration known to me of the relations between morality and other reasons which assumes that morality is a separate domain is S. Scheffler's *Human Morality* (New York: OUP, 1992). As he explains there can be other alternative interpretations of the situation described in the fourth proposition. But replacing this proposition with alternative variants will not affect my conclusions.

course, that the best alternative way of spending the day is not as attractive to me). Nevertheless, so the argument above goes, from the point of view of my own well-being it is better to lend the car and stay at home and (for example) listen to music, than to go to the country having refused to lend the car. The fact that the reason for lending the car is better than the reason for using it myself guarantees that my well-being is better served by lending it.

Consider now a big decision. Should I become a teacher or a lawyer? I will assume that both will provide a decent level of earning. It is well known, let us further assume, that there is a glut of lawyers but a great need for teachers, and that that is going to remain so for some time to come. This gives me a moral reason to be a teacher rather than a lawyer. Assume that on balance this is what I should do, but that but for that (moral) reason the best judgement would have been to become a lawyer. Again, it seems that on the classical view I should become a teacher, and I would not be making any sacrifice by doing so. I would simply be doing what I have reason to do, and my well-being depends on success in what I have reason to do. If so then considerations of morality and of well-being never conflict. Moral considerations do conflict with non-moral considerations, but they do not conflict with concern for my well-being. That concern is malleable. It is shaped by what I have reason to do, including moral reasons. Well-being cannot conflict with morality for it embraces it.

So far the difficulties. One weakness of the argument purporting to establish them is obvious. It assumes not only, as I claimed in the previous section, that responding to any moral consideration can contribute to one's well-being (i.e. would contribute in the absence of conflicting considerations), but also that the importance of any moral reason as a moral reason is the same as its importance as a possible contribution to the agent's well-being. Relying on that weakness we can see how a rebuttal of the argument suggests itself.

Consider a simplified example. I have a moral reason to volunteer as a driver for food convoys in a far-away country afflicted by starvation. According to the assumptions of the classical position, doing so willingly and successfully would contribute to my well-being. Alternatively I could start my university studies. I have gained a lucrative grant without which I cannot afford to go to university, but which has to be taken immediately. In other words, if I volunteer as a driver I will lose my chance of university education for the foreseeable future. What should I do? I should conform with the more stringent reason. Let us assume that the more stringent reason is the moral one. I do not mean that it is more stringent because it is a moral reason. I do not believe that moral reasons always defeat non-moral reasons. It is more stringent because many lives would be saved if I volunteer. The absence of drivers is the bottleneck in the fight against famine in that far-away country. Every week I work there I keep dozens of people alive, and if they survive a year, the new crops will give them a fair chance to enjoy a life of normal length. For the sake of the argument,[13] let us assume that in the circumstances prevailing the reason to volunteer easily defeats the very weighty reasons I have to take up the grant and go to university. Does it follow that according to the classical view doing what I have, both morally and rationally, to do would serve my well-being better than going to university? Surely it does not. While my volunteer work will contribute to my well-being it is plausible to assume that it would not do so nearly as much as would a university education. Therefore, so the rebuttal goes, the difficulty suggested above does not arise. The classical view does not lead to the conclusion that morality and the agent's well-being cannot conflict.

How convincing is the rebuttal? There is a doubt about its compatibility with the basic tenets of the classical approach, for it seems to reintroduce the fundamental division between considerations of well-being and of morality, as two distinct classes of normative considerations with their own internal structures, sources, and procedures for ranking the stringency of considerations which may diverge. Only thus, the doubters would say, does it make sense to suppose that one and the same reason would have one weight as a reason of the agent's own well-being and a different weight as a moral consideration.

This doubt is, however, misconceived. The rebuttal does not presuppose the division of so-called prudence and morality. It does not say that the moral consideration has two lives, a life as a 'prudential' consideration, where its weight is determined by its contribution to the well-being of the agent, and a different life, with different weight, as a moral consideration. Rather, the rebuttal assumes, consistently with the classical view, that the consideration is one and its weight or stringency is one. Its weight is determined by its nature, not as being an instance of a class of moral reasons, but as being what it is. And it does not have a different 'prudential' weight. We can say that conforming with it has certain consequences for one's well-being. But that does not imply that we have a separate reason of well-being not to follow it, or not to conform with it.

An analogy may help elucidate the point. Imagine that Mary, a renowned

---

[13] Various philosophers have argued that in the circumstances described the moral reason does not defeat the nonmoral one. See, among others, J. Griffin, *Value Judgement* (Oxford: OUP, 1996), Scheffler, *Human Morality*, Liam Murphy, 'The Demands of Beneficence', *Philosophy and Public Affairs*, 22 (1993), 267. I do not wish to take a position on this issue here. I am using this as an example only. So long as it is acknowledged that morality and well-being may conflict, examples which will serve to illustrate the rebuttal can be found.

painter, decides to move from Oxford to York. This will impoverish the art community in Oxford, with which Mary has been associated for many years. We can well imagine that both she and Jo, an Oxford art lover, will be sorry to see this happen. They may agree that Mary's decision is reasonable, perhaps it is even the best decision for her. Yet it results in a loss. Given that Jo knows it is the best he will not do anything to change Mary's mind. But he, as well as the arts in Oxford, are the losers as a result. The example shows that we are used to carving up the domain of value into smaller domains. We often assess events in terms of their significance to the sub-domains. We recognize that some may care about some subdomain more than about others. None of this requires attributing independent sources of normativity to the subdomains. Nor need those who care particularly about a subdomain think that they should prefer promoting its values over what is best over all.

This explanation is bound to appear very puzzling. It avoids the doubt at the cost of an apparently implausible claim, and quite apart from that it leaves a central question to be answered. The explanation assumes (*a*) that at least normally one's own well-being is not a reason for one's own action. Judgements of well-being, of how good a person's life is or was, are evaluative judgements, but they are not action-guiding, at least not for the person whose well-being is in question. It leaves unexplained (*b*) how it can be that, while following all reasons for action contributes to the agent's well-being, the significance of the contribution may be determined by considerations other than the stringency or weight of the reasons. To explain and test this explanation it is better to consider practical deliberation in cases to which no moral considerations apply.

3. MAKING SACRIFICES AND THE DISRUPTION FACTOR

I will start the process of dissolving the difficulties by considering the case of self-sacrifice. As was implied earlier, while it seems clear that people sometimes do and sometimes have to make sacrifices for moral reasons, I do not believe that we always harm our self-interest, or act against our expectations regarding our self-interest, when we make sacrifices. Once we see that self-sacrifice is not essentially[14] connected to well-being it will be

---

[14] This is not a claim about the meaning of the word. It is a normative claim about when it would be right to judge a person to be making a sacrifice. To a degree I accept that some will find claims concerning self-sacrifice, which I reject, convincing for—as I see it—they have a skewed understanding of values. At the same time my explanation fails if it does not capture the central elements in the common understanding of self-sacrifice.

easier to understand why an agent's well-being is not, normally, a reason for action for that agent.[15]

We need to focus on big decisions. Let us imagine a ballet dancer enjoying a reasonably successful career with a small provincial ballet company, the only one within hundreds of miles. Then dwindling audiences threaten the future of the company. If it is forced to disband our dancer will have to abandon ballet, to change career and look for something else to do. It does not surprise us that he regards the prospect as a great personal disaster. I think that it would be agreed that it is reasonable for him to try to prevent the collapse: he may urge all the dancers to accept a cut in earnings, and of course accept one himself. He may agree to volunteer some of his time for fund-raising in the community, etc. Let us assume that the company has to close. Our dancer looks for other possibilities and starts a new career as a theatre director with the local theatre company where he remains until his retirement. He quickly comes to like his new work, enjoying a success comparable to his success in his first career.

It is easy to imagine cases like this in which a person's life loses nothing by a forced change of career, and yet where this person is acting reasonably in trying to stave off the change, being willing to pay a considerable price in the process. Does it mean that people finding themselves in such situations are concerned by something other than their own well-being? There is certainly no suggestion that they are moved by concern for someone else, or for a cause. Their actions are self-regarding. But are they moved by concern for their own well-being? Yes, you may say. At the time they are trying to hang on to the life they have they are uncertain whether they will be able to find an alternative as good. That is what moves them. And no doubt in the vast majority of cases this is a factor. But it does not fully explain why people try to hang on to the life they have.

One way of bringing out this fact is by imagining an ideal situation: imagine that our dancer knows that a career in the theatre is his for the asking. The director of the theatre company is a friend, all the way back from school days, and remembering how the dancer was directing school plays and knowing of the precarious position of the dance company he offers him a job as an assistant director, with promotion after a learning period. This no doubt affects the situation, and it affects the type of sacrifice it would be reasonable for the dancer to accept in order to stay with the life he has. But it is still reasonable for him to regard the threat to his dancing career as a disaster for him. He wants to be a dancer not a theatre director. He knows that if he is forced into the theatre he will come to like

---

[15] I am not claiming that all self-sacrifices can be explained in this way, that is, without invoking the fact that the sacrificing act affects the agent's self-interest adversely. I will briefly comment on other kinds of self-sacrifice below.

it and be reasonably successful. But that is not what he wants and he is willing to try hard to stay with dancing. These admissions of his entail, on the assumption that his feelings and actions are rational,[16] that he is not concerned with his well-being. His concern is to have the life he wants to have, meaning the life he has become committed to.[17]

Here is another example. Jane faces a difficult choice. She has a uniquely challenging and rewarding job, but her employer is moving the business to another place a great distance away. Her partner cannot move. What is she to do? Both she and her partner are attractive people who will find no difficulty in establishing new relationships, should this one end. They know this from past experience, and they are a confident, positive sort of people. If they decide to break up the overwhelming odds are that they will have as good a life overall as they would have had had the move not occurred. They may well decide to part. But they may not, or at least not that easily. I suspect that we will have a feeling that something has gone awry if they find it easy to part, on the ground that their well-being is not at stake. This will show that they were not really very committed to each other. If they are, if they love each other deeply, or are very much in love, they will want to continue together, and they will try to find ways to do so, making serious sacrifices to do so, possibly even sacrificing their careers to do so. This is a reasonable, and rational, human response to such situations. But it cannot be explained by their concern for their own well-being.

Familiar as the feelings and conduct I illustrated are, are they really rational? Can they be defended by theoretical considerations? I believe that they can, though 'defending', here as elsewhere, does not mean deriving from first principles. It means explaining the way these feelings fit with other aspects of practical reason, thus showing how they make sense to us. The analysis I suggested for these examples sees them as illustrating the fact that normally our own well-being is not an independent factor in our deliberations.[18] In most cases when people refer to their well-being or their interests they refer either to their chances of succeeding with worthwhile goals or relationships which they have, or want to have, or to their possession of the means (money, education, etc.) which will enable them to pursue whatever worthwhile goal or relationship they may at some time come

---

[16] That is, not irrational. I am not implying that he would have been irrational to conclude that it is time to give up and change. We ought to remember that some people change in mid-career just because they feel like a change.

[17] I put the point in this, linguistically somewhat awkward, way in order to underline the fact that what matters is not how he has come to have that career (did he freely choose it?), but what it has come to mean to him.

[18] Strictly speaking it illustrates only that well-being is not always an overriding factor. But the phenomenology of such cases does, at least in some of them, point to the absence of any separate weight being given to one's well-being at all.

to want to pursue. Goals and relationships they have or may want to have are what people have reason to care about, not their well-being as such. That is why it is rational for them to behave in the ways described in the examples.[19]

The classical view, as set out in the previous section, provides a ready explanation of the rationality of this behaviour, and of the correctness of the analysis. We saw that the explanation of how—according to the classical view—agents' well-being can conflict with moral requirements which apply to them depends on the fact that normally agents' well-being is not a factor in their deliberations. The examples complement the explanation by showing, first, how people may feel torn about following morality on grounds other than the conflict with their well-being; and second, why they feel that they are making sacrifices to follow morality for reasons which do not depend on the impact of their action on their well-being. Both are explained by the fact that moral requirements may force people to give up goals, careers, and relationships that they care about. Crucial to the explanation is the fact that conflict between moral and non-moral considerations is just like conflict between various non-moral considerations. The demands of one's chosen and happy career may conflict with one's goal of pursuing certain hobbies, or with some of one's relationships, etc. In such cases we sacrifice careers for family, or the other way round.

Sacrifices for morality's sake are like all sacrifices, like sacrifices where no moral considerations are involved, a matter of giving up something one cares a lot about for the sake of something else one cares about. Both in cases which involve moral considerations, and in those which do not, the fact that one is making a sacrifice does not mean that one's action is setting back one's well-being. It means perhaps that one's life is not going to be as good as it might have been had circumstances been different, had one not been forced by circumstances to make sacrifices, but it does not mean that one's life is less good because of one's decision or action.

Moreover, while it is true that when making a sacrifice one's action may set back one's well-being, that can happen both in cases which involve moral considerations and in those which do not. Acting reasonably, even where no moral considerations are involved, need not serve one's well-being best. Let me develop the dancer's example to illustrate the point. We can imagine that the dancer's efforts to save the dance company are successful. After three or four years of hard struggle the future of the company is made

---

[19] We mark types, or degree of sacrifice. Whenever we give up (for what appears a good reason) something that we deeply care about we are making a sacrifice. Normally this would warrant saying that we are sacrificing the goal or relationship we are giving up (e.g. our career). When we do so with great reluctance we also sacrifice ourselves or (in slightly different circumstances) our life.

secure. The dancer continues his successful career, but he has paid a price. He is embittered, he has lost much of his zest and energy, his *joie de vivre*. Had he recognized defeat he would have made a relatively painless transition, and would even have taken pride in his ability to change direction. He would have had a better life. Yet his decision to struggle for his life as he had it is not unreasonable.[20]

Let us take stock of the conclusions so far. My main aim is to defend the classical view against the twin objections that it cannot make sense of (*a*) self-sacrifice, and of (*b*) the conflict between morality and self-interest. To reply to the objections one has to show that the explanation of self-sacrifice and of conflicts between morality and self-interest does not require the assumption that practical reason has (at least) two sources of reasons: morality and the agent's well-being.

I have argued that the notion of self-sacrifice does not involve essential reference to the agent's well-being. It is simply a special case of conflict of reasons. Reasons conflict when they cannot all be conformed with. Conflict can be said to be the manifestation of scarcity, when this last term is understood broadly and metaphorically. Again speaking metaphorically the response to scarcity is efficiency. It does not overcome scarcity but it reduces its impact. The efficient solution to a conflict is one in which the loss made inescapable by scarcity is as small as possible, or of as small a significance as possible. The terminology of scarcity, loss, and efficiency is obviously inept for many practical conflicts. I use it to make the point that while there is something undesirable about every conflict, some regret that it had to happen, there is normally no sacrifice made when one's response to conflicts is reasonable.

Some conflicts do call for sacrifices. A common explanation has it that conflicts between considerations whose normativity derives exclusively from concern for the well-being of the agent do not call for sacrifices. They involve only efficiency in the pursuit of one's well-being. On the other hand, when morality conflicts with the agent's well-being sacrifices may be called for. I suggested that this view is mistaken on both counts. Sacrifices are involved when the rational response to conflict involves abandoning one of one's cherished goals or relationships. This can happen when the conflict involves no moral considerations (as I tried to show by the examples at the beginning of this section) as well as when one or more of the considerations involved is moral. Either way there is no general reason to think that sacrifice will lead to diminution of the agent's well-being. Disruption, by

---

[20] I am not claiming that no sacrifice would have been too much. There is a point where dedication turns into irrational obstinacy. My claim is only that there are sacrifices it is not irrational of people to make in such situations which in fact diminish their well-being, and where uncertainty about the outcome is not a complete explanation of their actions.

one's own hand forced by circumstances, of the life one has is the context in which we normally feel forced to make sacrifices. For it is in such contexts that we find it most difficult to adjust to the actions and pursuits which reason imposes on us, when they require us to give up cherished aspects of our life. In this reluctance lies the essence of one central type of self-sacrifice.

The explanation of sacrifice is not yet complete. Before we return to it briefly, we have to address the second objection to the classical view by explaining the possibility of conflict between morality and well-being. For it is true that sacrifices may sometimes make one's life less good than it would have been without them. That possibility is yet to be explained.

4. ACTING AGAINST ONE'S INTEREST

Here is the difficulty. Even allowing that well-being has, for the agent, primarily an evaluative role, since right actions contribute to the well-being of those who undertake them how is it that they do not contribute to the agents' well-being in proportion to their value? Why does the perspective of well-being deviate from that of right reason?

The answer is very simple, and familiar. One consideration determines the distinct perspective of an agent's well-being. It allows the contribution of options to the agent's own well-being to diverge from the general verdict on their value over all. It is the fact that in assessing the contribution of actions, or anything else, to the well-being of a person we take that person's life as a whole as the measure. In assessing the value of actions and activities their ability to fill a span of time in the life of a person with worthwhile content is central. That means that while the more valuable options should be chosen over those of lesser value, those of lesser value may fill the life of the agent for longer, and thus contribute more to his well-being.

We already saw a simple illustration of the point in my conflict between volunteering to drive famine relief convoys and to go to university next year. While, by hypothesis, the value of my volunteering is greater than the value of going to study (since it will save lives which otherwise would perish), it will occupy me only for a few months. My failure to study in university will affect the rest of my life. That is why doing the right thing is, in the circumstances, against my self-interest. Paradoxically, had the volunteer work been life-long (as in some circumstances it may well be) then volunteering may not have been against my interest. (We need more information to judge this possibility.)

Naturally the short duration of some options, in as much as it reduces their contribution to the well-being of the agent, also reduces their value.

But given that their value does not (at least not entirely) depend on their contribution to the well-being of the agent, that fact cannot restore the coincidence of the perspective of the well-being of the agent with the value of his options over all.

The dependence of the perspective of the agent's well-being on the temporal dimension explains why we tend to find it natural to think that morally valuable activities, such as tending the sick or teaching the young, do not necessarily detract from the agent's well-being, whereas actions, such as giving to charity, do. Typically actions have shorter duration than activities, and therefore, other things being equal, contribute less to the agent's well-being. These are of course gross generalizations, to which counter-examples are easy to find.

We can now briefly return to complete the analysis of self-sacrifice. It was acknowledged earlier that cases where we are forced to give up the life we have form only one type of self-sacrifice. It is common to regard every case in which a person knowingly acts against his own interest in following what he regards as right reason as a case of self-sacrifice. The analysis of this section and the previous ones explains their nature. It does so without drawing any deep divide between prudential and moral or other reasons. This vindicates the classical view against the objection that it is incapable of explaining self-sacrifice.

Finally, it is important to emphasize that while cases in which self-interest is at odds with morality provide one context in which reason sometimes requires agents to act in ways detrimental to their self-interest this is not the only context where this can happen. Part of the reason that some moral considerations can set back one's well-being is that they are categorical. Categorical reasons are those whose weight or stringency is independent of the agent's will. Many of the reasons which apply to us arise out of our goals and relationships, and depend on our will in choosing and wishing to maintain those goals and relationships. That is why David, the composer, has a greater reason to complete a good musical composition this year than I have. Categorical reasons, such as the reason we have not to kill people, have stringency which is unaffected by whether or not they serve our goals.

All categorical requirements have the potential to conflict with well-being. This includes considerations of self-respect, personal integrity, and respect for the shape of meaningful activities and relationships, and others. An example is the requirement to respect what is of value, and this includes the possibility of engaging in valuable activities, including those one does not care for personally (the common example is respect for works of art, for cultural or historical heritage, but I have in mind a wider category, which includes the more abstract respect for the preconditions which make valuable activities possible). On the common use of 'morality' not all these requirements are moral ones. Moreover, I suspect that there is not much common to all categorical requirements. They include requirements of good manners, such as not spitting on the floor (where this is a customary requirement), common taboos (against adults playing with excrement, etc.). I am not suggesting that conformity with them commonly conflicts with self-interest, though they can conflict. My point is that categorical requirements are a diverse class, and that many of them are not commonly thought of as moral.

To these we should add that even goals and relationships which are voluntarily undertaken or sustained give rise to requirements, which while they apply only to people with those goals or relationships can conflict with those people's well-being. The commitments of loyalty which are the concomitants of friendship can make one liable to anything from inconvenience (having to forgo a pleasant evening to calm down a distressed friend) to torture (having to refuse to betray the friend to the tyrant's police). Other goals potentially have similar consequences. Finally, where circumstances threaten one of our central goals we may strive to protect it in ways which are not conducive to our well-being, and act reasonably while doing so. This was the burden of the examples in the last section.

5. WELL-BEING AND THE BIFURCATED VIEW OF PRACTICAL REASON

The general account of well-being also supports the analysis of sacrifice and of conflict between morality and well-being. I have argued that both explanations presuppose that normally an agent's well-being is not, for him, a reason for action. In the present section I hope to lend some support to that view by showing that an agent's well-being is not the fountain of that agent's 'self-regarding' reasons for action.

As we saw, one's well-being depends on success in worthwhile and wholeheartedly engaged-in goals and relationships. Other things being equal so long as one is successful in the pursuit of one's goals and the conduct of one's relationships one's life goes well. That makes judgements of well-being depend on the goals people have. Neither I nor David have ever composed a musical work. This has no bearing on my well-being, since being a composer is not an aim of mine. But it casts a long shadow on David's life, since he resigned his job five years ago to devote himself to musical composition.

Prima facie, and I will start with a simple claim and qualify it later, it follows that when I deliberate about what goals to have, concern for my well-being cannot guide me. I need to have goals before I can consult my well-being when pursuing them. But in that case pursuing my goals and pursuing my well-being are normally one and the same thing. Cases of disruption, as illustrated above, concentrate on the occasions when the two come apart: when I need to make decisions about abandoning one goal in favour of another. In such cases concern for our well-being cannot help.

I am not saying that there are no reasons to guide us in the choice of goals and relationships whose success will make our life go well for us. First, we are guided by the relative value of the goals that we can choose. Second, we are also guided in our choice of goals by the chances that we will be successful in them. Some may argue that these two points show that we are guided by the pursuit of our well-being after all. How can we assess the relative value of two goals save by their contribution to our own well-being? Why should one's success in the pursuit of one's goals and relationships matter except that it matters to one's well-being?

But neither objection is justified. Starting with the second point: there is an obvious reason for preferring an option one is more likely to succeed in than one where the prospect of success is less, a reason independent of any impact of success or failure on one's well-being. The reason is the very same reason we have for pursuing the option at all, namely that it is good in one way or another. If I have reason to go to the cinema to see a Tarantino film, I have no reason to go to the cinema if I will arrive too late for the film. Failure means failure to realize the reason for the action. So a reason for an option is a reason for the successful pursuit of the option, and not for a failed attempt to pursue it. Consider playing tennis. If my reason for playing John is the value of beating him at tennis then, other things being equal, I have no reason to play if I am certain that I will lose.[21] If, on the other hand, my reason for playing John is to have a stimulating vigorous afternoon playing good tennis, then I should play even if I lose, but not if, because of an injury, the match will not be good tennis, nor invigorating, and so on. Reasons for action are reasons for successful actions, and they determine what constitutes success.

Turning now to the first point above. Far from being able to assess the relative value of options for an agent by their possible contribution to his well-being, we cannot judge their contribution to his well-being except by reference to their value (i.e. their value independently of such contribution), for the more valuable they are the more their successful pursuit contributes to his well-being. If they do not have a value independent of their value to

---

[21] Other things are often not equal. I may have independent reasons to play him even if I lose—e.g. it may improve my game.

us how can they be valuable to us? Because we chose them? Can anything we choose be good for us just because we choose it? And how can we choose it except because we believe it to be valuable? I have discussed these matters elsewhere and will not repeat the arguments here. Their conclusion is that we can only choose what we believe to be of value, and that that value is independent of our choice. The contribution of options to our well-being is determined by their value, and by our success in pursuing them.[22]

Therefore, normally considerations of well-being cannot help with choice of goals. Nor can they determine when is the right time to abandon one goal and look for, or adopt, another. The fact that we know that our well-being will not be harmed if we abandon our goal is neither here nor there. We persist with one goal, or abandon another, or take up a new one, because these are attractive to us, and not because of concern for our well-being. That was the main lesson from the examples.

These conclusions are reinforced by the fact that there are independent reasons for allowing that some of the more important reasons people have need have no impact on their well-being. Judgements of well-being are judgements of how well a person's life goes. Not everything which happens to a person, or which he does, affects the course of his life. To do so it must be significant for the life as a whole, or for non-negligible parts of it. If I break off from writing and have a cup of coffee my well-being will not be affected at all. I have suggested elsewhere that only what affects our comprehensive goals and relationships, that is, those within which much of our short-term goals nest, affects our well-being.[23] Some resist this view, saying that the coffee matters a tiny little bit, and we do not notice this because it matters so little. But that misses the point. I may have a strong reason for having coffee now. I may need a break and some hot liquid inside me quite badly. Nevertheless, so long as my having or not having the coffee has no long-term consequences, my having the coffee does not affect my well-being at all.

The point may be clearer if we turn from coffee to pain and physical suffering. We have a very strong reason to avoid pain, but most episodes of pain, even very severe pain, horrible though they are, do not affect our well-being. It is difficult vividly to remember pain, and while persistent pain is paralysing and affects well-being by reducing a person's ability to function, and while even momentary pain can traumatize a person and thus affect his or her well-being, most pain episodes pass without trace, without affecting

---

[22] These comments about the value of options and of success in them will be qualified when we come to examine the possibility of adopting a goal of pursuing one's well-being. Griffin's analysis in *Well-Being* is in general consonant with these points.

[23] I am relying here on my analysis of well-being in 'Duties of Well-Being', in *Ethics in the Public Domain*, Ch. 1.

a person's well-being. The same is true of hedonic pleasure (that is the pleasures of the senses). We have strong reasons to pursue intense pleasures, but unless they fit in with our life's goals and ambitions (as they do for Don Juan, and others), they do not affect our well-being.

I have argued in the present section that well-being cannot be the fountain of all our 'self-regarding' reasons. First, what serves our well-being depends on our goals and relationships, and they cannot, normally, be chosen for the sake of promoting our well-being. Second, we may have reasons for 'self-regarding' actions which have no bearing on our well-being. It follows that the pursuit of well-being can at best be one goal of several one may have. That possibility has now to be examined.

6. ONE'S WELL-BEING AS AN OPTIONAL GOAL

Several points are fairly straightforward:

1. Subject to the following point, we advance our well-being by succeeding in the worthwhile goals and relationships that we care about, whether or not we aim to serve our well-being by pursuing them.

2. Some, including some of the most important, goals and relationships cannot be successfully pursued with the aim of improving one's well-being. Loving relationships are motivated by mutual love, and one cannot love another because doing so improves one's life. There are other goals and relationships which have to be undertaken for certain motives, which are other-regarding, rather than self-concerned.

3. As was pointed out above, since largely we promote our well-being by succeeding in worthwhile goals and relationships there is normally no difference between saying 'I want to have a good life' and 'I want to succeed in the goals and relationships that I care about'. But the second statement is close to analytical: if it is my goal then I want to succeed in it, that is what it means for it to be my goal. The same is true of voluntary relationships, and of all the relationships that are important to us in the sense that we really care about them. Caring about them means, among other things, that we want them to succeed, and that we want to succeed in conducting them. Of course we may have conflicting desires. Some people are unable to want anything badly without being ambiguous about it, and so on and so forth. Still, in most contexts what we want when we want our own good is to succeed with our worthwhile goals and relationships.

Is it not the case, though, that there is more to caring about how good one's life is than that? Is it not the case that we want to succeed in worthwhile goals and relationships because we care how well our life goes, because we want to have a good life? What we basically care about is our life. This dependence of the way goals matter to us on the fact that our life matters to us would suggest that concern for our well-being is rational, and is the foundation of our concern for anything else, including (if the classical view is right) morality.

I believe this view to be mistaken. To make progress here we need to distinguish various 'thick' uses of the expression 'being concerned with how good one's own life is' from its minimal meaning. People may or may not be inclined to engage in reflection about their life and its direction. People who are concerned with the quality of their life in this sense have, if you like, super projects (i.e. goals of pursuing other goals simultaneously or in succession). They are not merely dedicated teachers, parents, friends, etc. They are also pursuing the super-goal of dividing their lives equally between work and pleasure, friends and vocation, or some other super-goal. They may decide to be stockbrokers till they are 30 and duck farmers later. And so on. Possibly in our culture most people have some super-goals of this kind, mostly of an inchoate and open-ended kind (I want my life to be useful to others, to be honourable, etc.).

Super-goals differ from ordinary goals in degree only. They are marked by having components which are commonly and rationally taken as independent goals. The partial goals involved with ordinary goals are not commonly taken as goals in themselves. Some want to be duck farmers, others want to be stockbrokers. If you want to be both you have a super-goal. Whereas training every day for the London Marathon and running the Marathon are two components of the goal of winning the London Marathon.

Super-goals do not change the analysis: when deliberating about their life people are still concerned with their goals and relationships, including super-goals. The existence of super-goals does not remove the need to choose[24] goals, or to decide between goals one has, in ways which are not totally dictated by the super-goals. In part this is a result of the fact that super-goals are themselves subject to rational assessment, and to the vagaries of emotional attachment. For example, a person dedicated to a life of achievement may lose the taste for it and come to prefer a quiet life. They are also as liable to conflict as are ground-level goals. For most people it is also the result of the fact that their super-goals are, as was mentioned above, inchoate and do not provide complete guidance about their ground-level goals.

[24] For the sake of brevity I use 'choosing goals' in a way which may mislead. I do not mean to say that goals we have are always chosen after deliberation. We usually drift into them. The point is that keeping with them depends on holding them to be worthwhile, and in many cases, on their continued emotional and imaginative appeal.

People sometimes think of their concern for their success with their super-goals as concern with their own well-being. While the two often coincide, and it is therefore tempting not to distinguish between them, they are not the same. Anyone who has super-goals is concerned with their success, but not everyone who has them need be concerned with his own well-being. As the examples of Jane and the dancer show, the two may come apart.

Interestingly, one of the super-goals people may have is the pursuit of their own well-being. How is this possible? Does it not follow from my previous arguments that promoting one's well-being within reason is a by-product of pursuing one's goals and super-goals, and that giving one's well-being any additional weight would be irrational? Not quite.

There is reason to pursue anything of value. People may make it their goal to see that the musical life of Oxford flourishes. It is good that it does, and while, other things being equal, there is nothing wrong in not taking this good to one's heart, it is perfectly reasonable to care about this and make the prosperity of musical life in Oxford one of one's goals. Can one do the same with one's own well-being? But is it not redundant to do so? One's well-being consists in the successful pursuit of one's valuable goals, that is, we already pursue them as goals and there is no more we can do. There is no doubt that many who are concerned with their own well-being give it an unreasonable role in their deliberations. But there are (at least) three or four ways in which making the promotion of one's well-being one of one's goals can affect one's attitude and deliberations without committing one to acting against reason.

First, one will then be concerned that one should have worthwhile goals at all times of one's life and that one should have the means of satisfying them.[25] Second, while one's efforts in pursuit of one's goals need not be motivated by concern for one's well-being they can be (except—as mentioned above—where this would be self-defeating). Those who make their own well-being one of their goals do tend to think of many of their decisions in this way. It may not make a difference to what they decide nor to what they do, but it makes a big difference to how and why they decide and behave the way they do.

The third way in which having one's well-being among one's goals may affect one's conduct is, from the point of view of my general analysis, an oddity. To the extent that success in one's pursuits depends on one's effort and skills one will come to give success a greater weight in one's decisions than one would otherwise do. We saw before that having a goal imports the

---

[25] In part this concern overlaps the concern for self which will be discussed in the last section. But it goes beyond it.

desire to succeed in it, and that the value of one's activities depends both on the value of one's pursuits and on one's success in them. If all the goods involved were impersonal (number of people a doctor heals, etc.) these factors would not be affected by one's concern for one's well-being. But some of them are personal. They involve judgement, effort, dexterity, skill, etc. The overall value of one combination of value of activity plus success in it compared with another (e.g. being a good corporate lawyer—i.e. high success in a not very valuable activity—as against a quite but not as good career as a teacher—less success in a more valuable activity) is often undetermined by reason and is a matter of personal preference. I believe that in general we can expect those very much concerned with their well-being to prefer pursuits where they are reasonably confident of success and where that success depends on their efforts and skills over other pursuits. I described this as an oddity for I am aware of this as an empirical generalization, but am unable to provide a rationally compelling explanation of this phenomenon.

Finally, a fourth way in which the goal of pursuing one's well-being can affect one is a consequence of the fact that concern for one's well-being ranges over one's past as well as over one's future. While we cannot change the past, that does not mean that we are indifferent to how well we did in it. Moreover, it is not the case that our concern about the past cannot be action-guiding. Some people have the super-goal of shaping their future to suit their past, to continue its path, complement it, make up for it, etc. in order to make their life better as a whole. They may, for example., wish to compensate for past errors or failures by having another go at the same objectives, hoping that future success will redeem past failures.

It is, therefore, possible to have as one of one's goals the advancement of one's well-being. This leaves intact the following conclusions I argued for above:

(1) Such a goal is optional. There is nothing wrong in not having it, nor any defect or deficiency in the character of those who do not embrace it.

This point is most clearly illustrated by the attitude to one's past which pursuit of one's well-being brings. As we know past commitments, formal or informal, may shape our future. They generate reasons for action through which one's past controls one's future. They may be grounded on nothing more than integrity, the need not to betray oneself and one's past. But these are the exceptions. For the most part there is nothing wrong in turning our back on our past or just not paying much attention to it when charting our future. As we saw, some people are different. But apart from the fact that not all such goals are sensible, none of them is required.

There is nothing wrong with a life which does not include such goals. For goals these are. Hence pursuit of one's well-being is only an optional goal.

(2) It is not necessary to have that goal in order to have a good life. Those who do not have it are as likely to have a good life as those who do.
(3) Certain important human goods such as love and friendship cannot be pursued with the aim of improving one's well-being.
(4) One cannot have only the goal of having a good life. One succeeds in it only by succeeding in other goals. But the goal of having a good life does not provide rational guidance in the choice of one's other goals.
(5) These are just one aspect of the fact that pursuit of one's own well-being does not serve the pivotal role that it is assigned both in some philosophical writing and in popular thought.

The pursuit of one's well-being, at least when given prominence in one's life, is not a very attractive goal to have. In general one's well-being should be an unintended (though obviously not unwelcome) result of the way one leads one's life, rather than one's goal or reason for being concerned with whatever one is. This is true not only regarding those activities and relationships whose success depends on their being undertaken for a specific motive (see point 2 above). The point is often made regarding activities for a cause: it is unseemly to volunteer to help rescue seals threatened by an oil spill because concern for the quality of one's own life makes one realize that some more time spent working for green causes will improve it. The same is true of most activities, including those one does for 'self-regarding' reasons. Mountaineers climb mountains for the thrill of the climb, for the skill displayed, the challenge overcome, the camaraderie and for other reasons, but it somehow shows the wrong spirit to do it for the sake of one's well-being. One likes spending time with a friend because she is funny and entertaining to be with, not because laughing or being entertained improves the quality of one's life.

This argument about the unattractive aspect of pursuing goals in order to advance one's well-being in the narrow sense does not extend to showing that the pursuit of the super-goals which are often referred to as the pursuit of one's well-being in the broad sense is also tainted. There is nothing wrong in having super-goals. Wishing to be a stockbroker in the morning, a duck farmer in the afternoon, and a poet in the evening is no different from wishing to break both the 800 metre and the 1500 metre world records and to win Olympic gold medals in both events four times running. Super-goals are not everyone's taste, but in principle we judge them in the same way we judge other goals. This means, of course, that generally even when pursuing super-goals one should do so for the sake of the goal and not for the sake of one's well-being. The taint of narcissism does not attach to super-goals as such, but it may attach to them if pursued out of concern for one's well-being.

Nor does it attach to all aspects of the pursuit of one's well-being. In particular, while there is nothing wrong with a carefree attitude of a person who does not bother to provide himself the wherewithal to pursue goals which he may have in the future, there is equally nothing wrong with someone who does.

7. CARING ABOUT ONE'S WELL-BEING

Those who adopt the goal of pursuing their own well-being can adopt it in part only, and they can give it more or less importance in their lives. At a minimum it is not a goal at all, merely a focus of evaluative concern. In some ways this is the most attractive stance to take towards one's well-being (though this is a matter of individual preference).

It is only when we consider concern for one's well-being as an evaluative attitude that we conceive its full scope. We care, if we do at all, about the well-being of our life as a whole, past, present, and future. As already commented, those who adopt the pursuit of their well-being as a goal very often do not go as far as setting themselves the goal of bending the future to complement or compensate for their past. In the minimal sense, saying that people are concerned not merely with their goals but with how good their life is means that they are not indifferent to evaluative assessments of their life as a whole. They are sad or disappointed if their life turned out to be riddled with conflict between them and members of their family, happy if it was basking in the warmth of good friendships, etc. This in itself does not show that concern for our well-being is the foundation for all other concerns. It may be just one concern among others. Moreover, while it is reasonable for people to care about how well their life goes this may be merely an evaluative attitude. Parents are familiar with situations in which, while they are anxious that their children will do well on their own, any attempt by them to help their children to do well on their own will be self-defeating.

The point is a delicate one for two reasons. First, since success in worthwhile activities contributes to one's well-being, people who know that know that what they do for pleasure, or for a thrill will, other things being equal, be good for their life. The point I am making here is merely that that is not normally the motivating thought, nor should it be. Second, I am not claiming that it is always wrong, let alone self-defeating, to be motivated by concern for one's well-being (in the minimal sense), merely that, especially if this is the general attitude one has towards all one's activities and relationships, it shows a defect in one's personality, a form of narcissism which impairs one's ability to be fully engaged with anything other than oneself. For our purpose the lesson is that concern for one's well-being (in the minimal sense) is indeed primarily evaluative and not action-guiding. Many reasonable people want their life to go well as a result of their success with goals and relationships undertaken for other reasons. A life which is not outward-looking, which is entirely inward-looking, being ultimately concerned only with itself, is diminished by this fact.

All these explanations make sense, yet something is still missing. For one thing, in saying that 'many reasonable people want their life to go well' I have grossly understated the case. People care a lot whether their lives go well or not. But all I can claim, consistently with the general position I am advocating, is that concern for one's own well-being is just one normative concern one may have, on a par with concern for how well opera as a form of art is doing today. It is no good, the objector will claim, to assign to biology the explanation of why people's concern for their own well-being is nearly universal whereas caring about the state of the opera is a minority taste. In fact, the objection proceeds, concern for one's well-being is part of what makes persons persons.

There is some truth in the objection. Evaluative concern for one's well-being, I will claim, is neither as central as the traditional philosophical understanding of prudence makes it, nor as accidental as a concern about the state of the opera. There is a concern which is essential to being a person, but it is not a concern for one's well-being. It is a concern for one's self. Agents who are persons are aware of themselves as conscious beings, with a capacity for rational action, and with a body, a character, and a life. A certain (at least minimal) concern for one's functioning as a person is part of being a person. Persons care about their ability to act and lead their life while they are alive. That means, though they need not think of it in these terms, caring about their ability to control and guide their lives in the light of reason. They also care about their success in their actions, for as we saw aiming to succeed is part and parcel of being motivated to act. What else is included in the concern of a person for himself which is an essential aspect of being a person? Exploring this question cannot be undertaken here, but two points need to be made.

First, while concern for oneself is essential, its expression is not constant and it varies with ethical or religious beliefs, and with one's general culturally influenced view of what is of value in the world. For some, for example, concern for themselves involves primarily concern that their soul escape eternal damnation. For others, it may lie in perfecting their character as a virtuous character. Concern for one's well-being is just one possible, and culturally conditioned, manifestation of people's concern for themselves. One way in which the fundamental concern for oneself differs from concern for one's well-being is in being manifested in a variety of different ways, not necessarily including caring about well-being, in different people.

Second, there is another way in which the fundamental concern for oneself differs from caring about one's well-being. The fundamental concern is not exhausted by caring about one's well-being even in people who do so care. One's concern about one's ability to function as a person, for example, is not exhausted in caring about one's well-being. It is deeper. It may even conflict with one's well-being, in that preserving one's ability to act as a person while one is alive may require action which is detrimental to one's well-being overall.

If one's well-being is not normally an important reason for oneself, should it be of moral concern to others? If so does concern for the well-being of others encompass all that is morally relevant in one's relations with them? If, as seems likely, it does not, how does it relate to other concerns? In so far as one has reason to be concerned with the well-being of others how does that concern manifest itself? And, most directly relevant to the theme of this chapter, where people's concern with their own goals and relationships is at variance with what is best for their own well-being does moral concern for others require us to help people with their goals and relationships, or is it fashioned by what is needed for their well-being? Scrutiny of these questions is necessary to complete the account of the meaning and normative role of well-being.

As for the question, 'How is it that people sometimes act for moral reasons in ways detrimental to their well-being?' the answer turns out to be simple. People act for reasons, that is, for what appear to them to be adequate reasons, regardless of whether or not they serve their well-being. Sometimes the reasons which appear to be conclusive, even when conforming with them affects the agent adversely, are moral reasons.

INDEX

Boldface type indicates those chapters in which the subject is treated at length.

acculturation 193, 194
acting for a reason 22, 23, 32, 36, 37, 40, 41, 43, 44, 47, 231–5, 332
action:
  and points of view 24, 25, 27, 34, 37, 38, 43
  and the good 23, 24, 28, 30, 32
  explanation of 27, 28, 47
  expressive 36, 37, 39–44, 54
  intelligibility of 24, 25, 27, 31, 33, 34, 40, 65, 66
  intentional 23, 24, 27, 36–44, 48, 109–11
  involuntary 109
  justification of 31
  semi-voluntary 42, 109
  subjectivity of 19, 20
active and passive **ch. 1**
  and emotions 12
  objectivity of the active 17, 18
  phenomenology of 21
acts and activities 309, 310
agency **chs. 1–3**
  classical approach 22–8, 35, 39, 40, 42, 44, 47, 48, 65
  common assumption in explanation of 24, 26, 27, 31, 43
  core account of activity 19
  rationalist conception 47–9
akrasia, *see* weakness of will
amoralist **ch. 12**, 248, 273
  and egoism 275, 277
anomic reasons 25, 31–5, 37, 40
Anscombe, G. E. M. 22, 47, 285
appearance and reality 150
Aquinas 10
Aristotle 10, 22, 47, 304
Audi, R. 105
axiology 31

Baier, K. 247, 248
belief-formation 11–13
beliefs 11–13, 15, 23, 25, 26, 92, 110, 112, 113
  and virtue 9, 10
  responsiveness to truth 7, 8
  voluntariness of 7, 11, 12
Benacerraf, P. 223
Bennett, J. 7, 13
Brink, D. 105
Bulloch, P. 287

character and expressive action 38, 39
charity 309
Chisholm, R. 13
choice 48, 49
  institutional context 48
choosing to believe 7, 8, 12–14, 20, 278
circular arguments 31, 171, 174
Cohen, L. J. 278
commitments 243, 244
conceptual schemes 223, 224
constructivism 279
contractarianism 120, 302
contrariness 33, 34
control:
  and beliefs 53
  and intentional action 38, 40–4
convergence, *see* Peirce, C. S.
Crisp, R. 227
cultures, understanding other 156–8

Dancy, J. 219, 226, 228–30, 232, 234–8
Davidson, D. 17, 105, 156
deciding to believe, *see* choosing to believe
decision theory 48, 49
defeasibility 70
deontic considerations 25, 47, 252
Descartes and Cartesianism 140, 280
desires 8, 49, 54

desires (*cont.*):
  and pathological abnormalities 54, 55, 197, 262
  and reasons 56–62
  brute 50–2
  frustrated 58, 59, 61
  instrumental 261
  thin wants 115, 117
dissociation 21
Dummett, M. 128
duties 269
  imperfect 270
Dworkin, R. M. 126, 127, 131

emotions 12
epistemic issues:
  absolutes 139–42
  justification 141, 155, 159
  luck 141, 155
  multiculturalism 161, 162, 181
  objectivity 142–4
epistemology, moral 161
evaluation 31
  intelligibility of 223, 225, 229, 230
examples:
  amoralist's apple tree 289, 290, 292, 293
  beautiful sunsets 150, 151
  Billy Budd 239–45
  chess 148, 153
  chess club 144
  counting blades of grass/sheep's hairs 55, 262
  gay marriages 190
  Inuit face in Beverly Hills 215, 216
  Inuits and types of snow 139
  Jane's baby 269, 270
  Javanese jokes 205, 206, 208
  job application to Somali hospital 250, 251
  just rate of tax 208
  keep smoking, stay witty 287, 288
  learning the piano in retirement 56, 57
  New York Jewish jokes 149
  promises and John's cacti 237, 238
  sacrificing your child for $1,000 a year 61
  Sylvia's repeated door-locking 71, 72
  toddler on edge of road 218, 232, 233, 235
  uncontrary Mary 90–2, 98–103
  unfaithful husband's photograph 23, 36
exclusionary 93

exclusionary reasons 98
explanatory reasons 23

facts, social 144–6
Field, H. 131
Frankfurt, H. 5–7, 18–20, 55, 262
friendship 283, 286–9, 294, 295, 297, 298
  desert account of 292
  reciprocity 293

generalism 218, 220
goals 63, 64
grammatical/logical analysis 22, 30, 315
Griffin, J. 3, 197–201, 303–6, 314, 324
good, the **ch. 2**; *see also* value

Hacker, P. M. S. 150, 156
Hales, S. D. 126
Hampton, J. 105, 174
Hare, R. M. 105
Hart, H. L. A. 195
Hume and Humeanism 7, 113
Hursthouse, R. 23

impartiality 275
impetuosity 113, 116, 117
incommensurability **chs. 3 & 8**, 26, 46, 48, 65, 66, 83–5, 99, 102–4, 241, 243, 246, 248
  and personality-based reasons 196
  and the common measure 183–5
  and the good 46, 47
  Griffin on 197–201
  mixed value goods 185–8, 190, 191, 193–5, 197, 199, 212, 217
  of literary works 197–200
  of meaning 86, 88, 156–9
interests 132, 133, 200
irrationality 16, 17, 20, 28, 35, 37, 108, 127, 261, 276, 279, 317
  motivated 9, 72, 74, 232

justification, content-independent 195

Kant and Kantianism 227, 277, 305
Kenny, A. J. P. 114, 115, 267, 309

Larmore, C. 271
leading one's own life 16, 21
  and proper functioning of processes governing mental life 19, 20
Leiter, B. 130

MacIntyre, A. 156
Mackie, J. L. 129, 131
Marmor, A. 121, 130
mathematical properties, knowledge of 131
McDowell, J. 137, 139, 140, 221, 222
Meiland, J. 9
Mele, A. 105
moral change ch. 7
   intelligibility of 167–72
moral point of view ch. 11
morality ch. 13
   conventionalist interpretation 165, 210, 211
   eternal truths? 175–9
   intelligibility 163, 172–7, 181
   knowledge of 131
   moral character 242, 243, 246
   rule-utilitarian 168
   universality 167, 168, 279; *see also* value
Müller, A. 22, 23
Murphy, L. 314

Nagel, T. 78, 79, 86, 133–6, 273, 275–82, 302
Neurath's boat 142
Nietzsche 264
normativity chs. 4–5
   and capacity rationality 68, 69, 71, 73, 74, 76, 113–17
   and justification 77–81, 89
   and rationality 67–75

objectivity ch. 6, 6, 89, 224
   domain objectivity 120–9, 132, 142
   epistemic sense 119, 120, 122, 123
   impartiality 120
   and parochial concepts 132–40, 142, 159
   and reasons for action 78
   and subjectivity 118, 121–3

paradoxes of reason 80, 82, 84, 85, 87–9
Pareto superiority 185–7, 191
Parfit, D. 72, 73, 105
particularism ch. 10
Peirce, C. S., and Peircean convergence 136–8, 142, 143, 155, 158, 222
persons:
   nature of 5, 6, 17, 67, 68, 72, 151, 171, 179, 242, 263, 276, 331
   value of 274, 275, 278, 279, 282, 283, 287–90, 294–7, 299–301
Pettit, P. 130

phobias 21
Plato and Platonism 22, 125, 189, 190, 304
pleasure 27, 58, 204, 226, 229, 235, 308, 310, 325
pluralism:
   cultural 161
   value 159, 180, 196
practical concepts:
   parochial nature 119
   social dependence 119
practical reason:
   bifurcated view 322; *see also* acting for a reason; reason; reasons for action
practices, social ch. 9, 83, 153–5, 162–4, 166, 187–91, 194, 197, 199
   causal explanations 217
   evolution of 208, 209
presumptions, burden of proof 280
Price, H. H. 7
principles 219, 225–8, 245, 246
propositions 121, 124
   believing and accepting 278
prudence 288, 303, 314
Putnam, H. 137, 139

Quinn, W. 26, 174, 305

rationality:
   and ability to reason 75–7
   and proper functioning 71, 72
   and reasoning about ends 73
   substantive and procedural 73
Raz, J. 93, 98, 102, 143, 174, 185, 192, 227, 243, 264, 268, 274, 280, 290, 305, 324
realism 125, 144
reason chs. 2, 4, 5
   belief in 20
   choosing for a 8, 9
   epistemic reasons 95, 96
   formal 81, 82, 87–9
   responsiveness to is core of the active 19, 20, 39, 72
   sometimes underdetermines choice and beliefs 12, 15, 139, 242
   substantive principles of 81–7
   unconditional reasons 98; *see also* reasons for action
reasons for action 22, 23, 25–8, 30, 31, 33, 34, 38, 40, 41, 43, 44, 47, 48, 182, 219, 228, 229, 256, 304, 323, 328

reasons for action (*cont.*):
  agent-relative 249, 257
  and desires 26, 47
  belief/desire account of 50–3, 61
  categorical 321, 322
  complete 228, 229
  conformity with 90–4
  enticing and requiring 101, 102
  facts as 22–5
  intelligibility of 219
  internal and external 249
  neutral reasons 29
  normativity of 28, 33, 35
  optional nature? 94–105
  prudential 265, 304
  relational reasons 264, 265, 267
  self-regarding 322, 325, 329
  universal 257; *see also* stringency of reasons
Regan, D. 226
relativism 126
relativism, social ch. 7, 152, 161, 190, 213
  and moral change 163–7, 179–81
  and moral knowledge 161–3
responsibility 6, 122, 151
routines 36, 37, 192, 232

Scheffler, S. 174, 268, 312, 314
secondary qualities, knowledge of 131, 136, 151
self, concern for 331, 332
self-deception 16, 17, 25, 28
self-interest ch. 13, 264, 280, 303, 311
self-sacrifice 304, 312, 315, 316, 318–21
stringency of reasons 98, 248, 268, 269, 271, 272, 304, 306, 311, 313–15, 321
Stroud, B. 98
supererogation 243, 252, 269, 270
supervenience 170, 171, 219–25

thick concepts 133, 144–6, 153, 206, 207, 210, 326
  and non-cognitivism 210
  and objectivity 155–60
  thick wants 110
toleration and rights 308
tragedy 308
truth 122–4, 129

undefeated reasons 99, 103
universalizability 239, 246, 277
universality, and reasons for action 78
urges 73, 261, 262
utilitarians 301

value **chs. 6 & 8**, 22–5, 33, 46, 47, 53, 63, 64, 105
  accessibility of 148, 150–4, 204, 216
  dependent 258
  higher and lower 195, 196
  instrumental 266
  and instrumental goods 255
  intelligibility of 209, 210
  intrinsic 265, 266, 296, 297
  knowledge of 145, 202, 203
  of novels 213, 214
  prudential 199, 258
  relational goods 251–4, 256–60, 263, 264, 272, 285
  small and big values 30
  social creation of 203–7
  social dependence of 146–9, 153
  structure of 191–3
  unconditional goods 106
  universality 152, 208
volition 46
von Wright, G. H. 267, 309

weakness of will 16, 17, 35–8, 43, 55, 63, 108, 110, 113, 116, 117, 262, 271, 291
well-being 29, 64, 200, 258, 265, 283, 298, 303, 304, 306, 307, 308, 317, 324
  classical view 304, 312, 314, 318, 319, 321, 326
  as optional goal 325, 328, 329
  and pain 324
  and supergoals 326, 327, 329, 330
Wiggins, D. 121, 125, 128, 239
will, the ch. 5, 10, 15, 44, 48, 49, 52, 109–11, 116, 117, 192
  and normative beliefs 105–8, 112
  and reason 65, 66
Williams, B. 7–10, 12, 105, 125–9, 136–40, 144, 145, 282–6, 301
Winch, P. 3, 219, 239–42, 244–6
Wright, C. 128, 129, 131, 138, 139

CPSIA information can be obtained
at www.ICGtesting.com
Printed in the USA
BVHW071836120922
646819BV00007B/124